69/7.

EUROPE'S FUTURE CONSUMPTION

ASEPELT

ASSOCIATION SCIENTIFIQUE EUROPÉENNE

POUR LA PRÉVISION ÉCONOMIQUE

À MOYEN ET À LONG TERME

VOLUME II

EUROPE'S FUTURE CONSUMPTION

CONTRIBUTORS

A. AMUNDSEN   H. LINNEMANN
R. BENTZEL   N. NOVACCO
A. BROWN   F. PILLOTON
V. CAO-PINNA   J. POELMANS
H. DEN HARTOG   D. A. ROWE
C. FOURGEAUD   J. SANDEE
G. GEHRIG   R. STONE
L. M. GOREUX   J. G. VAN BEECK

Edited by

J. SANDEE

Central Planning Bureau, The Hague

1964

NORTH-HOLLAND PUBLISHING COMPANY – AMSTERDAM

FOREWORD

This is the second volume in a series started one year ago, with the publication of "Europe's Future in Figures", editor R.C. Geary. A third volume, on future European trade, is also well in hand. ASEPELT is living up to its own medium-term projections.

Like the first book, this one contains both actual forecasts and methodology. These are often intermingled, but there are some chapters composed entirely of figures and others representing the distilled experience of veterans in economic projection.

In any international undertaking, language presents a problem. While most contributions in this volume are in English, three are in French, with English summaries. Authors from so many European countries writing in languages related but not identical to their own may be expected to offend unwittingly against grammar, syntax or idiom. Outright errors in the English were corrected, however, by Miss Marjorie Deane of The Economist, and for the French the same service was rendered by Mr. A. Adam of the Université Libre de Bruxelles.

EDITOR

The European Scientific Association for Medium and Long Term Forecasting (ASEPELT) was founded on March 21, 1961.

An English translation of the statutes, together with a list of members of the Association and members of the Bureau, are annexed to the book.

CONTENTS

Page

FOREWORD V

Chapter 1

J. SANDEE: Introduction 1

Chapter 2

J. POELMANS: Consumption Forecasts for Belgium 16

Chapter 3

C. FOURGEAUD: Les Projections de Consommation en France 18

Summary in English 46

Chapter 4

N. NOVACCO and F. PILLOTON: Structural Changes in Italy's Private Consumption Expenditures Projections for the Next Ten Years . . . 50

Chapter 5

J. G. VAN BEECK and H. DEN HARTOG: Consumption Forecasts for the Netherlands 83

Chapter 6

A. AMUNDSEN: Private Consumption in Norway 1930–1970 131

Chapter 7

R. BENTZEL: Future Consumption in Sweden 170

Chapter 8

R. STONE, A. BROWN and D. A. ROWE: Demand Analysis and Projections for Britain: 1900–1970; a Study in Method 200

Chapter 9

G. GEHRIG: Gross National Product and Private Consumption in the Federal Republic of Germany in 1960 and 1970 226

Chapter 10

V. CAO-PINNA: Critiques des Méthodes de Prévision de la Consommation
  et Suggestions Pratiques   245

Summary in English 261

Chapter 11

L. M. GOREUX: Projections de la Demande des Produits Agricoles en Europe
  Occidentale en 1970 262

Summary in English 284

Chapter 12

H. LINNEMANN: An Attempt at Forecasting the Demand for Higher Education in the Netherlands   288

Chapter 13

J. POELMANS: Evolution de l'Alimentation Belge par Nature et Origine des
  Produits 304

Summary in English 338

EXTRACT FROM THE STATUTES   341

LIST OF MEMBERS 343

Appendices   345

CHAPTER 1

INTRODUCTION

BY

J. SANDEE

Netherlands Central Planning Bureau, The Hague, Netherlands

Those who hope to find in this introduction a convenient summary of the eleven chapters our book contains will be disappointed. They should read the whole book. It is thinner than most symposia, it is written in 11 different but equally pleasant styles, and it is really all about one subject: forecasting consumption in the longer run. This introduction contains some more or less connected thoughts about the same subject, largely picked (consciously or unconsciously) from the papers of our eleven distinguished contributors (or teams of contributors, but I hope the reader will allow me to ignore that complication from now on).

The purpose of consumption analysis

How did ASEPELT come to choose Consumption as its second topic, after Production as the first one? What happened was that we held a sort of census amongst members present at one of our meetings, and found that so many of them had been working on consumption that together they could easily fill a book. Apparently, the subject was 'in the air', and little effort was indeed needed to find eleven authors ready to cooperate.

The study of consumer behaviour has always had a large share of the attention of practical econometricians. For every one supply function, hundreds of demand functions have been fitted by least squares or other means. Could it be that regression analysis is better suited to the aggregate reactions of large numbers of freely choosing consumers than to the calculated behaviour of a few suppliers? Will supply functions always be filled with average or a priori or 'technological' coefficients because the true marginal coefficients cannot be statistically determined? (Unregulated diversified small-scale agriculture has, of course, been subjected to regression analysis ever since Hanau's hog cycle study).

Keen interest in demand rather than in supply certainly does not result from the supremacy of the consumer in the developed economy. One wonders how far the consumer is king even there, but insofar as he is, he will have little use for consumption studies. Except, of course, when he turns investor, and buys durables, or determines his liquidity preference. As anyone knows who ever bought a car, a good forecast about the state of the car market one year ahead could have been extremely useful.

The main interest in demand studies comes from producers rather than consumers. The uncertainty in future demand for an individual product is indeed appallingly large, by any statistical test. Investing and producing for the consumer market comes near to gambling, the difference being that the mathematical expectation of the gain is usually positive. There will generally be an asymmetric preference function: large losses are strongly disliked, large profits not particularly aimed at. Such an asymmetric preference function makes for 'playing safe', giving up profits to reduce risk. If uncertainties were smaller, profits could be higher.

The fickleness of consumers not only plagues entrepreneurs who risk the money of their shareholders, and their own livelihood, but also officials in countries where Governments care about economic expansion. Uncertainty and risk are stressed in the introductory pages by our Italian and French contributors, and our detailed forecasts for other countries are closely linked to similar work on Government account. The biggest gap in this respect in Western Europe is to be found in Federal Germany, where sentiment is still stronger than reason. We have been lucky enough, however, to secure a forecast of *total* German private consumption by Gehrig, and we may hope this will be detailed later on.

Uncertainty and rapid changes in consumer demand may even affect the employment of individuals with particular skills, although changes in technology are probably more important in this respect. This constitutes a link between demand analysis and vocational training policies. Our educational contributor, Linnemann, however, treats university education as part of consumer demand, which is a different sort of link, and one more suitable to university education in general than to those individual types of it that are largely vocational training.

Optimum breakdown of private consumption

This book is concerned with the analysis of private consumption of individual (groups of) commodities. The curious behaviour of total private consumption (and its complements, called either saving or hoarding as the cyclical situation dictates) is not discussed. In fact, most contributors assume total consumption given, and link the forecasts for components to this 'given' total. Nevertheless, Friedman will be invoked on one occasion.

If we want to discuss detailed consumer behaviour, the immediate problem before us is *which* details should be discussed. From early on, econometricians have studied demand for single commodities, such as sugar, or tram rides. Their choice was often governed by the source of finance for their research, or by statistical convenience (long, well-defined, easy-to-find time-series), or by theoretical interest, e.g. in problems of substitution, or of stocks versus flows of durables. This book contains two studies on food, and one on university education. It also contains, however, six forecasts of the breakdown of total consumption by groups of commodities. We agreed on a reasonably uniform breakdown into 15 categories; this will be discussed at the end of this introduction. Here, I should like to ponder over the *optimum* breakdown that could have been used.

Such an optimum breakdown assumes beforehand that there is a limit to the number of categories that can be distinguished. For if there were no such limit, the optimum breakdown would be very fine indeed. It would run far beyond the detailed distributions underlying the studies of most of our six country-specialists. Forecasts for one thousand commodities, for instance, could have been easily printed, in small type, on 30 pages. They would have been a mine of information for everybody, and could have been aggregated at will by those who prefer bigger groups. Econometric analysis of consumption is not an instrument like an optical microscope, which beyond a certain point loses on definition what it gains on magnification (there is a limit to the 'resolving power' of such an instrument). Relative uncertainty is independent of size, unless one goes down to commodities that in a whole year in a whole country are bought by so few consumers that the number of the latter begins to matter (data could be found in import statistics of certain countries). The more detail, the more additional information on individual items (e.g. price trends, or technological changes) can be employed.

It might be thought a waste of time and effort to distinguish so many categories, some of which would be very small indeed. Modern computer equipment, however, makes the (marginal) cost of one more category very low, and nearly always trifling in comparison to the costs of production and distribution of the item considered.

Often enough, the first limit to the fineness of the division is statistical data. Statistics collected by statistical agencies can never give more detail than the schedules employed contained themselves. Such schedules could sometimes ask for more detail than they habitually do. The respondent will often appreciate a very detailed schedule, which makes it immediately clear where each part of his data goes, and which requires less adding up than a more compact questionnaire would do. In fact, some agencies intentionally distinguish in their schedules more categories than they ever intend to use, solely for the convenience of respondents.

Most of the information is, in fact, only generated to be suppressed by statistical agencies. A small part they may deem so unreliable as to be of no use, or even positively dangerous. The greater part is forced into the straightjacket of a two or three digit code, and on tabulation and printing one or two of these digits may be lost. Punch-cards and tape help, of course, to reduce the cost of fineness of breakdown. But punch-cards are used less frequently than is often believed, and the cost of tabulation and printing is roughly proportional to the size of the tables provided. Several agencies generously allow the use of their basic data, so that analysts are not restricted to printed statistics only. Even so, the arrangement of the data on the cards (if those have been used at all) and the manner of storage of the cards will often put an effective stop to attempts to unearth more detail.

If a uniform breakdown for a number of countries is wanted, the highest common denominator of national breakdowns will have to be used. This will further reduce definition.

The next cause of coarser breakdown is fear of standard errors. Where budget studies are used as sources of income elasticities of demand, relative standard errors tend to increase as the items get smaller, because fewer purchases are represented by the budget observations. Substitution between consumption items becomes more frequent as items get smaller, and the estimated total of two or more items may have a much smaller relative error than the individual items it contains. This would also apply when time-series are used as statistical evidence.

While fear of standard errors may be a cause of coarser breakdowns, I do not think it a valid reason. Standard errors should, of course, be estimated and appended to the forecasts, wherever possible. In some cases they may be so high that the forecast has little practical value. This is something worth knowing; one might, in fact, give the standard error only, to show that the forecast, which is omitted, cannot be given with sufficient precision. But often a number of such minor and uncertain forecasts could be combined in more than one way to give a reasonably accurate total, and it should be left to the user of the analysis to decide which combination suited him best.

Unless, of course, the analyst is himself the main user (as will often be the case). For then he can decide for himself which combination suits him best, and he will see no need to estimate each of the components. This analysis has been attempted by Fourgeaud, who found that a great part of the uncertainty of detailed forecasts did not affect aggregates that had a real meaning in the planning process. Instead of consolidating close substitutes on the demand side one should in such a case try to consolidate substitutes on the supply side. It does not matter then that butter and margarine are demand substitutes, for the one requires cattle, and the other whales. But liquid milk and cheese are substitutes on the supply side, and it is their combined consumption that affects cattle policy. Tea, cocoa, and coffee could be combined with tobacco and spices, for these must all be imported, but beer can be produced in each European country, and wine in only some, so that they should be kept separate. This idea has been carried to its extreme by Goreux, who reduced all foods to their crude agricultural contents. Planners interested in the food industry or food retail trades could learn something from Jacqueline Poelmans who studied changes in manufacturing and selling margins in foods in Belgium over 10 years.

To many demand analysts it may seem a bit odd to distribute demand on the basis of considerations of supply, but if it is supply policy that benefits most from demand analysis, there is much to be said for an orientation on supply.

In one instance, however, demand will always reign supreme, and that is where 'want-independence' is invoked to convert income-elasticities to price-elasticities. The formulae derived by Frisch are given in the papers by Amundsen and by Van Beeck and Den Hartog; their derivation rests on the assumption that the consumption categories considered are 'want-independent'. In this connexion, Amundsen shows 'some willingness to rely on intuition', and this tells him that certain categories are sufficiently want-independent but other categories are not. Some people's intuitions will in this way lead to finer breakdowns than other people's. Van Beeck and Den Hartog do not use their intuition except to conclude that the price elasticities derived in this fashion are approximate only. This attitude would not affect the breakdown of consumption, except that finer breakdowns would probably separate more and more substitutes (and complementary goods) so that the Frisch assumption would be more and more approximate.

Finally, even electronic computers have their limits, and the aggregate estimation procedure preferred (on theoretical grounds) by Stone, Brown and Rowe allows the use of only a few expenditure categories. If these were chosen so as to be intuitively 'want-independent' the procedure might be repeated to sub-divide the want-independent categories (once only, of course).

Methods of consumption forecasting

Eleven papers on consumption forecasting enable us to arrive at some conclusions about contemporary methodology. It will be found that income (or total consumption) is generally considered the main determinant of consumption of individual commodities. Income elasticities are consequently much sought after. Those authors that have detailed long-time series of consumption generally prefer them to budget studies; those that have not sometimes explain why budget studies are better anyway. In three cases, both sources of information were used. Some contributors to our volume looked across frontiers to make international comparisons. Goreux systematically included all data from all countries. Vera Cao-Pinna has much to say about time-series and budget studies, and I shall permit myself to use her arguments wherever they suit me.

Statistically, *time-series* have their weaker sides; they are often badly linked to independent supply data, though generally better so than budget data. Their main drawback is the low number of observations (one for every year, and if the series are prolonged into the past, red flannel and candles will be used to forecast the consumption of nylons and tube-lamps). So much changes over time: relative prices and habits, supply of new and still newer products, income distribution by classes and regions. A few of these influences may be represented by suitable indicators, and introduced in the regression analysis, in the hope that thereby the income elasticity will be estimated with less bias and more accuracy. For the remainder, it must be hoped that the relationships between income and those 'other' variables will remain the same in the forecast period. If more explanatory variables were used in the regression (such as prices, or a trend, or specific indicators) it must be hoped that each of the hidden determinants is related to one of those additional variables only, and that

that relationship will continue in the forecast period. Where would time-series analysis be without hope? Readers are advised to read the Norwegian and Swedish contributions with particular attention; such optimism is often infectious.

Budget data are not troubled by changes over time, but then the elasticities they provide with respect to income and size of family, separately for regions and social groups, may be less suitable for forecasting changes over time. Fourgeaud puts forward the hypothesis that their income elasticities represent long-term influences rather than short-term effects. It is here that the name of Friedman appears. On price-elasticities budget data cannot say anything, unless one uses the Frisch expedient. According to Fourgeaud, the information they provide about consumption habits by social and regional groups hardly affect forecasts for the nation as a whole. Vera Cao-Pinna draws our attention to their statistical weaknesses. Everybody knows that according to budget studies the consumption of strong drinks is rather lower than the real level shown by excise figures. One can only hope that the income elasticities are not affected.

The larger number of observations allows the use of fairly complicated functions to link consumption to income. Goreux lists five different functions, some of which are also used by other authors, and Van Beeck and Den Hartog prefer a sixth variety. To apply non-linear functions over time, assumptions must be made concerning the distribution of income over the forecast period. Even in cases where little solid ground can be found for these assumptions, it is interesting to see which consumption components are most affected, and in which direction, by the use of more sophisticated functions and different hypotheses about income distribution. Van Beeck and Den Hartog provide some indications of such effects.

Non-linear functions should essentially be fitted to observations for individual families rather than to group averages. Statistical agencies are often able to provide the data, especially if they keep them on punch-cards, and modern computers make light work even of the most complicated formula. While some of our authors hint at the use of computers, others seem still to be hampered by computational limitations. The next ASEPELT consumption book will probably be based entirely on electronic results.

Actual *forecasting* seems to demand less effort than the estimation of elasticities from observations, if the number of pages devoted to either is an adequate indicator. Apart from income, or total consumption, some of our authors introduce prices, trends and family size. The prices come from either a more qualitative consideration of possible productivity and competition (including imports) on the supply side, or they are linked to income again by means of partial time-series analysis. The general impression is that labour-intensive commodities, above all services, will rise in relative price. Trends are partially based on experience, modified by intuition. Family size is taken from demographic analysis, which neatly shifts the burden. As long as these additional influences have modest effects, however uncertain, their introduction can only improve our forecasts.

Some instances are given of possible effects of supply rather than demand. Rent is, of course, the most obvious case: as long as few dwellings are left empty, the consumption of housing space must depend on supply. Hospital services come under the same description. For other commodities, the price mechanism must be called in to equate supply and demand, and we are back to the influence of relative prices. Bentzel has given more attention to these aspects than most other authors. Goreux has, of course, introduced dietetic considerations. Applying elasticities to food would make people add weight, which in most countries is frowned upon (in well-fed classes only?). And Fourgeaud mentions special treatment of durables including motor-cars where the 'parc' (stock) of durables was forecast first, and expansion and replacement were derived from it. In countries where expansion of the stock is nowadays particularly fast because incomes have risen faster than stocks, such a refined method has much to say for it. In any case, the consumption of durables in 1960, which all authors (except Fourgeaud) used as a base, should have been checked for cyclical peculiarities before 1970 was derived from it. Presumably there were few such peculiarities.

Special mention should be made of the forecasts, by Novacco and Pilloton, of the distribution of Italian consumption over the Northern and Southern halves of the country. Consumption by the nation as a whole was estimated first, and this was distributed assuming that for each consumption item Northern and Southern *per capita* consumption at identical income levels would differ by an amount that would not depend on the level of income. These differentials were estimated from linear regressions on post-war time-series.

International comparison

The use of a uniform breakdown enables us to compare estimates for six countries, by six authors. The following table groups them all together. The figures have been derived from those given on pp. 16, 36, 59, 118, 160, 198 and have been checked by the authors. It is left to the reader to compute the percentages and index numbers he thinks most helpful; tastes vary considerably in this respect. Such a table calls for comments of various kinds, and the first question may well be what ends such a table may serve.

The main purpose is mutual encouragement. It will appear that nearly all of these estimates follow closely related patterns. They therefore reinforce each other, and encourage forecasters to persevere in their attempts. Those who forecast strong increases for certain items will be pleased to see that richer countries have already reached the high levels they foresee in 1970, and similar satisfaction can be had by a contemplation of less income-elastic commodities.

We agreed on this breakdown without any discussion on principles of the type entertained above. Items were defined rather for practical convenience, and this implicitly incorporated the wisdom and experience of earlier distributors of consumer expenditure. Special care was taken to split the bigger items into lumps of comparable size. As a result the categories have roughly the same order of magnitude, except the transport items which with general approval obtained special treatment.

Some authors had to make small exceptions to uniformity which are indicated in footnotes to their tables. These will hardly affect such large categories as ours. Fats gave a lot of trouble: butter, lard, and margarine tended to get mixed up. Preserved meat or vegetables necessitated other exceptions. One wonders how continental statisticians would treat a tinned English plum pudding.

This experience is very encouraging. If it is possible without long debates or new statistical enquiries, to split European consumption into 15 roughly equal lumps, further refinements must be feasible with little additional effort. But how comparable are the figures in this table? Obviously, the contents of the items vary from country to country: 'beverages' means tea in the Netherlands, beer in Belgium, and wine in France. The greater differences are probably concentrated in food, but an item like 'health' must also vary considerably from one country to another.

Besides, even the totals differ, because expenditure by foreigners has

TABLE 1 – Consumption expenditures in six countries in dollars *per capita* at 1960 prices and exchange rates

	Belgium		France[a]		Italy		Netherlands		Norway		Sweden	
	1960	1970	1959	1970	1960	1970	1960	1970	1960	1970	1960	1970
1. Cereals and products	25.7	32.3	32.9	38.4	36.0	36.6	22.0	24.4	22.7	22.2	37.1	40.4
2. Milk and products	40.9	45.4	44.8	53.5	19.5	25.2	30.5	37.8	37.9	39.4	58.8	57.4
3. Meat, fish, eggs	97.9	121.0	93.2	124.1	55.9	73.1	47.7	60.4	59.8	71.2	82.4	96.5
4. Vegetables and fruits	40.7	53.7	32.5	44.8	36.2	50.0	19.5	22.4	39.4	58.7	43.0	56.1
5. Other food	37.2	46.8	19.9	30.7	22.2	30.5	33.0	40.4	46.9	56.3	28.3	36.1
6. Beverages	83.2	110.4	45.3	55.8	29.1	40.4	24.1	37.1	53.7	73.0	76.6	99.1
7.* Tobacco	18.9	23.0	15.3	18.1	17.9	26.6	22.5	28.8	22.0	24.6	32.4	40.1
8. Clothing	84.6	118.5	93.2	143.0	41.0	59.7	75.4	110.5	116.6	149.2	117.6	176.7
9. Durables	79.6	113.5	51.8	113.2	9.6	18.4	64.9	123.1	103.7	157.6	90.7	146.4
10. Heat & light	43.0	58.8	36.4	57.2	11.3	20.0	28.7	38.5	25.0	34.8	47.4	62.3
11. Rent	97.5	104.5	37.3	60.0	15.0	21.4	36.7	46.6	50.7	72.5	95.8	153.0
12. Health	43.7	66.8	68.6	138.6	17.2	26.5	23.6	41.5	29.5	39.2	30.4	49.8
13. Public transport	27.1	35.4	20.7	28.7	14.4	26.1	13.8	16.7	34.1	41.6	34.8	42.4
14. Transport equipment	} 51.8	} 92.7	15.0	34.3	6.3	13.4	12.1	26.2	15.9	60.4	42.9	81.9
15. Private transport operation			20.4	46.2	12.7	30.2	4.1	8.7	8.3	27.1	46.2	85.4
16. Other expenditure including tourism abroad	148.7	242.5	102.6	168.3	53.1	91.3	88.7	143.9	90.8	119.9	112.5	152.3
Total consumption[b]	920.5	1265.3	729.9	1154.9	397.4	589.4	547.3	807.0	757.0	1017.4	976.9	1376.5

[a] 1959 prices
[b] Items do not always add up to totals obtained separately

sometimes been deducted item by item, sometimes as a lump sum at the end of the classification (in which case our composite table blandly gives 'domestic' consumption plus tourism expenditures), and sometimes one does not quite know what happened. In the countries we consider this unevenness will hardly affect the comparison of the forecasts.

To convert all country data to common units, 1960 'official' rates of exchange have been used. We know, of course, that price levels of total consumption and its components vary from country to country. Gilbert and Kravis have not worked in vain. But by 1960 it is hardly possible to use their results; their breakdown was different from ours, and the partial price indices that should have been used to bring them up to date are distributed differently again.

Nevertheless, here lies a big problem, and not only a statistical problem. For even if we had price comparisons between countries, should we have 'deflated' our individual expenditure items to bring each of them to a common price level? It all depends on the price elasticities of demand one assumes. If these were all -1, obviously values would be more 'comparable' than volumes. One should then still deflate, but rather by overall deflators relating to total consumption. Previous experience has told us that price differentials are concentrated in services (and some foods with regulated prices). Other prices are little different, and tend to converge with trade liberalisation. This should be borne in mind when figures are read row-wise. It is probably advisable to skip the 'rent' row altogether, unless one is interested in seeing how much rent other people pay as a percentage of total expenditure – an interesting comparison, but of little importance for forecasters.

Going through the table row-wise (I made some graphs to help me in doing so) I was surprised to find how well these utterly unrelated estimates fitted together. I found a particularly high share (taking the general welfare level into account) for vegetables in Italy and for health in France, and low shares for durables in Italy, and for vegetables, public transport, and transport operation in the Netherlands. The first thing one thinks of in such a case is relative prices again. Are expenditures high because prices are high (and price elasticity low)? Or because prices are low, and elasticities high? One wonders, considers the price elasticities used by Van Beeck and Den Hartog, and wonders again.

To a small extent these differences may reflect idiosyncrasies of statisticians rather than consumers (and producers). Norwegian 'cereal' consumption may be low because 'pastry' is low. Pastry statistics are

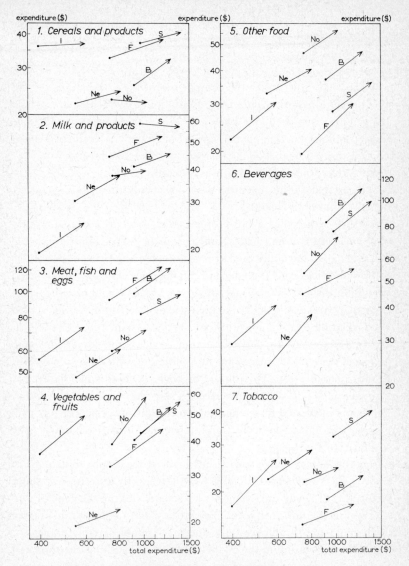

FIG. 1–7. Consumption expenditures in six countries (in dollars per capita at 1960 prices and exchange rates).

pretty dubious in most countries. Where is the borderline between pastry and sweets anyway? One also wonders how Italian consumption statistics can give such extremely low figures for durables, when their budget en-quiries are much more 'normal' in this respect.

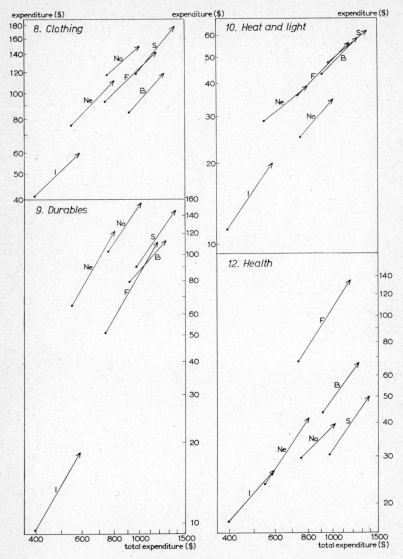

F<small>IG</small>. 8, 9, 10, 12. Consumption expenditures in six countries (in dollars per capita at 1960 prices and exchange rates).

The main conclusion is, however, that consumption functions are nearly the same all over Europe. This also holds for the changes as forecast by our authors. I compared the 'apparent' elasticities that can be derived from our table, and found them very similar indeed. Low ap-

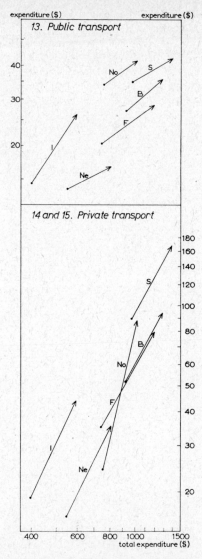

FIG. 13–15. Consumption expenditures in six countries (in dollars per capita at 1960 prices and exchange rates).

parent elasticities are encountered in cases like vegetables and private transport operation in the Netherlands, beverages in France, and milk in Sweden (leading to a *per capita* decline!). A high apparent elasticity is assumed for public transport in Italy and private transport expenditures

in Norway, while rents in Sweden are expected to rise faster than any-
where else. It is sometimes amusing to read what our authors have themselves to say about these very estimates.

I have seen hundreds of forecasts go wrong, and quite a few come true
by sheer luck. 'Naive models' have often been superior to sophisticated
econometric models (though the most sophisticated of those sometimes
came out best of all). Nevertheless I am willing to back each one of the
forecasts of our ASEPELT authors, including the 'outliers', rather than
go by the hunches of those that say they know best, but never stick their
necks out far enough to be caught by reality. For at this moment we have
no better methods than those applied in this book.

CHAPTER 2

CONSUMPTION FORECASTS FOR BELGIUM

BY

JACQUELINE POELMANS

Centre Interuniversitaire pour les Etudes de la Consommation Privée, Bruxelles, Belgique

The following table contains a revision of our earlier consumption forecasts (see Chapter I of Volume I of this ASEPELT series), arranged according to the distribution used in this Volume.

Prévisions de dépenses de consommation privée aux prix de 1960
(en millions de francs belges)

	1960	1970	Commentaires concernant le contenu des rubriques
1. Céréales et produits à base de céréales	11.766	15.296	Comprend la pâtisserie
2. Lait et produits laitiers	18.704	21.544	Ne comprend pas la crème glacée
3. Viande – poisson – œufs	44.790	57.374	Comprend la viande et les charcuteries conservées, y compris celles qui sont en boîte
4. Fruits et légumes	18.628	25.456	Comprend les fruits et les légumes secs mais ne comprend pas les fruits et légumes conservés, qui sont dans la rubrique 5
5. Autres produits alimentaires	17.036	22.204	—
6. Boissons	38.079	52.315	Ne comprend pas le cacao, qui est repris dans la rubrique 5
7. Tabac	8.650	10.899	
8. Habillement textile et cuir	38.704	56.171	Comprend toutes les dépenses relatives aux achats d'habillement textile et de cuir, à l'exclusion des réparations qui sont dans la rubrique 16
9. Biens durables	36.412	53.789	Ne comprend pas les réparations qui sont dans la rubrique 16
10. Chauffage – éclairage	19.653	27.869	—
	252.422	342.917	

	1960	1970	Commentaires concernant le contenu des rubriques
	252.422	342.917	
11. Loyers	44.636	49.546	—
12. Soins médicaux	20.007	31.671	—
13. Transports publics	12.395	16.802	En dehors des P.T.T. et des services de transport public. Cette rubrique comprend aussi les dépenses de transport par avions, bateaux et taxis
14. Autres dépenses } 15. de transport }	23.715	43.933	Il n'a pas été possible de faire la distinction demandée entre les rubriques 14 et 15
16. Divers	66.045	107.031	Ont été classés dans cette rubrique non seulement toutes les réparations mais aussi les services de soins personnels
17. Dépenses belges à l'étranger	7.500	15.810	
18. Dépenses des étrangers en Belgique	— 5.500	— 7.893	
Total	421.220	599.817	

CHAPTER 3

LES PROJECTIONS DE CONSOMMATION EN FRANCE

PAR

C. FOURGEAUD

Service des Etudes Economiques et Financières du Ministère des Finances, Paris, France

I. INTRODUCTION

1. La place des prévisions de consommation dans l'élaboration des plans de développement en France

Les deux premiers plans de modernisation et d'équipement s'étaient surtout proposé le relèvement du potentiel industriel et énergétique de la France.

Les destructions de l'appareil productif de base étaient telles, aux lendemains de la guerre que la priorité qui lui était accordée ne pouvait guère prêter à contestation.

Cette reconstitution, sinon totalement achevée, du moins suffisamment entreprise pour limiter les risques de pénuries essentielles, il devenait nécessaire d'orienter l'économie vers un développement beaucoup plus diversifié. Le 3ème Plan (1957–1961) s'est donc largement préoccupé d'établir des perspectives, déjà détaillées, de consommation des Particuliers de façon à mettre en évidence les rythmes de croissance possibles des différentes branches de l'économie et d'étudier les moyens d'action correspondants pour les atteindre.

Parallèlement, les études sur le comportement des consommateurs et les techniques de prévision ont été poursuivies. Notons toutefois que l'information statistique de base et même l'aspect théorique des problèmes de la consommation demeurent encore très en deça des nécessités de la projection.

Mais c'est véritablement pour l'élaboration du 4ème Plan (1961–1965) que les études de consommation à moyen terme ont été le plus «intégrées» aux travaux de planification proprement dits et que certaines de leurs insuffisances sont ainsi apparues. Afin de situer leur place dans la préparation du Plan, on rappellera très brièvement les étapes de l'élaboration du 4ème Plan.

2. Les étapes de la préparation du Plan

2.1. LES ESQUISSES PRÉLIMINAIRES

Pour préparer un Plan, il faudrait théoriquement envisager les diverses voies de développement offertes et choisir parmi elles celle (ou celles) jugées préférables d'après des critères appropriés. En raison de leur nombre, le simple recensement de ces voies est pratiquement impossible. On peut toutefois espérer mettre en évidence des «familles» relativement homogènes caractérisées chacune par l'existence de problèmes ou de choix particulièrement importants.

Une façon d'aborder cette recherche est d'étudier les implications de différents taux de croissance à long terme. Préalablement à l'étude proprement dite sur la période de planification, on est donc conduit à des perspectives à plus long terme. On espère ainsi que le grossissement dû au prolongement d'un même taux de croissance permettra de faire surgir les risques qui pèseront dans les années prochaines sur l'expansion.

C'est l'année 1975 qui a été choisie comme horizon du IVème Plan et pour laquelle on a étudié les conséquences de trois taux différents de progression de la production intérieure brute $-3, 4^1/_2, 6\%$ par an à partir de l'année 1961. Pour chacune de ces variantes on a défini un niveau de consommation des particuliers, compte tenu des investissements jugés nécessaires à la poursuite de l'expansion et d'hypothèses concernant la demande des administrations et le solde des échanges extérieurs.

Cette première étape était destinée à éclairer le Gouvernement sur le choix du taux de croissance souhaitable pour la période 1961–1965 et celui des grandes orientations de l'économie. A cette occasion des prévisions de consommation ont été établies dans la nomenclature d'étude de la production utilisée par la Comptabilité Nationale, le SEEF[1]) agissant comme bureau d'Etudes du Commissariat Général du Plan. En utilisant un système de relations interindustrielles, on a estimé les conséquences de la répartition de la demande finale sur les niveaux de production des différentes branches.

---

[1]) Service des Etudes Economiques et Financières – Ministère des Finances.

Le résultat de ces esquisses a été transmis au Conseil Economique et Social, Assemblée représentant les divers groupes sociaux, chargé par le Gouvernement de lui présenter un rapport d'orientation.

Les délibérations du Conseil Economique ont porté notamment sur les problèmes de consommation et le choix du taux de croissance. Elles ont conclu à la nécessité d'un effort supplémentaire en faveur des besoins collectifs (urbanisme, enseignement) et d'une expansion élevée. Le Gouvernement a alors choisi d'orienter les travaux du 4ème Plan sur la base d'une augmentation annuelle de 5% de la production intérieure brute. Une nouvelle esquisse plus précise et plus détaillée de consommation et de production fut alors établie pour l'année 1965 qui tenait compte des recommandations du Conseil Economique et devait guider les travaux des Commissions de Modernisation du Plan chargées de l'élaboration proprement dite.

3.   Les travaux des commissions de modernisation

Les grandes orientations globales fixées, le travail d'élaboration du Plan est décentralisé entre des Commissions «verticales», appelées Commissions de Modernisation qui groupent, pour une même branche de l'Economie, des représentants des entreprises, de l'Administration, des syndicats ouvriers, du Commissariat au Plan. Ces commissions sont elles-mêmes «démultipliées» en un grand nombre de groupes de travail ayant compétence pour un nombre plus restreint de produits dont ils étudient les perspectives de débouchés.

Les études préliminaires leur sont communiquées, en particulier les prévisions de consommation, importantes dans les secteurs orientés à titre principal vers la demande finale. Les divers groupes de travail élaborent leurs propres perspectives compte tenu des orientations générales définies dans les travaux préliminaires qui acquièrent ainsi une coloration plus concrète.

Une équipe de synthèse examine la cohérence des divers programmes et propose éventuellement les arbitrages nécessaires. Lorsque la synthèse définitive est achevée, après plusieurs mois, il existe par produit une balance mettant en regard les ressources (production et importation) et les emplois (consommation intermédiaire, investissement, consommation des ménages, des administrations, exportations) et qui représente les objectifs du Plan.

A ce stade les prévisions de consommation sont en principe communes à tous. Elles peuvent différer de celles contenues dans les esquisses préliminaires en raison de l'apport des groupes de travail.

Ceci montre déjà que les méthodes de prévision de la consommation ne reposent pas seulement sur des relations économétriques. Certaines informations, opinions d'expert, introduisent en fait un grand nombre de relations ou de contraintes entre les variables qui ne sont pas toujours susceptibles d'une formalisation précise. En réalité toute prévision à long terme, même si elle doit nécessairement s'appuyer sur un ensemble de relations économétriques vérifiées dans le passé, ne se réduit pas à l'application mécanique d'un modèle mais est aussi un travail d'imagination dans lequel la confrontation des points de vue joue un grand rôle, même dans le choix des paramètres du modèle.

Cet article se propose à l'occasion des prévisions 1970, non de dresser un catalogue exhaustif des méthodes de projection, mais de souligner les difficultés concrètes rencontrées dans la préparation du 4ème Plan.

Les chiffres proposées pour 1970 résultent d'une interpolation entre les évaluations assez détaillées pour 1965 et les esquisses plus globales pour 1975, fondées sur la variante moyenne. Malgré notre souci de respecter la nomenclature commune proposée pour ce livre de ASEPELT (assez différente de la nomenclature de travail française) nous nous sommes trouvés parfois dans l'obligation de nous en écarter légèrement – ou de renoncer à des ventilations utiles.

Après avoir examiné les facteurs qui influencent l'évolution de la consommation nous nous interrogerons sur l'incertitude qui peut affecter la prévision en tentant d'associer a chaque évolution une distribution de probabilité subjective. Un problème concret très important est d'apprécier si les incertitudes sont de nature à remettre en cause les perspectives de production des grands secteurs de base et donc leur programme d'équipement. L'auteur pour sa part ne le pense pas.

Enfin, à la lumière de la comparaison entre prévision et réalisation pour le plan 1957–1961 seront évoqués quelques axes de recherche, utiles à la poursuite de ces travaux.

II. LES METHODES DE PREVISION

1. **L'évaluation des besoins: Le partage entre consommation publique et consommation privée**

La satisfaction des besoins des individus est analysée par la Comptabilité Nationale au moyen de deux notions que l'on peut juger arbitraires mais qui sont commodes parce qu'elles correspondent à des achats de biens et services: la «consommation des Ménages» et la «consommation des Administrations».

La consommation des administrations a la nature d'une consommation intermédiaire destinée à permettre la «production» de services dont beaucoup ont un caractère collectif (défense nationale, enseignement, équipement urbain etc.). On ne peut pas en général, évaluer ces services par référence à un prix de marché car ils sont le plus souvent uniques dans leur genre ou cédés gratuitement.

L'estimation des besoins qui doivent être dans l'avenir satisfaits par des modes collectifs est du domaine éthique ou politique. L'évolution du partage de la consommation publique et privée a fait l'objet d'hypothèses encore provisoires qui apparaissent dans Tableau 1.

TABLEAU 1 – Evolution de la consommation des Ménages et des Administrations[a])

	Milliards de NF			
	1959	1965	1970	1975
Consommation des ménages	161,40			
Indices	100	136	172	220
Consommation et investissement des Administrations	19,10			
Indices	100	146	180	226
Ensemble	180,50			
Indice	100	137	173	221

[a]) Concept territorial

Compte tenu des autres hypothèses de l'équilibre global, la consommation des ménages serait à l'indice 172 en 1970, donnée de base pour l'ensemble des études.

2. Les facteurs qui influencent la structure de la demande

2.1. LES DONNÉES DÉMOGRAPHIQUES

2.1.a. *La population totale*

L'évolution naturelle de la population est une variable exogène. Elle peut être caractérisée par les éléments suivants:
— croissance d'ensemble au rythme de 0,8% par an
— distorsions importantes dans la répartition par âge: de 1959 à 1970 la population de moins de 20 ans doit s'accroître de 11% celle de plus de 60 ans de 16% alors que la population de 20 à 59 ans où se situe la majorité de la population active n'augmenterait que de 5%. La répartition par âge intervient dans le nombre d'unités de consommation et joue un rôle assez important dans la demande de certains biens (textiles par exemple).

Tableau 2 précise les perspectives qui tiennent compte, dans la mesure du possible, des mouvements migratoires consécutifs à la libre circulation de la main-d'œuvre dans les pays du Marché Commun et d'une hypothèse d'évolution politique favorable des rapports avec les pays de la zone franc.

2.1.b. *Population active et répartition par catégories socio-professionnelles*

Compte tenu des taux d'activité par âge, de la prolongation de la scolarité, des variations de l'activité féminine, on peut évaluer la population active occupée à 20,370 millions en 1970 et à 21,400 en 1975 soit une augmentation respective de 8 et de 13% par rapport à 1959.

On doit normalement prévoir une salarisation croissante de la population active (74% en 1970 contre 68% en 1959) au détriment des entrepreneurs individuels principalement des agriculteurs. La part de la population active employée dans l'agriculture (exploitants et salariés) pourrait décroître de 25% en 1959 à 19% en 1970. Ces facteurs ont certainement une influence sur la structure de la consommation le comportement de la population agricole étant sensiblement différent de celui de la population non agricole.

TABLEAU 2 – Evolution de la population totale de 1959 à 1975 – population moyenne de l'année – taux de mortalité décroissants

	Effectifs				Indice 1959 = 100			Taux de croissance annuel	
	1959	1965	1970	1975	1965	1970	1975	1959–1965	1965–1975
Population totale									
0– 4 ans	3965	3870	4060	4490	97,6	102,4	113,2	−0,4	1,5
5–14 ans	7750	8020	7950	8050	103,5	102,6	103,9	0,6	–
15–19 ans	2725	4050	4020	4080	148,6	147,5	149,7	6,8	–
20–59 ans	23170	23110	24380	25860	99,7	105,2	111,6	−0,1	1,1
60–64 ans	2270	2560	2560	2330	112,8	112,8	102,6	2,0	−1,0
65 et plus	5220	5690	6160	6570	109,0	118,0	125,9	1,5	1,5
Total	45100	47300	49130	51380	104,9	108,9	113,9	0,8	0,8
dont immigration depuis le 1.1.60	–	660	1200	1790					
Répartition en pourcentages									
0–19 ans	32,0	33,7	32,6	32,3					
20–59 ans	51,4	48,9	49,7	50,3					
60 et plus	16,6	17,4	17,7	17,4					

2.2. REVENU, PRIX ET CONSOMMATION

2.2.a. Revenu et consommation

Les perspectives d'augmentation de la consommation totale sur lesquelles s'appuient toutes les études particulières résultent d'équilibres physiques (à prix constants 1959), la consommation des ménages étant définie comme le solde des autres emplois de la production.

L'équilibre entre consommation et épargne c'est-à-dire l'étude des circuits de revenus ne peut être pris en compte au stade des travaux préliminaires. Il est lié à l'ensemble des problèmes de financement du plan et ne peut être résolu, que simultanément avec l'équilibre financier des entreprises et des administrations, une fois achevés les travaux de synthèse détaillés à prix constant.[2])

L'indicateur du niveau de vie retenu ici est la consommation globale en volume dont l'évolution serait:

	1959	1965	1970	1975
Consommation totale	100	136	172	220
Consommation par tête	100	130	158	193

2.2.b. La distribution des revenus

La croissance s'accompagne de modifications dans la structure des revenus. L'expansion inégale des différentes branches modifie la répartition globale de la valeur ajoutée entre revenus d'entreprises et salaires. A l'intérieur d'une même branche, les progrès de productivité devront s'accompagner de variations dans la structure hiérarchique des qualifications au profit du personnel le plus qualifié qui peuvent modifier l'échelle des rémunérations. Enfin, la puissance publique peut elle-même infléchir la distribution des revenus par la fiscalité et les transferts sociaux ou la politique des prix, par exemple des prix agricoles.

Il est bien connu que l'évolution des différentes consommations n'est pas insensible à la plus ou moins grande inégalité dans la distribution des revenus. Encore conviendra-t-il d'apprécier numériquement cette influence.

---

[2]) Voir à ce sujet «Modèle à moyen terme à prix variables» A. NATAF et P. THIONET, Etudes Comptabilité Nationale N° 3, 1962.

2.2.c. *La structure des prix*

La structure des prix se modifie en fonction de l'évolution technique d'une part, des interventions publiques (subventions – fiscalité etc.) et du comportement financier des entreprises d'autre part. On connaît les distorsions les plus importantes observées au cours des dix dernières années mais il n'est pas certain que les évolutions passées se poursuivent dans l'avenir. Il n'est d'ailleurs pas possible de préciser au départ l'ampleur des variations de prix relatifs. Il est certes, très probable que le prix des services et des loyers s'accroîtra par rapport à celui des biens industriels, mais l'évolution du niveau relatif des prix agricoles dépend à la fois de la politique nationale et de contraintes internationales. La prévision de la consommation devrait aussi prendre en compte ces éléments, même en faisant sur les plus incertains des hypothèses provisoires.

2.3. LES AUTRES FACTEURS EXOGÉNES

Bien d'autres facteurs sont susceptibles d'influencer la structure de la consommation. Citons parmi eux.
– L'urbanisation
  La structure des consommations varie suivant la taille de la commune. Si l'on est capable de poser des hypothèses sur l'intensité de l'urbanisation, elles devraient se traduire sur l'évolution de la consommation.
– Les effets de diffusion pour certains biens durables
  On sait que pour un même niveau de revenu les taux de possession de certains biens durables s'accroissent au cours du temps. Cet effet de diffusion lié à des comportements de patrimoine joue un grand rôle dans la demande de biens nouveaux.
  Dans quelle mesure sommes-nous capables de tenir compte de tous les facteurs cités?

3.   La prise en compte des facteurs de développement

3.1. L'IMPOSSIBILITÉ DE TENIR COMPTE SIMULTANÉMENT DE TOUS LES FACTEURS EXPLICATIFS

La prise en compte de façon numérique des différents facteurs énumérés au paragraphe précédent n'est pas possible en l'état actuel de notre information statistique et du niveau atteint par la théorie de la consommation.

Théoriquement il faudrait, pour chaque produit de la nomenclature exprimer l'évolution de sa consommation par une fonction des différentes variables, soit symboliquement

$$f(R, P, E)$$

R = désignant le revenu des différentes catégories socio-profession-nelles considérées,

P = l'ensemble des prix relatifs,

E = l'ensemble des autres variables exogènes.

En se limitant aux seuls facteurs revenu et prix et en résumant leur influence par des coefficients d'élasticité, dans une nomenclature comprenant n biens il serait nécessaire de déterminer statistiquement $(n^2 - n)$ coefficients indépendants – et ceci par catégorie socio-professionelle. Or on ne dispose en France que d'une seule grande enquête de consommation et d'une série de comptes nationaux portant sur 10 ans. On peut certes songer à imposer aux fonctions de consommation des propriétés qui limitent le nombre de paramètres indépendants, comme l'existence de fonctions d'utilité. Des tentatives faites dans ce sens n'ont pas encore abouti à des solutions concrètes bien satisfaisantes. On est donc conduit à négliger l'influence de certains facteurs en espérant que ceux qui sont retenus sont les plus importants.

Or il semble bien qu'en première approximation, pour un horizon pas trop éloigné, la croissance des revenus soit de loin le facteur essentiel d'évolution pour un grand nombre de produits.

3.2. L'IMPORTANCE DES FACTEURS NÉGLIGÉS

3.2.*a*. La distribution des revenus est approximativement connue pour l'année de base. Les premiers travaux de projection, notamment pour 1965, ont été effectués sous l'hypothèse d'une distribution de revenus inchangée. Cette hypothèse de travail était destinée à faciliter les calculs, indépendamment de toute option sur le sens et l'ampleur d'éventuelles distorsions dans la répartition. On a alors tenté de vérifier si l'évolution de la consommation totale par produit était susceptible de varier très sensiblement lorsqu'on modifiait la répartition initiale des revenus, le niveau global restant inchangé. Les calculs ont montré que des modifications dans la distribution dont l'ampleur ne met pas en cause le système social actuel n'avaient qu'une influence assez secondaire sur la consommation totale de la plupart des produits. Les exceptions les plus notables concernent l'acquisition de certains biens d'équipement ménager et les dépenses de vacances. Les projections de consommation établies dans l'hypothèse d'une distribution de revenu inchangée seraient donc peu affectées par des mesures sociales en faveur des catégories les moins favorisées de la population titulaires de bas salaires et revenus agricoles, familles nombreuses, par exemple.

3.2.*b*. Les variations dans la structure des prix doivent être, tout au moins si l'on considère des groupes de biens suffisamment agrégés, d'une ampleur limitée. Les informations relatives aux élasticités-prix demeurent fragmentaires ou incohérentes dans leur ensemble, sauf dans quelques cas particuliers (substitution charbon-fuel par exemple). On a choisi en règle générale de les négliger, bien que cette attitude soit critiquable. Précisons toutefois que les méthodes de projection tenant compte, comme nous le verrons, des séries temporelles, intègrent partiellement l'influence d'une variation de la structure des prix voisine de celle observée dans le passé.

En fait les facteurs généraux retenus dans la projection sont essentiellement:
— l'évolution démographique de la population et sa répartition entre agricoles et non agricoles,
— la croissance de la consommation totale, choisie comme indicateur de niveau de vie.
— des variables spécifiques à certains produits: parcs des biens durables, facteurs de diffusion pour des biens nouveaux par exemple.

3.3.   LES INFORMATIONS DISPONIBLES

Trois sources principales ont été utilisées pour estimer le développement futur de la consommation.

3.3.*a. Les séries de comptabilité nationale française*

On dispose d'une série homogène de comptabilité nationale depuis 1949[3]) en prix courants et prix 1956 qui comporte une décomposition de la consommation par fonction et produits établie en commun par le SEEF et le CREDOC[4]).

---

[3]) Les comptes de la Nation, Volume 1, 1960, Imprimerie Nationale. Voir aussi «Consommation» Revue du CREDOC, Volume 2, 1958.
[4]) INSEE Institut National de la Statistique et des Etudes Economiques. CREDOC Centre de Recherches et de Documentation sur la consommation.

3.3.*b. Les résultats d'une enquête sur les budgets familiaux* effectuée en 1956 par l'INSEE et le CREDOC[5]). Son exploitation a été effectuée en ajustant aux résultats, des «lois de consommation» de deux types différents suivant la nature des produits.

$$C_j = a_j \log R + b_j \text{ pour les prouits alimentaires} \qquad (1)$$

$$\log C_j = a_j \log R + b_j \text{ pour les autres produits} \qquad (2)$$

ou C_j = désigne la consommation par produit et par unité de consommation.

R = la consommation totale.

L'autoconsommation a fait l'objet d'analyses séparées.

Les exploitations ont été réalisées en classant les ménages enquêtés suivant divers critères:
— Taille du ménage,
— Catégorie socio-professionnelle,
— Catégories de communes.

3.3.*c. Les comparaisons internationales*

Les annuaires de comptabilité nationale des organismes internationaux contiennent des évaluations de la consommation privée qui, utilisées avec précaution, peuvent aider à la prévision. On dispose aussi de travaux de projection effectués dans le cadre de l'OCDE et d'autres organismes internationaux. Une attention toute particulière a été portée à l'évolution de la consommation aux Etats-Unis. Malgré toutes les réserves qu'appellene ces comparaisons, il semble que le niveau de la consommation française en 1956 soit voisin de celui des Etats-Unis vers 1929. Les perspectives pour 1965 nous conduiraient à une consommation proche de celle des Etats-Unis vers la fin de la guerre. L'histoire du développement américain fournit donc un point de repère pour l'évolution future des pays européens à niveau de vie actuel moins élevé. Malgré les différences de mode de vie, une telle référence peut servir à apprécier la vraisemblance de certaines projections à long terme, mais ne peut être utilisée que comme complément d'information.

---

[5]) INSEE Institut National de la Statistique et des Etudes Economiques. CREDOC Centre de Recherches et de Documentation sur la consommation.

La base importante de la projection demeure l'analyse des enquêtes de budgets familiaux et des séries temporelles dont on est conduit maintenant à interpréter les résultats.

4.   La comparaison des analyses de budgets familiaux et des séries temporelles

4.1.   EXPOSÉ DU PROBLÈME

Les analyses de budgets familiaux et de séries temporelles sont de nature différente.

Si l'on adopte pour la prévision les «lois de consommation» résultant de l'analyse des budgets familiaux on admet implicitement qu'à revenus égaux le comportement des différents consommateurs présente un caractère permanent. La structure de la consommation des individus les plus riches actuellement constituerait une image satisfaisante de la consommation des individus les moins riches lorsqu'ils bénéficieront ultérieurement des mêmes revenus réels.

Au contraire, en faisant choix d'élasticités de consommation obtenues dans les séries temporelles, on admet que les liaisons globales observées dans le passé ont un caractère structurel qui se maintiendra dans la période couverte par la prévision.

L'ajustement statistique de lois de consommation de l'un ou l'autre type n'a donc a priori pas de raisons de conduire aux mêmes résultats numériques.

Tableau 3 compare les coefficients d'élasticité.

L'écart entre les coefficients d'élasticité, faible pour certains produits est d'une ampleur telle pour d'autres que leur utilisation conduirait à des évolutions très différentes (énergie – textile par exemple). Même pour les biens alimentaires l'écart apparaît significatif.

Certaines explications viennent immédiatement à l'esprit. Les analyses de budgets familiaux ne tiennent pas compte d'éléments dynamiques présents dans les séries temporelles: modification dans la structure des prix relatifs et la distribution des revenus, modification des comportements, apparition de produits nouveaux, ou plus élaborés, et subissant une part plus importante de frais de commercialisation etc. De plus, les enquêtes de budgets familiaux portent en général sur une période très courte et leurs résultats peuvent être entachés d'erreurs accidentelles.

Ces raisons n'apparaissent pas suffisantes. On peut en effet penser que

TABLEAU 3 – Comparaison des coefficients d'élasticité

Fonctions de consommation	Série en prix 1956 1949/59[a])	Enquête budgets de famille 1956	
		Population agricole	Population non-agricole
ALIMENTATION	0,70	0,65	0,55
Produits à base de céréales	0,20	0,50	0,20
Légumes et fruits	0,40	0,75	0,95
Viande, volailles, œufs, poissons	0,70	0,85	0,72
Produits laitiers et corps gras	0,60	0,45	0,30
Sucre et produits divers	1,30	0,58	0,20
Boissons	0,40	0,65	0,60
HABILLEMENT	1,10	0,90	1,35
Vêtements	1,20	0,95	1,40
Chaussures	0,70	0,50	0,90
HABITATION	1,30		
Logement	—	—	1,46
Equipement du logement	2,20	1,72	1,64
Energie et produits d'entretien	1,00	0,93	0,60
HYGIÈNE ET SOINS	1,70	1,20	0,98
Hygiène et soins personnels	1,30	1,40	1,95
Consommation médicale	1,80	1,10	0,70
TRANSPORTS ET COMMUNICATIONS	1,70	—	—
Transports individuels	2,10		—
Achats	2,00	2,70	
Utilisation	2,10	3,40	3,74
Transports collectifs	0,50⎫	1,15	1,97
Télécommunications	1,40⎭		
CULTURE ET LOISIRS		1,30	1,65
Hôtels, cafés, restaurants, divers	0,90	—	—

[a]) Ajustement graphique.

les élasticités revenu des budgets familiaux sont affectés d'une erreur systématique. On présentera ci-dessous une hypothèse susceptible, nous semble-t-il, d'éclairer cette question, très importante pour les travaux de projection.

Malgré le caractère incertain des statistiques disponibles et la difficulté de comparaisons précises – il semble que l'on puisse faire l'hypothèse suivante:

Pour des biens que nous qualifierons de 1ère nécessité, l'élasticité (par rapport au revenu ou à la consommation globale) est en général plus élevée dans les séries temporelles que dans les budgets familiaux, elle serait au contraire moins élevée pour les autres biens.

Une théorie même provisoire justifiant cette hypothèse permettrait ainsi d'interprêter de façon cohérente les coefficients d'élasticité – tout au moins pour les biens de consommation dont l'évolution est correctement expliquée par le revenu courant de l'année.

Nous exposerons ci-dessous très brièvement une justification de cette hypothèse généralisant les idées de M. FRIEDMAN qui a expliqué le fait que l'élasticité globale de la consommation soit très inférieure à l'unité dans les enquêtes de budgets familiaux (alors qu'elle est voisine de 1 dans les séries temporelles) par l'existence de variations accidentelles dans le revenu et la consommation des individus enquêtés.

Les observations de l'enquête sont donc «biaisées» par rapport aux composantes permanentes du revenu et de la consommation et l'ajustement d'une loi globale minore l'élasticité réelle de la consommation.

Cette hypothèse peut être étendue aux divers biens de consommation. L'idée simple qui va être formalisée est que les variations accidentelles de revenu ont peu d'influence sur la demande des biens de 1ère nécessité, mais jouent au contraire un grand rôle dans celle des autres biens.

4.2. FORMALISATION

Considérons un échantillon de N individus ($1 \leq i \leq N$) et désignons par R_{it} et C_{it}^k, la consommation totale et la consommation d'un bien k au cours d'une période t pour l'individu i.

Posons

$$\text{I} \quad \begin{cases} R_{it} = R_{p,\,it}(1 + \varepsilon_{it}) \\ C_{it}^k = C_{p,\,it}^k (1 + \eta_{it}^k) \end{cases}$$

— $R_{p,it}$ et $C_{p,it}$ représentent la composante systématique, ou permanente, du revenu et de la consommation.

— $\varepsilon_{it} R_{p,it}$ et $\eta_{it}^k C_{p,it}^k$ les composantes aléatoires.

En posant Log $R_{it} = r_{it}$

Log $C_{it}^k = c_{it}^k$

les perturbations ε et η étant supposées petites on obtient

$$r_{it} = r_{p,it} + \varepsilon_{it}$$

$$c_{it}^k = c_{p,it}^k + \eta^k{}_t.$$

On impose aux composantes ε et η des propriétés suivantes:

a) Les variables aléatoires ε_{it} et η_{it}^k sont de moyenne nulle, indépendantes des composantes systématiques.

b) Il existe une relation fonctionnelle entre les composantes systématiques du revenu et de la consommation.

$$c_{p,it}^k = A_k r_{p,it} + B_k.$$

A_k est la véritable élasticité de consommation que l'on devrait utiliser dans les projections.

En raison des hypothèses (a) les moyennes par tête (pour l'ensemble de la population) du revenu et de la consommation sont peu différentes des composantes systématiques moyennes correspondantes. A_k peut être assimilé à l'élasticité constatée dans les séries chronologiques en faisant abstraction des autres influences (celle des prix par exemple).

c) la régression de η_{it}^k en ε_{it} est linéaire.

$$E[\eta_{it}^k/\varepsilon_{it}] = \eta_{it}^k \varepsilon_{it}.$$

Le coefficient $\mu_{it}^k = \mu_k$, supposé indépendant de i et t, peut être interprêté comme l'élasticité du bien k pour une variation aléatoire du revenu.

Si, sur les données de l'enquête de budgets familiaux on ajoute une loi de la forme

$$c_{it}^k = \alpha_{k,t} r_{it} + \beta_{k,t}$$

par la méthode des moindres carrés,

α_k est l'élasticité de consommation relative aux budgets familiaux à comparer avec A_k élasticité réelle.

On peut alors classer les biens en 3 groupes.

$$G_1 : \mu^k < A_k$$
$$G_2 : \mu^k = A_k$$
$$G_3 : \mu^k > A_k.$$

— Le groupe G_1 comprend les biens pour lesquels l'élasticité relative a des variations aléatoires de revenu est inférieure à l'élasticité à long terme. Cette propriété caractérise assez bien les produits de première nécessité assez insensibles aux variations conjoncturelles de revenu – par exemple les produits alimentaires.

— Le groupe G_3 comprend les biens de luxe, très sensibles au contraire à des variations inattendues de revenu.

— Le groupe G_2 est intermédiaire.

On peut démontrer alors que[6])

pour les biens du groupe $G_1 : \alpha_k < A_k$
pour les biens du groupe $G_2 : \alpha_k = A_k$
pour les biens du groupe $G_3 : \alpha_k > A_k$.

Cette théorie, rudimentaire, permet de mieux interpréter les résultats des enquêtes de budgets familiaux dont les avantages essentiels, et à notre avis irremplaçables, sont d'une part, de permettre des études dans une nomenclature détaillée, et d'autre part de pouvoir mettre en évidence l'influence de facteurs sociologiques :
– Taille des ménages,
– Catégorie sociale,
– Catégorie de communes,
utiles et relativement aisés à prendre en compte dans les projections de consommation.

Cette théorie s'est trouvée assez bien vérifiée par l'analyse de la consommation en France durant la période de stagnation des revenus 1958–1959.

5.   Les méthodes de projection proprement dites

On a procédé en deux étapes.
1) Projection par unité de consommation ou par ménage, de la consommation exprimée dans une nomenclature de besoins ou fonctions. Cette projection est effectuée en faisant la synthèse des informations disponibles sur les lois de consommation.

L'évolution de la demande des biens durables, automobile et équipement du logement, a été estimée en tenant compte simultanément de l'accroissement du parc en fonction du revenu et de la durée de vie probable des différents équipements. Les ventes relatives à une année déterminée sont la somme de l'accroissement annuel du parc et de la demande de remplacement.

Pour la plupart des produits les projections ont été établies par grandes catégories socio-professionelles, essentiellement les ménages agricoles et non-agricoles. Les analyses de budgets familiaux ont montré que les différences de comportement étaient surtout sensibles à ce niveau, la population non-agricole ayant dans son ensemble un comportement plus

---

[6]) Voir démonstration en annexe.

homogène. Les résultats ont été ensuite extrapolés à la population totale en tenant compte de l'évolution prévisible de sa structure.

2) Répartition du total de la consommation par «fonction» selon les produits classés dans une nomenclature de production.

C'est en cours de cette seconde étape que devrait être prise en compte explicitement l'influence des prix relatifs sur les substitutions entre produits satisfaisant les mêmes besoins. Cette répartition par produit a été effectuée en fonction des tendances observées dans le passé et d'hypothèses jugées raisonnables sur l'évolution des prix relatifs, pour l'énergie, par exemple.

Les deux étapes de la projection ne sont d'ailleurs pas indépendantes en ce sens qu'une analyse par produit a pu conduire à réviser l'analyse par fonction et inversement.

III. LES RESULTATS D'UNE PROJECTION 1970

1. Remarques préliminaires

1.1. Comme on l'a déjà signalé, l'année 1970 n'a pas fait l'objet de pro jection particulière. Des études détaillées ont été réalisées pour 1965, échéance du 4ème Plan, ainsi que des perspectives plus globales pour 1975.

Les évaluations relatives à 1970, proposées dans cet article ont été obtenues par extrapolation sans que soient bien pris en compte toutes les caractéristiques de l'année 1970.

1.2. Les nomenclatures utilisées en France sont différentes de celle proposée pour ce livre de l'ASEPELT. Si pour 1965 la correspondance entre elles ne pose pas de difficultés, l'utilisation des travaux sur 1975, plus globaux, implique que la nomenclature n'a pu être entièrement respectée. Les écarts seront signalés.

Le concept de consommation est lui-même différent. La consommation alimentaire est la consommation à domicile. La consommation hors domicile (restaurant, cantine etc.) est incluse dans la demande de services et les achats alimentaires apparaissent dans la consommation intermédiaire des branches correspondantes. Ce traitement semble mieux traduire le comportement effectif des consommateurs et permet tout aussi bien de «remonter» à la production agricole ou d'établir des bilans alimentaires, la comptabilité française comprenant unensemble complètement intégré de relations.

Un tableau de passage sera présenté pour l'année 1965 seulement.

1.3. Les résultats de la projection

Tableau 4 indique les résultats de la projection en francs 1959.

TABLEAU 4 – Evolution de la consommation

	Valeur en milliards de NF 1959	Indices 1959 = 100		
		1965	1970	1975
1. Produits à base de céréales	7,350	117	127	139
2. Produits laitiers[1])	10,000	116	130	142
3. Viande – poissons – œufs[2])	20,810	122	145	172
4. Légumes et fruits[3])	7,270	124	150	179
5. Autres biens alimentaires[4])	4,440	138	168	220
6. Boissons[5])	10,110	117	134	152
7. Tabac[6])	3,420	121	129	137
8. Vêtements et produits en cuir[7])	20,810	135	167	208
9. Biens durables[8])	11,560	163	238	345
10. Chauffage, éclairage	8,140	136	171	214
11. Logement[9])	8,340	137	175	222
12. Santé[10])	15,310	152	220	290
13. Transports publics[11])	4,620	125	151	182
14. Achats de moyens de transport individuels	3,340	174	250	360
15. Dépenses de transport privé	4,550	172	247	353
16. Autres biens et services[12])	21,350	140	193	267
17. Dépenses des nationaux à l'extérieur[13])	5,580	115	150	210
18. Dépenses des non nationaux à l'intérieur[13])	—4,030	160	215	300
Ensemble 1–16	162,970	135	172	222

[1]) y compris huile margarine et graisses animales
[2]) y compris charcuterie et conserves de viande
[3]) non compris conserves
[4]) y compris conserves de fruits et légumes
[5]) y compris boissons alcoolisées
[6]) y compris allumettes
[7]) y compris maroquinerie
[8]) non compris jouets et articles de sport
[9]) y compris produits d'entretien
[10]) y compris dépenses d'hygiène et soins personnels
     y compris remboursements sécurité sociale et assistance.
[11]) y compris P.T.T.
[12]) y compris jouets et articles de sport.
     La valeur des denrées alimentaires consommées dans les restaurants n'est pas exclue.
     Non compris dépenses d'hygiène personnelle.
     Non compris services domestiques et assurances exclus des dépenses de consommation.
[13]) touristes et voyageurs, fonctionnaires et militaires, travailleurs temporaires.

1.4. Remarques

La part de la consommation alimentaire (à domicile) qui s'élevait à 37,2% en 1959 pourrait ne plus représenter que 27,2% de la consommation en 1975 et 30% en 1970. Mais corrélativement la consommation hors domicile liée d'une part à la généralisation de la journée continue et au développement des loisirs devrait s'accroître.

Pour 1965, la consommation totale de produits alimentaires évoluerait comme suit:

	Valeur 1959	Indice 65/59
Consommation à domicile [a]	63,25	119,4
Consommation hors domicile [a]	7,7	125
Consommation alimentaire totale	70,95	120

[a] Aux prix de détail y compris pour l'autoconsommation boissons comprises.

On sait que l'évolution des dépenses alimentaires aux prix de détail dépasse celle des dépenses évaluées aux prix à la ferme (ou à l'importation), l'élévation du niveau de vie se traduisant non seulement par une augmentation des quantités consommées mais aussi par une amélioration de leur qualité.

Cet «effet qualité» est difficile à apprécier. Pour 1965 l'augmentation des dépenses alimentaires évaluée au prix des produits de base pourrait être de 17% contre 20% évaluée aux prix de détail des produits transformés. L'écart est plus faible que celui qui apparaît dans les études de la FAO mais on doit considérer qu'une partie de l'effet qualité est déjà localisé au niveau de la production agricole.

Parmi les consommations non alimentaires le développement se porterait vers les biens durables, les dépenses de santé et celles de transport. En 1975 le parc de réfrigérateurs pourrait s'élever à 17 millions soit sensiblement 1 par ménage, contre 7 millions en 1965. Celui des machines à laver à 10,2 millions (0,6 par ménage) et celui des télévisions à 12 millions (0,7 par ménage). Parallèlement 7 ménages sur 10 possèderaient une automobile, certains en possédant plusieurs.

IV. L'INCERTITUDE DES PROJECTIONS DE CONSOMMATION

L'importance de la consommation dans la préparation des plans conduit tout naturellement à s'interroger sur l'incertitude qui peut les affecter.

L'incertitude se situe à deux niveaux:

— celui de l'évolution globale, objectif du plan, considérée comme une donnée,

— celui de la décomposition par produit, le volume de la consommation globale étant fixé.

On n'examinera ici que l'incertitude liée à la décomposition par fonction ou produit.

Le travail de projection achevé, on peut calculer à posteriori des élasticités apparentes de consommation qui résument les résultats des études sur les divers facteurs pris en compte.

Toutes les remarques antérieures concernant les méthodes de projection montrent bien que chaque élasticité apparente est entachée d'une certaine incertitude. On a tenté de la chiffrer dans le cadre des travaux du 4ème Plan pour l'année 1965.

L'idée peut être la plus naturelle est d'affecter à chaque coefficient d'élasticité une loi de probabilité subjective construite en tenant compte d'opinions (parfois contradictoires) exprimées par divers spécialistes ou de la propre incertitude dans laquelle se trouvaient les personnes qui ont effectué le travail de projection.

C'est ainsi que par exemple les dépenses alimentaires pourraient se développer à un rythme plus élevé; que les dépenses d'habillement pourraient être surestimées, que l'expansion prévue des achats de biens durables du logement représenterait un minimum etc.

Cette partie présente les résultats d'une tentative d'étude de «*variantes*» basées sur ce principe.

Elle a porté sur l'incertitude:

— au niveau des «fonctions» de consommation dans une nomenclature d'ailleurs différente de celle de cette étude.

— au niveau des produits de la nomenclature de production.

Enfin, on a calculé l'influence de cette incertitude sur les taux de progression des différentes branches.

1. Principes de la méthode

1.1. LES LOIS DE PROBABILITÉS

On a envisagé selon les produits considérés 2 cas :
— Le coefficient d'élasticité est tel que l'on peut lui associer un intervalle, chaque point étant équivraisemblable.
— On associe encore un intervalle au coefficient d'élasticité mais on pense que la valeur initiale est plus probable que les autres choix possibles dans l'intervalle.

A chaque cas on associe une loi de probabilité simple, de type uniforme dans le 1er cas, triangulaire dans le second.

Voici à titre d'exemple les bornes de quelques intervalles, définies par rapport à l'élasticité initiale :

Alimentation	− 10%	+ 20%
Habillement	− 20%	0
Equipement du logement	0	20%
Transports collectifs	− 20%	+ 20%
Culture et loisirs	− 10%	+ 30%

1.2. LA DÉFINITION DES VARIANTES

Le principe de la méthode est de construire des échantillons «fictifs» de l'ensemble des coefficients d'élasticité à l'aide d'une table de nombres aléatoires.[7]) Cette méthode simule d'autres projections possibles en fonction des lois de probabilité admises. A chaque échantillon correspond un «profil de consommation». On a obtenu 200 profils de consommation possibles parmi lesquels on en a sélectionné trois, choisis parmi les plus différents du profil initial, en introduisant une «distance» qui permet de les classer par rapport à ce profil initial.

Le commentaire qui suit est relatif à ces trois profils et aux conséquences que l'on peut en déduire concernant l'incertitude de la projection.
— par fonction de consommation
— par produit
— par branche.

---

[7]) Il faut tenir compte du fait que la moyenne pondérée (par les coefficients budgétaires) des élasticités est égale à l'unité, de telle sorte que les incertitudes sur chaque élasticité ne peuvent pas etre indépendantes.

2.   Les résultats

2.1.   PAR FONCTIONS

On trouvera sur Tableau 5 les écarts en pourcentages par rapport aux projections de base.

TABLEAU 5

	Variantes		
	1	2	3
Alimentation	0	+ 2	− 1
Habillement	− 4	− 7	0
Logement et petit entretien	+ 1	− 2	0
Equipement du logement	+ 7	+ 2	+ 4
Energie produits d'entretien	− 1	− 2	− 1
Hygiène santé	0	0	+ 5
Transports individuels	+ 2	− 9	0
Transports collectifs	+ 3	+ 2	− 2
Culture loisirs – divers	− 1	+ 6	− 2

L'incertitude, d'après ces résultats serait assez importante sur l'habillement, les transports individuels, les dépenses de culture et loisirs. Rappelons que pour chaque variante l'évolution globale de la consommation est identique.

2.2.   PAR PRODUIT

En répartissant *de la même façon* les dépenses globales des fonctions dans une nomenclature de produits on obtient pour chacune des variantes les écarts suivants (en pourcentages) (Tableau 6).

L'incertitude au niveau des produits dans cette nomenclature agrégée apparaît en général moins importante que sur les fonctions de consommation. En effet, à ce niveau d'agrégation les produits d'une même branche satisfont des besoins différents et la nomenclature regroupe en général les produits les plus substituables. Le total de la consommation étant fixé, il existe des compensations à l'intérieur des groupes de produits, par exemple ceux des industries mécaniques et électriques qui comprennent à la fois des biens d'équipement du logement et des automobiles.

Tableau 6

	Variantes		
	1	2	3
Produits de l'agriculture	0	2	− 3
Produits des industries agricoles et alimentaires	0	2	− 2
Energie	+ 1	− 3	− 1
Produits des industries mécaniques et électriques	+ 3	− 2	+ 1
Produits chimiques	0	− 1	+ 3
Textiles et cuirs	− 4	− 6	0
Industries diverses	+ 2	+ 3	+ 1
Bâtiment et T.P.	+ 4	− 7	+ 2
Transports et télécommunications	+ 3	+ 2	− 2
Loyers et services	0	+ 2	+ 1

2.3. SUR LES NIVEAUX DE PRODUCTION

Les répercussions de l'incertitude de la répartition de la consommation par produit sur le niveau de production des différentes branches ont été estimées en utilisant un système de relations technologiques du type Léontief.

Si y désigne le vecteur de la demande finale, la production x lui est liée par la relation :

$$(I - A)x = y.$$

A étant la matrice des coefficients techniques.

En conservant les mêmes coefficients techniques (matrice A) que dans la variante initiale ainsi que les composantes de la demande finale autre que la consommation des particuliers, on a pu calculer les niveaux de production correspondant à chaque variante de consommation.

Les écarts en pourcentages par rapport aux perspectives initiales apparaissent sur le tableau.

Compte tenu de toutes les interdépendances, l'incertitude au niveau des grandes branches est assez faible. Elle ne demeure sensible que pour les branches orientées à titre principal vers la demande finale comme le textile. Elle apparaît au contraire négligeable au niveau des industries de base, ou qui ont une activité très polyvalente (industrie mécanique par exemple).

Certes, ces conséquences dépendent des hypothèses, posées a priori sur les lois de probabilité des différentes élasticités de consommation. Mais il n'apparaissait pas que l'influence finale fut si faible même au niveau de branches agrégées, les lois de probabilité étant assez dispersées. Bien que

TABLEAU 7

	Ecarts en %		
	1	2	3
Agriculture	− 0,2	+ 1,6	− 0,8
Industries agricoles et alimentaires	− 0,2	+ 1,8	− 0,9
Energie	+ 0,3	− 1,6	0
Industries mécaniques et électriques	+ 0,5	− 0,3	+ 0,3
Chimie	− 0,2	− 0,4	+ 0,6
Textile et cuirs	− 0,3	− 4,7	+ 0,1
Industries diverses	+ 0,6	+ 0,8	+ 0,3
Bâtiment et T.P.	− 0,3	− 0,5	+ 0,2
Transports et télécommunications	+ 0,7	+ 0,3	− 0,4
Loyers − services divers	− 0,2	+ 1,2	− 0,5

ce travail expérimental doive être complété par une étude plus détaillée, on est tenté alors de penser que dans des limites raisonnables, l'imprécision de la répartition entre les différents biens d'un total de consommation *fixé* a peu d'influence sur le niveau de production des grandes branches et par conséquent sur le montant des investissements nécessaires. Cette conclusion serait d'un grand intérêt pratique. Elle justifierait l'emploi de modèles globaux où l'économie est divisée seulement endeux ou trois secteurs dans la phase préparatoire du Plan. Elle légitimerait aussi l'établissement de projections détaillées indispensables pour engager le dialogue avec les Commissions de Modernisation spécialisées.

V. COMPARAISON PREVISIONS-REALISATIONS POUR L'ANNEE 1961

Une projection de consommation a été effectuée en 1956–1957 pour l'année 1961, échéance du 3ème Plan – la base statistique étant 1954.

La comparaison entre prévisions et réalisations permettra de mettre en évidence quelques insuffisances.

La comparaison précise est d'ailleurs délicate, les objectifs d'augmentation de volume global de la consommation n'ayant pas été réalisés, bien que l'évolution démographique ait été sous-estimée.

Il importe donc de séparer par produit l'influence du taux de croissance de celle des autres facteurs.

Certes, l'erreur commise sur le niveau global affecte aussi la répartition des biens et services consommés. Toutefois, certaines dépenses (classées

	Prévisions	Réalisation
Consommation totale – indice 1961/1954	141	134
Consommation par tête – indice 1961/1954	134	125

dans un premier groupe) sont essentiellement liées à l'évolution des revenus alors que d'autres (classées dans un second groupe) en sont plus indépendantes (chauffage, éclairage, loyers, soins médicaux).

La comparaison a porté plus particulièrement sur les produits du premier groupe en ramenant le niveau global de la consommation à celui effectivement observé en 1961.

Pour chaque fonction de consommation ou catégorie de produits on peut définir une erreur relative de prévision. La moyenne de ces erreurs relatives (en valeur absolue) pondérées par les dépenses correspondantes en 1954 représente une «erreur moyenne»:

$$ E = \sum_j A_j \left| \frac{C_{jP} - C_{jR}}{C_{jP}} \right|. $$

A_j désigne le coefficient budgétaire de l'année de base, C_{jP} l'évolution prévue pour le groupe j et C_{jR} l'évolution réalisée.

1. Les résultats

L'erreur moyenne est de l'ordre de 3% pour les biens du premier groupe défini ci-dessus, de 7% pour ceux du second groupe, et de 4% pour l'ensemble de la consommation exprimée dans une nomenclature «fonctionelle» en 25 postes. If faut noter que l'erreur moyenne, toutes choses restant égales, est d'autant plus faible que la nomenclature de comparaison est plus agrégée.

Tableau 8 précise cette comparaison.

1.1. ALIMENTATION

L'erreur de prévision est en moyenne de 3%. En général, l'évolution a été sous-estimée sauf pour les produits à base de céréales et les boissons (vins et boissons alcoolisées). Pour l'ensemble des viandes, volailles, l'erreur est faible mais la substitution de la viande de porc et la volaille à la viande de bœuf accompagnée de fortes variations de prix, n'avait pas été prévue.

TABLEAU 8 – Comparaison pour l'année 1961

	Dépenses 1954 aux prix 1956[1])	Indices 1961/1954		Erreurs relatives en %
		Prévisions 3ème Plan	Réali- sations[3])	
Produits à base de céréales	5,910	112,2	107,8	3,95
Légumes	3,820	116,6	115,6	0,83
Fruits	2,690	131,5	135,2	— 2,83
Viandes, volailles, œufs, poissons	14,990	121,8	122,8	— 0,89
Produits laitiers et corps gras	7,490	114,1	119,7	— 4,92
Produits d'alimentation divers	2,440	121,0	130,0	— 7,43
Boissons et stimulants	6,620	115,8	113,3	2,11
ALIMENTATION	43,950	118,4	119,4	2,65
Vêtements	12,050	138,2	140,5	— 1,62
Chaussures et articles chaus- sants	2,190	124,1	118,2	4,93
HABILLEMENT	14,240	136,0	137,1	2,13[2])
Logement	4,010	147,2	136,4	7,36
Réparations et petit entretien	1,100	162,8	139,8	14,13
Equipement du logement	5,040	164,5	166,9	— 1,48
Energie	4,070	142,1	134,5	5,29
Produits d'entretien	1,210	128,2	123,7	3,48
HABITATION	15,440	151,1	145,1	5,07
Hygiène et soins personnels	1,650	139,8	140,3	— 0,35
Pharmacie, lunetterie, ortho- pédie	1,950	160,0	172,8	— 8,05
Soins médicaux, hospitalisation, cure	4,910	171,3	161,4	5,79
HYGIENE ET SANTE	8,510	162,6	159,9	5,25
Transports individuels	4,650	158,4	159,8	— 0,86
Transports collectifs	2,520	125,9	123,9	1,61
Télécommunications	340	148,3	141,0	4,90
TRANSPORTS ET TELECOMMUNICATIONS	7,520	147,0	146,8	1,29[2])
CULTURE ET LOISIRS	7,310	148,2	152,5	— 2,80
Services hôteliers	7,590	138,4	131,4	5,05
Biens et services divers	2,900	139,0	115,4	16,50
HOTELS, CAFES, RESTAURANTS ET DIVERS	10,490	138,6	127,0	8,21[2])
CONSOMMATION TOTALE	107,460		133,5	3,59[2])

[1]) En milliards de NF.　　[2]) Moyenne pondérée.　　[3]) Comptes provisoires.

1.2. Les dépenses d'HABILLEMENT ont été assez correctement prévues sauf l'évolution de la demande de chaussures surestimée de 5%.

1.3. HABITATION

L'erreur d'ensemble est de 5% environ l'évolution générale ayant été surestimée.

Les dépenses de loyers ont moins augmenté que prévu les objectifs de construction de logements neufs n'ayant pas été entièrement réalisés. Celles de chauffage et d'éclairage dépassent de 5% les prévisions mais analysées en détail font apparaître des écarts beaucoup plus importants. La demande de charbon a été surestimée de 15% ainsi que celle des produits pétroliers, par contre les possibilités de distribution de gaz de ville avaient été minorées.

Les dépenses d'équipement du logement ont été réalisées dans leur ensemble mais les achats de réfrigérateurs ont été sous-estimés au profit de ceux de machines à laver et de meubles dont le taux d'expansion n'a pas été atteint.

1.4. AUTRES BIENS

Les dépenses de matériel de transport se sont moins développées que prévu. Ce fait n'est pas imputable à la demande d'automobiles mais plutôt à celle de motocycles dont le marché en 1958 s'est brusquement effondré ce qui n'avait pas été imaginé.

On notera aussi la plus forte expansion des dépenses de culture et loisirs qui intéresse les ventes de livres et de récepteurs de télévision.

CONCLUSION

Cet article n'avait pas pour ambition de faire le point des méthodes d'économétrie de la demande, mais d'attirer l'attention sur les difficultés concrètes des projections effectivement réalisées pour l'élaboration des Plans en France. En fait, il apparait que la nature de ces difficultés est liée au fossé qui sépare actuellement la théorie du comportement du consommateur et les soucis des praticiens. Et ceci dépasse même semble-t-il, le problème de l'information statistique.

La comparaison entre prévision et réalisation pour l'année 1961 a montré que si, au niveau des besoins, l'appréciation avait été relativement correcte, des erreurs assez importantes apparaissaient au niveau des produits substituables. Un effort devrait donc être accompli dans la définition d'un ensemble complet de fonctions de consommation introduisant l'influence des prix relatifs, suffisamment élaborées pour être réalistes et suffisamment simples pour pouvoir faire l'objet de déterminations statistiques. Ce juste milieu ne semble pas avoir encore été atteint.

Même en ce qui concerne l'effet revenu, les problèmes de comparaison entre analyses de budgets familiaux et séries temporelles sont loin d'être résolus. Des comparaisons systématiques restent à faire qui sont très délicates en raison des différences de nomenclature et de champ couvert, même à l'intérieur d'un même pays. La généralisation des enquêtes permanentes telle qu'on l'envisage actuellement est certainement un instrument très précieux.

Enfin, lorsque la projection en «volume» est achevée, il est nécessaire de lui associer une projection des circuits de revenu dont on n'a pas parlé ici. Les études de financement entreprises pour le 4ème Plan ont mis en évidence la grande importance du comportement financier des ménages, d'une part globalement et d'autre part à l'égard des différentes natures de placement, monnaie, semi-liquidités, valeurs mobilières etc. Ce comportement de patrimoine, auxquels se rattachent les achats de biens durables, demeure encore incertain. Les enquêtes sur l'épargne qui commencent à se développer pourraient éclairer cette question de première importance pour l'espect financier du Plan.

SUMMARY

Consumption forecasts are becoming more and more important parts of the French Four Year Plans. The Fourth Plan (1961–1965) in particular was based on a detailed discussion of estimates for 1965 and 1975 in a large number of working groups. The 1970 forecasts given in Table 4 are interpolations between these two sets of estimates.

While rising incomes will be the most important factor determining future consumption, some attention should be given to such matters as the distribution of disposable income, the price structure, and the growth of the cities.

Time series of consumption since 1949 and a large budget study undertaken in 1956 are the main sources of data, which, however, often result in different income elasticities (Table 3). An attempt is made to explain these differences by a generalisation of Friedman's permanent income theory. The development of consumer expenditure in the United States can also serve as a guide.

Most of the estimates have been made separately for rural and urban households.

Experience has shown that forecasts are very uncertain indeed, and a special study has been made of the impact of this uncertainty on future production levels. From 200 artificially constructed 'variants' of the consumption pattern three were selected that differed most in various directions. These variants were translated into differential production patterns by means of a Leontief model. The result was that discrepancies in the consumption pattern will affect production of broad sectors to a lesser extent, except for typical consumer goods industries such as textiles.

One practical example of uncertainty in forecasting is given in Table 8 where forecasts for the 1954–1961 expansion of consumer expenditure are set against the provisional estimates for 1961 as now available.

Demonstration de la propriété liant l'élasticité revenu des enquêtes de budgets familiaux et des séries temporelles

En utilisant la méthode des moindres carrés on sait que:

$$\alpha_{k,t} = \frac{\sum_i (c_{it}^k - \bar{c}_t^k)(r_{it} - \bar{r}_t)}{\sum_i (r_{it} - \bar{r}_t)^2} \tag{1}$$

ou $\bar{c}_t^k$ et $\bar{r}_t$ sont respectivement les moyennes de c_{it}^k et r_{it} dans l'enquête. En remplaçant dans (1) c_{it}^k et r_{it} par leur valeur

$$r_{it} = r_{p,it} + \varepsilon_{it}$$
$$c_{it}^k = c_{p,it}^k + \eta_{it}^k$$

et en tenant compte de l'hypothèse

$$c_{p,it} = A_k r_{p,it} + B_k$$

on trouve:

$$\alpha_{kt} = \frac{A_k \sum_i (r_{p,it} - \bar{r}_{pt})^2 + \sum_i (\eta_{it}^k - \bar{\eta}_{it}^k)(r_{p,it} - \bar{r}_{p,t}) +}{\sum_i (r_{p,it} - \bar{r}_{p,t})^2 + 2\sum_i (\varepsilon_{it} - \varepsilon_t)(r_{p,it} - \bar{r}_{p,t}) + \sum (\varepsilon_{it} - \bar{\varepsilon}_t)^2}$$

$$\frac{+ A_k \sum_i (r_{p,it} - \bar{r}_{pt})(\varepsilon_{it} - \bar{\varepsilon}_t) + \sum_i (\eta_{it}^k - \bar{\eta}_i^k)(\varepsilon_{it} - \bar{\varepsilon}_t)}{\sum_i (r_{p,it} - \bar{r}_{p,t})^2 + 2\sum_i (\varepsilon_{it} - \varepsilon_t)(r_{p,it} - \bar{r}_{p,t}) + \sum (\varepsilon_{it} - \bar{\varepsilon}_t)^2}$$

qui peut se mettre sous la forme:

$$= \frac{F}{G}.$$

En vertu des hypothèses posées et en divisant par N (nombre de consommateurs) le numérateur et le dénominateur,

$$\frac{F}{N} \to A_k \operatorname{Var}(r_{p,t}) + \operatorname{Cov}(\varepsilon_t \eta_t^k) \qquad \text{(presque sûrement)}$$

$$\frac{G}{N} \to \operatorname{Var}(r_{p,t}) + \operatorname{Var}(\varepsilon_t) \qquad \text{(presque sûrement)}$$

[1]) Cette annexe est issue d'un article publié par l'auteur: «Lois de consommation statiques et dynamiques», Etudes de Comptabilité nationale, Imprimerie Nationale Paris, No. 2, 1961.

on sait alors, d'après un théorème de calcul de probabilités, que:

$$\alpha_{k,t} \rightarrow \frac{\lim F}{\lim G} \qquad \text{(presque sûrement)}$$

soit, le nombre N d'individus enquêtés étant grand:

$$\alpha_{k,t} \simeq \frac{A_k \operatorname{Var}(r_{p,t}) + \operatorname{Cov}(\varepsilon_t \eta_t^k)}{\operatorname{Var}(r_{t\ t}) + \operatorname{Var}(\varepsilon_t)}$$

$$\alpha_{k,t} - A_k = \frac{\operatorname{Cov}(\varepsilon_t \eta_t^k) - A_k \operatorname{Var}(\varepsilon_t)}{\operatorname{Var}(r_{p,t}) + \operatorname{Var}(\varepsilon_t)} =$$

$$= \frac{\dfrac{\operatorname{Cov}(\varepsilon_t \eta_t^k)}{\operatorname{Var}(\varepsilon_t)} - A_k}{\dfrac{\operatorname{Var}(r_{p,t})}{\operatorname{Var}(\varepsilon_t)} + 1}. \qquad (2)$$

Cette relation montre que $\alpha_{k,t} - A_k$ est de même signe que $\mu_t^k - A_k$.

1. *Pour le groupe G_1:*
   d'après sa définition:

$$\mu_t^k < A_k$$

   d'où:

$$\alpha_{k,t} < A_k.$$

2. *Pour le groupe G_2:*
   alors:

$$\mu_t^k = A_k$$

   d'où

$$\alpha_{k,t} = A_k.$$

3. *Pour le groupe G_3:*
   d'après sa définition:

$$\mu_t^k > A_k$$

   d'où:

$$\alpha_{k,t} > A_k.$$

STRUCTURAL CHANGES IN ITALY'S PRIVATE CONSUMPTION EXPENDITURES PROJECTIONS FOR THE NEXT TEN YEARS*)

BY

NINO NOVACCO AND FRANCO PILLOTON†)

SVIMEZ, Rome, Italy

1. INTRODUCTION

Since the end of World War II, there has been a growing interest – in many Western countries -- in studies of economic development prospects based on so-called 'projection' methods. These studies – which are generally at the macro-economic level – have often a dual purpose. On the one hand, they promote a deeper knowledge of development problems, a need growingly felt by economists; on the other, there is a tendency to put the results of these projections to such practical ends as orientating the decisions of the business world or providing a guideline to policy makers in their choice of economic measures to promote growth or to maintain a sustained growth rate.

Some of the most interesting projections concern developments in private consumption. Their importance is self-evident if one thinks of the influence exerted by the size, structure and geographical location of consumer demand variations on the level, and distribution, of investment by industry and area, and consequently, over the whole structure of the economy and its potential expansion rates.

Consumption projections may be obtained from general equilibrium econometric models, comprising simultaneous equation systems which explain the relations among different aggregates considered of relevance for the description of a given economic system. With reference to the

*) For Appendix B see p. 347.
†) This study was conducted as part of the Authors' work with SVIMEZ, Associazione per lo sviluppo dell'industria nel Mezzogiorno, 'Centro per gli studi sullo sviluppo economico' (Association for the Industrial Development of Southern Italy, 'Center for Studies on Economic Development').

autonomous variations assumed for certain aggregates (exogenous variables), and on the basis of empirically determined parameters, these models enable the economist to estimate the values acquired by all other aggregates (endogenous variables), among which there is also private consumption; its breakdown by type of expenditure is then perforce strictly connected to the dimensions of the model itself[1]).

Another type of projection of private consumption leads to an entirely autonomous evaluation of possible consumption developments, disregarding general equilibrium relations and utilizing empirically determined functional relations between the consumption of a given product or service and the national income level. In this case the projections – although in general less aggregated than those obtainable from the previous method – represent only the first stage of a study aimed at the formulation of detailed development forecasts for a given economic system[2]) by means of successive approximations *(iterative analysis)*.

We have used the latter projection method in this study of the development of private consumption in Italy from 1960 to 1970. We are fully aware that it may provide us with only first approximation results, which should be checked – before being accepted – by means of a consistency test, such as the iterative analysis mentioned before. It must be noted, however, that in Italy some experience has been acquired in the use of these projection methods. In fact – notwithstanding the methodological innovations introduced from time to time and the qualitative improvements of the basic statistical evidence – these projections have always led to results reflecting the same trends outlined in this study[3]). We have

---

[1]) Cf., e.g.: F. PILLOTON, Analisi degli effetti indotti nello schema leontieviano delle interdipendenze strutturali, in 'L'Industria', nr. 4, 1952.

[2]) Cf. V. CAO PINNA, Validité théorique et empirique d'une prévision globale de la croissance de l'économie italienne de 1958 à 1970, in 'Europe's Future in Figures', Edited by R. C. GEARY, North-Holland Publishing Company, Amsterdam, 1962; and Méthode de prévision du développement économique à long terme; Rapport d'un groupe d'experts, in 'Informations Statistiques', nr. 6, Office Statistique des Communautés Européennes, Bruxelles.

[3]) Cf., in this connection: V. CAO PINNA, Struttura ed elasticità dei consumi delle famiglie italiane; Contributo alla preparazione dello schema di sviluppo dell'occupazione e del reddito in Italia nel decennio 1954–64, Roma, 1954 (proof prints); Id., Struttura ed elasticità dei consumi di un campione di famiglie italiane; Analisi dei risultati di una indagine su 1600 famiglie italiane, Roma, 1958 (mimeographed); SVIMEZ, Stime sui consumi privati in Italia nel prossimo decennio, Giuffrè, Roma, 1960; F. PILLOTON, Redditi e consumi della famiglia italiana in relazione allo sviluppo economico del paese, in 'Quaderni di azione sociale', ACLI, nr. 4–5, 1961; V. CAO PINNA, Le prospettive dei consumi alimentari in Italia: 1965, 1970, 1975, Istituto italiano per gli studi sui consumi, Giuffrè, Roma, 1962.

thus good reason to believe that the projections illustrated in the following pages are sufficiently reliable, especially in respect of the structural
changes which should take place in the next ten years.

For a better understanding of the range of these changes, we must keep
in mind that Italy's present consumption level and structure constitute
an absolute novelty in the country's economy, which had been previously
characterized by living standards not too dissimilar from those prevailing
in non-industrialized countries.

In 1950, that is in the year marking the end of the postwar reconstruction period, Italy's average *per capita* consumption – according to national accounts data – amounted to about 132000 lire annually[4]. In the
same year, food accounted for 49% of total consumption expenditure, as
against 39% in France, 33% in the Netherlands, 29% in Belgium and 24%
in the United States. In these countries, *per capita* private consumption
expenditures was considerably higher than in Italy: from 50% higher in
the Netherlands up to a maximum of 500% in the United States[5]).

Although the value of these international comparisons is doubtful, the
magnitude of the differences leaves no doubt that in 1950 Italy's standard
of consumption was still one of the lowest of the Western Countries, with
regard to both the absolute level and the share absorbed by food expenditures.

During the following ten years, the situation improved substantially,
thanks to Italy's economic development. In the last decade, private consumption – in real terms – expanded at an annual rate of 4.7%[6]). If we
consider that, in the same period, the population grew at an annual rate
averaging 0.55–0.60%, we see that the increase in *per capita* consumption
averaged more than 4% annually.

---

[4]) If we consider the shape assumed by the frequency distribution of the variable
under consideration, we estimate the 1950 modal *per capita* consumption to be of the
order of magnitude of 100000 lire annually. For tentative comparison purposes, it
should be remembered that the official lira-dollar exchange rate was 625 lire to the dol-
lar during the last ten years – although the lira purchasing power has proved higher
than that indicated by the exchange rate (Cf.: M.GILBERT and J.B.KRAVIS, An International Comparison of National Products and the Purchasing Power of Currencies,
OEEC, Paris, 1954, and M.GILBERT and Associates, Comparative National Products
and Price Levels, OEEC, Paris, 1958).

[5]) Cf.: OECE, 'Bulletins statistiques de l'OECE, Statistiques générales', nr.1, 1960.

[6]) The expansion of investment was considerably higher than that of consumption.
During the fifties, gross investment – in real terms – grew by 9.1% annually, and its
share of gross domestic expenditure grew from 18.9% in 1950 to 25.9% in 1960, with a
marginal ratio of 35.3% (all percentages are calculated on the basis of 1954 lire).

To have an idea of what these figures mean for a country like Italy, it may suffice to underline that from the political unification to the eve of the Second World War, overall consumption in Italy grew at an average annual rate of less than 1.2% and *per capita* consumption at an annual average of only about 0.5%. In this long period, the lack of any real development in private consumption kept the composition of expenditure practically unchanged: up to the thirties at least, with the exception of a few changes caused mainly by relative price fluctuations, about two thirds of expenditure was steadily absorbed by food, beverages and tobacco. This happened when other countries – thanks to industrialization – were enjoying an increase in income which led to a considerable expansion in private consumption and a radical improvement in its composition expecially since the turn of the century. The share accounted for by essential consumer goods (food, in particular) was gradually declining, whereas the consumption of goods and services typical of higher living standards[7]) was acquiring a growing importance.

As the reconstruction period following the Second World War reached its end, and thanks to the general improvement of economic conditions, Italy also underwent a radical change in the pattern of consumer expenditure, such as that which had already occurred, at least half a century before, in industrial countries. According to the results of this study, provided that the national income keeps on growing steadily, as we hope, this process of change should be further intensified in the near future.

2. METHODS FOLLOWED AND WORKING ASSUMPTIONS FOR PROJECTIONS

The projections contained in this study were made on the basis of the elasticities presented by *per capita* expenditures on certain classes of goods and services set against the change in aggregate *per capita* private consumption expenditure. The evaluation of such elasticities was based on:

a) the results of a SVIMEZ study on the development of private consumption expenditure from 1958 to 1970[8]);

b) the results of Prof. Cao Pinna's study on the development of food consumption expenditure from 1955–1957 to 1975[9]);

---

[7]) Cf.: SVIMEZ, Stime sui consumi privati, ecc., *op. cit.*, Chapter I; ONU-ECE, Etude sur la situation économique de l'Europe en 1958, Chapter V, Genève, 1959.

[8]) Cf.: SVIMEZ, Stime sui consumi privati, ecc., *op. cit.*

[9]) Cf.: V. CAO PINNA, Le prospettive dei consumi alimentari, ecc., *op. cit.*

c) a number of Engel consumption equations, specifically fitted – for the purpose of this study – on the *regional historical series* (North and Mezzogiorno) of Italy's territorial economic accounts from 1951 to 1961.

A brief discussion of the methods of analysis followed in the SVIMEZ study is necessary since it provided most of the material we used.

The SVIMEZ study is based on some functional relations between *per capita* expenditure on certain classes of goods and services and the overall *per capita* expenditure on private consumption. These relations were empirically fitted on data drawn from two different statistical sources, namely:

a) the 1953 survey of family budgets made by the DOXA institute on a random sample of 1 599 families[10];

b) the *national historical series* of Italy's economic accounts from 1950 to 1958.

The use of both sources was prompted by the fact that each presented individual advantages and shortcomings according to the specific application. As stated in the SVIMEZ study, 'in the analysis of household budgets it is generally considered advantageous to have a grouping of households by *per capita* expenditure class leading to a differentiation of consumption among the different classes, in which qualitative factors play an important role. This circumstance is particularly useful when, employing functions for forecasting purposes, one is confronted with situations in which a considerable increase in consumer expenditures is highly probable. The functions obtained on this basis present, however, the serious shortcoming of being essentially static, since they disregard all those dynamic elements which are implicitly present in time series and which should be taken into account in the drafting of long term forecasts (five or ten years); these dynamic elements consist essentially of changes in income distribution, price structure variations, effects of technological progress, changes in the average consumer preferences, etc.'

'Owing to these considerations, and taking into account the fact that the Italian situation – in spite of the substantial increases of recent years – is still characterized by relatively low *per capita* consumption levels, it was deemed necessary to forecast the changes in expenditure composition with due regard to both the qualitative substitution processes emphasized by the equations obtained from household budgets and those dynamic

---

[10] The survey was financed by the Mutual Security Agency, Cassa per il Mezzogiorno and SVIMEZ.

factors that are always included in the analysis of historical series, even if only implicitly when the equations are characterized by only one independent variable' (overall *per capita* expenditure on private consumption).

Moreover, considering that the above mentioned qualitative substitution process presents some limits, beyond which it becomes less important, the SVIMEZ study resorted to special calculations, based on data drawn from household budgets, for the determination of certain kinds of sigmoidal functions. These functions are characterized by the fact that they never exceed some given consumption levels, which are consequently called saturation levels[11]).

In conclusion, we may say that the projections made by SVIMEZ were based on three series of expenditure functions, of which two were determined from household budgets and one from the analysis of historical series. The projections made with these three types of functions were subsequently averaged out in order to obtain a unified series of evaluations jointly complying with the above mentioned requirements.

In the present study, on the other hand, we have calculated the elasticity values from the results obtained from the three series of functions. We have then critically analyzed their differences, taking into account also the results provided by the expenditure functions calculated from the above mentioned regional historical series. On the basis of this critical analysis we have finally selected the elasticities used in our projections.

Prof. Cao Pinna's study[12]) was used in order to supplement the results of our projections in the food sector, for which no details are supplied by the SVIMEZ survey. Cao Pinna's evaluation of the developments of food consumption in the next ten years is of a very analytical nature and utilizes the following basic statistical material:

a) the historical series of *per capita* food availability and aggregate expenditure on private consumption calculated by the Central Institute of Statistics (ISTAT);

b) the sample survey of the budgets of 1599 Italian households, already mentioned in connection with the SVIMEZ study;

---

[11]) Among the many essays on this subject, cf.: F. PILLOTON and E. MALFATTI, Note sull'impiego della funzione sigmoide nello studio delle curve engeliane, in SVIMEZ, 'Stime sui consumi privati, ecc.', *op. cit.* Appendix C.

[12]) This study was promoted by the US Department of Agriculture within the framework of a wider programme aimed at analyzing medium and long term development prospects of the supply and demand of agricultural produce in some countries of the Western hemisphere.

c) the ISTAT sample survey of the budgets of 8207 non agricultural households carried out in 1953 and 1954[13]).

We have used Cao Pinna's results in our study in the same manner as we did for those of the SVIMEZ study: the evaluation of individual *per capita* expenditure on food products enabled us to calculate elasticities in respect of the total *per capita* expenditure on food, and these elasticities were then used in our projections.

A few remarks are in order as to the working assumptions adopted in estimating the development of the total *per capita* expenditure on private consumption. They relate to the foreseeable increase in gross domestic expenditure, the foreseeable changes in the propensity to consume and in the total population[14]).

With regard to domestic expenditure, we have assumed an average annual increase of 5% for the whole projection period. If we consider the Italian balance of payments situation, we see that such a rate is roughly equal to that of the gross national product. Moreover, if we take into account that the past ten years have recorded an average annual growth rate of GNP (in 1954 lire) approximating 6% (5.55% in the period 1950 to 1955 and 6.85% in 1956–1961), and that present development prospects in the Mezzogiorno are much brighter than in the early fifties, we find that the assumption of a 5% average growth rate for the whole period considered in our projection is sufficiently reliable and substantially consistent with the assumption made by SVIMEZ in 1960[15]).

[13]) Cf.: ISTAT, Indagine statistica di bilanci di famiglie non agricole negli anni 1953–54, in 'Annali di statistica', Anno 89, Serie VIII, Vol. 11, Roma, 1960.

[14]) It should be noted that, as in the case of Italian national accounts, private consumption expenditures are defined, in this study, in terms of national and not domestic consumption expenditures: they include, therefore, the consumption expenditures of members of households residing in the country (even though temporarily abroad) and they exclude the consumption expenditures of those residing abroad (even though temporarily in Italy). In view of this fact, *per capita* consumption should be calculated on the basis of *de jure* population; however, since we have good reason to believe that the annual population data calculated by ISTAT are overestimated (owing to the difficulties involved in keeping current registrations and cancellations at the Register Office (Anagrafe)), we have preferred to use Italian *de facto* population data which – as is well known – does not take account of tourist movements.

[15]) In the SVIMEZ study already mentioned the assumptions on income envisaged a 5% annual increase from 1958 to 1964 and a 4.5% increase for the subsequent period. It is also interesting to note that in the study prepared by V. CAO PINNA for the first ASEPELT volume (Validité théorique et empirique d'une prévision, etc., *op. cit.*), the average growth rate of the gross domestic expenditure was assumed to be 4.6% annually from 1959 to 1970, whereas, according to a recent OECD study, the average growth rate of Italian income from 1961 to 1975 should be 5.6% (cf.: OCDE, Perspective de croissance des principaux partenaires de l'OCDE, Rapport du Groupe de

As far as private consumption is concerned, its average share of the gross domestic expenditure should gradually decline – according to our assumptions – from 66.1% in 1960 (at current prices), to 63.9% in 1965 and 63.4% in 1970. The marginal propensity to private consumption should thus amount to 56% in the first five years, to 61.2% in the second five-year period, and to 58.9% over the whole decade (marginal propensity averaged 57.9% from 1950 to 1960). This point is discussed further in Appendix A[16]).

With regard to population, we have accepted the assumptions adopted in a forecast of population growth made during the last months of 1961[17]). According to this assumption, the Italian *de facto* population should grow at an average rate of 0.51% from 1960 to 1970. Since our projection period is made up of two sub-periods, we had to divide this rate between 1960–1965 and 1965–1970, respectively. We have thus assumed an average annual rate of 0.53% for the first five years and an average annual rate (calculated as a residual) of 0.49% for the second five-year period. Moreover, since we wanted to forecast the geographical distribution of private consumption, we also had to estimate the population growth rates of the two five-year periods for the North and the Mezzogiorno respectively. Relying largely on the experience of the last decade, we have made the following assumptions (annual growth rate, in percent):

	1960–65	1965–70	1960–70
Mezzogiorno	0.48	0.48	0.48
North	0.56	0.50	0.53
Italy	0.53	0.49	0.51

travail nr.2, Document intérieur: Doc. CPE/WP 2-62-7, Paris, 1962); conversely the EEC Commission makes two assumptions for the next ten-year period: in the first assumption the annual growth rate is 5.25% whereas in the second one it is 5.85% (cf: COMMISSIONE CEE, Relazione sulle prospettive di sviluppo economico nella CEE dal 1960 al 1970, Gruppo di lavoro per i problemi strutturali e di sviluppo a lungo termine, Doc. II/4344/62-I, Bruxelles, 1962). To support our assumption further, it is interesting to note that the 'Commissione nazionale per la programmazione economica' (Italian National Economic Planning Commission), which was recently set up in Italy, seems to be of the opinion that a 5% annual rate of increase should be adopted.

[16]) See note 1 of Appendix A, Foreword.

[17]) Cf.: F. PILLOTON, Stime della popolazione e delle forze di lavoro in Italia al 1970, Commisione per l'elaborazione di uno schema organico di sviluppo nazionale dell'occupazione e del reddito, Gruppo di lavoro econometrico, Confidential working paper, Roma, 1961 (mimeographed), and: Id., Prima revisione delle proiezioni demografiche al 1970, Commissione per l'elaborazione ecc., Gruppo di lavoro demografia economica, Confidential working paper, Roma, 1961 (mimeographed).

Still with reference to the regional aspects of our projections, we have assumed that the total *per capita* expenditure on consumption will grow in the near future relatively faster in the Mezzogiorno than in the North. Such a differential, however, should not be too great, because of the need to increase future investment in the Mezzogiorno and the likelihood of a relative reduction of resource transfers from the North to the Mezzogiorno. Since the 1960 total *per capita* expenditure on consumption in the Mezzogiorno amounted to 62% of that in the North, we have assumed that this percentage may grow to 63% in 1965 and to 65% in 1970.

On the basis of these assumptions, the total *per capita* expenditure on private consumption should undergo the following changes in the coming years:

Regions	Absolute values (1960 lire)			Annual growth rates (%)		
	1960	1965	1970	1960–65	1965–70	1960–70
Mezzogiorno	178 990	217 700	274 734	4.00	4.75	4.35
North	288 843	345 556	422 667	3.65	4.10	3.90
Italy	248 374	298 574	368 349	3.75	4.30	4.00

3. RESULTS OF PROJECTIONS

Private consumption projections for the next ten years were calculated with reference to a 'base' consisting of Italy's 1960 national account data, duly reclassified, for uniformity's sake, in accordance with the classification used in this book[18]).

The results, which are shown in Table 1 on a national basis, and in Table 2 in their geographical breakdown, provide an indication of the important changes which are likely to take place in the sixties; in particular, as evidenced by the index numbers contained in the last two columns of the above mentioned tables, the demand for food products should record rather limited increases, whereas expenditure on other goods and services should expand at a rate considerably higher than the average[19]).

---

[18]) For the differences between the original classification of the data used in our study and the ASEPELT classification, see notes 1 and 2 of Appendix A, Foreword, and Table I of Appendix B.

[19]) It should be noted that the results of our projections are especially interesting in connection with the expected structural changes of private consumption expenditures due to the differing expansion rates characterizing each expenditure group. To emphasize this point and to make it easier to reconstruct the data (for any reader desiring to do so), we have decided not to use round figures in the presentation of results.

TABLE 1 – Projections of private consumption expenditure in 1965 and 1970, at 1960 prices

Expenditure item	Overall expenditure (billion lire)			Per capita expenditure					
				Absolute value (lire)			Index (1960 = 100)	
	1960	1965	1970	1960	1965	1970	1965	1970
1. Food	5254	6097	7017	106120	119938	134677	113.02	126.91
— cereals and products a)	1115	1151	1192	22521	22649	22882	100.57	101.60
— meat, fish, eggs b)	1729	2044	2382	34927	40212	45712	115.13	130.88
— milk and products c)	605	703	820	12215	13826	15736	113.19	128.83
— vegetables and fruits d)	1120	1404	1629	22613	27613	31275	112.12	138.31
— other foods	685	795	994	13844	15638	19072	112.96	137.76
2. Beverages	899	1062	1315	18158	20882	25248	115.00	139.05
— alcoholic	701	820	1008	14159	16116	19355	113.84	136.70
— non-alcoholic	198	242	307	3999	4764	5893	119.13	147.36
3. Tobacco	555	685	867	11210	13479	16637	120.24	148.41
4. Clothing and footwear e)	1268	1537	1943	25611	30225	37288	118.02	145.59
5. Household durables	297	417	599	5999	8204	11494	136.76	191.60
6. Non-durable household products and miscellaneous personal services	452	560	705	9129	11014	13538	120.65	148.30
7. Fuel and electric power	349	472	650	7049	9291	12482	131.81	177.07
8. Dwellings f)	465	561	698	9392	11043	13390	117.58	142.57
9. Health and hygiene g)	531	661	864	10725	13013	16574	121.33	154.54
10. Communications	447	611	849	9028	12008	16305	133.01	180.60
11. Private transport (purchase)	196	288	436	3959	5658	8371	143.17	211.44
12. Private transport (operation) e)	392	620	982	7918	12203	18842	154.12	237.96
13. Miscellaneous	1192	1607	2266	24076	31606	43503	131.28	180.69
Total	12297	15178	19191	248374	298574	368349	120.21	148.30

a) Including pastry.
b) Including: poultry, frozen and tinned meat and fish, bacon and lard.
c) Excluding ice cream.
d) Excluding processed tomatoes.
e) Including repairs.
f) For 'Dwellings' no account was taken of the corrections made by ISTAT on national accounts data inasmuch as they appeared after the publication of the SVIMEZ study. This explains the low levels of the expenditure, not only in the 'base' year, but also in the years covered by our projections. For some further clarification of this point, see footnote 1, Appendix A, Foreword.
g) Excluding voluntary or compulsory insurance.

TABLE 2 – Projections of regional private consumption expenditure in 1965 and 1970 at 1960 prices

Expenditure item	Overall expenditure (billion lire)			Per capita expenditure				
				Absolute value (lire)			Index (1960 = 100)	
	1960	1965	1970	1960	1965	1970	1965	1970
A. MEZZOGIORNO								
1-2. Food and beverages	1770.2	2103.0	2535.8	97056	112576	132559	115.99	136.58
3. Tobacco	156.8	195.2	252.5	8597	10455	13194	121.61	153.47
4. Clothing and footwear	328.4	397.7	507.5	18005	21285	26254	118.22	147.31
5–8. Dwellings and related expenditures[a]	374.6	499.5	693.3	20538	26751	36242	130.25	176.46
9. Health and hygiene	145.7	183.2	245.4	7989	9813	12823	122.83	160.51
10–12. Transport and communications	214.0	326.8	517.5	11733	17494	27056	149.10	230.60
13. Miscellaneous	274.9	361.1	503.7	15072	19326	26336	128.22	174.73
Total	3264.6	4066.6	5255.6	178990	217700	274734	121.63	153.49
B. NORTH								
1–2. Food and beverages	4382.8	5056.0	5796.2	140156	157228	175805	112.18	125.44
3. Tobacco	398.2	489.8	614.5	12734	15236	18635	119.65	146.34
4. Clothing and footwear	939.6	1139.3	1435.5	30047	34419	43533	117.88	144.88
5–8. Dwellings and related expenditures[a]	1188.4	1510.5	1958.7	38003	46988	59411	123.64	156.33
9. Health and hygiene	385.3	477.8	618.6	12321	14872	18750	120.70	152.18
10–12. Transport and communications	821.0	1192.2	1749.5	26254	37073	53069	141.21	202.14
13. Miscellaneous	917.1	1245.9	1762.3	29328	38740	53464	132.09	182.30
Total	9032.4	11111.4	13935.4	288843	345556	422667	119.63	146.33

a) See footnote f), Table 1.

TABLE 2 – (contd.)

| Expenditure item | Overall expenditure (billion lire) | | | Per capita expenditure | | | | |
| | | | | Absolute value (lire) | | | Index (1960 = 100) | |
	1960	1965	1970	1960	1965	1970	1965	1970
C. ITALY								
1–2. Food and beverages	6153.0	7159.0	8332.0	124278	140820	159925	113.31	128.68
3. Tobacco	555.0	685.0	867.0	11210	13479	16637	120.24	148.41
4. Clothing and footwear	1278.0	1537.0	1943.0	25611	30225	37288	118.02	145.59
5–8. Dwellings and related expenditures[a]	1563.0	2010.0	2652.0	31569	39552	50904	125.29	161.25
9. Health and hygiene	531.0	661.0	864.0	10725	13013	16574	121.33	154.54
10–12. Transport and communications	1035.0	1519.0	2267.0	20905	29879	43518	142.93	208.17
13. Miscellaneous	1192.0	1607.0	2266.0	24076	31606	43503	131.28	180.69
Total	12297.0	15178.0	19191.0	248374	298574	368349	120.21	148.30

a) See footnote f), Table 1.

These structural changes can be seen even more clearly in Tables 3 and 4, which indicate the percentage composition of total expenditure and the elasticity values in the projection periods. According to the data contained in these tables (one referring to the whole of Italy, and the other containing a regional breakdown), the share of food expenditure should

TABLE 3 – Structure and elasticity of private consumption expenditure from 1960 to 1970[a])

Expenditure item	% Composition			Elasticity[b])		
	1960	1965	1970	1960–65	1965–70	1960–70
1. Food	42.73	40.17	36.56	0.66	0.55	0.60
— cereals and products[c])	9.07	7.59	6.21	0.03	0.05	0.04
— meat, fish, eggs[d])	14.06	13.47	12.41	0.77	0.61	0.68
— milk and products[e])	4.92	4.63	4.27	0.67	0.62	0.64
— vegetables and fruits[f])	9.11	9.25	8.49	1.09	0.59	0.82
— other foods	5.57	5.23	5.18	0.66	0.94	0.81
2. Beverages	7.31	6.99	6.86	0.80	0.90	0.84
— alcoholic	5.70	5.40	5.26	0.70	0.87	0.79
— non-alcoholic	1.61	1.59	1.60	0.95	1.01	0.98
3. Tobacco	4.51	4.51	4.51	1.00	1.00	1.00
4. Clothing and footwear[g])	10.31	10.12	10.12	0.90	1.00	0.95
5. Household durables	2.41	2.75	3.12	1.70	1.60	1.65
6. Non-durable household products and miscellaneous personal services	3.68	3.69	3.68	1.02	0.98	1.00
7. Fuel and electric power	2.84	3.11	3.39	1.50	1.40	1.45
8. Dwellings[h])	3.78	3.70	3.64	0.88	0.92	0.90
9. Health and hygiene[i])	4.32	4.36	4.50	1.05	1.15	1.00
10. Communications	3.64	4.02	4.43	1.55	1.45	1.50
11. Private transport (purchase)	1.59	1.90	2.27	1.95	1.85	1.90
12. Private transport (operation)[g])	3.19	4.09	5.11	2.35	2.07	2.20
13. Miscellaneous	9.69	10.59	11.81	1.48	1.52	1.50
Total	100.00	100.00	100.00	1.00	1.00	1.00

[a]) Composition percentages and elasticities were calculated in 1960 lire.
[b]) Calculated on *per capita* values with the formula $\Delta \log y / \Delta \log x$.
[c]) Including pastry.
[d]) Including: poultry, frozen and tinned meat and fish, bacon and lard.
[e]) Including ice cream.
[f]) Excluding processed tomatoes.
[g]) Including repairs.
[h]) See footnote [f]), Table 1.
[i]) Excluding voluntary or compulsory insurance.

TABLE 4 – Structure and elasticity of regional private consumption expenditure from 1960 to 1970[a])

Expenditure item	% Composition			Elasticity[b])		
	1960	1965	1970	1960–65	1965–70	1960–70
A. MEZZOGIORNO						
1–2. Food and beverages	54.22	51.71	48.25	0.76	0.70	0.73
3. Tobacco	4.80	4.80	4.80	1.00	1.00	1.00
4. Clothing and foot-wear	10.06	9.78	9.65	0.85	0.95	0.90
5–8. Dwellings and re-lated expenditures[c])	11.48	12.29	13.19	1.35	1.31	1.33
9. Health and hygiene	4.46	4.51	4.67	1.05	1.15	1.10
10–12. Transport and communications	6.56	8.04	9.85	2.04	1.87	1.95
13. Miscellaneous	8.42	8.87	9.59	1.27	1.33	1.30
Total	100.00	100.00	100.00	1.00	1.00	1.00
B. NORTH						
1–2. Food and beverages	48.52	45.50	41.59	0.64	0.55	0.60
3. Tobacco	4.41	4.41	4.41	1.00	1.00	1.00
4. Clothing and foot-wear	10.40	10.25	10.30	0.92	1.02	0.97
5–8. Dwellings and re-lated expenditures[c])	13.16	13.60	14.06	1.18	1.16	1.17
9. Health and hygiene	4.27	4.30	4.44	1.05	1.15	1.10
10–12. Transport and communications	9.09	10.73	12.55	1.93	1.78	1.85
13. Miscellaneous	10.15	11.21	12.65	1.55	1.60	1.58
Total	100.00	100.00	100.00	1.00	1.00	1.00
C. ITALY						
1–2. Food and beverages	50.01	47.16	43.42	0.68	0.61	0.64
3. Tobacco	4.51	4.51	4.51	1.00	1.00	1.00
4. Clothing and foot-wear	10.31	10.12	10.12	0.90	1.00	0.95
5–8. Dwellings and re-lated expenditures[c])	12.71	13.25	13.83	1.22	1.20	1.21
9. Health and hygiene	4.32	4.36	4.50	1.05	1.15	1.10
10–12. Transport and communications	8.42	10.01	11.81	1.94	1.79	1.86
13. Miscellaneous	9.69	10.59	11.81	1.48	1.52	1.50
Total	100.00	100.00	100.00	1.00	1.00	1.00

[a]) Composition percentages and elasticities were calculated in 1960 lire.
[b]) Calculated on *per capita* values with the formula $\Delta \log y / \Delta \log x$.
[c]) See footnote [f]), Table 1.

gradually decline, until – by 1970 – it reaches, in the North, levels comparable to those now characterizing industrialized economies and, in the Mezzogiorno, levels similar to those presently characteristic of Northern Italy.

The reduction of the food expenditure share will lead to an increase in the percentages attributed to other goods and services, especially marked in fuel and electric power, household durables and transport. All these items should show a considerable expansion particularly in the South, where the expenditure composition should be, by 1970, even better than that prevailing today in the North.

To demonstrate the reliability of our projections, we have shown in Table 5 the developments which should take place in the next ten years and those which actually occurred in the fifties, for each item of expenditure and in terms of average annual growth rates. Comparison between the two series of data leads us to a number of general considerations which may be of some interest.

During the projection period, the largest expenditure increments are expected for those items which grew fastest in the last ten years. Future growth rates, however, should be generally slower, especially for those items whose past expansion was considerably influenced by special factors, as was the case with durables, fuel and electric power and transport expenditures.

The sustained growth rates recorded for durables in the fifties were mostly due to the progressively increasing use of household electric appliances in general, and of radio and television sets[20]) in particular.

This is one of the most typical examples of the radical changes which technological progress – especially through relative price variations – produces on consumer preferences. We must not forget, however, that such preferences are also considerably affected by the so-called imitative or 'keep up with the Joneses' tendency. Consumers want to bring their standards up to those of persons living in the same environment but

---

[20]) According to the available statistics, the number of subscribers to the Italian radio network grew from 3 648 139 at the end of 1951 to 7 839 794 at the end of 1960, thus recording an average annual increase of 8.87%. Television subscribers increased from 147 516 in 1955 (one year after the beginning of regular television broadcasts) to 2 019 925 in 1960, thus recording an average annual increase of 33.74%. The regional breakdown of these developments is: radio subscribers, 11.09% in the Mezzogiorno and 8.18% in the Center-North; television subscribers, 140.64% in the Mezzogiorno and 29.94% in the Center-North. Cf.: RAI, Gli abbonamenti alla radiodiffusione nel 1960, Torino, 1961.

TABLE 5 – Pattern of *per capita* private consumption expenditure from 1951 to 1960 and forecasts for 1970[a])

Expenditure item	Index (1951 = 100)		Average annual growth rate (%)	
	1960	1970	1951–60	1960–70
1–2. FOOD AND BEVERAGES				
Mezzogiorno	133.81	182.76	3.29	3.17
North	131.95	165.52	3.13	2.29
Italy	132.54	170.55	3.18	2.55
3. TOBACCO				
Mezzogiorno	153.42	235.45	4.87	4.37
North	146.59	214.52	4.34	3.88
Italy	148.54	220.45	4.49	4.03
4. CLOTHING AND FOOTWEAR				
Mezzogiorno	127.51	187.83	2.74	3.95
North	124.90	180.96	2.50	3.78
Italy	125.64	182.92	2.57	3.83
5–8. DWELLINGS AND RELATED EXPENDITURES				
Mezzogiorno	175.41	309.53	6.44	5.84
North	172.18	269.17	6.22	4.57
Italy	173.06	279.06	6.28	4.88
of which				
5. Household durables	246.92	473.10	10.56	6.72
6. Non-durable household products and miscellaneous personal services	144.45	214.22	4.17	4.02
7. Fuel and electric power	248.72	440.41	10.65	5.88
8. Dwellings	127.86	182.29	2.77	3.61
9. HEALTH AND HYGIENE				
Mezzogiorno	202.41	324.89	8.15	4.85
North	166.65	253.61	5.84	4.29
Italy	175.29	270.89	6.44	4.45
10–12. TRANSPORT AND COMMUNICATIONS				
Mezzogiorno	232.83	536.91	9.80	8.71
North	216.04	436.70	8.94	7.29
Italy	219.50	456.93	9.13	7.61
of which				
10. Communications	157.67	284.75	5.19	6.09
11. Private transport (purchase)	228.22	482.55	9.60	7.78
12. Private transport (operation)	357.72	851.23	15.21	9.06

a) We had to choose 1951 as a base year, because the necessary statistical documentation was available on a regional basis (territorial economic accounts) only from 1951 onwards.

TABLE 5 – (contd.)

Expenditure item	Index (1951 = 100)		Average annual growth rate (%)	
	1960	1970	1951–60	1960–70
13. MISCELLANEOUS				
Mezzogiorno	158.65	277.21	5.26	5.74
North	140.26	255.69	3.83	6.19
Italy	144.27	260.68	4.16	6.09
TOTAL				
Mezzogiorno	145.85	223.87	4.28	4.35
North	143.30	209.69	4.08	3.90
Italy	144.08	213.67	4.15	4.00

TABLE 6 – Relative price changes by expenditure group from 1950 to 1960[a]) (index numbers, 1950 = 100)

Expenditure item	Evaluations made	
	including dwellings	excluding dwellings
1–2. Food and beverages	97.84	100.76
3. Tobacco	98.36	101.30
4. Clothing and footwear	94.14	96.95
5. Household durables	75.43	77.68
6. Non-durable household products and miscellaneous personal services	84.88	87.41
7. Fuel and electric power	95.72	98.57
8. Dwellings	321.04	—
9. Health and hygiene	109.59	112.86
10. Communications	105.30	108.44
11. Private transport (purchase)	68.97	71.03
12. Private transport (operation)	94.28	97.09
13. Miscellaneous	106.43	109.60
Total	100.00	100.00

[a]) Relative price changes were calculated by means of ratios between the price indexes of the different expenditure items and the aggregate index of private consumption prices. These price indexes were calculated from national account data, at both constant prices (1954 lire) and current prices (see Tables V and VI of Appendix B).

enjoying larger incomes. In future years, since it may be reasonably assumed that the relative price trends of the past decade will continue (see Table 6) and since the imitative effect should also continue to play an important role, the elasticity of this expenditure should remain at rather high levels. According to our projections, the consumption of durable goods should grow at a rate of 6.7% annually, as against 10.6% in the past decade.

These considerations may apply also to transport expenditure, especially for the purchase and operation of private transport means. We have therefore estimated a 7.6% annual growth rate for this item, as against 9.1% in the last decade.

With regard to fuel and electric power expenditure, there is no reason to believe that the same factors which have contributed to the considerable increase in the past should not continue to exert their influence – even if to a more limited extent. A basic source of past developments was the considerable expansion in the number of dwellings; another important factor was the changes in energy sources for household purposes: there has been a progressive reduction in the percentage of energy requirements supplied by inferior fuels (such as firewood). This decline should continue in the future, especially in urban centres, thus promoting a further expansion of more costly energy sources, such as coal, fuel oil, electric power and LP-gas. With electric power in particular, we must bear in mind that the considerable increase in consumption which took place in the past decade was substantially enhanced by the expansion of distribution networks over country and mountain villages, and – especially in urban centres – by the growing use of electrical household appliances. According to our projection, the expenditure for this item should grow at an average annual rate of 5.9% as against 10.7% in the past decade.

Among the remaining items, special reference must be made to 'clothing and footwear' and to 'miscellaneous' expenditures.

With regard to the former, we must keep in mind that the limited expansion in the past was probably due to the fact that expenditures on other goods and services – for the reasons discussed above – have grown at a very fast rate. It is reasonable to expect, therefore, that the next decade will mark a return to more regular elasticity values. According to our projections, this item should expand at an average annual rate of 3.8% in the next decade, as against 2.6% in the fifties.

With regard to miscellaneous expenditures, which largely comprise expenditure on recreation and cultural pursuits (entertainment, books, newspapers, etc.), the expansion forecast in our projections is considerably greater than in the past decade, since these pursuits constitute a type of consumption with a rather high elasticity, and whose *per capita* levels are still considerably low in our country. We must, however, stress that the expansion rate forecast for the North is higher than in the Mezzogiorno, where most of the increase in recreation expenditures should be absorbed in the next ten years by the purchase of radio and television sets and of cars which are classified, respectively, under household durables and under transport and communications.

On the basis of what we have said so far, it may be concluded that expenditures on goods and services classified as private consumption are likely to grow at widely differing rates in the next ten years. This should lead to a considerable change in the pattern of expenditure which – by 1970 – should show a pattern similar to that prevailing today in countries enjoying higher *per capita* incomes.

Technical description of projection methods

1. FOREWORD

As previously stated (see section 3 of the paper), the projections of private consumption over the next decade were calculated with reference to a 'base' consisting of Italy's 1960 national account data[1]), conveniently re-classified for uniformity's sake, in accordance with the recommendations[2]) for this volume.

---

[1]) In order to arrive at a better interpretation of the results obtained, it must be borne in mind that, with regard to the expenditure on dwellings, the 'base' does not take into account the corrections that ISTAT made after the publication of the SVIMEZ study. This explains the low levels of the expenditure, not only in 1960, but also in the years covered by our projections. On the other hand, no alternative was available, since, as we have stated earlier, we have made an extensive use, in this report, of the SVIMEZ results based on the uncorrected data. An idea of the degree of under-estimation involved is given by the following data: after correction, the expenditure on dwellings in the base year was estimated by ISTAT at 945 billion lire, as against 465 billions in Table 1, i.e. an increase of 103.2%. A similar correction was made also for private consumption which grew from 12 297 billions, in Table 1, to 12 777, i.e. an increase of 3.9% (the regional increase was 4.0% in the South and 3.9% in the North). Similar changes should be made for 1965 and 1970. With regard to the elasticities shown in Table 3, the expenditure on dwellings should grow from 1 141 billions in 1965 (as against 561 billions in Table 1) to 1418 billions in 1970 (as against 698 billions in Table 1), whereas overall consumption expenditure in the two years considered should amount to 15 758 and to 19 911 billions respectively. If we correct also the gross domestic expenditure, the share covered by private consumption would drop from 67.0% in 1960 to 64.8% in 1965 and to 64.2% in 1970, while marginal shares would be 56.8% from 1960 to 1965, 62.0% from 1965 to 1970, and 59.7% over the whole decade.

[2]) The differences between the original classifications followed by our sources and the ASEPELT classification are shown in Table 1 of Appendix B. Owing to these dif-ferences, we had to reclassify – for the base year – some expenditures grouped by the national accounts under items differing from those used in this volume. Because of this we had to resort to very tentative estimates for the following consumption items:

— pastry, reclassified from 'other foods' (in national accounts) to 'cereals and pro-ducts';

— ice cream, reclassified from 'other foods' (in national accounts) to 'milk and pro-ducts';

— lard and bacon, reclassified from 'oils and fats' (in national accounts) to 'meat, fish, eggs';

In making these projections, we have widely drawn on the results of a study conducted by SVIMEZ in 1960, with the same purpose of forecasting the development of private consumption over the next ten years.

The results of the SVIMEZ study were based on three series of functional relations between the *per capita* expenditure on a given group of goods and services and the total *per capita* expenditure on private consumption:

a) the first series comprised 37 parametrically linear equations, fitted on data drawn from the 1953 DOXA survey on household budgets[3]);

— eggs, reclassified from 'milk, cheese and eggs' (in national accounts) to 'meat, fish, eggs';

— tomato products, reclassified from 'potatoes, vegetables and fruits' (in national accounts) to 'other foods'.
  In spite of these reclassifications, some differences still remain between the ASEPELT classification and the one we have used in our study. These differences concern the following items of expenditure:

— tinned meat, tinned fish, sausages, which were grouped under 'meat, fish, eggs' since it was not possible to estimate the expenditure classifiable under 'other foods';

— compulsory insurance, which was excluded from 'health' since the classification followed by Italy's national accounts excludes it also from private consumption expenditures;

— voluntary insurance, which was included in 'miscellaneous' since it was not possible to estimate the amount of voluntary insurance classifiable under 'health';

— hygiene (and also cosmetics, etc.), which, owing to the lack of statistical documentation, was associated with health under 'health and hygiene', in accordance with the classification adopted in Italy's national accounts.

— tourism abroad, which, in accordance with the method used in Italy's national accounts, is distributed among the various items of our projections, and not classified separately, as requested by ASEPELT (Italy's national accounts do not include the foreign tourists' expenditures; see footnote 14 of Section 2 of the paper). The classifications used in our sources permitted us to isolate 'non-durable household goods and miscellaneous personal services', which according to ASEPELT's suggestions – are grouped under 'miscellaneous'.

[3]) The following functions were used (see Appendix B, Tables III and VIII):

$$y = a + bx$$

$$y = a + bx + cx^2$$

$$y = a + b \log x,$$

where:

y $\quad = $ *per capita* expenditure on a given group of goods and services;

x $\quad = $ *per capita* expenditure on private consumption;

$a, b, c = $ empirically determined parameters (least squares method).

b) the second series comprised 37 sigmoidal functions, fitted on the same data[4]);

c) the third series comprised 18 parametrically linear equations, fitted on the series of 1950–1958 Italian national account data, expressed in *per capita* values and at constant prices[3]) (1954 lire).

We had some doubts as to the direct use of these functions in our study, especially since it would have required a considerable amount of work (for instance the difficult calculation of data from sigmoidal functions) and would have supplied three series of values which could have served only to give a range of actual projections.

We thus tried to bypass the obstacle by utilizing, instead of the functions, the elasticity values calculated on the three series of *per capita* projections made by SVIMEZ. A comprehensive critical analysis of the three series of these values enabled us to choose one elasticity series only, and we have used it for the projections made in our study. Our choice was also influenced by the results obtained from the regional expenditure functions, which we shall discuss below.

The information provided by the SVIMEZ study does not contain, however, any details as to the various expenditure items classified under 'food'. In order to close this gap, we have utilized the results of Prof. Cao Pinna's study, relating to the development of food consumption from 1955–1957 to 1975. In this case also, we resorted to the useful tool of elasticity; the only difference being that elasticities were determined this time with respect to *per capita* expenditures on food and beverages rather than to the total *per capita* expenditure on consumption.

Since we required a regional breakdown of our forecasts, we have also

---

[4]) The functions adopted were (see Appendix B, Table IV):

$$y = K \frac{1}{\sqrt{2\pi}} \int_0^{\xi} e^{-\frac{1}{2}t^2} \, dt,$$

where:

y = *per capita* expenditure on a given group of goods and services;

K = saturation level of expenditure y, empirically determined (graphic interpolation);

$\xi = a + b \log x$, where x is total *per capita* expenditure on private consumption and a and b are empirically determined parameters (least squares method).

For some further information on the graphic-analytical method used to determine K, a and b, Cf.: F. PILLOTON and E. MALFATTI, Note sull'impiego della funzione sigmoide, etc., *op. cit.*, p. 81.

utilized some functional relations determined on a regional basis between
the *per capita* expenditures on the different groups of goods and services
and the total *per capita* expenditure on private consumption. These relations were fitted on the historical series of the territorial economic accounts from 1951 to 1961, expressed in *per capita* values at constant prices
(1954 lire). To quantify parameters in these relations, we have resorted to a
joint utilization of the data concerning the two geographical areas, so as
to formulate a unified expenditure function applicable to both the Mezzogiorno and the North, such as:

$$y = hM + kN + f(x)$$

where:

y = *per capita* expenditure on a given group of goods and services;
M = intercept of the function for the Mezzogiorno;
N = intercept of the function for the North;
h = 1 and $k = 0$, in the function for the Mezzogiorno;
h = 0 and $k = 1$, in the function for the North;
x = total *per capita* expenditure on private consumption.

The above function presents the following characteristics:

a) for a given value of x, the y/x value is influenced by h and k. As a
consequence, if $M \neq N$, the average propensity to consume a given
group of goods and services would prove different in the two geographical
areas;

b) the first derivative with respect to x does not contain constants M
and N, so that the marginal propensity to consume a given group of goods
and services (for a given value of x) is the same for both geographical
areas.

We may thus conclude that, for equal values of x and Δx, both the
'mean' and 'point' elasticities differ in the two geographical areas (save in
the case that $M = N$).

2. UTILIZATION OF SVIMEZ RESULTS

Appendix B (from Table II to Table VIII) carries the statistical material
used and the forecasts made in the SVIMEZ study, reclassified in accordance with the ASEPELT system.

In reorganizing the presentation of this material, we have made some
corrections to the national account data which ISTAT had brought up to

date after the publication of the SVIMEZ study[5]). For this reason we had to refit the expenditure functions (utilizing this time data covering the whole period from 1950 to 1960), with reference, however, to the following items[6]) only:

a) alcoholic beverages;
b) tobacco;
c) non-durable household products and miscellaneous personal services;
d) private transport (purchase);
e) private transport (operation);
f) other transport;
g) books and newspapers;
h) entertainment;
i) other recreational and cultural expenditures;
l) miscellaneous.

Table IX of Appendix B summarizes the results of the SVIMEZ study, and indicates, for each year considered, the projected expenditure levels of each group of goods and services. These levels were calculated from the three series of functions mentioned in the preceding section 1. On the basis of these levels we have derived the three series of average elasticities contained in Table A (see next page).

Table A shows that the food expenditure elasticity presents very similar values regardless of the method adopted. Non-food products and services, on the other hand, show – in general – elasticities of the same order of magnitude when calculated on the basis of household budgets (1st and 2nd method) and somewhat different values when calculated from national account data. The main differences are found in the expenditure elasticities for clothing and footwear, non-durable household products, fuel and electric power, dwellings and miscellaneous expenses. Some of these differences may be attributed to a lack of uniformity between the two different statistical sources from which the expenditure functions were calculated. For instance, the expenditures on clothing and footwear, dwellings and durable goods, as covered in the surveys of household budgets, include a number of detailed items which are normally classified under miscellaneous expenditures in the national accounts (time series).

---

[5]) We did not take into account the 'corrections' made for 'dwellings' (see note 1 of this Appendix, Foreword).

[6]) On the basis of the new functions, we calculated the new values of expenditure for the projection years and used them to replace the values originally indicated in the SVIMEZ study.

N. NOVACCO AND F. PILLOTON

TABLE A – Average elasticities of *per capita* expenditure calculated with the three methods of analysis adopted in the SVIMEZ study[a])

Expenditure item	1st method		2nd method		3rd method	
	1958–65	1958–70	1958–65	1958–70	1958–65	1958–70
1–2. Food and beverages	0.68	0.68	0.65	0.64	0.66	0.63
3. Tobacco	0.88	0.86	0.83	0.79	1.09	1.08
4. Clothing and foot-wear	1.37	1.33	1.21	1.20	0.78	0.71
5–8. Dwellings and related expenditures of which	1.11	1.11	1.03	1.09	1.25	1.22
5. Household durables	1.42	1.32	1.60	1.57	1.66	1.58
6. Non-durable household products and miscellaneous personal services	0.60	0.64	0.75	0.75	1.03	1.02
7. Fuel and electric power	0.87	0.87	0.89	0.88	1.72	1.63
8. Dwellings	1.29	1.23	1.31	1.29	0.44	0.47
9. Health and hygiene	1.07	1.04	1.09	1.07	0.88	0.89
10–12. Transport and communications of which	1.77	1.74	1.95	1.92	1.78	1.68
10. Communications	1.47	1.42	1.61	1.59	1.24	1.22
11. Private transport (purchase)	1.83	1.84	2.10	2.05	1.70	1.63
12. Private transport (operation)	2.13	2.02	2.21	2.17	2.36	2.14
13. Miscellaneous	1.55	1.50	1.73	1.70	1.12	1.11

[a]) The elasticities were calculated with the formula $\Delta \log y / \Delta \log x$ (the values of x and y were taken from Table IX of Appendix B).

This lack of uniformity in classification, although having some influence, does not play a major role in explaining differences between elasticities. Actually the differentiation between the three series of data arises from the differences in the three methods of analysis, and it is on this very differentiation that we have based our choice of the elasticities adopted in our projections.

We are summarizing below the results of a comparative analysis we made for this purpose of the data contained in Table A. In order to simplify our exposition, we shall limit the comparison to the elasticity values calculated for the whole projection period. The figures following each expenditure item in parentheses are the elasticity values calculated over the whole projection period with the 1st, 2nd, and 3rd method, respectively. As previously indicated, these three methods were based – respectively – on the results given by: the parametrically linear equations determined from household budgets; the sigmoid functions determined from household budgets; and the parametrically linear equations determined from the historical series of national accounts. In our final choice of elasticities we have also considered the results obtained with the regional expenditure functions.

1–2. Food and beverages (0.68; 0.64; 0.63).

As it is well known the results obtained from the household budgets survey normally underestimate the elasticities concerning this item. In our case however, the historical series, probably due to the remarkable increase in total private consumption during the decade from 1950 to 1960, gave the lowest elasticity values. During the next ten-year period the rate of expansion of private consumption is not likely to be much lower than it was in the past; consequently the elasticity adopted for the projections is of the same order of magnitude as that obtained with the third method. The slight increase (0.64 as against 0.63) was suggested by the consideration that in the next few years, the Southern regions (where the elasticities are higher) shall participate more actively in the formation of the national demand for products listed under this item, while the qualitative improvement in consumption shall exert some influence, especially in the Central and Northern regions.

3. Tobacco (0.86; 0.79; 1.08).

A detailed analysis of the data obtained from the household budgets leads to the conclusion that – when the survey was being made – the farmers producing tobacco, especially in the Mezzogiorno, did not report the real consumption of this product. Owing to this, the elasticity based on the first and second methods is probably overestimated. The third method, however, gives higher values, probably due to the recent expansion of tobacco consumption, especially among women. In this study we have adopted an elasticity of 1.0, which is slightly less than that calculated from the third method.

4. Clothing and footwear (1.33; 1.20; 0.71).

The results obtained with the first and second methods do not differ widely from the values commonly accepted as normal by many economists. The third method, on the other hand, presents much lower values reflecting a ten-year experience which recorded a radical change in the preferences of Italian consumers, who were more attracted by durable consumer goods and private transport. The assumption of a gradual return to more regular elasticity values however, seems reasonable enough, even though the Southern regions will have to face many difficulties as a result of this change. Accordingly we chose an elasticity of 0.95 for the whole decade from 1960 to 1970.

5. Household durables (1.32; 1.57; 1.58).

The developments of the fifties have affected the high results obtained with the third method. No slowdown of present trends is likely to take place in the next decade and taking into account the expected effects of the Common Market on the relative prices of these products, we have adopted an elasticity of 1.65. This value is slightly higher than that obtained with the third method, due to the increased importance that the Southern regions (where the elasticity is higher) will gain during the next few years in the formation of the national demand for the products considered.

6. Non-durable household products and miscellaneous personal services (0.64; 0.65; 1.02).

The same considerations apply for this item. Nevertheless, to take into account the progressive decline in domestic services, we have assumed for 1960–1970 an elasticity of 1.00, which is lower than that obtained with the third method.

7. Fuel and electric power (0.87; 0.88; 1.63).

At the end of section 3 of the paper, we indicated why the last decade witnessed a considerable increase in expenditure on this item. These same reasons also explain why the third method provides an elasticity value higher than the other two. In section 3 we also said that the very causes which affected the growth of this expenditure item in the fifties should still exert some influence in the future. This is why we have chosen an elasticity of 1.47, which is not much below that obtained with the third method.

8. Dwellings (1.23; 1.29; 0.47).

The situation for this item is theoretically the opposite of that for food products. Nevertheless, the values obtained with the third method are strongly distorted by current rent freezing regulations. Allowing for the return to normality which should take place during the projection period, we have adopted an elasticity of 0.83, i.e. an intermediate value between first and second method results on the one hand, and third method results on the other.

9. Health and hygiene (1.04; 1.07; 0.89).

If we consider the level reached by the *per capita* expenditure on this item, the first two methods seem to provide more realistic results, especially if we take into account the need for reorganization in the social security services which are listed, in the Italian national accounts, under the expenditure on hygiene and health (medical services and medicines). We have therefore adopted an elasticity of 1.10.

10–11–12. Communications (1.42; 1.59; 1.22); Private transport (purchase) (1.84; 2.05; 1.63); Private transport (operation) (2.02; 2.17; 2.14).

The same considerations made for durables apply to these three items. We have therefore adopted elasticity values higher than those obtained with the third method, namely: 1.50 for communications; 1.90 for private transport (purchase); and 2.20 for private transport (operation).

13. Miscellaneous (1.50; 1.70; 1.11).

A considerable part of this item is accounted for by entertainment and recreation expenditures, the elasticity of which tends to be underestimated in the analysis based on historical series, because of the marked development of television broadcasts in the period from 1955 to 1960. The elasticities provided by the first and second methods are thus considered to be of more significance especially for the Central and Northern regions. In the Mezzogiorno on the other hand, we feel that radio and television broadcasts shall continue to exert some influence, although somewhat less than in the past, on the expenditure on this item. Accordingly we have adopted an elasticity of 1.50.

3. UTILIZATION OF PROF. CAO PINNA'S RESULTS

The use of results from Prof. Cao Pinna's study does not require any particular comment. The great detail presented by these projections for the expenditure items classified under 'food' also simplified the classification recommended by ASEPELT. On the basis of the changes forecast

for the periods from 1955–1957 to 1965 and from 1965 to 1970 we have
calculated the elasticities (see Table B) of each group of *per capita* expenditure in respect of total *per capita* expenditure on food and beverages.
These elasticities were then used for the projections made in this study.

TABLE B – *Per capita* expenditures on food products; changes forecast in Cao Pinna's
study and elasticities calculated in relation thereto[a])

Expenditure item	Index of *per capita* expenditure		Elasticity	
	1965 (1955–57 = 100)	1970 (1965 = 100)	1955/57–1965	1965–1970
Cereals and products	100.47	100.52	0.02	0.05
Meat[b])	135.94	111.03	1.38	1.08
Fish	105.45	105.26	0.24	0.53
Eggs	119.70	108.86	0.81	0.87
Milk and products	125.22	110.04	1.01	0.98
Vegetables and fruits	143.87	109.92	1.63	0.97
Tomato products	142.86	130.00	1.60	2.70
Fats	118.25	113.12	0.75	1.27
of which bacon and lard	(115.63)	(108.11)	(0.65)	(0.80)
Sugar and jam	132.63	115.77	1.27	1.51
Pastry and ice cream	136.89	113.25	1.41	1.28
Other food products	116.34	107.77	0.68	0.75
Alcoholic beverages	126.74	114.68	1.06	1.41
Non alcoholic beverages	137.49	117.24	1.43	1.64
Total food and beverages	124.99	110.22	1.00	1.00

[a]) Elasticities were calculated with the formula $\Delta \log y / \Delta \log x$.
[b]) Including: poultry, frozen and tinned meat and fish, sausages.

The reason why we used the elasticities in respect of total *per capita* expenditure on food and beverages rather than of total *per capita* expenditure on private consumption was that the overall results obtained
through the analytical method by Prof. Cao Pinna do not differ substantially from those we have obtained by employing an aggregate function relating to total expenditures on food and beverages.

4. UTILIZATION OF REGIONAL EXPENDITURE FUNCTIONS

The functions used for regional projections were fitted on the statistical data obtained from territorial economic accounts (see Tables X and XI of Appendix B).

⸱ The parameters of the different expenditure functions were as follows:

1-2. Food and
beverages
$$y = 13449h + 11790k + 518.83x - 0.26x^2$$
$$y = -314988h - 318446k + 184612.981 \log_{10} x$$

3. Tobacco
$$y = -206h - 101k + 47.46x$$

4. Clothing and
footwear
$$y = 3986h + 7227k + 81.27x$$

5-8. Dwellings and
related expen-
ditures
$$y = -8560h - 8560k + 152.31x$$

9. Health and
hygiene
$$y = -4521h - 7098k + 69.31x$$
$$y = -1621h - 1621k + 46.84x$$

10-12. Transp. and
comm.
$$y = -12845h - 14959k + 149.80x$$

13. Miscellaneous $y = -753h + 343k + 82.55x.$

Since the functions were fitted on data expressed in 1954 lire, the values which may be attributed to the independent variable (*per capita* expenditure on consumption) for the years 1960, 1965, and 1970 must be expressed in a currency characterized by an equal purchasing power. These values (in thousand lire) are:

	1960	1965	1970
Mezzogiorno	167.4	203.6	256.9
North	269.1	321.9	393.8

By putting these values in the place of the independent variable of the equations mentioned above, we obtained, for the period covered by the projections, the changes in the expenditure levels and the regional elasticities shown in Table C. These elasticities were subsequently amended (see Table 4), according to the criteria summarized below. To simplify our exposition, and in accordance to what was done at the national level, we are taking into account only the elasticities related to the whole period

(1960–1970). These values are placed in parentheses right after each expenditure item, in the following order: Mezzogiorno, North.

1–2. Food and beverages (2nd degree polynomial: 0.77; 0.74; semilogarithmic function: 0.72; 0.55).

Among the various functions used for this expenditure, the best fit was given by a polynomial of the second degree. Two circumstances, how-

TABLE C – *Per capita* expenditure changes and related elasticities estimated on the basis of regional functions[a])

Expenditure item	Index of *per capita* expenditure (1960 = 100)		Elasticity	
	1965	1970	1960–1965	1960–1970
A. MEZZOGIORNO				
1–2. Food and beverages				
(2nd degree polynomial)	116.39	139.17	0.78	0.77
(semilog. function)	116.43	135.94	0.78	0.72
3. Tobacco	122.20	154.88	1.02	1.02
4. Clothing and footwear	116.75	141.42	0.79	0.81
5–8. Dwellings and related				
expenditures	132.55	180.48	1.44	1.38
9. Health and hygiene $(M \neq N)$	135.45	187.61	1.55	1.65
$(M = N)$	126.66	165.96	1.21	1.18
10–12. Transport and commu-				
nications	144.33	209.61	1.87	1.73
13. Miscellaneous	122.87	156.54	1.05	1.05
Total	121.63	153.49	1.00	1.00
B. NORTH				
1; 2. Food and beverages				
(2nd degree polynomial)	114.48	132.41	0.75	0.74
(semilog. function)	111.04	123.46	0.58	0.55
3. Tobacco	119.78	146.72	1.01	1.01
4. Clothing and footwear	114.78	134.89	0.78	0.79
5–8. Dwellings and related				
expenditures	124.80	158.57	1.24	1.21
9. Health and hygiene $(M \neq N)$	131.68	174.81	1.54	1.47
$(M = N)$	122.02	151.91	1.11	1.10
10–12. Transport and commu-				
nications	131.20	173.68	1.52	1.45
13. Miscellaneous	119.32	145.64	0.99	0.99
Total	119.63	146.33	1.00	1.00

[a]) The elasticities were calculated with the formula $\Delta \log y / \Delta \log x$.

ever, have discouraged us from using this function for regional projections. In the first place, contrary to what experience may teach, the elasticities obtained for the sixties do not show marked regional differences; in the second place, these values seem to be too high both at the regional and at the national level[7]).

Among other functions which may be used for our purpose, the semilogarithmic one seems to be the one preferred – at the theoretical level – by econometricians; however, if we take into account the differences between calculated and actual data in the period from 1951 to 1960 we may come to the conclusion that the elasticities obtained with this function are overestimated for the Mezzogiorno and underestimated for the North. Nevertheless the average national elasticity which may be obtained by weighting the regional values is of the same order of magnitude as the elasticity adopted at the national level[8]); consequently we feel that it might prove useful in deciding the values to be adopted for the Mezzogiorno and the North, to take into account the results obtained with the semilogarithmic function. A few corrections have been made to these data in order to eliminate the drawbacks mentioned above and also in view of the fact that the quality of consumption is likely to be improved during a process of income growth. We have thus adopted an elasticity value of 0.73 for the Mezzogiorno and of 0.60 for the North.

3. Tobacco (1.02; 1.01).

This expenditure item does not require any particular comment since the regional elasticity values obtained from the expenditure function are practically the same as those obtained at the national level. The value adopted for the projections is 1.0 for both the Mezzogiorno and the North.

4. Clothing and footwear (0.81; 0.79).

We have already stated that during the next few years a return to more regular elasticity values seems reasonable enough, especially if we bear in mind the reasons which have influenced the behaviour of Italian consumers in the fifties. This evolution, however, will be slower in the Southern regions where the marginal propensity to food consumption will continue to be rather high and where future consumer behaviour with

---

[7]) The national elasticity value found by calculating the weighted average of the two regional elasticities is 0.75.

[8]) The national elasticity value found by calculating the weighted average of the two regional elasticities is 0.61.

regard to durables is expected to be almost the same as in the North during the period from 1951 to 1960. Consequently the elasticities adopted for the projection are 0.90 for the Mezzogiorno and 0.97 for the North.

5–8. Dwellings and related expenditures (1.38; 1.21).

This item requires no particular comments, since the two regional elasticities provide a weighted average whose value does not differ widely from that adopted at the national level[9]). The corrections which we then made to the results obtained from the two groups of regions are proportionate to those relating to the country as a whole. We thus obtained the following elasticities: Mezzogiorno 1.33; North 1.17.

9. Health and hygiene ($M \neq N$: 1.65; 1.47; $M = N$: 1.18; 1.10).

The function with different regional parameters gives rather high elasticities. If we adopt a function where $M = N$, the approximation of actual to calculated data during the period from 1951 to 1960 is not very satisfactory; the elasticity values however, seem normal enough, even though the Southern regions have a slight tendency of being overestimated. Consequently we have decided to use the same elasticity adopted for the nation as a whole, i.e. 1.10.

10–12. Transport and communications (1.73; 1.45).

We have already mentioned the reasons why the elasticities adopted for the projections of this expenditure item are higher, for the country as a whole, than those obtained from the functions which were fitted on the time series. In making the necessary adjustments to the elasticities obtained at the regional level, the North was placed in a more favourable position than the South since it is expected that with regard to food and beverages, the marginal propensity to consume in the latter region will remain at rather high levels during the next few years. The values adopted are 1.95 for the Mezzogiorno and 1.85 for the North.

13. Miscellaneous expenditures (1.05; 0.99).

With regard to this item the reader should refer back to what was stated on the values indicated for the country as a whole. The elasticities adopted are 1.30 for the Mezzogiorno and 1.58 for the North.

---

[9]) The national average elasticity obtained by weighting the two regional elasticities is 1.25 as against 1.21 indicated in the preceding pages. It is interesting to note that the data used for this expenditure item have permitted the adoption of a function where $M = N$.

CHAPTER 5

CONSUMPTION FORECASTS
FOR THE NETHERLANDS*)

BY

J. G. VAN BEECK and H. DEN HARTOG

Central Planning Bureau, The Hague, Netherlands

Introduction

In the first volume of the ASEPELT-series "Europe's Future in Figures" Sandee deals with the possible economic growth of the economy of the Netherlands up to 1970 [21]. His paper is mainly concerned with providing forecasts of macro economic entities. Those forecasts are based on an annual increase of productivity per man-hour of 4%. For total private consumption per head this implies about the same increase annually. This hypothesis is the starting point of the forecasts to be given in the present paper. More specifically, this paper is to be considered as an exercise in breaking down a given macro figure for total private consumption into a number of expenditure categories. This is done for the years 1970 and 1980. The forecasts presented for 1970 (see Table 5.1) should be regarded as an extension of Sandee's paper on a more detailed level. The forecasts for 1980 are included to demonstrate the consequences of the property of decreasing elasticities of the demand functions used. The macro figure for total private consumption which is assumed to be given for 1980 is obtained by extrapolation on the basis of the 1970 forecast.

To break down the given totals the authors have used the system of demand equations as suggested by TÖRNQVIST [23] (see section 2, paragraph 2.1).

Considerable attention was given to the estimation procedure for the parameters of this system (see section 2, paragraph 2.2) from data obtained from the National Budget Inquiry held by the Central Bureau of

---

*) This paper has benefited on many points from the comments and constant guidance of Professor Dr. P. J. Verdoorn in the course of our work on it. Our thanks are due to him.

Statistics in 1951 [5; 6; 7], more specifically the budgets of salaried employees and civil servants (see section 3, paragraph 3.1). The nature of these data made it necessary to include in the Törnqvist equations a variable representing family-size. This means that account must be taken of eventual changes in family size when forecasting for 1970 and 1980.

Account has also been taken of possible trend developments. The annual trend percentages are computed from data going back to 1929 with the help of a method which gives weight to the influence of total expenditure as the Törnqvist equations describe it, as well as to the influence of relative prices (see section 4, paragraph 4.2).

In conclusion the forecasts for the different expenditure categories in 1970 and 1980 are given in table 5.1. These forecasts are briefly discussed see section 5, paragraphs 5.2, 5.3 and 5.4).

1. A DISCUSSION OF THE METHOD FOR BREAKING DOWN TOTAL PRIVATE CONSUMPTION INTO CATEGORIES

Breaking down a given total for private consumption into a number of expenditure categories can be carried out in different ways. In principle two possibilities present themselves. One depends on a compilation of previous results for individual expenditure categories, the other on a complete and coherent system of demand equations.

1.1. THE COMPILATION OF PREVIOUS RESULTS FOR INDIVIDUAL EXPENDITURE CATEGORIES

It is possible in the first case to compile the results of previous empirical analyses and studies on consumer behaviour with respect to one or more individual expenditure categories and from this compilation, make some estimate of the expenditure functions to be used for the different categories. This might be done conceivably with the help of investigations carried out for the Netherlands, other European countries or for the United States. On the basis of the adopted functions total private consumption could be distributed over the expenditure categories.

This method has some drawbacks for the present purpose. First, the expenditure categories for which the functions have been actually computed will not always correspond with the categories adopted in this book, for which the functions are supposed to provide the forecasts.

Secondly, the available studies do not cover the whole realm of private consumption; some studies deal only with expenditure on foods [9], while others cover only, perhaps durables [10] or textiles [13]. The individual character of these studies is a drawback; it accounts for an undesirable measure of incompleteness in the description of consumer behaviour. Thirdly, the individual character of the studies involved causes a lack of uniformity and a lack of coherence in the estimated functions. On the one hand the estimation procedures used will probably not be uniform, while on the other hand the functions probably do not refer to one coherent system of Engel curves.

In view of these drawbacks this method will not be followed in this paper. It will appear that the second method has some features which make it definitely superior.

1.2. THE USE OF A COMPLETE AND COHERENT SYSTEM OF DEMAND RELATIONS

In the second case it is possible to break down total private consumption according to a complete and coherent system of demand equations of which the parameters are estimated with the help of consistent basic material. This method does not suffer from possible incompleteness and heterogeneity. However, the use of an already estimated system (such as the budget distribution models for the Netherlands of SOMERMEIJER [22] and WIT [24]) has the first mentioned drawback of the previous method: the lack of correspondence between the expenditure categories for which the system is estimated and the categories to be distinguished in the present paper. To get over this difficulty it is necessary to choose some system of demand equations especially suited for forecasting over long periods involving relatively large changes in total private consumption and to estimate it separately on the basis of consistent basic material grouped into expenditure categories according to the uniform classification adopted in this book. This method will be followed for the forecasts to be given in this paper.

Having chosen the method of forecasting, it is next necessary to choose the system of demand equations for breaking down the given macro figures for total private consumption. In making this choice it is useful to apply some criteria.

The most important criterion is the requirement that the equations of the system all have decreasing expenditure elasticities. This requirement is based on the consideration that in the long run, when total expenditure (or income) is rising, all commodities rated as luxuries in the consumer's budget will gradually become less and less a luxury, even, perhaps, becoming 'necessities'; also all commodities classified as necessities will become even more necessary, that is to say, their consumption will have a saturation level (the case of inferior commodities is left out of consideration here).

This required property of the system of Engel curves is confirmed in many recent empirical investigations into consumer behaviour [1; 2; 12; 13; 19; 20; 22; 23; 24]. From these investigations it is apparent that, technically speaking, there are quite a few conceivable systems of Engel curves which possess the property of a decreasing expenditure elasticity. PRAIS [19, p.93] mentions a few such types of Engel curves; moreover, the system of cumulative lognormal frequency curves introduced by AITCHISON and BROWN [1; 2] in the analysis of budgets, the system of hyperbolic Engel curves suggested by Törnqvist and the budget distribution model used by SOMERMEIJER [22] and WIT [24] all possess this property.

This summing up is not limitative and the choice of a system comprising one or more of the mentioned Engel curves on the basis of the property of a decreasing expenditure elasticity alone would be difficult. Therefore the choice is limited, more or less arbitrarily, to those Engel curves which are suggested in the framework of a coherent system describing all expenditures in the consumer's budget, leaving out of consideration the Engel curves suggested as some partial description of expenditures in the consumer's budget. This limitation leaves the systems of Aitchison and Brown and of Törnqvist and the budget distribution model used by Somermeijer and Wit for further comparison.

These three systems all possess the property of decreasing expenditure elasticities, but it must be investigated to what extent this property is a main feature of the systems as distinct from a purely formal one. Further inspection shows that in the budget distribution model used by Somermeijer and Wit the expenditure elasticities decrease only very slowly when total expenditure increases. Moreover, the elasticities decrease in a rather unusual way: they all decrease with the same constant absolute amount per percent increase of total expenditure. Apart from the unusual way in which the elasticities in the model used by Somermeijer and Wit decrease, the magnitude of the decrease is in general materially insignificant. In other words, the decreasing elasticities in this budget distribution model do not show the essential changes in the relative positions of the commodities in the consumer's budget when large changes in the level of total expenditures are involved. When using the budget distribution model for practical purposes the property of decreasing elasticities can be regarded as purely formal and the elasticities themselves as practically invariable. On these grounds the budget distribution model used by Somermeijer and Wit must be rejected for forecasting.

On the other hand, this budget distribution model possesses the useful property of satisfying the additivity criterion, which the systems of demand equations of Aitchison and Brown and of Törnqvist (and many other conceivable non-linear systems) do not possess. The additivity criterion should, however, not be overstressed to the extent of letting the choice of the system of equations depend on it. In practice the budget identity will be very nearly fulfilled over a large part of the range of observed data regardless of the system chosen, the discrepancies not being significant. This is ensured because the estimation procedure of the relevant Engel curves is applied to observations which themselves satisfy the budget identity. The divergence between total expenditure and the sum of expected expenditures on different items will not therefore be too great. What has to be done with a divergence, if it occurs, will be explained in section 3, paragraph 3.3.

The choice is now limited to the systems of Aitchison and Brown and of Törnqvist. The present authors are of the opinion that this choice should be determined by the flexibility of the system of demand equations in describing consumer behaviour. Bearing in mind that the total of consumption expenditures is regarded as the explanatory variable in the equations, this flexibility can be judged with respect to two aspects of the Engel curve.

First, the system of demand equations should allow for the description of expenditure categories having a saturation level as well as of expenditure categories having *no* apparent saturation level. On the one hand the desirability of having a parameter in the equations representing the saturation level of consumption is most apparent in the case of necessities, since the Engel curve flattens considerably in the upper ranges of total expenditure and the expenditure elasticity falls fairly rapidly towards zero. On the other hand, there are for some expenditure categories no a priori grounds for postulating a saturation level of consumption; examples are Entertainment, Tourism, and the hybrid category Other expenditures [19, p. 89].

Secondly, the system of demand equations to be chosen should allow for a parameter representing some total expenditure below which the commodity in question is not purchased, as well as for the possibility that there is no such initial expenditure total. Of course items such as farinaceous food will indeed be purchased at very low incomes, but it is not implausible to suggest that some commodities are purchased only above a certain total expenditure [12, p. 33]. This might be suggested on the basis of the existence of indivisibilities alone.

Considering the flexibility of the system of demand equations with respect to these two aspects of the Engel curves, the choice between the system of Aitchison and Brown and the system of Törnqvist is now practically determined. The system of Aitchison and Brown does not allow for the flexibility in the sense defined above. The property of an expenditure category having a saturation level is generalised by Aitchison and Brown for *all* expenditure categories [1, pp. 35–36]. Apart from the inflexibility implied thereby, Prais and Houthakker point out that, theoretically, such a generalisation violates the additivity criterion [20, pp. 83–84], that is, when total expenditure is the explanatory variable in the Engel curves. For the same reason it is not possible to accept the 'modified Törnqvist curve' suggested by FISK [12]; in fact, Fisk replaces the system of curves suggested by Törnqvist by a modification of the basic equation of the Törnqvist system which results in an Engel curve based on the logistic distribution [12, p. 45]. Besides, the cumulative lognormal frequency curves as Aitchison and Brown use them do not allow for a parameter in the Engel curve representing a non-zero initial expenditure total below which the commodity in question is not consumed. It is implied that as long as total expenditure is positive, however small, there is always some expenditure on each of the items making up the total expenditure. This exclusion of the parameter representing a positive initial expenditure total in the Engel curve also affects the flexibility of the system. Of course, these objections to the system of Aitchison and Brown have a purely theoretical character; they probably have no practical significance.

The Törnqvist system of hyperbolic demand relations, however, is flexible in all respects mentioned above, including the saturation level as well as the initial expenditure total; moreover, the lack of computational capacity made it necessary to restrict the regression analysis to relatively simple relations such as those suggested by Törnqvist. Therefore this system is chosen for setting up the forecasts in this paper.

2. THE TÖRNQVIST SYSTEM
AND ITS ESTIMATION PROCEDURE

2.1. THE SYSTEM OF DEMAND EQUATIONS

The Törnqvist system of demand equations as it is presented in the literature [23; 25, pp. 107–108] is given in Table 2.1. In this system y denotes the expenditure on, or the quantity of the commodity considered; x denotes total expenditure or income. For the purpose of the forecasts. y is taken as the expenditure on the commodity considered and x as total expenditure[1]). By definition, the budget identity $\Sigma y = x$ applies. Regarding the conditions set to the parameters α, β and γ, the non-negativity of α and γ is decided on a priori grounds, while the condition set to the parameter β is implied – as can be proved – by the required property of decreasing expenditure elasticities.

TABLE 2.1 – The Törnqvist system of demand equations

For:	Relation	Elasticity	Conditions
Necessities	$y = \dfrac{\alpha x}{x + \beta}$	$\eta = \dfrac{\beta}{x + \beta}$	$\alpha > 0, \beta > 0$
Semi-luxuries	$y = \alpha \dfrac{x - \gamma}{x + \beta}$	$\eta = \dfrac{\beta}{x + \beta} + \dfrac{\gamma}{x - \gamma}$	$\alpha > 0, \gamma > 0,$ $\beta > -\gamma, x \geq \gamma$
Luxuries	$y = \alpha x \dfrac{x - \gamma}{x + \beta}$	$\eta = 1 + \dfrac{\beta}{x + \beta} + \dfrac{\gamma}{x - \gamma}$	$\alpha > 0, \gamma > 0,$ $\beta > -\gamma, x \geq \gamma$

A comparison of the elasticity formulae shows how necessities, semi-luxuries and luxuries are distinguished: they are defined with respect to the level of their expenditure elasticity. For luxuries, the expenditure elasticity is always above unity and converges to unity when total expenditure x increases. For necessities, the expenditure elasticity is always below unity and becomes ultimately zero for very high levels of total expenditure x. For semi-luxuries, the expenditure elasticity ranges from infinity (as is the case for luxuries) to zero (as is the case for necessities), when total expenditure x ranges from γ to very high.

---

[1]) This implies that $y = pq$ (where $p =$ the price of the commodity and $q =$ the quantity of the commodity) so that the parameters α, β and γ of the Törnqvist equations can be regarded as involving the price p of the commodity considered [25, p. 107].

With y interpreted as expenditure on a particular commodity it can be seen that parameter α, in the formulae given for necessities and semi-luxuries, represents the saturation level either for expenditure of a necessary kind or for expenditures of a relatively luxurious character. In the case of semi-luxuries parameter γ denotes the initial level of total expenditure below which the consumer has no demand for the commodities in question. In fact, this parameter γ is the only difference between the formula for semi-luxuries and the formula for necessities. Thus parameter γ, being zero or greater than zero, gives the demarcation between necessities and semi-luxuries. Parameter β determines in both formulae the curvature of this type of Engel curve in such a way that the smaller the value of β the sooner the saturation level of expenditure α will be reached as total expenditure x increases.

In the formula given for luxuries, however, parameter α denotes the fraction of the consumer's total expenditure that he tends to spend on the commodity considered. In fact, y/x tends to α for very high levels of total expenditure. For this type of Engel curve there is thus no absolute saturation level, only a relative saturation level expressed as the fraction α of total expenditure. Again parameter γ indicates the initial level of total expenditure below which the consumer has no demand for the commodity in question. Here, too, parameter β determines the curvature of the Engel curve and how soon the relative saturation level α is reached.

For the estimation procedure of the Törnqvist demand equations outlined in the next paragraph the difference between the formulae for necessities and semi-luxuries is not material. As already pointed out, this difference amounts only to the parameter γ being zero or greater than zero. Therefore it is convenient to refer in the remainder of this paper only to two demand equations summarising the Törnqvist system, namely:

For necessities and semi-luxuries

$$y = \alpha \, \frac{x - \gamma}{x + \beta} \qquad (2.1.1.a)$$

with

$$\alpha > 0, \gamma \geqq 0, \beta > -\gamma, x \geqq \gamma.$$

For luxuries

$$y = \alpha x \, \frac{x - \gamma}{x + \beta} \qquad (2.1.1.b)$$

with

$$\alpha > 0, \gamma \geqq 0, \beta > -\gamma, x \geqq \gamma.$$

These two hyperbolic relations describe all special cases for necessities, semi-luxuries and luxuries. The condition set to the parameter β is again implied by the property of decreasing elasticities, while the other conditions are decided on a priori grounds.

The Törnqvist system of hyperbolas is logically consistent in the following sense: Let the items of the consumer's budget be lumped together in two aggregates, and suppose that the demand function of the first aggregate y_1 is of type (2.1.1.a) with $\gamma = 0$; then the demand function for the second aggregate $y_2 = x - y_1$ will be of type (2.1.1.b) of the given functions [25, p. 108].

FISK [12, p. 35] considers it a major shortcoming that the classification of commodities into three groups is rather rigid. However, equation (2.1.1.a) of the system with $\gamma > 0$ provides for a transition of the expenditure elasticity from a value above unity to a value below unity converging to zero, that is, a transition from luxuries to necessities. The Törnqvist system is thus not as rigid as it seems.

2.2. THE ESTIMATION PROCEDURE FOR THE TÖRNQVIST SYSTEM

Estimation of the Parameter β

To estimate the parameters of the different Törnqvist hyperbolas by linear regression analysis it is necessary to linearize the relations (2.1.1.a) and (2.1.1.b). This is only possible to a certain extent, namely to the extent that an a priori value of the parameter β is given. Linear regression in this case does not yield a least squares estimate for β. On the contrary, estimation of the other parameters is impossible if β is not given a priori. So, to estimate the other parameters a preliminary estimate of β is needed. This preliminary estimate is obtained as follows:

Given three equidistant expenditure totals $x_1, x_2(=2x_1)$ and $x_3(=3x_1)$, for which the corresponding demand values y_1, y_2 and y_3 are obtained from the available budget data by graphic interpolation or some other approximation, it is possible to solve β in terms of x_1, y_1, y_2 and y_3 by substituting (x_1, y_1), (x_2, y_2) and (x_3, y_3) successively in the relations (2.1.1.a) and (2.1.1.b). A system of three equations yields the following expression for β, respectively,

For necessities and semi-luxuries

$$\beta = -\frac{y_1 - 4y_2 + 3y_3}{y_1 - 2y_2 + y_3} \cdot x_1. \qquad (2.2.1.a)$$

For luxuries

$$\beta = - \frac{3y_1 - 6y_2 + 3y_3}{3y_1 - 3y_2 + y_3} x_1. \qquad (2.2.1.b)$$

These two formulae can be written using the following notation (in which $x_0 = y_0 = 0$):

$$\Delta_1 = y_1 - y_0 = y_1 \left.\right\}$$
$$\Delta_2 = y_2 - y_1 \left.\right\} \quad \Delta_2^2 = \Delta_2 - \Delta_1 \left.\right\} \quad \Delta_3^3 = \Delta_3^2 - \Delta_2^2.$$
$$\Delta_3 = y_3 - y_2 \left.\right\} \quad \Delta_3^2 = \Delta_3 - \Delta_2 \left.\right\}$$

The formulae (2.2.1.a) and (2.2.1.b) then become:
For necessities and semi-luxuries

$$\beta = - \left(1 + 2 \cdot \frac{\Delta_3}{\Delta_3^2}\right) x_1. \qquad (2.2.2.a)$$

For luxuries

$$\beta = - 3 \cdot \frac{\Delta_3^2}{\Delta_3^3} x_1. \qquad (2.2.2.b)$$

It can be seen now that in this estimation procedure the parameter β is determined by the first, second and third differences of the values given for y.

This condition provides a device for distinguishing between type (2.1.1.a) and type (2.1.1.b). For formula (2.1.1.a) it is known that the first differences Δ between the successive y's must be positive and the second differences Δ^2 negative. For formula (2.1.1.b) the first differences Δ must be positive, the second differences Δ^2 also positive and the third differences Δ^3 negative. Thus, if the budget data reveal negative second differences Δ^2 the commodities considered are assumed to be either necessities or semi-luxuries; if, however, the budget data yield positive second differences the commodities in question are regarded as luxuries.

Estimation of the parameters α and γ [2])

The preliminary value of β being given and the choice between type (2.1.1.a) and type (2.1.1.b) being determined, it is now possible to cal-

---

[2]) The authors are indebted to Mr. A. J. Middelhoek of the Central Planning Bureau for his valuable advice on this part of the estimation procedure.

culate the regression between y and x to estimate the parameters α and γ. For the two types of the Törnqvist demand equations this estimation proceeds as follows.

For those expenditure categories for which the preliminary estimation of β suggest they are of type (2.1.1.a), these relations are estimated at first with the help of the regression equation:

$$y = \alpha - \alpha(\beta + \gamma) \frac{1}{x + \beta} + u \qquad (2.2.3)$$

where u is the residual term. The value of the parameter β is now varied in such a way as to maximise the squared correlation coefficient R^2. Because β is always given a priori and α is known as the constant in the regression, the parameter γ can be found from the regression coefficient $-\alpha(\beta + \gamma)$. It follows then that regression equation (2.2.3) provides the criterion for fixing the value of γ: If $\gamma > 0$ for that value of β where R^2 is a maximum then regression equation (2.2.3.) gives the estimates for the parameters α and γ of type (2.1.1.a). If, however, $\gamma < 0$ where R^2 is a maximum, then type (2.1.1.a) of the Törnqvist system will be re-estimated with $x/(x + \beta)$ as the independent variable. The regression equation then becomes

$$y = \alpha \cdot \frac{x}{x + \beta} + u. \qquad (2.2.4)$$

The regression analysis for this type of relation must be performed here in such a way as to yield a zero constant. This will be done with the help of a procedure for estimating regression equations with an a priori constant outlined by Barten and used in the Central Planning Bureau. This procedure rests on the hypothesis that the sum of residuals in the universe from which the regression sample is taken will be zero for the a priori value of the constant, i.e. zero, although the sum of residuals in the sample might not be zero. Denoting the dependent variable by y and the independent variable $x/(x + \beta)$ by z the procedure yields the following formulae for the regression coefficient α and the squared correlation coefficient R^2 respectively:

$$\alpha = \frac{\Sigma\, yz}{\Sigma\, z^2}, \qquad R^2 = \frac{\dfrac{(\Sigma\, yz)^2}{\Sigma\, z^2} - \left(\dfrac{\Sigma\, y}{n}\right)^2 \cdot \dfrac{1}{n}}{\Sigma\, y^2 - \left(\dfrac{\Sigma\, y}{n}\right)^2 \cdot \dfrac{1}{n}}$$

where n is the number of observations. Here too the value of β is varied in such a way as to maximize R^2.

For those expenditure categories for which the preliminary estimation of β indicates a type (2.1.1.b) relation, the parameters α and γ are estimated by a method similar to that used for type (2.1.1.a) of the system. Type (2.1.1.b) can also be written as

$$y/x = \alpha \frac{x - \gamma}{x + \beta}. \tag{2.2.5}$$

The regression equation to be used here then becomes

$$y/x = \alpha - \alpha(\beta + \gamma) \frac{1}{x + \beta} + u. \tag{2.2.6}$$

Here too the parameter γ can be found from the regression coefficient $-\alpha(\beta + \gamma)$. If $\gamma < 0$ for that value of β where R^2 is a maximum, then the regression is repeated with the equation

$$y/x = \alpha \frac{x}{x + \beta} + u. \tag{2.2.7}$$

The value of β is again varied in such a way as to minimize Σu^2, while the correlation must yield a zero constant.

Estimation of the parameters α and β when considering the influence of family size

When estimating the Törnqvist functions with the basic material available[3]) it seems useful to include another variable in the regression equation. This variable, g, represents family size expressed as the number of persons per household. Since the number of available observations is quite small, its purpose is only that of a 'cleaning variable', i.e. it mainly serves to improve the estimation of the influence of x. The regression coefficient of this variable, δ, will represent the influence on the expenditure in the category considered of an extra person in the family. The estimation procedure for the Törnqvist functions allowing for family size is then as follows.

---

[3]) See section 3, paragraph 3.1.

Type (2.1.1.a) of the system is estimated in the first instance with the help of the equation

$$y = \alpha - \alpha(\beta + \gamma) \frac{1}{x + \beta} + \delta g + u. \qquad (2.2.8)$$

If γ appears to be greater than zero, type (2.1.1.a) will be chosen with the values of the parameters such as the regression equation (2.2.8) yields for R^2 maximized. If, however, $\gamma < 0$ type (2.1.1.a) will be re-estimated according to the equation:

$$y/g = \alpha \frac{x}{g(x + \beta)} + \delta + u. \qquad (2.2.9)$$

It is not necessary that the constant δ in this regression equation should be made equal to zero, because if the equation is written explicitly in y, x and g then δ is the coefficient of the variable g. The value of the parameter β is varied in such a way as to maximize the squared correlation coefficient R^2. Allowing for the influence of family size, type (2.1.1.b) is estimated according to the equation

$$y/x = \alpha - \alpha(\beta + \gamma) \frac{1}{x + \beta} + \delta g + u. \qquad (2.2.10)$$

If $\gamma < 0$ for R^2 having a maximum value then type (2.1.1.b) is re-estimated with the help of the equation

$$y/gx = \alpha \frac{x}{g(x + \beta)} + \delta + u. \qquad (2.2.11)$$

Here, too, for the same reasons as mentioned for regression equation (2.2.9), the constant δ does not need to have a zero value. The squared correlation coefficient R^2 is maximised by varying the value of parameter β.

In general it is necessary to choose only a limited number of a priori values for β to maximize R^2. After correlating twice for different values of β (the first time for a value of β estimated with the formulae (2.2.1) information is already obtained about the direction in which R^2 changes. Parameter β is varied in that direction so that R^2 goes through the maximum value and begins to decrease. Then in small steps β is varied in the opposite direction so that R^2 again passes through the maximum. At this stage a good impression is obtained of the value of β where R^2 is a maximum. The definite guess of β will approximate the maximum of R^2 with sufficient accuracy [20, p. 137].

It should be borne in mind that the analysis as outlined above ignores the bias in the estimated parameters inherent in estimating them by regression of expenditures (y) on total expenditures ($\Sigma\, y$). Moreover it disregards possible bias originating from estimating the parameters α and γ with the help of a priori values of β.

The variable g in the regression equations is not treated symmetrically for the three types of Törnqvist functions. This is so because a symmetrical treatment of the variable g cannot be carried out easily without considerable intercorrelation between the explaining variables in the regression equations. Moreover the variable g is only included in the equations to estimate the influence of total expenditures as accurately as possible.

For the acceptance of the coefficient δ a standard has to be applied. More or less arbitrarily, this standard is fixed at $|\delta| \geqq \sigma_\delta$ (the standard error of δ). This wide margin is used because g is, as was said above, only included as a 'cleaning variable'. In addition, regarding the acceptability of the sign of the coefficient δ attention is given to the agreement with similar results in the literature [16].

If the coefficient δ cannot be accepted for the reasons mentioned above, the relation is re-estimated with the help of regression equations (2.2.3) or (2.2.4) and (2.2.6) or (2.2.7).

3. THE BASIC MATERIAL USED
AND THE RESULTS OF THE REGRESSION ANALYSIS

3.1. THE BASIC MATERIAL USED FOR THE ESTIMATION OF THE TÖRNQVIST SYSTEM

For the estimation of the system of Törnqvist demand equations, the data of the National Budget Inquiry in 1951 for the Netherlands [5; 6; 7] are available. From the compilation of the results of this inquiry [6] a choice can be made between two kinds of data:

a) the budgets given in Table 1 of [6]: expenditures, money income and money savings, per family, classified by income and by family size;
b) the budgets given in Table 2 of [6]; expenditures, money income and money savings, per family, classified by income and by occupational groups.

The difference between these two kinds of data lies in the subclassification by family size and by occupational group, respectively. In the first set of data the possible influence of family size can be traced explicitly, while the probable influence of the occupational group on expenditures is only implicitly included. In the second set of data exactly the opposite is true: the probable influence of the occupational group can be traced explicitly, while the possible influence of family size is implicitly present in the data.

A rough investigation shows that the numerical differences between the two kinds of data are not very large. Therefore the data arranged into classes of occupational groups are chosen for the estimation of the Törnqvist system, mainly on grounds of suitability. These grounds are: For the budgets classified into family groups the eventual influence of the occupational group on expenditures is – if present – less easy to quantify. On the other hand the probable influence of family size on the budgets arranged according to occupational groups is much easier to quantify, because the mean family size per income-class in every occupational group can be obtained [7, p. 5].

It could be argued that the budgets in *all* occupational groups should be involved in the estimation of the Engel curves. This would, however, give rise to considerable technical difficulties when estimating the relations. Therefore, again on grounds of suitability, only the budgets of *one* occupational group are chosen, namely the budgets of salaried employees and civil servants.

The authors are of opinion that interpolation for the purpose of forecasting is much more reliable than extrapolation. It appears that the range of total expenditures which is covered by the sample of the Budget Inquiry for the group of salaried employees and civil servants includes the range of average total expenditures per family (household) covered in the period 1960–1970; the range covered in the period 1960–1980 lies only for a very small part outside the range covered by the sample. For the other occupational groups, both total expenditure ranges covered for the forecasting periods 1960–1970 and 1960–1980 lie for a considerable part outside the ranges covered by the sample. Thus, when choosing the budgets of salaried employees and civil servants for estimating the system of demand equations the 1970 forecast will be obtained by interpolation, while only the 1980 forecasts will be obtained by extrapolation just outside the range covered by the sample. Furthermore, the number of observations in the group of salaried employees and civil servants is larger than in any other occupational group distinguished: For the group of salaried employees and civil servants six income classes are given, while for the other groups this number is four or even less.

Further, it can be argued that an occupational group such as manual workers will in the long run, if income increases, adopt the consumption pattern of salaried employees and civil servants as it prevails now. This implies that the consumption pattern of salaried employees and civil servants is representative in the long run of that of other occupational groups.

The budget data used in the estimation must be in line with the following definition of the given macro-total for private consumption: 'All expenditure for non-productive purposes on goods and services produced at home or imported' [8, p.37]. This means that all expenditures of a savings character [8, pp.14, 15, 17] in the budget must be omitted. In this way consistency is obtained, while the budget identity $\Sigma y = x$ applies.

The budget data so defined are now regrouped in expenditure categories as defined for the present volume. Thanks to the detailed subgrouping of the data in the Budget Inquiry this regrouping can be done with great exactness. For the estimation of the Engel curves the minimum classification into 17 ASEPELT expenditure categories is adopted. In section 5, where the forecasts are given some subgroupings of these 17 categories are discussed.

In Appendix I the 17 ASEPELT expenditure categories are listed with a rough summary of the kind of expenditures which each category is supposed to cover. Alongside are indicated the items in the National Budget Inquiry 1951 belonging to the expenditure categories considered; the code numbers used refer to those in the Budget Inquiry [6, pp.31–56].

The regrouping according to Appendix I provides the series for the y in the different expenditure categories. These series are given in Appendix II; also the series for $\Sigma y = x$ and the series g for the family size in the different (total) expenditure classes.

3.2. THE RESULTS OF THE REGRESSION ANALYSIS

On the y-series for the 17 expenditure categories and the x- and g-series given in Appendix II the regression analysis described in the previous section is applied[4]). The results of this analysis are given in Table 3.1, while their graphic presentation is given in the graphs of Fig.3.1, confronted with the actual data.

---

[4]) Computations were performed by Messrs. C. Kwinkelenberg, G. H. Lansink and L. Zieren of the Central Planning Bureau.

Fig. 3.1. Engel curves for 17 expenditure groups, allowing for differences
in family size (Salaried employees
and civil servants budgets 1951)

y = expenditures on the item consi-
    dered (guilders per household
    per year);
x = total expenditures Σy
    (1000 guilders per household per
    year);
●   data of the National Budget
    Inquiry 1951;
—   expenditures calculated from
    the estimated demand equations;
○   expenditures projected for 1970
    and 1980

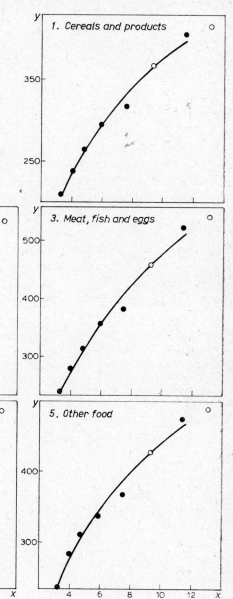

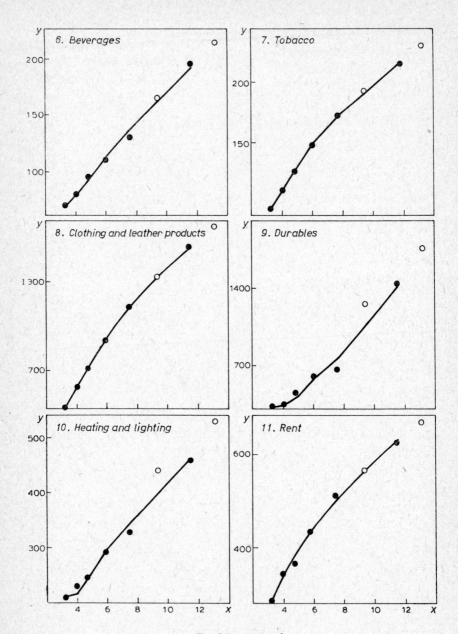

FIG. 3.1 *continued*

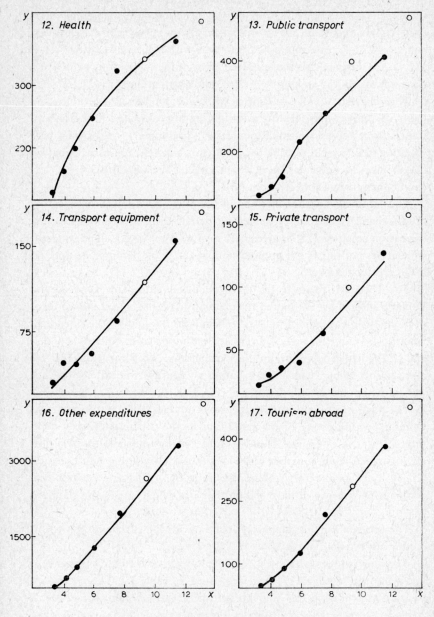

FIG. 3.1 *continued*

As is apparent from Table 3.1, column 3, the Törnqvist relations for the expenditure categories Cereals and products, Meat, fish and eggs, Other foods and Rent are estimated finally with the help of regression equation (2.2.4); preliminary calculations with equations (2.2.8), (2.2.9) and (2.2.3) indicate that the standard error of the regression coefficient δ does not satisfy the standard $|\delta| \geq \sigma_\delta$ and that parameter $\gamma \leq 0$.

The relations for the categories Milk and products, Vegetables and fruits, Beverages and Heating and lighting are estimated in the last instance from regression equation (2.2.9); preliminary regressions with equation (2.2.8) yield a value for γ which is smaller than zero; equation (2.2.9) gives a coefficient for δ which satisfies the standard $|\delta| \geq \sigma_\delta$, as can be seen from Table 3.1, column 3.

The parameters of the functions for the categories Clothing and leather products and Health are estimated ultimately from equation (2.2.3); the regression equation (2.2.8) gives here a value for δ with a standard error which does not satisfy the applied standard $|\delta| \geq \sigma_\delta$; parameter γ appears to be greater than zero.

The Törnqvist relations for the expenditure categories Tobacco and Public transport are estimated from equation (2.2.8); the standard error of δ satisfies the standard $|\delta| \geq \sigma_\delta$. The relations found for the categories Transport equipment and Tourism are estimated from equations (2.2.7) and (2.2.6) respectively; preliminary calculations with equations (2.2.11) and (2.2.10) show a value for δ with a standard error which does not satisfy the applied standard $|\delta| \geq \sigma_\delta$.

The relations found for the categories Durables, Private transport and Other expenditures are of the same type as the two relations last mentioned. For the categories Durables and Private transport the relations are estimated from equation (2.2.11), because estimation with equation (2.2.10) yield a value for γ smaller than zero; the coefficients found for the influence of family size have standard errors which satisfy the standard $|\delta| \geq \sigma_\delta$.

The relation for the category Other expenditure can be estimated directly with the help of equation (2.2.10).

The nine cases in which the coefficient δ was accepted on grounds of satisfying the standard $|\delta| \geq \sigma_\delta$ are listed in Table 3.2. The coefficient $dy/dg \cdot 1/\bar{y}$, showing the influence of one additional family member as a fraction of average expenditure on the item considered, is given to make comparison between the different δ's possible. The standard error σ_δ is expressed as a percentage of δ itself.

TABLE 3.1 – Estimated Törnqvist demand equations and expenditure elasticities

1	2 Expenditure category	3 Demand equations a)b)	Elasticities			
			4 1951	5 1960	6 1970	7 1980
1	Cereals and products	$630 \dfrac{x}{x+6750}$	0.56	0.50	0.42	0.34
2	Milk and products	$651 \dfrac{x}{x+10000} + \dfrac{7g}{(90)}$	0.58	0.54	0.48	0.41
3	Meat, fish and eggs	$962 \dfrac{x}{x+10200}$	0.66	0.60	0.52	0.44
4	Vegetables and fruits	$798 \dfrac{x}{x+9000} - \dfrac{5g}{(74)}$	0.68	0.61	0.51	0.42
5	Other foods	$757 \dfrac{x}{x+7200}$	0.58	0.52	0.43	0.36
6	Beverages	$744 \dfrac{x}{x+30000} - \dfrac{3g}{(67)}$	0.94	0.89	0.81	0.73
7	Tobacco	$406 \dfrac{x-343}{x+9000} - \dfrac{1g}{(82)}$	0.72	0.65	0.54	0.44
8	Clothing and leather products	$3712 \dfrac{x-1426}{x+12850}$	1.07	0.93	0.76	0.62

TABLE 3.1 – (continued)

1	2 Expenditure category	3 Demand equations a) b)	Elasticities 1951 (4)	1960 (5)	1970 (6)	1980 (7)
9	Durables	$0.2765x \dfrac{x}{x+2000} - 0.026g \cdot x$ (32)	1.56	1.43	1.30	1.21
10	Heating and lighting	$1044 \dfrac{x}{x+7000} - 44g$ (18)	0.92	0.76	0.58	0.45
11	Rent	$1217 \dfrac{x}{x+10650}$	0.67	0.62	0.53	0.45
12	Health	$608 \dfrac{x-1849}{x+4000}$	0.96	0.76	0.55	0.40
13	Public transport	$1004 \dfrac{x-1437}{x+3300} - 64g$ (14)	1.69	1.11	0.69	0.47
14	Transport equipment	$0.0179x \dfrac{x}{x+4000}$	1.43	1.37	1.30	1.23
15	Private transport	$0.0205x \dfrac{x}{x+3000} - 0.0014g \cdot x$ (68)	1.61	1.49	1.35	1.26
16	Other expenditures	$0.4559x \dfrac{x-1147}{x+2000} - 0.013gx$ (87)	1.69	1.53	1.35	1.14
17	Tourism abroad	$0.0675x \dfrac{x-614}{x+10000}$	1.78	1.70	1.59	1.48
			1.13	1.07	0.98	0.86

a) x = total expenditure in guilders, per family in 1951 prices; g = family size (number of persons per household)

As will be remembered from section 2, paragraph 2.2, the coefficient δ represents the influence on expenditure of one more member in the family. Only in one case, namely Milk and products is the sign of δ positive. This is in accordance with the results of investigations by HOUTHAKKER [16, pp. 18–19]. All other coefficients δ have a negative sign. For the expenditure categories Beverages, Tobacco, Durables, Heating and lighting, Public transport, Private transport and Other expenditures this is also

TABLE 3.2 – The influence of family size

Expenditure category	δ	$\dfrac{dy}{dg}\Big/\bar{y}$	σ_δ	Expenditure category	δ	$\dfrac{dy}{dg}\Big/\bar{y}$	σ_δ
2 Milk and products	$+7$	$+0.03$	90%	10 Heating and lighting	-44	-0.17	18%
4 Vegetables and fruits	-5	-0.02	74%	13 Public transport	-64	-0.36	14%
6 Beverages	-3	-0.03	67%	15 Private transport	-0.0014	-0.18	68%
7 Tobacco	-1	-0.01	82%	16 Other expenditures	-0.013	-0.06	87%
9 Durables	-0.026	-0.27	32%				

in agreement with other investigations [16, pp. 18–19]. On the other hand the sign of δ for the category Vegetables and fruits is in contradiction with what would be expected from Houthakker's results. The coefficient is maintained, however, because it satisfies the standard $|\delta| \geqq \sigma_\delta$, although its standard error is rather large.

Considering the squared correlation coefficients $\hat{R}^2$,[5]), corrected for bias according to BARTEN [3], given in Table 3.3, it can be concluded that the Törnqvist system of demand equations provides a satisfactory explanation and description of consumer behaviour as it appears from the budget data for salaried employees and civil servants. None of the correlation coefficients are lower than 0.960.

Another measure of the goodness of fit of the Törnqvist hyperbolas to the budget data is given alongside the correlation coefficients in Table 3.3. It measures the dispersion of the residuals u expressed as percentages of the relevant observations y. The value for each $\sigma_{u/y}$ is calculated accord-

---

[5]) All correlation coefficients R^2 are computed from the residuals $u = y - y^*$ according to the formula $R^2 = 1 - \sigma^2_{u}/\sigma^2_{y}$. Then they are corrected for bias so as to obtain $\hat{R}^2$. Thus, all correlation coefficients are brought on the same basis and are comparable with each other.

TABLE 3.3 – Squared correlation coefficients $\hat{R}^2$ and $\sigma_{u/y}$

Expenditure category	$\hat{R}^2$	$\sigma_{u/y}$ as a %	Expenditure category	$\hat{R}^2$	$\sigma_{u/y}$ as a %
1 Cereals and products	0.980	2.4	9 Durables	0.976	7.5
2 Milk and products	0.968	3.6	10 Heating and lighting	0.985	1.0
3 Meat, fish and eggs	0.972	3.4	11 Rent	0.993	2.2
4 Vegetables and fruits	0.996	1.5	12 Health	0.977	3.1
9 Other foods	0.969	3.1	13 Public transport	0.997	3.0
6 Beverages	0.988	3.7	14 Transport equipment	0.969	11.7
7 Tobacco	0.999	0.4	15 Private transport	0.979	9.3
8 Clothing and leather products	0.999	0.9	16 Other expenditures	0.997	2.6
			17 Tourism abroad	0.992	6.7

ing to the expression

$$\sigma_{u/y} = \sqrt{\sum \left(\frac{y - y^*}{y} \right)^2 \bigg/ n}$$

where n = the number of observations. As can be seen this measure gives an impression of the relative magnitude of residuals, while the expression $1 - R^2$ gives the absolute magnitude of the unexplained variance of y as a percentage of the total variance of y. The lower the standard deviation of the percentage residuals $\sigma_{u/y}$ the better is the fit. This measure supports the view that on the whole the Törnqvist system gives a satisfactory fit to the budget data.

This conclusion is also supported by the fact that in almost every case the fitted Törnqvist demand equation agrees with what might be expected on a priori grounds. An exception is probably the relation found for the category Beverages, which would seem to qualify as semi-luxuries rather than as necessities in the Törnqvist sense. It must be noted, however, that this category includes such items as expenditure on coffee and on tea.

3.3. THE ADDITIVITY OF THE ESTIMATED SYSTEM
AND ITS EXPENDITURE ELASTICITIES

How far does the estimated Törnqvist system deviate from the additivity criterion $\Sigma y = x$ mentioned in section 1, paragraph 1.2.? A graphical illustration of this deviation is given in the layer diagram of Fig.3.2, where the expected expenditures for the different categories are added for a range of supposed expenditure totals (family size is kept constant at the sample mean of the Budget Inquiry). The required budget identity $\Sigma y = x$ is represented by the 45° line.

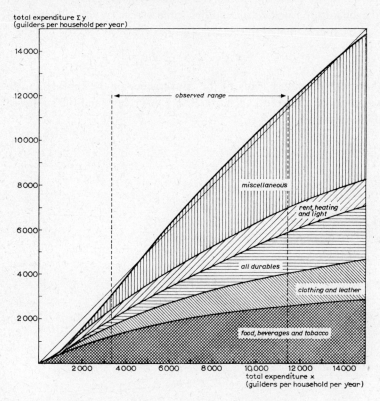

FIG.3.2. The Törnqvist Engel curves and the additivity problem.

For the range observed in the sample of the Budget Inquiry the system of estimated demand equations approximates fairly well to the identity required by the additivity criterion. In the range for which the forecasts are set up this conclusion is upheld, although it should be noted that the influence of changes in family size is not included in the graph.

If it appears, when handling the system of equations, that the additivity criterion is not sufficiently satisfied, then equality between Σy and x can be obtained by substituting a newly chosen expenditure total x' in the equations. This expenditure total x' is approximated by

$$x' = x + (x - \Sigma y). \tag{3.3.1}$$

If now the new total of expected expenditures $\Sigma y'$ according to the relations is still deviating appreciably from the original value for the supposed expenditure total x, still another value x'' can be substituted. This value x'' is approximated in the same way.

$$x'' = x' + (x - \Sigma y'). \tag{3.3.2}$$

This method ultimately leads to the convergence of the repeatedly calculated total of expected expenditures Σy, $\Sigma y'$, $\Sigma y''$ and the supposed expenditure total x.

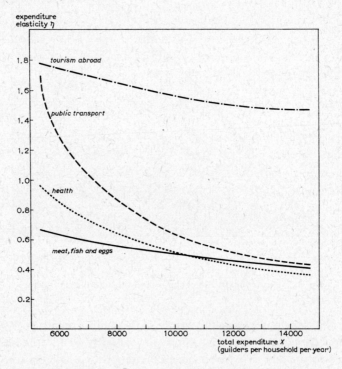

FIG. 3.3. The expenditure elasticity as a function of total expenditure.

The extent to which the system of Engel curves satisfies the additivity criterion can also be demonstrated by means of the weighted sum of expenditure elasticites which does not equal unity, as can be seen from

Table 3.1. The given elasticities are computed on the basis of total expenditures and family size for the years 1951, 1960, 1970 and 1980[6]). From this point of view the additivity of the system might seem more seriously in question than Fig.3.2 shows. The reason for this difference is that whereas changes over time in family size influence the level of elasticities and the weighting system of Table 3.1[7]), the graph of Fig.3.2 has been computed for the case that family size remains unchanged.

Incidentally it can be noted from Table 3.1 that all estimated Törnqvist demand functions possess the required property of decreasing expenditure elasticities. A graph showing the expenditure elasticity as a function of total expenditure is given in Fig.3.3 for four expenditure categories.

4. APPLICATION OF THE SYSTEM
AND COMPUTATION OF A TREND

4.1. THE APPLICATION OF THE SYSTEM OF DEMAND EQUATIONS

The application of the system of demand equations for forecasting presumes some variables to be given.

It is implicit in the data used for estimation that the system describes the consumer behaviour of an average Dutch family or household. Family or household is defined here as in the Methodological Introduction to the National Budget Inquiry of 1951 [5, p.38]. In short this definition is: A family or household consists of a married couple with unmarried children and relatives living in one dwelling, in so far as the consumptive expenditures of these persons are financed out of their joint incomes.

The figure for total private consumption as defined in this paper is obtained by multiplying the expenditures, as the system of demand equations gives them for an average Dutch household, by the total number of Dutch households. This last figure is based on data and forecasts of total population (migration included) of the Central Bureau of Statistics of the Netherlands and on data and forecasts concerning the mean Dutch family size as defined above[8]). For simplicity, the total number of Dutch

---

[6]) See table 4.1.
[7]) If family size appears in the Törnqvist formula it also appears in the elasticity formula.
[8]) The forecasts of the mean family size are provided by Messrs. G.E.Engberts and K.C.Bijkerk of the Central Planning Bureau.

families is computed by dividing the *total* population of the Netherlands by the mean family size. This means that people other than those living in families, such as those living in institutions and those living alone, are classed in units of average family size. For the application of the system of demand equations it is supposed that these units behave as 'real' households of the mean size. This hypothesis – even if completely unjustified – does not cause a large inaccuracy, because the numbers involved are relatively small.

TABLE 4.1 – Data for 1929, 1951, 1960, 1970 and 1980

	1929	1951	1960	1970	1980
Total private consumption (in mlns of guilders at 1951 prices)[a]	10403	13870	20360	33368	54685
Total population (× 1000 persons)[b]	7781	10264	11477	12757	14237
Mean family size[c]	4.39	3.94	3.76	3.58	3.41
Number of families (× 100 families)	17716	26079	30500	35635	41803
Total expenditure per family (in guilders at 1951 prices)	5870	5320	6680	9360	13080
Price index (1960 = 100)[d]	42	85	100	100	100

[a]) For 1929 obtained from [4]; for 1951 from [8]; for 1970 and 1980 from extrapolation on the basis of the hypothesis mentioned in the Introduction.

[b]) For 1929, 1951 and 1960 obtained from [8]; for 1970 and 1980 based on forecasts of the Central Bureau of Statistics of the Netherlands (not published).

[c]) For all years obtained from data and forecasts of the Central Planning Bureau.

[d]) For 1929 obtained from [4]; for 1951 and 1960 from [8].

The mean total expenditures per household required for handling the equations are found, of course, in the reverse way: By dividing the given figures for *total* private consumption by the number of families as defined above.

The data supposed to be given for handling the system of equations for the years 1929, 1951, 1960, 1970 and 1980 are presented in Table 4.1.

All value quantities are given in prices of 1951, because the system of equations is estimated with data given in 1951 prices. For the price indices, 1960 is chosen as the base year, because ultimately the forecast will be presented in 1960 prices.

4.2.   COMPUTATION OF TENTATIVE TREND VALUES

It is possible to compute a systematic trend for each expenditure category by means of a comparison of the outcomes of the system of demand equations with the actual figures for a certain period of time. Differences between the outcomes of the system and the actual figures for this period of time may be caused by

— the fact that the system of demand equations only traces the influence of total expenditure on expenditures in the different categories and consequently ignores the influence of relative prices and of possible trend developments on expenditures;
— more or less accidental deviations as a consequence of circumstances such as war, or an exceptional situation in a specific market;
— faulty measurements.

Leaving aside the last two factors, it is possible to regard the actual figures for the different expenditure categories as the result of the impact of total expenditure, of relative prices and of trend developments. The actual figures for each relevant expenditure category can be written as a function of total expenditure, relative prices and some trend

$$y(R) = \varphi \cdot y(M) \cdot p^{\varepsilon} \cdot e^{\theta \tau} \qquad (4.2.1)$$

where $y(R)$ is the actual figure, φ some constant, $y(M)$ the outcome of the system of demand equations, p the relative price (that is, absolute price P divided by a cost of living index Q), ε the price elasticity and $e^{\theta \tau}$ describing the trend component. If all the variables occurring in equation (4.2.1) $y(R)$, $y(M)$ and p are indices with the same base year the constant φ can be left out

$$y(R) = y(M) \cdot p^{\varepsilon} \cdot e^{\theta \tau}. \qquad (4.2.2)$$

If now the indices $y(R)$, $y(M)$ and p^{ε} are given, the term $e^{\theta \tau}$ can be solved from (4.2.2)

$$e^{\theta \tau} = \frac{y(R)}{y(M)} \cdot p^{-\varepsilon}. \qquad (4.2.3)$$

The annual trend τ can now be found with the help of compound interest tables. Considering the hypothesis from which τ is calculated, its character is purely residual and it should be regarded only as a tentative value for the trend.

This procedure was applied to data for two different periods: the period 1929–1960 and the period 1951–1960, respectively. The data and results for both periods are given in Table 4.2. All $y(M)$ are obtained from the system of demand equations. The $y(R)$ and p for the period 1929–1960 are calculated from data published by the Central Bureau of Statistics [8] and from a publication of the Econometric Institute of the Netherlands Economic School [4]; the $y(R)$ and p for the period 1951–1960 are calculated from sources published by the Central Bureau of Statistics [8]. The $y(M), y(R)$ and p are indexed with 1929 and 1951, respectively, as the base year.

The price elasticity ε_i with respect to the relative price p_i for the different expenditure categories $i (= 1, 2 \dots n)$ is derived with the help of a method devised by FRISCH [14; 15; 17, pp.87–95]. This method uses a demand function of the following form (for the ith expenditure category)

$$y_i = \varrho_i X^{\eta_i} P_i^{\lambda_i} \prod_{j \neq i} P_j^{\lambda_{ij}} \qquad (4.2.4)$$

where ϱ_i is some constant, X is total expenditure at current prices, η_i is the expenditure elasticity, P_i and the $P_j (j \neq i)$ are the absolute prices of the n expenditure categories in the budget and λ_i and $\lambda_{ij} (j \neq i)$ are respectively the direct price elasticity and the cross elasticities with respect to those prices. This function is different from function (4.2.1) with respect to the independent variables: Function (4.2.1) contains deflated total expenditure and relative price only, while function (4.2.4) contains total expenditure at current prices and all absolute prices.

The method of Frisch makes it possible to calculate λ_i and the λ_{ij} $(j \neq i)$ for all expenditure categories $i (= 1, 2 \dots n)$ simultaneously if all expenditure η_i, one direct price elasticity λ_0 and all budget shares w_i are given. From the so calculated $\lambda_i (i = 1, 2 \dots n)$ the price elasticities ε_i are derived. This derivation rests on the following deduction [11, pp.356 –358].

If it is assumed by way of approximation that all $P_j (j \neq i)$ in equation (4.2.4) always change equally and in the same direction then it is possible to rewrite (4.2.4) as (leaving out for convenience the suffix i)

$$y = \varrho X^\eta P^\lambda A^{\lambda_a} \qquad (4.2.5)$$

where A represents some average of the $P_j (j \neq i)$. Now a deflator or a cost of living index Q is defined as the weighted geometric average of P and A.

$$Q = P^w A^{1-w}. \qquad (4.2.6)$$

Then equation (4.2.5) can be written as

$$y = \varrho x^\eta P^{\lambda+w\eta} A^{\lambda a+(1-w)\eta} \tag{4.2.7}$$

where x is deflated total expenditure.

If it is assumed further that the consumer is fully aware of price changes and, moreover, reacts rationally this implies that in (4.2.7) the exponents of P and A respectively have the same numerical value but the opposite sign. Thus the absence of 'money illusion' makes it possible to write equation (4.2.7) as

$$y = \varrho x^\eta P^\mu A^{-\mu} \tag{4.2.8}$$

where $\mu = \lambda + w\eta$.

From the definition (4.2.6) it is known that

$$A = Q^{\frac{1}{1-w}} \cdot P^{\frac{-w}{1-w}}. \tag{4.2.9}$$

Substitution of (4.2.9) in equation (4.2.8) yields

$$y = \varrho x^\eta P^{\mu+\frac{\mu w}{1-w}} Q^{-\frac{\mu}{1-w}}$$

$$= \varrho x^\eta \left(\frac{P}{Q}\right)^{\frac{\mu}{1-w}}$$

$$= \varrho x^\eta p^\varepsilon. \tag{4.2.10}$$

This equation is of the type used for the computation of trends (equation (4.2.1)). Thus, the price elasticity ε with respect to the relative price p can be expressed in terms of the expenditure elasticity η, the budget share w and the calculated direct price elasticity λ with respect to the absolute price P:

$$\varepsilon = \frac{\lambda + w\eta}{1 - w}. \tag{4.2.11}$$

Moreover, the above deduction shows that the calculated cross elasticities λ_{ij} $(j \neq i)$ are implicit in the price elasticity ε, because equation (4.2.10) is identical with equation (4.2.4), but only in so far as (i) all P_j $(j \neq i)$ change equally and in the same direction; (ii) the deflator used is a reasonable approximation of the weighted geometric average of P and A, and (iii) there is no 'money illusion'. These requirements are taken for granted here.

For the calculation of the direct price elasticities λ_i the required ex-

TABLE 4.2 – Estimation of residual trends[a])

		The 1929–1960 period ($\theta = 31$)			
Expenditure category		Actual figures for 1960 (1929 = 100)	Outcomes of the system of equations (1929 = 100)	Relative price (1929 = 100)	Estimated price elasticity
		$y(R)$	$y(M)$	p	ε
1	2	3	4	5	6
1	Cereals and products	147.9	180.3	94.7	−0.4
2	Milk and products	168.0	177.2	97.6	−0.4
3	Meat, fish and eggs	179.2	181.9	96.0	−0.5
4	Vegetables and fruit	100.8	184.2	166.7	−0.5
5	Other food	199.1	180.4	103.8	−0.4
6	Beverages	110.5	189.5	135.1	−0.7
7	Tobacco	171.0	183.5	135.4	−0.5
8	Clothing and leather products	213.2	187.8	107.4	−0.8
9	Durables	171.2	231.5	112.4	−1.1
10	Heating and lighting	210.4	202.9	111.9	−0.7
11	Rent	203.2	182.1	72.6	−0.5
12	Health	—	—	—	—
13	Public transport	—	—	—	—
14	Transport equipment	499.7	193.9	91.9	−1.0
15	Private transport	—	—	—	—
16	Other expenditures	—	—	—	—
17	Tourism abroad	—	—	—	—
	12, 13, 15, 16 and 17[b])	209.2	205.5	97.1	−1.1

[a]) Sources mentioned in the text.

[b]) For these expenditure categories no specification per category can be given for the period 1929–1960 because of a lack of detailedness in the data.

penditure elasticities η_i are computed from the system of demand equations. Further, the price elasticity ε with respect to the relative price for the expenditure category Clothing and leather products is known from time series analyses and is fixed at −0.8 for the period 1929–1960, and at −0.7 for the period 1951–1960. For the calculation it is transformed to λ_θ with the help of (4.2.11).

It should be noted that the assumption of want independence [14, p.8; 15, p.177; 17, p.88] under which this method is valid does not apply to the expenditure categories used here. Therefore the values found for the price elasticities ε should be regarded as approximations to the actually prevailing price elasticities for each expenditure category.

	The 1951–1960 period ($\theta = 9$)					
Annual residual trend percentage	Actual figures for 1960 (1951=100)	Outcomes of the system of equations (1951=100)	Relative price (1951=100)	Estimated price elasticity	Annual residual trend percentage	Definite annual trend percentage chosen for prediction
τ	$y(R)$	$y(M)$	p	ε	τ	τ'
7	8	9	10	11	12	13
-0.70	106.1	130.4	106.4	-0.4	-2.02	-1.0
-0.20	102.2	130.5	130.5	-0.4	-1.53	—
-0.10	145.1	133.1	97.7	-0.5	$+0.82$	—
-1.12	102.5	133.8	118.6	-0.5	-2.02	-1.0
$+0.37$	126.2	130.5	98.5	-0.4	-0.44	—
-1.07	168.0	141.5	98.8	-0.7	$+1.81$	$+1.0$
$+0.27$	142.7	134.7	92.5	-0.5	$+0.21$	—
$+0.60$	184.9	143.7	72.8	-0.7	$+0.34$	$+0.5$
-0.56	208.1	165.6	86.6	-1.0	$+0.93$	$+1.0$
$+0.37$	134.3	142.5	116.9	-0.6	$+0.37$	—
-0.16	125.2	133.3	150.4	-0.5	$+1.57$	—
—	175.4	139.8	127.1	-0.6	$+4.12$	$+3.0$
—	115.4	164.0	110.2	-0.8	-3.03	-2.0
$+2.78$	219.2	153.9	96.3	-1.0	$+3.51$	$+3.0$
—	154.8	165.0	110.9	-1.1	$+0.56$	$+2.0$
—	120.2	164.1	108.9	-1.0	-2.52	-1.5
—	231.1	166.7	112.4	-1.3	$+5.31$	$+4.0$
-0.04						

The values found for τ are recapitulated in Table 4.3 together with the values for τ', which represent the annual trend percentages finally chosen for the forecast. The choice of τ' is discussed in section 5.

The computation of trends for each expenditure category might be considered as a demonstration of the operation of the system of demand equations. Taking account of the influence of changes in relative prices the results for the period 1929–1960 can be regarded as satisfactory. The residual ascribed to trend developments expressed as the trend percentage τ is in general not much larger than 1% per annum, except for the category Transport equipment where $+2.78\%$ is found. For this category, however, a strong positive trend development would be expected on grounds of increasing consumer acceptance. For the period 1951–1960 the results of the system of demand equations seem to be less satisfactory. The residual trends τ are larger than for the period 1929–1960.

TABLE 4.3 – Trend percentages τ and τ'

Expenditure category		τ 1929–1960	τ 1951–1960	τ'
1	Cereals and products	− 0.70	− 2.02	− 1.0
2	Milk and products	− 0.20	− 1.53	—
3	Meat, fish and eggs	− 0.10	+ 0.82	—
4	Vegetables and fruits	− 1.12	− 2.02	− 1.0
5	Other food	+ 0.37	− 0.44	—
6	Beverages	− 1.07	+ 1.81	+ 1.0
7	Tobacco	+ 0.27	+ 0.21	—
8	Clothing and leather products	+ 0.60	+ 0.34	+ 0.5
9	Durables	− 0.56	+ 0.93	+ 1.0

Expenditure category		τ 1929–1960	τ 1951–1960	τ'
10	Heating and lighting	+ 0.37	+ 0.37	—
11	Rent	− 0.16	+ 1.57	—
12	Health	—	+ 4.12	+ 3.0
13	Public transport	—	− 3.03	− 2.0
14	Transport equipment	+ 2.78	+ 3.51	+ 3.0
15	Private transport	—	+ 0.56	+ 2.0
16	Other expenditures	—	− 2.52	− 1.5
17	Tourism abroad	—	+ 5.31	+ 4.0
	12, 13, 15, 16 and 17	− 0.04		

This difference between the two periods can be explained in large measure by the difference in character of the two periods. In the period 1929 –1960 the influence of the trade cycle is not very significant. The year 1929 as well as the year 1960 are boom years, so that both years are of the same type from an economic point of view. Therefore this period is supposed to be representative for trend computation. The period 1951–1960, however, is completely different: 1951 was a year of stagnating activity and 1960 a boom year. Moreover, some recovery from the second world war is included in this period. The residual trend τ found for this period, therefore, probably includes a part to be ascribed to trade cycle movements, so that this period is less representative for trend computation.

It appears that in explaining the differences between the actual figures and the outcomes of the system of demand equations the development of relative prices cannot be left out of consideration. The negative correlation between $y(R)/y(M)$ and p is obvious in both periods. This means in fact that changes in the consumer price structure should be taken into consideration when forecasting. This, however, is not possible, because of the lack of information about future developments of relative prices.

5. CONSUMPTION FORECASTS
FOR THE YEARS 1970 AND 1980

5.1. GENERAL REMARKS

In the foregoing section tentative trend values τ are calculated for the periods 1929–1960 and 1951–1960. For trend estimation the first period is more representative than the second period. It is clear, therefore, that in choosing trends for prediction-purposes the results for the 1929–1960 period will be given more weight than those for the 1951–1960 period as can be deduced from Table 4.3. Apart from the computed trends, other aspects are sometimes taken into account in fixing the definite trends. In commenting on the forecasts for the different expenditure categories some further consideration will be given to this point.

In Table 5.1 the forecasts for 1970 and 1980 are presented as index numbers (basis 1960 = 100) while the actual expenditures for 1960 are given in millions of guilders in current prices.

The actual total for 1960 is in agreement with the definition of total

TABLE 5.1 – Consumption forecasts for 1970 and 1980 (trends τ' included)

Expenditure category	Expenditure in 1960 in current prices[a])	Consumption indices (1960 = 100)	
		1970	1980
1	2	3	4
1. Cereals and products	960	123	146
2. Milk and products	1330	138	183
3. Meat, fish and eggs	2080	142	190
4. Vegetables and fruit	850	128	156
5. Other food	1440	137	180
6. Beverages (incl. non alcoholics)	1050	171	285
7. Tobacco	980	142	194
8. Clothing and leather products	3290	163	250
9. Durables	2830	211	429
10. Heating and lighting	1250	149	208
11. Rent	1600	141	192
12. Health	1030	196	355
13. Public transport	600	135	160
14. Transport equipment	530	244	588
15. Private transport	180	233	529
16. Other expenditures	3410	164	261
17. Tourism abroad	460	298	873
	23870[b])	164	269

[a]) Millions of guilders. Source [8].
[b]) Later estimates of this total are slightly higher.

private consumption used in Sandee's paper [21][9]. Consumption by foreigners is subtracted from total consumption (including consumption by foreigners) as well as from the expenditures in the different categories. This is in accordance with the character of the system of equations, which describes only consumption behaviour of Dutch households. The equations disregard consumption by foreigners.

As far as possible, food and beverages consumed in places of refreshment are allocated to the relevant categories. The figures presented in Table 5.1, column 3 and 4 are computed in the following way[10]).

---

[9]) See the definition cited on page 98; excluding, however, expenditures by foreigners.
[10]) In Appendix III a more refined method is explained which, however, leads to nearly the same results.

With the help of the data given in Table 4.1 for 1960, 1970 and 1980 the index numbers $y(M)$ are computed for, respectively, 1970 and 1980 (base year 1960 = 100) with the equations given in Table 3.1, taking care that the budget identity $\Sigma y = x$ is fulfilled[11]). Next, these $y(M)$ are imposed on the actual consumption data for 1960.

In the figures for 1970 and 1980 calculated in this way allowance will be made eventually for a trend. After summation of the figures including trend, the possible difference between this sum and the given total of private consumption is distributed pro rata over the expenditure categories.

This is done to obtain equality between the given total of private consumption and the sum of expenditures in the different categories. The following totals give an idea of the magnitude of the applied correction. After this correction the index numbers given in Table 5.1 are calculated.

	Summation of figures before allowing for trend		Summation of figures after allowing for trend		Given total of private consumption (Table 4.1)	
	1970	1980	1970	1980	1970	1980
Sums of expenditures over categories	38 249	61 469	39 298	66 491	39 120	64 113
Sums as a percentage of the given totals	97.8	95.9	100.5	103.7	100	100

Before commenting on the different consumption categories it must be stressed again that in the given predictions no allowance is made for any future relative price developments. But from Table 4.2 it can be seen how important a role relative prices have played in the past.

The forecasts are now discussed briefly.

5.2. FOOD

Total food including non-alcoholic beverages

The expenditures for this sub-total increase by 80% in the period 1960 to 1980 (excluding trend: 84%). This means an annual increase per head of nearly 2%. This gives for an increase of 4% for total consumption an

---

[11]) According to the procedure described in section 3, paragraph 3.3.

elasticity of almost 0.5, a figure which is about 0.15 higher than the apparent elasticity for roughly the same group, in a recent study of the E.E.C. [9]. It must be noted, however, that consumption studies related to weight units often give lower elasticities than those on the basis of expenditure in constant prices. This results from the fact that at higher income levels it is often better-quality goods, rather than more of them, that are consumed. The gap of 0.15 between the elasticities can, therefore, be attributed to quality differences. Such a difference has also be taken into account when judging the elasticities of the different food-categories.

Cereals and products

For the postwar period as well as for the period 1929–1960 a negative trend is found. For the prediction period a negative trend of 1% per annum is assumed. The per head expenditures on cereals and products will then increase 0.8% yearly. Within this figure, consumption of bread will decrease somewhat, while consumption of pastry, cake and biscuits will increase.

Milk and products

For the period 1929–1960 predicted and actual figures for the consumption of dairy products do not differ much. Therefore no trend is introduced in the forecast. Expenditure per head will rise 2% annually. Probably the consumption of fresh milk will hardly rise, so that the increase must be attributed to products, such as cheese, butter and condensed milk.

Meat, fish and eggs

For this category also, no trend in the past is apparent. The expected growth of something over 2% yearly per head is more or less in accordance with what is accepted by other investigators, according to the literature.

Vegetables and fruit

In view of the development in the period 1929–1960, especially in the postwar period, the trend is fixed at − 1% per annum. The increase per head is still more than 1% per annum. This seems to be on the high side. However, because quality improvements play an important part in this category this figure looks plausible. The use of deep-freeze vegetables and better quality ones generally will probably expand a great deal.

Other food

The trend after the war is opposite to that since 1929. Because there are no special reasons to introduce a trend, the results as given by the equation are accepted. The annual growth rate per head amounts to 1.8%. The consumption of margarine, vegetable and mixed fats and oils will not deviate much from the present day level, while the consumption of preserved foods will show a continued increase.

5.3. BEVERAGES AND TOBACCO

Beverages including soft drinks

Between 1929 and 1960 a negative trend is observed, particularly for alcoholic beverages. This may have been the result of anti-alcoholic propaganda. After the war the trend is clearly positive for both alcoholic and soft drinks. In part this has to be regarded as a recovery from rationing, of coffee in particular, and the slackening of anti-alcohol propaganda. Moreover, there are indications that the consumption of beverages, especially alcoholic drinks, will tend towards the consumption level of the rest of Europe. This means that the consumption of non-alcoholic beverages per head will increase by 2.8% per annum and that of alcoholic drinks by 5.3%. The first figure is found with the help of a Törnqvist relation estimated separately for non-alcoholic beverages; the second figure by substracting this relation from the relation estimated for all beverages.

Tobacco

In the case of tobacco a small positive trend is observed. Probably this reflects the participation of women in smoking. This process is not yet ended. But on the other hand there might be some counter influence in the near future from the reports on lung cancer. So for the prediction period no trend is introduced. Consumption per head will increase by 2.3% per annum.

5.4. ALL OTHER EXPENDITURES

Clothing and leather products

Considering the development during 1929–1960, a positive trend of 0.5% per annum seems reasonable for the period up to 1980. This implies a rise in consumption per head of 3.5% annually.

Durables

The negative trend since 1929 cannot be explained. In the postwar period the trend is definitely positive. This can be attributed to the rise of new products such as television and other electrical appliances. Because a saturation level for these goods has not yet been reached and new products may turn up, the trend is fixed at 1% per annum.

Heating and lighting

Although a small positive trend is observed for this item, no trend is included here. The results without trend turned out to be in good agreement with the results of the energy model developed from time-series analysis by the Central Planning Bureau of the Netherlands [18].

Rent

For the 1929–1960 period no trend is found. The postwar trend is clearly a recovery one. Up to 1980 expenditure on rent will increase by more than 3% per annum. This is in agreement with the increase of the limited supply of the stock of dwellings in the last ten years, quality improvements included. This rate of increase in the supply is supposed to continue in the future.

Health

The postwar trend amounts to 4% per annum. Since the improvement of medical care is not expected to come to a standstill yet, the future trend is fixed at 3% per annum. This means that expenditures on health per head will increase 5.4% annually. This might seem to be high, but it is again stressed that changes in relative prices are not taken into account; if relative prices go up, the volume of demand will increase less steeply.

Public transport, transport equipment, private transport

These categories are treated here simultaneously, because Public transport on the one hand and Transport equipment and Private transport on the other hand are substitutes, one for the other. This appears, too, from the trends. The former has a negative sign, the latter a positive sign. It is assumed that these development patterns will continue in the future. The annual increase of the expenditure on transport equipment and on private transport per head amounts to 7.5 to 8%. This rise is about half the increase in these items in the last few years. A diminution of the growth-rate is to be expected.

Other expenditure

After the war this category – consisting mainly of services – has a negative trend. For instance, expenditures on entertainment, hotels, restaurants and domestic services have decreased. This is the result of the rise of television and domestic appliances (for the same reasons a positive trend was evident in the case of durables). This development will undoubtedly be continued, although perhaps at a slower rate.

Tourism abroad

For this category it is supposed that consumer acceptance is playing an important rôle. Therefore it is not surprising that the trend was so large. The growth rate of these expenditures is much greater than that of all other categories; it amounts to more than 10% per head per annum.

Breakdown of private consumption

Expenditure category	Including	Code number in the National Budget Inquiry 1951 [6]
1. Cereals and Products	Bread, pastry, cake, biscuits, rice, macaroni	1 2.1–2.2
2. Milk and products	Butter, milk, cheese, ice-cream, cocoa-milk	6.1.3–6.2 10.0 –13–14
3. Meat, fish and eggs	Animal fats, beef, veal, pork, game and poultry, bacon, ham, smoked and salted meat, sausages, fresh sea and fresh water-fish, shell fish, fried, smoked and steamed fish, dried and salted fish, eggs	10.1–10.2 10.3–11.0 11.1–11.2 11.3–11.4 11.5–11.6 11.7–11.8 12.0–12.1 12.2–12.3 12.4–12.5 12.6–15
4. Vegetables and fruits	Peas and beans, potatoes, vegetables, fresh herbs, sauerkraut, dried and deep-freeze vegetables, fruits (including dried, preserved and deep-freeze fruits)	2.0–3 4.0–4.1 4.2–4.3 4.4–4.5 4.7–4.8.1 4.9–5.0 5.1–5.2 5.3–5.4 5.5–5.6 5.8
5. Other foods	Pickled gherkins etc., preserved foods such as vegetables, fruit, meat, fish in tins or jars, sugar, jam, chocolate and confectionery, spices, vinegar, salt, sauces, vegetable and mixed fats and oils, margarine	4.6–4.8.0 5.7–7 8.1–8.2 8.4–8.5 8.6–8.7 9.0–9.1 11.9–12.7 12.8–12.9
6. Beverages	Alcoholic and non-alcoholic drinks (excl. milk; see 2) tea, coffee, cocoa	6.0–6.1.0 6.1.1–6.1.2. 8.0

APPENDIX I (cont.)

Expenditure category	Including	Code number in the National Budget Inquiry 1951 [6]
7. Tobacco	Cigars, cigarettes, shag, smokers' requisites	33
8. Clothing and leather products	Men's, ladies', children's outer- and underwear, leatherwork, cost of repairs	25.1–25.2 25.3–25.4 25.5–25.6.0 25.6.1–25.7.1 26–25.0
9. Durables	Furniture, jewellery, watches, umbrellas, radio and television sets, musical instruments, cameras, films, developing, printing	20–25.7.0 25.7.2–25.7.3 29.3.2–29.3.0 29.3.3
10. Heating and lighting	Gas, electricity, fuels	21
11. Rent	Rent, contribution to house-building society, maintenance cost on owner-occupied house, mortgage interest and other costs	17.0.0–17.0.1
12. Health	Sickness insurance, doctor, hospital, maternity care	28–35.1
13. Public transport	Train, tramway, taxi, boat, telephone, telegraph, postage, radio rediffusion, radio licence	29.3.1 34.2 34.3
14. Transport equipment	Bicycles, motorcars, motorcycles and parts	34.0.0–34.0.1 34.1.0
15. Private transport	Costs of repair, hire, tyres, sheltering, petrol, oil, parking, insurance	34.0.2–34.0.3 34.0.4–34.0.5 34.1.1–34.1.2 34.1.3–34.1.4 34.1.5–35.6
16. Other expenditures	Consumption not at home, water, maintenance of home (at tenant's expense), house cleaning and cleaning of clothes, domestic help, plants and animals, physical care, admission fees, subscriptions, donations, handicrafts, sporting goods, toys, newspapers, periodicals, books, education and training, religion, fire, burglary and glass insurance, charity gifts	16–17.0.3 19.0–22 23–24 25.6.2–25.7.4 27 29–29.1 29.4–30.0 30.1–31 32–35.5 36.0–36.1 38.1–39.0 39.1–38.0

APPENDIX I (cont.)

Expenditure category	Including	Code number in the National Budget Inquiry 1951 [6]
17. Tourism abroad	Holidays, excursions	29.2
Expenditure not included in the 17 groups	Life insurance, old-age insurance, education insurance, marriage and funeral ceremonies, taxes	35.0–35.2 35.3–35.4 37–38.2 39.2.1.

Family expenditure data for estimating Törnqvist demand equations
(grouped according to the breakdown given in Appendix I)

Expenditure category	Income class					
1. Cereals and products	209.8	237.6	264.0	295.8	316.5	405.3
2. Milk and products	187.2	224.8	243.7	263.6	296.7	385.7
3. Meat, fish and eggs	235.9	279.6	313.6	356.6	382.0	522.3
4. Vegetables and fruits	198.2	234.4	255.3	294.1	334.6	427.5
5. Other foods	238.1	283.8	310.3	338.5	366.5	474.5
6. Beverages	68.6	79.2	95.4	108.8	130.0	197.2
7. Tobacco	95.3	111.0	126.0	147.0	173.0	215.0
8. Clothing and leather products	434.5	571.7	717.1	887.3	1122.2	1527.0
9. Durables	323.6	350.5	448.8	597.6	662.3	1439.7
10. Heating and lighting	208.0	229.0	246.0	290.0	328.0	461.0
11. Rent	286.6	347.2	365.7	432.3	515.1	626.9
12. Health	129.1	160.0	194.2	247.3	322.9	368.0
13. Public transport	103.2	120.7	144.0	219.9	289.1	407.9
14. Transport equipment	30.4	47.8	46.4	56.0	83.7	153.5
15. Private transport	21.7	30.1	35.3	39.9	62.8	126.6
16. Other expenditures	502.3	677.1	888.9	1283.1	1962.8	3291.7
17. Tourism abroad	49.9	61.5	90.9	126.0	219.0	383.0
Total expenditure $\Sigma y = x$	3322.4	4046.0	4785.6	5983.8	7567.2	11412.8
Family size g (number of persons per household)	2.877	3.755	4.131	4.263	4.470	4.23 2

Computation of $y(M)$ with a shifting expenditure distribution

Because of the non-linearity of the estimated system of demand equations
it is interesting to investigate the possibility of computing the index numbers $y(M)$ with an expenditure distribution shifting over time when total
private consumption expenditures change over time. This procedure is
analogous to that of using a shifting income distribution.

From a theoretical point of view this more refined computation of
$y(M)$ may be preferred, because it gives more weight to the non-linearity
of the system of demand equations. From a practical point of view, however, there is the objection that a great deal of computational work is involved in applying this procedure. It is, therefore useful to investigate the
magnitude of the differences between the $y(M)$ computed according to
this procedure and computed as is done in the paper. This is carried out
for four expenditure categories. These categories are chosen with respect
to the degree of curvature of their Engel curves, measured on a linear scale.

The expenditure categories considered are Meat, fish and eggs, Health,
Public transport and Tourism abroad.

The expenditure distribution for 1951 is taken from the National Budget Inquiry 1951 [6]. The expenditure distributions for 1960 and 1970 are
derived from the one for 1951: The expenditure levels are adjusted in such
a way that the variation coefficient and the frequencies of the distribution
are held constant. This means that expenditure in every expenditure class
is increased with the percentage increase of the mean expenditures of the
distribution.

The $y(M)$ for 1970 (1951 $=$ 100) calculated according to both procedures are given below (the increase in the number of families is left out of
consideration):

Expenditure category	$y_1(M)$ for 1970 (without expen- diture distribution)	$y_2(M)$ for 1970 (with expenditure distribution)	Percentage Difference between $y_1(M)$ and $y_2(M)$
	1960 $=$ 100		
Meat, fish and eggs	121.0	120.8	-0.1
Health	124.3	125.5	1.0
Public Transport	139.1	142.5	2.4
Tourism abroad	173.7	174.8	0.6

As can be seen the differences are relatively small. This justifies the computation of $y(M)$ by means of substituting just one expenditure total x in the equations, as is done in the paper.

REFERENCES

[1] AITCHISON, J. and J.A.C. BROWN (1954), A Synthesis of Engel Curve Theory Review of Economic Studies, XXII (1), 57, pp. 35–46.

[2] AITCHISON, J. and J.A.C. BROWN (1957), The Lognormal Distribution. 1st edition, Cambridge, The University Press.

[3] BARTEN, A.P. (1962), Note on unbiased estimation of the squared multiple correlation coefficient. Statistica Neerlandica, XVI (2), pp. 151–163.

[4] BARTEN, A.P. and J.I. VORST (1962), De consumptieve bestedingen van gezinshuishoudingen in Nederland, 1921–1939 en 1948–1958 (Consumption Expenditure of Family Households in the Netherlands, 1921–1939 and 1948–1958. The Econometric Institute of the Netherlands Economic School.

[5] Centraal Bureau voor de Statistiek (1953), Nationaal Budgetonderzoek 1951, Methodologische Inleiding (National Budget Inquiry 1951, Methodological Introduction). Series A, no. 1. Publishing Company W. de Haan, Utrecht.

[6] Centraal Bureau voor de Statistiek, (1957), Nationaal Budgetonderzoek 1951, Samenvatting van de Resultaten (National Budget Inquiry 1951, Compilation of Results). Series A, no. 2. Publishing Company W. de Haan, Utrecht.

[7] CENTRAAL BUREAU VOOR DE STATISTIEK (1954), Nationaal Budgetonderzoek 1951, Uitgavenrekeningen van gezinnen van hoofdarbeiders, onderscheiden naar inkomen en gezinsgrootte (National Budget Inquiry 1951, Budgets of salaried employees and civil servants, distinguished according to income and family size). Series 2B, no. 3. Publishing Company W. de Haan, Utrecht.

[8] CENTRAAL BUREAU VOOR DE STATISTIEK (1961), Nationale Rekeningen 1960 (National Accounts 1960). Statistische en Econometrische Onderzoekingen, Supplement 1961 Publishing Company W. de Haan, Zeist.

[9] COMMUNAUTÉ ECONOMIQUE EUROPÉENNE (1960), Tendances de la production et de la consommation en denrées alimentaires dans la C.E.E. (1956 à 1965) Etudes, Série Agriculture no. 2, Bruxelles.

[10] CRAMER, J.S. (1958), Ownership Elasticities of Durable Consumer Goods. Review of Economic Studies, XXV (2), 67, pp. 87–96.

[11] FERBER, R. and P.J. VERDOORN (1962), Research Methods in Economics and Business, Macmillan Publishing Company, New York.

[12] FISK, P.R. (1958), Maximum Likelihood Estimation of Törnqvist Demand Equations. Review of Economic Studies, XXVI (1), 69, pp. 33–50.

[13] FRAENKEL, M. (1959), Een onderzoek naar het toekomstig verbruik van textielvezels en kleding in West-Europa (An Investigation into the Future Consumption of Textile Fibres and Clothing in Western Europe). Economisch-Statistische Berichten, 44 (2211), pp. 1014–1017.

[14] FRISCH, R. (1955), From National Accounts to Macro Economic Decision Models. Studies in Income and Wealth, Series IV, pp. 1–26. International Association for Research in Income and Wealth. Bowes & Bowes, London.

[15] FRISCH, R. (1959), A Complete Scheme for Computing All Direct and Cross Demand Elasticities in a Model with Many Sectors. Econometrica, XXVII, 2, pp. 177–196.

[16] HOUTHAKKER, H.S. (1952), The Econometrics of Family Budgets. Journal of the Royal Statistical Society, CXV, pp.1–21.

[17] JOHANSON, L. (1960), A Multi-Sectoral Study of Economic Growth. 1st edition. North-Holland Publishing Company, Amsterdam.

[18] MIDDELHOEK, A.J. (1962), Een sectormodel van het energieverbruik (A Sector-model for the Consumption of Energy), Statistica Neerlandica, XVI, 4, pp. 403–431.

[19] PRAIS, S.J. (1952), Non-linear Estimates of the Engel Curves. Review of Economic Studies, XX (2), 52, pp. 87–104.

[20] PRAIS, S.J. and H.S. HOUTHAKKER (1955), The Analysis of Family Budgets. 1st edition. The University Press, Cambridge.

[21] SANDEE, J. (1962), Possible Economic Growth in the Netherlands, Chapter V (pp.162–183) of Volume I of the ASEPELT publication Europe's Future in Figures. North-Holland Publishing Company, Amsterdam.

[22] SOMERMEIJER, W.H. and others (1961), Een methode voor de schatting van prijs- en inkomenselasticiteiten uit tijdreeksen en haar toepassing op consumptieve uitgaven in Nederland 1949–1959 (A method for estimating price and income elasticities from time series and its application to consumption expenditures in the Netherlands 1949–1959). Statistische en Econometrische Onderzoekingen, 4th quarter 1961, pp.205–228. Publishing Company W. de Haan, Zeist.

[23] TÖRNQVIST, L. (1941), Review article. Ekonomisk Tidskrift, 43, pp.216–225.

[24] WIT, J.W.W.A. (1957), Inkomenselasticiteiten in 1935/36 en 1951 voor Nederland: toepassing van een model voor inkomensbesteding (Income elasticities in 1935/36 and 1951 for the Netherlands: Application of a model for income spending). Statistische en Econometrische Onderzoekingen, 1st quarter 1957, pp.27–41. Publishing Company W. de Haan, Zeist.

[25] WOLD, J. and L. JUREEN (1953), Demand Analysis, 1st edition. John Wiley & Sons, Inc., New York.

CHAPTER 6

PRIVATE CONSUMPTION IN NORWAY 1930–1970[1])

BY

ARNE AMUNDSEN

Central Bureau of Statistics, Oslo, Norway

1. INTRODUCTION

The present study is a continuation of some research work on consumer demand that began in the Central Bureau of Statistics several years ago[2]). One of the chief aims of the research has been to develop a highly disaggregated consumer-demand model that fits into an already established input-output model to form a 'national budget model'[3]). The preparatory work on classification and computation of price indices, expenditures at constant prices, demand elasticities, etc. is, however, directly applicable

---

[1]) The author acknowledges with sincere thanks the assistance rendered by Miss Hilde Bojer and Mr. Eivind Bjøntegård of the Central Bureau of Statistics' Research Division, in connection with the preparation of data and tables and with the interpretation of results. He is also indebted to Mr. Finn Andersen, of the Computing Department, who was responsible for all computations.

[2]) Some results from regression analysis of cross section family budget data were published in Monthly Bulletin of Statistics No. 2, 1955 (Statistiske meldinger nr. 2; NOS, Central Bureau of Statistics of Norway, Oslo, 1955, pp. 39–55). Further regression results, covering all postwar surveys of consumer expenditure in Norway, were presented in Survey of Consumer Expenditure (1958), Third Volume, NOS A 41, Central Bureau of Statistics of Norway, Oslo, 1961. Computations of complete sets of direct and cross price elasticities, based on Frisch's method, date from 1958; the results have been used in analyses of year-to-year changes in the composition of private consumption; see Central Bureau of Statistics Economic Surveys for the years 1958 to 1961, Chapters on Private Consumption. Cf. also NOS A 41 (see above), pp. 16–24. Results of time series regressions based on National Accounts classifications of private consumption expenditures, mainly for the years 1930–39, were presented in: 'A Preliminary Report on Regression Studies of Consumer's Expenditures in Norway'; Central Bureau of Statistics of Norway, Oslo, May 1958 (mimeographed).

[3]) A first version of a budget model of this type has been used for the preparation of next-year national budgets in Norway since 1960. The main features of the model are described in a mimeographed paper: 'An inter-industry model of production and consumption for economic planning in Norway' by PER SEVALDSON. Presented at the Conference of the International Association for Research in Income and Wealth, Tutzing, August 1961. (Preliminary, to be published).

to the construction of a separate consumer demand model that specifies demand equations for the 123 item classification of private consumption expenditures in the Norwegian National Accounts system, or for any aggregation into expenditure groups of these items. It is the separate model, applied to the ASEPELT breakdown and to other groupings of private consumption, that is used here for analysing changes in the composition of consumer demand in Norway since 1930 and for projecting the composition in 1970.

The adequacy – for analytical purposes – of existing standard classifications of consumer expenditure data is by no means evident, and much empirical work of the trial-and-error type is probably a prerequisite for a more systematic search for optimum classifications. The detailed item specification of the data underlying this study offers rich possibilities for experiments with different classifications. These possibilities have not been thoroughly explored. However, some vague ideas and tentative conclusions as regards possible directions for further work have emerged and some comments on these complex problems are given in connection with the description of data in section 2.

Econometric research rests ultimately on the belief that suitably chosen statistical methods applied to highly simplified versions of economic models may give useful information on structural features of economic behaviour. Not infrequently, however, the econometrician feels obliged to draw the conclusion that his methods or his model specifications, or both, have failed and that the results obtained cannot be utilized for forecasting purposes or for practical policy-making decisions.

The possibility exists that the economic interpretation of the specified model is wrong, and that a reinterpretation can be given that attaches meaning to the results obtained. The long list of estimates of demand elasticities for various groups and items presented in section 4 illustrates this point. The logarithmic-linear regression model used is a familiar one in econometric studies, having total *per capita* consumption expenditure and a group or item price index as explanatory (independent) variables. If the coefficients are interpreted as 'pure' or 'net' elasticities, intuition suggests that many of them are of questionable value for practical applications. However, if interpreted as 'gross' elasticities, as is done explicitly in the model specifications of section 3, they may be of some value.

In section 5 an attempt has been made to draw conclusions about trends in the consumption pattern since 1930 on the basis of the estimates of gross elasticities and information from other sources.

Section 6 presents 1970 projections for 16 ASEPELT groups and for certain national accounts groups. It is assumed here that total *per capita* private consumption increases by 3 per cent annually and that all relative prices remain unchanged. In several cases intuition, information from other sources and guesswork have suggested certain adjustments to the regression coefficients, when utilized for projection purposes. I have not hesitated to act on these suggestions. It is the adjusted coefficients that form the basis for projections. It is not difficult, I believe, to see that these corrections may represent improvements.

The last three sections present results of a highly experimental character. Section 7 gives complete sets of estimates of direct and cross price elasticities for groups supposed to be 'want independent'. This is a straight-forward application of Frisch's method[4]). Section 8 presents the assumptions made about price changes over the next decade, and section 9 gives a 1970-projection, where also the effects of assumed price changes are taken into account.

2. CLASSIFICATIONS; SOURCES OF DATA; ETC.

The Norwegian national accounts provide tables of annual data on the composition of private consumers' expenditure in considerable detail back to 1930.[5]) A two-way breakdown is available, by sector of origin and by categories of goods and services. Only the latter type of breakdown will be considered here.

The item classification for which figures of expenditures at current as well as constant prices are available, specifies 78 items for the years 1930–1939 and 123 from 1949 onwards. The latter item classification permits easy aggregation to the 78 'combined items' – to be called 'subgroups' in the following text and tables. The national accounts classification system includes aggregation to a 30-group classification and a 10-group classification[6]). For all items and aggregations, price indices, of the Paasche

---

[4]) RAGNAR FRISCH, A Complete Scheme for Computing All Direct and Cross Demand Elasticities in a Model with Many Sectors, Econometrica, April 1959.

[5]) Sources: National Accounts, NOS XI. 109 and NOS XI. 185, Central Bureau of Statistics of Norway, Oslo, 1952 and 1954; punched cards of manuscript tables (unpublished).

[6]) The national accounts classification code is as follows:
XOO = 10-group classification; XXO = 30-group classification; XXX = item classification.

The 30-group classification has not been used in the present study.

type, have been computed as ratios of value figures at current prices to
value figures at constant prices. All value figures at constant prices are
evaluated in terms of 1955-prices[7]).

The standard minimum breakdown of private consumption, recommended for all studies to appear in the present book – the ASEPELT
breakdown – has been derived from the item classification mentioned
above[8]). The groups 17 and 18, Tourism abroad and Expenditures by
tourists, have been left out. Nor are these groups included in total private consumption[9]).

Easy access to details of the composition of consumers' expenditure
invites empirical studies of the problems of classification. It is conceivable,
on a priori grounds, that structural elements in the composition of consumers' expenditure might be adequately described by simple relationships when the expenditure items are grouped in one way, but not when
they are grouped in another way.

Systematic search for optimum classifications presupposes, however,
some knowledge about the class of a priori admissible hypotheses, and it
is hard to see how one can avoid starting with experimental work of the
trial-and-error type.

In order to facilitate such experiments data were arranged (on
punched cards) in a way that easily permitted regression computations for
any grouping of expenditure items. In the present study priority has been
given to the ASEPELT 16 group classification with items arranged as a
subclassification of the ASEPELT groups, and to the 10-group national
accounts classification. An aggregation of the ten groups to a 4-group
classification has also been considered. Regressions have been computed
for all groups and items. There is no individual treatment of any group or
item; the regression equation is of one particular form and has total

---

[7]) There is a break between 1939 and 1949; prewar series were prepared in terms
of 1938-prices, and postwar series in terms of 1955-prices. To provide a link between
the volume expenditures of the two periods all figures at 1938-prices were, for the purposes of the present study, multiplied by the factor 2.56, which is the ratio of the 1955
price index to the 1938 price index of total private consumption.

[8]) There are some minor deviations. Ice cream is in group 5 (Other food), not in
group 2 (Milk and milk products). Repairs of bicycles is in group 14 (Transport
equipment), not in group 15 (Private transport). Group 9 (Durables) includes not only
repairs, but also washing, cleaning, dyeing and related materials.

[9]) In the present study the term 'total private consumption' corresponds to 'Total
specified items' in the national accounts publications. A few correction items and Tourism have to be added in order to obtain all consumers' expenditure on goods and services.

expenditure and the direct price as explanatory variables in all cases (see next section). All expenditure data are on a *per capita* basis.

Regressions for all items would hardly have been planned and carried out, were it not for the belief that regression coefficients, standard errors, etc. may give *some* useful information on the structure, regardless of the plausibility of the a priori assumed model. There is a wide range of possibilities for statistical tests on the basis of our transformations of the observation matrix.

Such 'statistics' may be helpful in experimental work even if we do not apply the whole apparatus of statistical testing, but rely to some extent on intuitive judgment and information from other sources. A reference to Table 1 below may illustrate this point. For the group Clothing and leather products we find highly varying estimates of the expenditure elasticity for the various periods considered and large standard errors (not shown in Table 1) in postwar years. Inspection of the columns of estimates of expenditure elasticities for individual items suggests quite clearly that a remarkable change in the composition of the group is taking place. The share of items like sewing services, knitting yarn, and materials decreases with increasing total expenditure, and there is an opposite movement in the shares of ready-made goods. From'this observation we can safely infer that substitutions take place within the group. But these substitutions seem to influence the regularity (stability) of the expenditure elasticity for the group total, and perhaps this should be taken as a warning that our group classification should be reconsidered. There are no compelling reasons for considering the aggregate of all clothing items as a significant group. Large-scale regression computations for individual items and for various aggregations of items may reveal information of this type and serve as a guide for further research.

Prewar data (1930–1939) and postwar data (1949–1959) have been treated, both separately and combined, in the computations. For postwar data the period 1952–1959 has also been considered separately.

3. MODEL SPECIFICATIONS

The following notation will be used throughout:

x_i = per capita expenditure, at constant (1955) prices, on expenditure group or item no. i

x = total per capita expenditure

P_i = price index of group or item no. i

P = price index of total expenditure

p_i = relative price of group or item no. i $\left(= \dfrac{P_i}{P} \right)$

log = 'natural logarithm of'.

For simplicity of notation subscript indication for time has been omitted.

The model equations underlying the regressions in section 4 are of the form:

$$\log x_i = C_i^T \log x + c_{ii}^T \log p_i + C_{oi}^T + u_i \qquad (3.1)$$

where u_i is a residual term, and where C_i^T, c_{ii}^T and C_{oi}^T are assumed to be constants for a given period T, but may take other values in other periods[10]).
C_i^T will be referred to as 'the gross expenditure elasticity' and c_{ii}^T as 'the gross direct price elasticity', for group or item no. i, in period T.

Two non-overlapping periods are considered, the prewar years 1930–1939 and the postwar years 1949–1959. Exclusion of the years 1949–1951 from the latter period gives the third period considered. Finally, as an alternative to this period grouping, all years for which data are available, i.e. the years 1930–1959, with the exclusion of the years 1940–1948, are included in one period with the modification, however, of (3.1) that the constant term, C_{oi}^T, may take a different value in postwar years to that in prewar years[11]).

The reference to the coefficients in (3.1) as gross elasticities implies an assumption to the effect that they may be different from the corresponding 'net' or 'pure' elasticities developed in theories on consumer demand. The net elasticities are considered as the stable elements in consumer behaviour, and further model specifications have, therefore, to be made in order to establish a meaningful economic interpretation of the gross elasticities. A fundamental difficulty is, however, that many different economic interpretations are possible.

My choice has been to interpret the gross elasticities in (3.1) as coefficients in some kind of 'reduced form' equations, derived from a somewhat more general form of approximation than (3.1) to traditional textbook demand equations and from certain other relationships to be described shortly.

---

[10]) The double subscript for the coefficient of log p_i has been chosen in order to avoid a change in notation, when also cross price elasticities are introduced.

[11]) This implies that, for the combined period, (3.1) may be written with an additional term, dz (say), where z is a dummy variable, taking the value zero in prewar years and the value one in postwar years, and where d is a constant 'shift' parameter.

TABLE 1 – Time series regressions based on National Accounts private consumption data. Selected periods 1930–1959, varying classifications

	Budget proportions, geometric average in period 1949–1959	Expenditure elasticities, estimates based on period				Direct price elasticities, estimates based on period			
		1930–1939	1930–1959 excl. 1940–1948	1949–1959	1952–1959	1930–1939	1930–1959 excl. 1940–1948	1949–1959	1952–1959
	1	2	3	4	5	6	7	8	9
1. CEREALS AND PRODUCTS	0.037								
151 Flour, etc.	0.009	0.5	—	−0.3	−0.3	—	—	−0.7	−0.6
152 Biscuits, etc.	0.003	—	−0.1	−1.0	−0.2	−0.7	−0.8	−0.9	−1.2
153 Bread, cakes	0.024	—	—	1.9	4.0	—	—	−1.3	−1.8
154 Macaroni, cornflakes, etc.	0.001	—	—	−1.2	−1.7	—	—	−0.0	0.3
152–154	0.028	1.0	0.9	4.0	1.6	−0.1	−0.9	0.2	−0.1
Weighted average of items				−0.5	−0.9			−0.1	0.2
Weighted average of sub-groups		0.9	0.5	−0.8	−0.8				
2. MILK AND PRODUCTS[a]	0.055			−0.6	−0.4				
131 Butter	0.007	0.2	−0.6	−1.0	−0.5	−1.0	—	0.2	0.2
141 Milk, cream	0.035	0.4	0.0	−0.9	−0.4	0.5	−0.4	−0.4	−0.9
142 Condensed and powdered milk	0.002	0.5	−0.1	−1.2	−1.6	—	0.1	0.1	−0.1
143 Cheese	0.011	1.6	0.5	0.9	−0.5	−1.3	−2.6	−2.0	−1.9
Weighted average of items		0.4	0.1	−0.6	−0.5	−1.3	0.2	0.3	1.2

[a] Ice cream included in group 5: Other food.

Table 1 – (continued)

	Budget proportions, geometric average in period 1949–1959	Expenditure elasticities, estimates based on period				Direct price elasticities, estimates based on period			
	1	1930–1939	1930–1959 excl. 1940–1948	1949–1959	1952–1959	1930–1939	1930–1959 excl. 1940–1948	1949–1959	1952–1959
		2	3	4	5	6	7	8	9
3. MEAT, FISH, EGGS	0.086	—	—	0.7	0.9	—	—	−0.6	−0.3
111 Meat	0.059	—	—	0.7	0.7	—	—	−0.2	0.1
121 Fish	0.017	0.2	0.3	0.8	1.1	−0.4	−0.5	−0.9	−0.5
144 Eggs	0.010	0.8	0.6	1.0	1.2	−0.7	−0.4	−0.1	−0.3
Weighted average of items				0.8	0.8				
4. VEGETABLES AND FRUITS	0.046	—	—	3.6	2.6	—	—	−0.8	−0.5
161 Potatoes	0.010	−0.1	−0.2	−0.3	−0.1	0.0	0.1	0.1	0.0
162 Fresh vegetables, Norwegian	0.011	—	—	1.5	0.8	—	—	−0.3	−0.3
163 Fresh vegetables, imported	0.001	—	—	9.8	7.5	—	—	−0.5	−0.4
164 Fresh fruits, Norwegian	0.006	—	—	−0.2	0.1	—	—	−1.0	−0.9
165 Fresh fruits, imported	0.008	—	—	12.6	5.4	—	—	−0.9	2.5
166 Dried fruits	0.003	−0.0	1.1	3.2	−0.6	−0.2	−3.5	−4.3	−2.3
167 Berries	0.007	—	—	−0.4	0.1	—	—	−0.4	−0.4
162, 163	0.012	1.2	1.7	2.3	1.5	−0.1	−0.3	−0.4	−0.4
164, 165, 167	0.021	1.2	2.7	5.2	3.8	−0.6	−0.3	−1.0	−0.3
Weighted average of items				2.8	1.3				
Weighted average of sub-groups		0.8	1.7						

Table 1 – (continued)

	Budget proportions, geometric average in period 1949–1959	Expenditure elasticities, estimates based on period				Direct price elasticities, estimates based on period			
		1930–1939	1930–1959 excl. 1940–1948	1949–1959	1952–1959	1930–1939	1930–1959 excl. 1940–1948	1949–1959	1952–1959
	1	2	3	4	5	6	7	8	9
5. OTHER FOOD	0.063								
112 Canned meat	0.002	—	—	0.7	2.0	—	—	0.2	1.4
122 Canned fish, dinner	0.002	—	—	2.0	5.9	—	—	-2.2	0.4
123 Other canned fish	0.003	—	—	-0.2	-0.1	—	—	0.8	-0.2
132 Margarine, oils, etc.	0.013	0.7	0.7	-2.0	0.2	-0.2	0.3	0.9	-0.6
168 Preserved fruits, vegetables	0.006	2.0	2.0	1.1	0.6	-0.3	-0.4	0.3	-0.1
171 Sugar	0.008	0.9	1.1	1.7	1.4	-0.3	0.6	-0.5	-1.6
172 Syrup	0.001	0.5	-1.1	0.8	0.1	-0.9	-1.3	0.7	0.3
176 Chocolate, confectionery	0.016	2.0	1.4	-2.9	-1.9	-1.2	-0.6	-1.6	-0.6
177 Other	0.012	1.1	0.9	-0.2	-1.2	2.0	-0.4	-0.2	-1.5
122, 123	0.005	2.7	1.3	0.3	0.3	0.4	2.4	-1.0	-0.2
Weighted average of items				0.4	-0.0			1.8	-0.1
6. BEVERAGES	0.069	—	—			—	—		
173 Coffee	0.019	0.0	1.3	1.1	0.9	-0.4	0.1	-0.6	-0.4
174 Tea	0.001	0.0	1.2	3.2	2.1	-0.6	0.7	-0.1	-0.3
175 Cocoa, etc.	0.003	-0.5	0.4	4.4	3.4	-2.6	0.3	-0.7	-0.1
211 Mineral water, etc.	0.004	1.6	3.2	-2.7	-4.5	-1.6	-0.8	1.1	-0.7
212 Beer	0.013	0.3	0.4	5.0	4.7	-1.7	-1.1	-0.6	-1.6
213 Wines, spirits	0.029	1.1	1.1	0.9	1.1	-0.4	0.7	-0.5	-0.7
Weighted average of items		0.6	1.1	1.0	0.6			-0.2	-0.8

Table 1 – (continued)

	Budget proportions, geometric average in period 1949–1959	Expenditure elasticities, estimates based on period				Direct price elasticities, estimates based on period			
		1930–1939	1930–1959 excl. 1940–1948	1949–1959	1952–1959	1930–1939	1930–1959 excl. 1940–1948	1949–1959	1952–1959
	1	2	3	4	5	6	7	8	9
7. TOBACCO	0.031	—	—	0.2	0.4	—	—	−0.2	−0.6
221 Cigars	0.001	0.6	0.4	−3.4	1.9	−2.1	−0.9	−1.4	−0.9
222 Cigarettes	0.015	2.2	1.4	0.3	0.3	−0.2	−0.5	0.4	−0.7
223 Pipe tobacco	0.013	1.7	1.1	0.5	0.6	0.3	−0.2	−0.4	−0.4
224 Chewing tobacco	0.001	1.6	−2.5	−3.9	−3.0	−1.1	−0.9	−1.5	0.2
225 Snuff	0.001	0.0	−0.5	−1.4	−1.3	−1.2	−0.6	−0.3	−0.4
Weighted average of items				0.1	0.3				
Weighted average of subgroups		2.0	1.0						
8. CLOTHING AND LEATHER PRODUCTS	0.158	1.3	1.2	0.6	2.0	0.1	0.3	−0.1	1.1
511 Ready-made clothing	0.054	2.3	2.1	2.2	1.4	−1.8	−1.1	−1.0	−0.3
512 Knitware	0.028	1.5	1.6	2.9	0.8	−0.7	−0.7	0.2	−1.6
513 Hats, gloves, umbrellas, etc.	0.005	—	—	0.8	−0.1			−1.1	−0.9
514 Furs	0.003	—	—	−1.4	−1.9			0.6	−0.5
521 Materials	0.025	—	—	−1.5	0.0			0.1	0.7
522 Knitting yarn	0.006	—	—	−5.2	−1.1			0.7	−0.8
523 Sewing services	0.008	—	—	−3.1	−3.3			−2.1	0.4
524 Other clothing items	0.004	—	—	−0.8	−0.2			0.4	0.6
531 Footwear, excl. rubber footwear	0.017	1.4	0.5	−0.4	1.1	0.9	−0.8	−0.3	−0.4
532 Rubber footwear	0.005	3.6	1.4	−2.1	−1.6	−1.6	−1.2	−0.9	−0.6
533 Repairs	0.003	0.1	−1.1	−2.4	0.8	0.3	0.0	−0.8	2.3
513, 514	0.008	2.9	1.5	−0.9	−0.9	0.2	0.1	0.2	−0.8
521–524	0.043	0.6	−0.4	−2.9	0.4	0.2	0.4	−0.5	0.9
Weighted average of items				0.5	0.5			−0.4	
Weighted average of subgroups		1.6	1.0						

Table 1 – *(continued)*

	Budget proportions, geometric average in period 1949–1959	Expenditure elasticities, estimates based on period				Direct price elasticities, estimates based on period			
		1930–1939	1930–1959 excl. 1940–1948	1949–1959	1952–1959	1930–1939	1930–1959 excl. 1940–1948	1949–1959	1952–1959
	1	2	3	4	5	6	7	8	9
9. DURABLES	0.125	–	–	1.7	2.0	–	–	−0.4	0.3
411 Furniture, etc.	0.021	3.2	3.1	1.4	3.7	−1.0	0.1	−0.6	1.4
412 Hot-plates, stoves	0.003	–	–	−1.3	−0.5	–	–	−1.2	−0.0
413 Vacuum cleaners	0.001	–	–	12.7	13.4	–	–	2.4	3.0
414 Electric heaters	0.001	–	–	4.0	3.0	–	–	−0.7	0.7
415 Other electric equipment	0.005	–	–	−8.6	4.2	–	–	−7.1	0.0
416 Bed clothing, carpets, etc.	0.005	3.3	3.2	1.9	0.7	−1.1	−1.1	−1.5	−1.9
417 Sewing machines, etc.	0.001	–	–	−2.2	−3.4	–	–	−2.2	−2.2
418 Gold, silver and pewter ware	0.005	–	–	2.7	2.8	–	–	1.3	1.7
419 Decorative articles	0.002	–	–	0.3	2.1	–	–	−1.2	−3.4
421 China and pottery	0.003	–	–	−2.8	−4.2	–	–	0.9	1.8
422 Glassware	0.003	–	–	0.8	−0.3	–	–	−0.3	0.0
423 Earthen ware, ceramic	0.001	–	–	−5.7	−4.2	–	–	2.0	2.0
424 Kitchen utensils	0.014	2.7	1.2	−0.2	0.4	0.6	0.5	−0.6	−1.2
425 Other durable household goods	0.002	–	–	−4.7	−5.1	–	–	−1.6	−3.9
430 Cleaning materials	0.005	3.0	1.8	0.7	2.4	0.5	−1.0	−1.4	−0.5
431 Washing, cleaning, dyeing	0.003	–	–	0.7	−1.5	–	–	−0.2	1.6

TABLE 1 – (continued)

	Budget proportions, geometric average in period 1949–1959	Expenditure elasticities, estimates based on period				Direct price elasticities, estimates based on period			
	1	1930–1939	1930–1959 excl. 1940–1948	1949–1959	1952–1959	1930–1939	1930–1959 excl. 1940–1948	1949–1959	1952–1959
		2	3	4	5	6	7	8	9
9. DURABLES *(continued)*									
432 Repair of durable household goods	0.004	—	—	− 0.8	0.4	—	—	0.4	0.7
433 Incandescent lamps	0.002	13.5	2.8	3.0	3.6	5.9	− 0.5	− 0.7	− 0.6
434 Other household goods	0.008	—	—	1.0	− 0.4	—	—	0.9	0.9
412–415, 417	0.011	4.3	5.3	− 1.8	3.6	− 0.3	− 1.0	− 4.3	0.5
421–423	0.007	2.1	1.0	− 0.6	− 1.4	− 1.8	− 1.0	0.4	0.8
418, 419, 425	0.009	1.9	0.4	0.6	1.7	− 1.8	− 0.4	0.7	1.0
432, 434	0.012	2.2	1.0	0.3	− 0.4	− 0.9	1.0	0.9	0.7
841 Radio receivers, TV, etc.	0.005	6.1	5.4	4.4	1.0	− 1.1	− 0.2	0.1	− 2.9
842 Radio licences	0.001	4.3	2.5	1.3	2.8	− 2.0	− 2.3	− 0.4	− 2.0
843 Musical instruments	0.001	—	—	7.9	8.0	—	—	− 2.3	− 1.5
844 Sport and photo equipment, etc.	0.015	—	—	1.2	1.6	—	—	− 1.0	− 1.6
961 Travelling equipment, etc.	0.004	—	—	2.1	3.8	—	—	0.5	0.1
964 Watches	0.002	—	—	4.5	3.6	—	—	− 0.4	− 0.7
965 Stationary, paper, printed matter	0.003	—	—	2.0	1.7	—	—	− 1.2	− 1.2
966 Coffins, tomb-stones, etc.	0.001	—	—	− 0.2	− 0.1	—	—	0.1	− 0.2
967 Other goods	0.004	—	—	− 0.1	0.6	—	—	− 0.7	− 0.5
961–967	0.014	1.8	1.6	1.2	1.7	− 2.1	− 0.6	− 0.6	− 0.7
843, 844	0.016	1.9	1.9	1.8	2.1	− 1.3	− 1.1	− 1.1	− 1.9
Weighted average of items				0.5	1.5				
Weighted average of subgroups		2.9	1.6						

TABLE 1 – (continued)

	Budget proportions, geometric average in period 1949-1959	Expenditure elasticities, estimates based on period				Direct price elasticities, estimates based on period			
		1930-1939	1930-1959 excl. 1940-1948	1949-1959	1952-1959	1930-1939	1930-1959 excl. 1940-1948	1949-1959	1952-1959
	1	2	3	4	5	6	7	8	9
10. FUEL AND LIGHT	0.038								
321 Firewood	0.008	—	—	2.0	2.2	—	—	-0.3	-0.1
322 Peat	0.001	—	—	-1.2	-1.3	—	—	0.3	0.0
323 Coal and coke	0.003	—	—	-6.7	-8.0	—	—	-0.1	-0.2
324 Fuel oils	0.005	-0.4	2.3	-2.9	-2.6	-1.1	0.3	0.0	0.5
325 Gas	0.004	-1.0	-1.8	5.6	3.7	-0.3	-0.2	-0.3	0.2
326 Electricity	0.017	0.4	2.4	-3.3	4.0	-0.8	0.0	-0.4	-0.8
321–323	0.012	1.4	-0.4	4.0	4.0	-0.2	0.3	-0.4	1.2
Weighted average of items				1.5	2.0			0.0	0.2
11. RENT	0.068	0.7	0.7	1.7	0.1	0.4	0.2		
311 Dwellings	0.067			1.6	0.1			-0.1	0.3
312 Crews' quarters on ships	0.001			2.8	3.1			-0.1	0.3
Weighted average of items				1.6	0.1			-0.6	-0.8
12. HEALTH	0.038	0.7	0.9	1.5	1.6	-0.2	0.1		
641 Physicians, etc.	0.008			1.3	2.0			-0.2	-0.0
642 Dentists	0.006			0.2	0.7			0.1	0.4
643 Hospital fees	0.016			0.8	-0.2			-0.6	-0.7
644 Nursing at home	0.001			-0.2	0.1			-0.0	0.3
645 Drugs, instruments, etc.	0.007			3.0	-2.9			-0.3	-0.9
Weighted average of items				1.2	-0.1			-0.9	-4.1

TABLE 1 – *(continued)*

	Budget proportions, geometric average in period 1949-1959	Expenditure elasticities, estimates based on period				Direct price elasticities, estimates based on period			
		1930-1939	1930-1959 excl. 1940-1948	1949-1959	1952-1959	1930-1939	1930-1959 excl. 1940-1948	1949-1959	1952-1959
	1	2	3	4	5	6	7	8	9
13. PUBLIC TRANSPORT	0.048	—	—	0.8	0.9	—	—		
711 Railways	0.010	1.4	0.4	-0.9	-0.4	—	—	0.1	-0.7
712 Trams, suburban trains	0.004	0.4	0.2	-0.5	-0.4	-0.7	-0.8	-0.7	-0.6
713 Sea transport	0.005	—	—	0.7	0.8	-0.8	-1.3	-1.0	-1.0
714 Air transport	0.002	2.7	2.1	4.4	2.5	—	—	-0.2	-0.1
715 Buses	0.010	—	—	1.8	1.7	-0.7	-1.1	-1.9	-3.2
716 Taxis	0.008	2.5	2.5	-1.5	-1.4	—	—	-0.9	-1.4
717 Freight expenses	0.003	—	—	1.5	1.3	-1.7	-0.6	-0.2	-0.2
941 Postage	0.002	—	—	0.9	0.7	—	—	-0.9	-2.8
942 Telephone	0.003	—	—	1.9	2.5	—	—	0.6	0.7
943 Telegrams	0.001	—	—	1.1	1.3	—	—	0.1	0.0
713, 714, 716	0.015	0.8	0.7	0.2	-0.0	-0.5	-0.1	-1.0	-1.5
941-943	0.006	0.8	1.3	1.4	1.7	-0.5	0.3	-0.4	-1.3
Weighted average of items				0.4	0.5			0.3	0.3
14. TRANSPORT EQUIPMENT	0.010			6.8	4.7				
721 New cars, motorcycles	0.006	5.2	2.5	7.3	7.7	-1.1	-3.5	-0.5	0.2
723 New bicycles and maintenance b)	0.004			-2.7	0.7			-3.1	-0.0
Weighted average of items				3.3	4.9			0.1	3.3

b) Not possible to split this item.

TABLE 1 – (continued)

	Budget proportions, geometric average in period 1949–1959	Expenditure elasticities estimates based on period				Direct price elasticities, estimates based on period			
		1930–1939	1930–1959 excl. 1940–1948	1949–1959	1952–1959	1930–1939	1930–1959 excl. 1940–1948	1949–1959	1952–1959
	1	2	3	4	5	6	7	8	9
15. PRIVATE TRANSPORT	0.009	—	—	2.3	1.4	—	—	−1.2	−0.7
722 Maintenance of cars, motorcycles	0.003	—	—	3.1	1.8	—	—	−1.7	−2.3
724 Petrol, oil	0.006	6.4	6.2	2.0	1.6	−2.2	0.3	−1.0	0.0
Weighted average of items				2.4	1.7				
16. OTHER	0.119	—	—	0.6	1.0	—	—	0.1	−0.4
651 Cosmetics, etc.	0.003	4.1	3.7	4.6	5.8	0.8	−0.7	−1.1	−1.8
652 Soap	0.002	1.6	1.1	0.3	0.5	−1.2	−0.6	−0.6	−0.7
653 Other toilet articles	0.002	—	—	2.5	2.0	—	—	−1.3	−1.4
654 Hairdressing, etc.	0.004	—	—	0.6	2.2	—	—	0.1	−1.5
811 Schools	0.003	0.9	1.1	0.7	0.7	−1.6	−0.9	0.1	0.1
821 Books	0.006	—	—	0.2	2.1	—	—	0.4	−0.4
822 Magazines, newspapers, periodicals	0.012	—	—	1.2	2.1	—	—	−0.0	−0.3
831 Cinemas	0.004	1.8	1.0	−1.1	−0.9	−2.0	−1.4	−0.2	−0.4
832 Theatres	0.001	1.6	0.5	−0.3	0.9	−0.9	−1.5	−1.5	−2.4
833 Concerts, etc.	0.001	1.8	2.2	2.0	−0.0	−1.9	−1.1	−1.0	−0.3
911 Hotel and restaurant services, etc.	0.016	1.1	1.3	1.2	1.1	0.2	−0.4	−0.5	−0.1
921 Other food preparation services	0.007	—	—	0.8	0.8	—	—	−1.0	−0.8
922 Services of establishment welfare institutions	0.001	—	—	−4.1	−3.1	—	—	−0.6	−0.1

TABLE 1 – *(continued)*

	Budget proportions, geometric average in period 1949–1959	Expenditure elasticities, estimates based on period				Direct price elasticities, estimates based on period			
		1930–1939	1930–1959 excl. 1940–1948	1949–1959	1952–1959	1930–1939	1930–1959 excl. 1940–1948	1949–1959	1952–1959
	1	2	3	4	5	6	7	8	9
16. OTHER *(continued)*									
923 Services of local government welfare institutions	0.002	—	—	1.1	1.3	·.	—	0.3	0.3
951 Domestic services	0.018	—	—	– 3.3	– 1.8	—	—	– 0.4	– 1.3
971 Insurance services	0.006	—	—	1.8	1.8	—	—	0.0	0.1
972 Banking services	0.018	—	—	2.1	2.3	—	—	– 0.1	0.5
973 Public lottery services	0.005	—	—	1.8	1.5	—	—	– 1.3	– 1.1
974 Other services	0.008	—	—	0.8	0.6	0.6	—	– 0.2	0.1
653, 654	0.006	1.5	1.5	1.7	2.4	– 1.3	– 0.1	– 1.2	– 2.1
821, 822	0.018	0.7	0.7	1.0	2.8	0.7	0.1	0.0	– 0.8
921–923	0.010	– 0.2	– 0.0	0.8	0.7	– 0.3	– 0.2	– 1.1	– 0.6
971–974	0.037	0.3	1.4	1.8	1.7		0.5	0.1	0.4
Weighted average of items				0.5	1.0				
National Accounts groups:									
A. TEN-GROUP CLASSIFICATION									
100 Food	0.310	1.0	0.9	0.9	0.9	– 0.8	– 0.4	– 0.3	– 0.4
200 Beverages a) and tobacco	0.077	0.9	0.9	0.8	0.5	– 1.3	– 0.2	0.4	– 0.4
300 Rents, light and fuel	0.106	0.8	0.9	1.8	0.8	0.5	0.3	– 0.1	0.4
400 Durable household goods, household operation b)	0.107	2.1	1.4	1.2	1.0	– 1.0	0.5	0.3	0.7
500 Clothing and footwear	0.158	1.3	1.2	0.6	2.0	0.1	0.3	– 0.1	1.1

a) Items 173–175 (coffee, tea, cocoa) included in the food group in this classification.

b) Domestic services, item 951, classified in group 400 in period 1930–1939. For comparison purposes this classification has been used here also for postwar periods.

TABLE 1 – (continued)

	Budget proportions, geometric average in period 1949–1959	Expenditure elasticities, estimates based on period				Direct price elasticities, estimates based on period			
		1930–1939	1930–1959 excl. 1940–1948	1949–1959	1952–1959	1930–1939	1930–1959 excl. 1940–1948	1949–1959	1952–1959
	1	2	3	4	5	6	7	8	9
A. TEN-GROUP CLASSIFICATION (continued)									
600 Personal hygiene and medical care	0.049	1.0	1.3	1.7	1.8	0.4	0.2	−0.3	−0.1
700 Travel and transportation	0.061	2.4	2.5	1.2	1.3	−0.9	−0.2	−1.2	−0.6
800 Education, literature, entertainment	0.049	1.6	1.7	1.6	2.0	−1.5	−0.0	0.2	−0.2
900 Hotel and restaurant services, etc.[c]	0.026	0.6	0.8	0.8	0.9	0.5	−0.1	−0.3	−0.4
000 Other[d]	0.057	0.5	1.5	1.9	2.0	−0.7	0.3	−0.3	0.3
Weighted average of groups 100–000	1.000	1.2	1.2	1.1	1.2				
B. FOUR-GROUP CLASSIFICATION									
100, 200 Food, beverages, tobacco	0.387	0.9	0.9	0.9	0.8	−0.7	−0.7	−0.7	−0.4
300 Rents, light and fuel	0.106	0.8	0.9	1.8	0.8	0.5	0.3	−0.1	0.4
500 Clothing and footwear	0.158	1.3	1.2	0.6	2.0	0.1	0.3	−0.1	1.1
400, 600, 700, 800, 900, 000 Other	0.349	1.5	1.5	1.3	1.3	−0.5	−0.5	−0.7	−0.3
Weighted average of groups 100, 200	0.387	1.0	0.9	0.9	0.8				
Weighted average of groups 400, 600, 700–000	0.349	1.6	1.6	1.4	1.5				

c) The group 900 includes items 911–923.
d) The group 000 includes items 941–974, with the exception of item 951 (domestic services), which is transferred to group 400, cf. footnote b).

As a somewhat more general form of demand equations than (3.1) consider

$$\log x_i = E_i \log x + e_{ii} \log p_i + h_i q_i + e_{oi} + v_i \tag{3.2}$$

where v_i is a residual and q_i is an additional explanatory variable in the demand equation for group no. i,[12]). Suppose this is the form that we would have chosen as a basis for estimation, if we had believed that our short and, as a rule, highly intercorrelated series of data would give reliable estimates of as many as four parameters. Suppose furthermore that in this form all important demand-influencing variables in the periods considered are explicitly taken into account, and accordingly, that the effects of less important variables are 'absorbed' by the residual variable v_i (without disturbing the randomness of this term). On these assumptions it seems justified to interpret the coefficients E_i and e_{ii} as net elasticities, and as constants within a time-span of the length considered here.

For the sake of argument suppose now that, for a given period T, relationships of the form

$$q_i = A_i^T \log x + B_i^T \log p_i + B_{oi}^T + w_i \tag{3.3}$$

where w_i is a residual term, hold for each expenditure group[13]). As in (3.1) the superscript T indicates that the value of the coefficients depends on the period considered. Substitution of (3.3) into (3.2) would then give (3.1) provided we interpret the coefficients, the constant term and the residual in (3.1) as follows:

$$C_i^T = E_i + h_i A_i^T$$

$$c_{ii}^T = e_{ii} + h_i B_i^T$$

$$C_{oi}^T = e_{oi} + h_i B_{oi}^T \tag{3.4}$$

$$u_i = v_i + h_i w_i.$$

Formally, a link has in this way been established between the net elasticities in the preferred form (3.2) and the gross elasticities in the more

---

[12]) The economic interpretation of q_i may vary from one group to the next; say (the logarithm of) an additional price variable in one equation, a stock variable in another, a trend variable in a third, etc. The concrete interpretation is unimportant in the present context. Indeed, the arguments to be developed apply equally well, or better, if the term $h_i q_i$ is replaced by a set of additional variables $\Sigma_k h_{ik} q_{ik}$ ($k = 1, 2, \ldots$); however, the one-variable case illustrates the main points.

[13]) The statement that these relations hold implies certain restrictions on the variability of the residual term, w_i.

simplified form (3.1). The gross elasticities of (3.1) are coefficients of a reduced form obtained from (3.2) and (3.3).

The existence of relationships of the type (3.3) is in many cases implicit in analysis of time series of consumption data. As an illustration
consider the simple case where q_i in (3.2) is a trend variable, and where an
exponential trend 'dominates' the growth pattern of total *per capita* consumption x. The latter statement implies some kind of relationship between two of the explanatory variables in (3.2); this relationship may be
written:

$$\log x = H_i^T q_i + \text{a constant} + \text{a residual}$$

or

$$q_i = \frac{1}{H_i^T} (\log x + \text{a constant} + \text{a residual}),$$

which is a particular form of (3.3), with $A_i^T = 1/H_i^T$ and $B_i^T = 0$. We note
that the gross expenditure elasticity in (3.1) becomes $C_i^T = E_i + h_i/H_i^T$ and
that the ratio of h_i to H_i^T must be known in order to obtain the value of
E_i from a given value of C_i^T.

The idea of making use of supplementary relations like (3.3) in economic analysis is not new; it was presented in a paper by HAAVELMO in 1938
and referred to as 'the method of supplementary confluent relations'[14]).
Put very briefly a *confluent relation* is a relation derived by an elimination
process from two or more other relations supposed to represent the 'true'
structure. To quote HAAVELMO (p. 206): 'The introduction of (these) supplementary confluent relations is a way of letting the situation in the total
system influence our study of the partial system'[15]).

---

[14]) Published in Econometrica, Vol. 6, 1938, pp. 203–218. See also Report of the
meeting of the Econometrica Society at Oxford, 1936, Econometrica, Vol. 5, 1937,
pp. 373–374.

[15]) A further quotation may be illuminating (pp. 206, 207):
'If we *had* worked with the total system, we could have obtained the confluent relations
considered by an elimination process. The point now is that *we do not carry through*
this elimination process, but take the elementary confluent relations directly as they are
observed in statistical data.

This procedure may be justified by the following considerations:
(a) The elimination process in the complicated total system may lead to certain simple
confluent relations between a small number of variates. By consideration of the observed variates it is more easy to discover these simple connections than the system of
complicated underlying structural relations. On the other hand, these simple observed
facts are certainly *realistic* elements in the economic system. If we start with the construction of a total system of structural equations, these elementary confluent relations

A trend in total *per capita* consumption may be looked at as a confluent relation in this sense; the time shape – or an approximation to it – is the result of the interaction of many structural relations in the economic system. The observed intercorrelations between explanatory variables in regression equations – when interpreted with caution – are other sources for information on confluent relations that may take the form (3.3), and may contribute to an adequate interpretation of results obtained by applying regression methods to (3.1).

It follows from (3.4) that the coefficients in (3.1), for a period θ different from T, may be written as follows

$$C_i^\theta = C_i^T + h_i(A_i^\theta - A_i^T)$$

$$c_{ii}^\theta = c_{ii}^T + h_i(B_i^\theta - B_i^T) \tag{3.5}$$

$$C_{oi}^\theta = C_{oi}^T + h_i(B_{io}^\theta - B_{io}^T).$$

These formulae give in explicit form the differences between gross coefficients in two different periods. It follows that estimates of these differences can be obtained indirectly by subtraction, if data are available for the periods T and θ. If θ represents the projection period, (3.5) gives no rule for obtaining estimates, but tells us only what kind of guesses have to be made in order to derive the gross coefficients to be applied in the projection formulae. However, estimates of gross coefficients in earlier periods may in many cases suggest 'plausible guesses'[16]).

The complete set of direct and cross price elasticities introduced in section 7 is related to the model considered here through the residual term of (3.2); we have

$$v_i = \sum_{k \neq i} e_{ik} \log p_k + v_i' \tag{3.6}$$

---

ought to come out as elimination results. Taking the elementary confluent relations as they are *observed* is therefore equivalent to having assumed an underlying *realistic* structure and to having carried out a *correct* elimination process.

(b) The compound coefficients in the elementary confluent relations may have relatively *smaller* error terms than the individual structural coefficients. This may be precisely the reason why they are easily discovered in the observations. This is of importance for the statistical verification as discussed in the section below.

(c) Taking certain elementary confluent relations as a datum is not so great a reduction in generality as taking the whole *time shape* of certain variates as given. The same confluent relation between several variates may indeed hold for different time shapes.'

[16]) More or less in the same way as the past time series of $\log x$ and $\log p_i$ serve as the empirical basis for guesses on the value of these variables in the projection period.

where v_i' is a new residual term[17]) and where the summation includes all expenditure groups with the exception of group no. i (the price term of which is included in (3.2)). The coefficients e_{ik} $(k \neq i)$ are the cross price elasticities[18]).

4. TIME SERIES REGRESSIONS, 1930–1959

The estimates of gross expenditure elasticities and gross direct price elasticities presented in this section are based on least squares regressions applied to (3.1)[19]). Scarcity of space prevents the inclusion of estimates of all relevant parameters. Only budget proportions and gross elasticities are shown in Table 1.

Budget proportions, a_i, for all items and groups are given for the period 1949–1959 only. The formula used is

$$a_i = \text{antilog of } \frac{1}{N^T} \left(\Sigma_t \log X_{it} - \Sigma_t \log X_t \right) \tag{4.1}$$

where N^T is the number of observations in period $T = 1949$–1959 and where the summation is over all observations in period T,[20]).

---

[17]) The assumption is implicit that 'the combined effect of all other prices' does not disturb unduly the random character of v_i'.

[18]) The elasticities E_i and e_{ij} are the ordinary (Cournot-Hicks-Allen) elasticities, satisfying the homogeneity conditions (7.1) and the budget restraints (7.2) and (7.3) of section 7. These parameters, although defined in terms of partial changes in *absolute* prices, are permissible as coefficients also when the demand equations are written in terms of relative prices, as is done above. However, there are an infinite number of other permissible sets of such coefficients.

It can be shown that any set of coefficients

$$g_{ij} = e_{ij} + F_i a_j \tag{3.7}$$

where F_i is arbitrary and where a_j is the weight in the price index of group no. j, is permissible, provided the price index of total consumption, in differential notation, is of the form:

$$\frac{dP}{P} = \Sigma_j a_j \frac{dP_j}{P_j} \; ; \text{i.e. } \Sigma_j a_j \frac{dp_j}{p_j} = 0. \tag{3.8}$$

$\left(\text{By definition, } \dfrac{dp_j}{p_j} = \dfrac{dP_j}{P_j} - \dfrac{dP}{P} = \text{d} \log p_j \right).$

A more fundamental problem is what interpretation can be given to regression coefficients based on equations specified in terms of relative prices. This problem will not be discussed here (see, however, remark in footnote [36]).

[19]) For the period that includes prewar and postwar data (1930–1959, the years 1940–1948 excluded) a dummy variable is also present; see footnote 11). The coefficients of the dummy variable are not included in the table.

[20]) A few minor adjustments in the third decimal were necessary in order to obtain consistency between budget proportions for items and for groups.

TABLE 2 – Tabulation of projections 10 years ahead of budget proportions and *per capita* item expenditures for given values of expenditure elasticities. (Arranged so as to have 'regular' intervals in column 2 below.)
Assumption: *Per capita* total consumption expenditure at constant prices increases by 34.4 per cent in 10 years (i.e. by 3 per cent annually); other explanatory variables assumed unchanged.

For an item having the expenditure elasticity	A projection 10 years ahead – on assumptions stated above – gives the following	
	ratio of: budget proportion 1970 / budget proportion 1960	ratio of: item expenditure 1970 / item expenditure 1960
−2.75	0.33	0.44
−1.34	0.50	0.67
−0.35	0.67	0.90
0.03	0.75	1.01
0.53	0.87	1.17
1.00	1.00	1.34
1.41	1.13	1.52
1.75	1.25	1.68
1.96	1.33	1.79
2.37	1.50	2.02
3.34	2.00	2.69
4.72	3.00	4.03
5.70	4.00	5.38
6.44	5.00	6.72
8.79	10.00	13.44
10.16	15.00	20.16

Estimates of gross expenditure elasticities and of gross price elasticities are shown for all periods considered.

For each of the 16 ASEPELT groups an *average* expenditure elasticity estimate is also given. It is an average of estimates for all items or subgroups within the group. The weights are derived from the budget proportions in column 1.

The arguments of previous sections imply that estimates of gross elasticities may need adjustment before they are entered into a projection formula. There is, however, a simple relationship between regression coefficients and conditional projections for a given time-span and for given projection values of the right-hand side variables in a regression equation, and it may be of interest to have tabulations of such relationships. Table 2 provides answers to the following question: If *per capita* total consumption increases by 3 per cent annually in 10 years, and if relative prices

TABLE 3 – Standard errors of regression coefficients, residual standard errors and multiple correlation coefficients. ASEPELT groups and National Accounts groups, 1949–1959 and 1952–1959

	Standard errors of estimates of:				Residual standard errors		Multiple correlation coefficients	
	Expenditure elasticities		Direct price elasticities					
	1949–1959	1952–1959	1949–1959	1952–1959	1949–1959	1952–1959	1949–1959	1952–1959
ASEPELT GROUPS:								
1 Cereals and products	0.4	0.6	0.4	0.5	0.03	0.04	0.89	0.81
2 Milk and products	0.2	0.2	0.2	0.1	0.02	0.02	0.79	0.62
3 Meat, fish, eggs	0.2	0.2	0.3	0.3	0.03	0.03	0.83	0.85
4 Vegetables and fruits	0.5	0.7	0.3	0.4	0.07	0.07	0.94	0.84
5 Other foods	0.3	0.5	0.3	0.7	0.05	0.03	0.67	0.90
6 Beverages	0.2	0.3	0.6	0.3	0.04	0.02	0.91	0.91
7 Tobacco	0.3	0.3	0.3	0.5	0.05	0.04	0.30	0.63
8 Clothing and leather products	0.3	1.2	0.4	0.9	0.03	0.03	0.78	0.72
9 Durables	0.4	0.5	0.2	0.5	0.03	0.03	0.97	0.96
10 Fuel and light	0.2	0.4	0.1	0.4	0.04	0.04	0.96	0.93
11 Rent	0.3	0.2	0.4	0.1	0.02	0.01	0.97	0.99
12 Health	0.2	0.3	0.4	0.4	0.03	0.03	0.95	0.94
13 Public transport	0.2	0.2	0.3	0.7	0.02	0.02	0.92	0.94
14 Transport equipment	3.7	2.2	1.7	1.0	0.23	0.13	0.90	0.86
15 Private transport	1.1	0.9	0.7	0.6	0.09	0.06	0.94	0.88
16 Other	0.1	0.3	0.3	0.4	0.02	0.01	0.93	0.94
NATIONAL ACCOUNTS GROUPS:								
100 Food	0.2	0.2	0.2	0.3	0.02	0.01	0.94	0.95
200 Beverages and tobacco	0.5	0.3	0.5	0.4	0.04	0.02	0.67	0.88
300 Rents, light and fuel	0.3	0.6	0.2	0.2	0.03	0.02	0.97	0.87

TABLE 3 – *(continued)*

| | Standard errors of estimates of: | | | | Residual standard errors | | Multiple correlation coefficients | |
| | Expenditure elasticities | | Direct price elasticities | | | | | |
	1949–1959	1952–1959	1949–1959	1952–1959	1949–1959	1952–1959	1949–1959	1952–1959
NATIONAL ACCOUNTS GROUPS *(continued)*								
400 Durable household goods, household operation	0.4	0.5	0.5	0.6	0.04	0.03	0.86	0.69
500 Clothing and footwear	0.3	1.1	0.2	0.8	0.03	0.03	0.79	0.75
600 Personal hygiene and medical care	0.2	0.3	0.3	0.5	0.03	0.03	0.97	0.96
700 Travel and transportation	0.6	0.8	0.7	1.0	0.04	0.04	0.96	0.91
800 Education, literature, entertainment	0.1	0.3	0.2	0.4	0.02	0.01	0.98	0.99
900 Hotel and restaurant services, etc.	0.1	0.3	0.2	0.7	0.02	0.02	0.96	0.88
000 Other	0.2	0.2	0.6	0.9	0.03	0.03	0.97	0.97
100, 200	0.1	0.1	0.3	0.4	0.01	0.01	0.97	0.97
400, 600, 700, 800, 900, 000	0.1	0.1	0.2	0.7	0.01	0.01	0.99	0.99

remain unchanged, what are the projections 10 years ahead of the change in volume and the change in the budget proportion of an item having the expenditure elasticity C_i?

Table 3 gives standard errors of gross elasticities, residual standard errors and multiple correlation coefficients for the ASEPELT and national accounts groups, and Table 4 summarises information on standard errors of regression coefficient for subgroups and items.

TABLE 4 – Frequency distributions of standard errors of regression coefficients

Interval	Frequencies of standard errors of estimates of:							
	Expenditure elasticities				Direct price elasticities			
	1930 –39	1930 –59	1949 –59	1952 –59	1930 –39	1930 –59	1949 –59	1952 –59
	2	3	4	5	6	7	8	9
Less than 0.25	32	21	13	9	24	22	27	25
0.25–0.44	22	26	32	27	18	31	41	30
0.45–0.64	8	11	26	17	16	12	33	24
0.65–0.84	3	5	18	12	3	5	16	18
0.85–1.04	3	5	12	15	3	3	6	13
higher	6	6	41	62	10	1	19	32
Total frequencies[a])	74	74	142	142	74	74	142	142

[a]) The total number of subgroups is 78; however, 4 of them have been excluded from the tables, because they do not fit into the ASEPELT classification. There are only 19 subgroups that represent more than one item; the total 142 includes these subgroups in addition to the 123 items.

5. COMMENTS ON TRENDS IN THE CONSUMPTION PATTERN, 1930–1959

Our period begins with the years of the great depression. There are not, however, many visible signs of these unhappy years in the national aggregates[21]). The overall picture of the period 1930–1939 is dominated by the years of steady growth that began in 1933 and ended with the occupation of the country early in 1940. The purchasing power of consumers directed the expansion in the consumer goods market, well below the upper bound set by existing capacity.

[21]) The volume of gross domestic product declined from 81.6 in 1930 to 75.2 in 1931 (0.7 index points lower than in 1929) and increased to 79.0 in 1932, and to 80.8 in 1933. For private consumption the corresponding figures are for the years 1930–1933: 85.4, 83.3, 83.3, 84.6.

Market imperfections – rationing, short supply, etc. – were outstanding features of the early postwar years, and were still to some extent influencing consumers' demand as late as the start of the fifties. Little of use can be learnt about consumer demand from short time series that include the years 1946–1948, and data for these years are omitted here. The inclusion of the years 1949–1951 is also of questionable value, and this has to be taken into account when results for the periods 1949–1959 and 1952–1959 are compared. Of course, the shortcomings of the statistical data have also to be borne in mind[22]).

A simple formula can be given for the growth rate of total private consumption in the thirties and the fifties. It equals, on the average, three fourths of the percentage growth rate of the gross national product. The elasticity of total private consumption with respect to the gross national product is very close to 0.75 for both periods, and the residual standard error is of the order of magnitude of 1.7 per cent.

Nothing simple, however, characterizes the changes in the composition of consumption over the same period.

The range of estimates of gross expenditure elasticities in Table 1 extends from negative values to positive values as high as 12, and individual estimates vary in many cases considerably from one period to another. Furthermore, almost all broad groups of expenditures include both high-elasticity items and low-elasticity items.

If, to begin with, we look at the broader groups, e.g. the four-group and the ten-group classification, we see that there are only small differences between periods in the expenditure elasticities for food, beverages and tobacco combined, for food alone and for the fourth group of the four-group classification. For the other broad categories the differences are quite large.

It is of interest to compare these results with those obtained from studies of postwar family budget data. This is possible for the following groups[23]):

---

[22]) Indicators of the reliability of the various data estimates are given in the published tables; see e.g. Table 4 of 'National Accounts 1930–1939 and 1946–1951', NOS XI 109, Oslo 1952.

[23]) For results obtained in cross section studies see: Survey of Consumer Expenditure (1958), Third Volume, NOS, A 41, Central Bureau of Statistics of Norway, Oslo, 1961. The studies cover the following budget surveys: Industrial workers 1951–52, higher salaried employees 1952–53, farmers 1954, fishermen 1954, workers 1958, salaried employees 1958, self-employed 1958 (and old age pensioners 1955–56; not taken into consideration here).

		Range of expenditure elasticity estimates:	
		Cross section studies	Time series studies
100	Food	0.3–0.5	0.9–1.0
200	Beverages and tobacco	0.4–1.5	0.5–0.9
300	Rent, light and fuel	0.5–1.4	0.8–1.8
400	Durable household goods	1.5–2.5	1.0–2.1
500	Clothing and footwear	0.2–1.4	0.6–2.0
600	Personal hygiene and medical care	0.7–0.9	1.0–1.8
700	Travel and transportation	1.3–3.0	1.2–2.4

We see that cross section estimates also vary considerably, but this is probably due to factors such as family size, habits, social background etc. which vary substantially between social groups but only slightly within short periods. We also note that there are certain differences in level, in particular for the food group, for which estimates of expenditure elasticity from time series are 2 to 3 times as large as those from cross section analysis.

Our discussion so far suggests two main conclusions: (i) that the changes observed in the composition of private consumption in the periods considered are rather unsatisfactorily described by a constant elasticity model in terms of broad groups and (ii) that the effects of total expenditure changes over time are significantly different from the effects of inter-household changes in total expenditure, at least for some groups (e.g. food). We shall examine these provisional conclusions in the light of the model specifications in section 3,[24]).

We shall make use of the definitive relationship between group elasticities and component part elasticities[25]). The results for the food group

---

[24]) The discussion here is confined to expenditure elasticities. A discussion of the significance of the price variables is considerably more difficult. In section 7 we shall be concerned with estimates of complete sets of price elasticities, and it will be seen that the estimates of direct elasticities given there differ somewhat from those shown in Table 1. These differences may be ascribed to the presence of confluent relations (and random elements).

[25]) The group elasticity is a weighted average of component part elasticities, with the group proportions as weights. There is no corresponding exact relationship between the least squares estimates of these elasticities, but Table 1 illustrates that this relationship holds to a good approximation in most cases. In cases where the approximation is poor, *some* useful information can sometimes be derived also from this fact.

serve as an illustration. Table 1 discloses that many of the fruit and vegetable items, particularly imported goods in postwar years, come out
with 'abnormally' high gross expenditure elasticity estimates, and easy
calculations show that a correction to cross section levels would also
imply a reduction of the elasticity estimate for the food group to a level
much closer to the cross section level.

The demand for vegetable and fruit items, particularly in postwar
years, was influenced by special factors that were highly intercorrelated
with total expenditure (gradual removal of import restrictions and other
market imperfections, gradual changes in tastes, etc.). Such effects are, of
course, absent in cross section data, but are present in the form of confluent relations in time series data and produce high values of gross expenditure elasticities. On the basis of this interpretation we cannot conclude that the expenditure elasticity estimates for vegetables and fruits –
and for the food group – are inconsistent with results obtained in cross
section studies. Nor can we conclude that they are abnormally high. As
long as the confluent relationships hold good we can make use of the
gross elasticity estimates as if they were estimates of 'regular' elasticities.
Moreover, if we keep an eye on what happens in the market for vegetables
and fruits, it does not seem too difficult to adjust at this disaggregated
level, for the effects of gradual changes in the 'supplementary factors[26]').

Similar points of view can be applied to other groups and other items.
For the group clothing and footwear we find gross expenditure elasticity
estimates that vary considerably between periods. A study of the results
obtained for the items suggests that this is partly due to rather fundamental changes in household habits. Negative values of elasticities reflect
gradual substitution effects; materials lose their importance and are
replaced by ready-made goods.

It is much more difficult to interpret results for close substitutes, e.g.
margarine and butter, but it can be done if this is of particular interest.

Space does not allow discussion of all the results presented in Table 1 or
examination of standard errors, confidence intervals, statistical tests, etc.

---

[26]) The discussion is here in terms of 'intuitive adjustments'. It follows from the
discussion in section 3, however, that one can do a little better than that in many cases,
cf. the formulae (3.5).

6. PROJECTIONS 1960–1970, PRICES ASSUMED UNCHANGED

In this section projections of the composition of private consumption in 1970 are given for ASEPELT groups and for the ten-group and the four-group classification of the Norwegian national accounts system. The assumptions made on the values of the variables considered as exogenous are: (a) that relative prices (the ratios of each group price index to the price index of total private consumption) remain unchanged; and (b) that total *per capita* consumption at constant (1955) prices increases by 34.4 per cent from 1960 to 1970, i.e. by 3 per cent annually[27]).

Projection values for 1970, at 1955-prices, have been calculated from the formula

$$\log x_i (1970) = \log x_i (1960) + 0.2956 C_i^\theta \ . \tag{6.1}$$

where the first term on the right-hand side is the *observed* 1960 value of $\log x_i$, and where C_i^θ is an adjusted estimate of the gross expenditure elasticity for the group i,[28]). The coefficient 0.2956 is the logarithm of the factor 1.34 (which is the ratio of the assumed total *per capita* expenditure in 1970 to the observed total *per capita* expenditure in 1960).

Table 5 presents the projection values obtained for *per capita* group expenditures in 1970 (at 1955-prices) in the form of index numbers (1960 = 100)[29]), and in the form of ratios of budget proportions in 1970 to 1960 budget proportions.

The adjusted estimates of gross expenditure elasticities applied in the projections are given in column 2 of Table 5. The adjustments were carried out in connection with preparatory work on the Norwegian national budget model, and were based on the detailed item classification. The figures shown in column 2 are weighted averages, with budget proportions as weights, of adjusted estimates of the items' elasticities. The discussion of techniques in section 3, in particular the relationships in (3.5), has served as the analytical basis for carrying out these adjustments.

---

[27]) In the period 1949–1959 the average annual rate of growth of total *per capita* private consumption was 2.5 per cent.

[28]) The choice of observed 1960 values as a starting point for projections was found suitable for practical reasons. This choice has consequences for the stochastic properties (e.g. for the calculation of tolerance intervals etc.) of the projections. The superscript θ of C_i refers in this context to the projection period, compare (3.5). No separate notation has been used to distinguish estimates from parameters.

[29]) The expected population growth between 1960 and 1970 is 9 per cent. Projection values for total group expenditure in 1970 (1960 = 100) can be obtained by multiplying 1970 *per capita* figures by the factor 1.09.

TABLE 5 – Projections of private consumption in 1970, ASEPELT groups and National Accounts groups. *Per capita* figures at constant (1955) prices. Assumptions: a) Unchanged relative prices; b) Total private *per capita* consumption expenditure (at 1955-prices) increases by 3 per cent annually; i.e. by 34.4 per cent in 10 years

	Budget proportions in 1960 (at 1955-prices)	Adjusted (see text) expenditure elasticity estimates	Group expenditure in 1970, 1960=100 (at 1955-prices)	Ratios: budg. prop. 1970/budg. prop. 1960
	1	2	3	4
Asepelt Groups:				
1 Cereals and products	0.030	−0.08	98	0.73
2 Milk and products	0.050	0.13	104	0.77
3 Meat, fish, eggs	0.079	0.58	119	0.89
4 Vegetables and fruits	0.052	1.36	149	1.11
5 Other food	0.062	0.62	120	0.89
6 Beverages	0.071	1.03	136	1.01
7 Tobacco	0.029	0.39	112	0.83
8 Clothing and leather products	0.154	0.83	128	0.95
9 Durables	0.137	1.42	152	1.13
10 Fuel and light	0.033	1.12	139	1.03
11 Rent	0.067	1.20	143	1.06
12 Health	0.039	0.96	133	0.99
13 Public transport	0.045	0.66	122	0.91
14 Transport equipment	0.021	4.52	380	2.83
15 Private transport	0.011	4.00	326	2.43
16 Other	0.120	0.93	132	0.98
Total	1.000	1.00	134	1.00
National Accounts Groups:				
A. TEN-GROUP CLASSIFICATION				
100 Food	0.299	0.68	122	0.91
200 Beverages and tobacco	0.074	0.53	117	0.87
300 Rents, light and fuel	0.100	1.17	141	1.05
400 Durable household goods, household operation	0.089	1.17	141	1.05
500 Clothing and footwear	0.154	0.83	128	0.95
600 Personal hygiene and medical care	0.051	1.18	142	1.06
700 Travel and transportation	0.070	2.26	195	1.45
800 Education, literature, entertainment	0.064	1.47	154	1.15
900 Hotel and restaurant services, etc.	0.025	1.08	138	1.03
000 Other	0.074	0.94	132	0.98
Total	1.000	1.00	134	1.00

TABLE 5 – *(continued)*

	Budget proportions in 1960 (at 1955-prices)	Adjusted (see text) expenditure elasticity estimates	Group expenditure in 1970, 1960=100 (at 1955-prices)	Ratios: budg. prop. 1970/budg. prop. 1960
	1	2	3	4
B. FOUR-GROUP CLASSIFICATION				
100, 200 Food, beverages, tobacco	0.373	0.65	121	0.90
300 Rents, light and fuel	0.100	1.17	141	1.05
500 Clothing and footwear	0.154	0.83	128	0.95
400, 600, 700, 800, 900, 000 Other	0.373	1.37	150	1.12
Total	1.000	1.00	134	1.00

A detailed discussion of the adjustment procedure cannot be given here. But it can be said that most corrections were within the limits of the confidence intervals and that the small team responsible for the adjustments did not find it too difficult to reach agreement[30]).

It will be left to the reader to draw his own conclusions from the figures in Table 5. There is probably no need of warnings about the reliability of the projections presented. Statistical assessments confirm what is intuitively obvious: that random elements produce rather wide tolerance intervals[31]).

7. DIRECT AND CROSS PRICE ELASTICITIES

Frisch's method for computing complete sets of price elasticities is applicable for 'want-independent groups', provided all *net* expenditure elasticities (E_i), all budget proportions (a_i) and at least one direct *net* price elasticity (e_{ii}) are known[32]). The want-independence assumption is unnecessary if only two complementary groups are considered, say food and non-food. The restraints on elasticities following from the homogeneity

---

[30]) A similar adjustment process is almost always involved in input-output studies, where 'estimates' of structural coefficients, as a rule, are obtained from observations for one single year only.

[31]) A number of 'nuisance problems' had to be solved in connection with the preparation of Table 5 in order to obtain consistent aggregations of elasticity estimates.

[32]) See his article in Econometrica, *op. cit.*

postulate and from the budget equation,

$$\Sigma_j e_{ij} = - E_i \qquad (7.1)$$

$$\Sigma_i a_i E_i = 1 \qquad (7.2)$$

$$\Sigma_i a_i e_{ij} = - a_j \qquad (7.3)$$

allow us in this case to derive the values of the remaining three price elasticities. Table 6 illustrates the computations involved. If the two budget proportions, the two expenditure elasticities and either the direct price elasticity of food (-0.24) or of non-food (-0.93) are known it is easy to derive the numerical values of the remaining three price elasticities with the help of (7.1) and (7.3).

These results could also have been obtained from the formulae[33]

$$e_{ii} = - E_i \left(a_i - \frac{1 - a_i E_i}{\breve{\omega}} \right) \qquad (7.4)$$

$$e_{ij} = - a_j E_i \left(1 + \frac{E_i}{\breve{\omega}} \right), \quad i \neq j, \qquad (7.5)$$

for direct and cross price elasticities respectively, where the parameter $\breve{\omega}$, the money flexibility (which is independent of the subscript i), is given by

$$\breve{\omega} = \frac{E_i(1 - a_i E_i)}{e_{ii} + a_i E_i}. \qquad (7.6)$$

With appropriate values inserted from Table 6, we obtain the value -3 for the money flexibility, and we note that there is a simple correspondence between direct elasticities and the parameter $\breve{\omega}$, for given values of the budget proportions and the expenditure elasticities[34]. There is, of course, no particular need for the parameter $\breve{\omega}$ and for the formulae (7.4) and (7.5) in cases where only two complementary groups are involved. The equations (7.1) – (7.3) can be solved in a much simpler way.

If we have more than two groups, it is not sufficient to know all budget proportions, all net expenditure elasticities and one direct price elasticity in order to derive the remaining ones from (7.1)–(7.3). But if in addition

---

[33] See FRISCH's article; op. cit., formulae (61), (62), (64).
[34] To a direct price elasticity of -0.30 for food there corresponds a value of -2 for $\breve{\omega}$, and to a direct food price elasticity of -0.17 corresponds the value of -7 for the money flexibility. We note that the parameter is rather sensitive to small changes in the value of the direct price elasticity for food.

we *assume* that (7.6) holds for *all* expenditure groups, these conditions are again sufficient. Frisch has derived (7.6) from the assumption that the groups are want-independent, a property which is defined in terms of utility concepts. From a practical viewpoint it is difficult (impossible?) to lay down operational criteria for want independence, and the method presupposes therefore some willingness to rely on intuition in this respect. Once established, however, the values obtained for price elasticities may be tested, and in this way we are directed towards empiricism again, towards the time-honoured method of trial-and-error.

TABLE 6 – Direct and cross price elasticities, budget proportions and (net) expenditure elasticities, Food and Non-food.

i \ j	Food 1	Non-food 2	Net expenditure elasticites
1. Food	− 0.24	− 0.16	0.40
2. Non-food	− 0.33	− 0.93	1.26
Budget proportions	0.30	0.70	

The element in row no. i, column no. j is the price elasticity e_{ij} of the expenditure (at constant prices) on group no. i with respect to the price index of group no. j.

It has been assumed that the groups of the ten-group classification, and *a fortiori* the groups of the four-group classification, can be considered as want independent. Intuition suggests, however, that this assumption cannot be made for all ASEPELT groups.

It is, as already mentioned, the net elasticities that enter the formulae given above. We have probably no better source for information on net expenditure elasticities than the family budget studies. The net expenditure elasticities shown in Tables 7 and 8 for the four-group and the ten-group classifications have been obtained from postwar cross section studies.

It is considerably more difficult to derive useful information about the value of net direct price elasticities. The numerical illustration in Table 6 may serve as a starting point for speculation. If we accept the figures entered for net expenditure elasticities and budget proportions, and if in addition we make the plausible guess that all four price elasticities take negative values, there is a rather limited range for admissible values; the most plausible range for the direct price elasticity for food cannot be wide. The mid-point of such an interval cannot be very far from -0.25. This is somewhat lower in absolute values than our point estimates of the *gross* direct price elasticity in Table 1,[35]). The value of the parameter $\breve{\omega}$ corresponding to this estimate is -3.

The value -3 chosen for the parameter $\breve{\omega}$ is a compromise value which, when inserted in (7.6), produces a set of direct net price elasticities

TABLE 7 – Direct and cross price elasticities, budget proportions and (net) expenditure elasticities, four-group classification.

i \ j	Food, beverages, tobacco 1	Rents, light and fuel 2	Clothing and footwear 3	Other 4	Net expenditure elasticities
1. Food, beverages, tobacco	-0.32	-0.04	-0.05	-0.09	0.50
2. Rents, light and fuel	-0.27	-0.36	-0.09	-0.16	0.88
3. Clothing and footwear	-0.34	-0.08	-0.47	-0.20	1.09
4. Other	-0.48	-0.11	-0.15	-0.80	1.54
Budget proportions	0.38	0.10	0.16	0.38	

The element in row no. i, column no. j is the price elasticity e_{ij} of the expenditure (at constant prices) on group no. i with respect to the price index of group no. j.

that in an approximate sense complies with the results obtained for direct gross price elasticities[36]). Other values of $\breve{\omega}$ within a range from, say, -4 to -2 could, with no less empirical justification, have been chosen.

Inspection of Tables 7 and 8 suggests that the effects of price changes on consumption cannot be taken adequately into account by demand models that include only direct price elasticities. The results obtained for the effects of changes in the price of food ('necessities') are particularly illustrative. An increase in the price of food (relative to the price of all

---

[35]) The value -0.25 is within the range of the confidence intervals for the *gross* price elasticities in Table 1.

[36]) FRISCH, *op. cit.*, p. 189, quotes Mr. Leif Johansen's results based on Norwegian data, giving values close to -2. PEARCE, in Econometrica, October 1961, p. 507, states that 'experiments on British Consumer data suggest a value ... not very different from ... -2'. However, empirical evidence on the values of price elasticities is scanty and there are, as far as I can see, unsolved problems in connection with the interpretation and the empirical determination of coefficients in demand equations specified in terms of relative prices. Least squares regressions give unique regression coefficients, but the discussion in footnote [18]) suggests that the interpretation is troublesome. For this reason I am not prepared to defend my own choice of -3 for $\breve{\omega}$ very strongly.

TABLE 8 – Direct and cross price elasticities, budget proportions and (net) expenditure elasticities, ten-group classification.

i \ j	Food	Beverages and tobacco	Rents, light and fuel	Durable household goods, household operation	Clothing and footwear	Personal hygiene and medical care	Travel and transportation	Education, literature, entertainment	Hotel and restaurant services etc.	Other	Net expenditure elasticities
	1	2	3	4	5	6	7	8	9	10	
1. Food	−0.24	−0.02	−0.03	−0.01	−0.04	−0.01	−0.01	−0.01	−0.01	−0.02	0.40
2. Beverages and tobacco	−0.23	−0.35	−0.07	−0.03	−0.08	−0.03	−0.01	−0.03	−0.02	−0.05	0.90
3. Rents, light and fuel	−0.23	−0.04	−0.36	−0.03	−0.08	−0.03	−0.01	−0.03	−0.02	−0.05	0.88
4. Durable household goods, household operation	−0.52	−0.10	−0.14	−0.73	−0.19	−0.07	−0.03	−0.07	−0.04	−0.11	2.00
5. Clothing and footwear	−0.27	−0.06	−0.08	−0.03	−0.47	−0.04	−0.02	−0.04	−0.02	−0.06	1.09
6. Personal hygiene and medical care	−0.28	−0.06	−0.08	−0.03	−0.10	−0.40	−0.02	−0.04	−0.02	−0.06	1.09
7. Travel and transportation	−0.62	−0.12	−0.17	−0.07	−0.22	−0.08	−0.82	−0.09	−0.04	−0.13	2.36
8. Education, literature, entertainment	−0.35	−0.07	−0.10	−0.04	−0.13	−0.05	−0.02	−0.50	−0.02	−0.07	1.35
9. Hotel and restaurant services etc.	−0.27	−0.05	−0.08	−0.03	−0.10	−0.03	−0.02	−0.04	−0.37	−0.06	1.05
10. Other	−0.23	−0.05	−0.06	−0.03	−0.08	−0.03	−0.01	−0.03	−0.02	−0.34	0.88
Budget proportions	0.30	0.07	0.10	0.09	0.15	0.05	0.07	0.06	0.03	0.08	

The element in row no. i, column no. j is the price elasticity e_{ij} of the expenditure (at constant prices) on group no. i with respect to the price index of group no. j.

consumption goods) has stronger effects on the demand for several non-food groups (in particular for 'luxuries') than on the demand for food.

It is the purpose of the following two sections to illustrate the importance of taking into account the effects of price changes in projections.

8. PRICE CHANGES 1960–1970, EXTRAPOLATIONS OF POSTWAR TRENDS

In Norway relative prices of consumer goods changed considerably in postwar years, partly as a consequence of changes in indirect taxes and government subsidies. However, there are certain trend-like movements in relative prices for broad categories of goods, and the possibility exists that these trends will persist in the next decade also.

Since total *per capita* consumption expenditure has developed on an exponential trend, it is permissible and convenient for our purpose to measure postwar trends in relative prices by regressions of the form

$$\log p_i = \varepsilon_i \log x + \text{a constant term} \tag{8.1}$$

where ε_i has to be interpreted as an elasticity of the relative price index for group no. i with respect to total *per capita* consumption expenditure. Table 9 presents the regression coefficients obtained for the various periods. The values of ε_i chosen to represent the trends over the next decade are shown in the last column of the table. There is a declining trend for clothing and durables and for transportation services.

It follows from (8.1) and (3.6) that, for each group, the combined effect of all price changes is represented by the term

$$D_i \log x = (\Sigma_j e_{ij} \varepsilon_j) \log x. \tag{8.2}$$

9. PROJECTIONS 1960–1970, PRICE CHANGES TAKEN INTO ACCOUNT

Projections that take price changes into account can be given only for want independent groups. The assumptions underlying the projections for the ten-group classification and the four-group classification are: (a) that relative prices change in accordance with the elasticities ε_i (which relate relative price changes to changes in total *per capita* expenditure); and (b) that total *per capita* consumption at constant prices increases as specified in section 6, i.e. by 3 per cent annually.

The projection formula is (6.1) also in this case; the only change is that the coefficient C_i^0 has to be replaced by $(C_i^0 + D_i)$, where D_i is given by (8.2).

TABLE 9 – Time series regressions of logarithm of relative group prices on logarithm of *per capita* total expenditure at constant prices, National accounts groups. Selected periods, 1930–59

	Elasticities; regression coefficients based on period:				Adjusted (see text) elasticities ε_i
	1930–39	1930–59 excl. 1940–48	1949–59	1952–59	
A. TEN-GROUP CLASSIFICATION					
100 Food	0.5	0.1	0.6	0.4	0.4
200 Beverages and tobacco	− 0.3	− 0.0	− 0.8	− 0.5	− 0.5
300 Rents, light and fuel	− 0.5	− 0.2	1.6	2.1	1.5
400 Durable household goods, household operation	0.4	0.1	− 0.7	− 0.7	− 0.7
500 Clothing and footwear	− 0.1	− 0.1	− 0.9	− 1.4	− 1.2
600 Personal hygiene and medical care	0.1	0.1	0.3	0.4	0.4
700 Travel and transportation	− 0.5	− 0.1	− 0.9	− 0.8	− 0.8
800 Education, literature, entertainment	− 0.1	0.0	0.1	0.6	0.6
900 Hotel and restaurant services, etc.	0.3	0.2	− 0.1	0.3	0.3
000 Other	− 0.8	− 0.3	0.0	0.1	0.0
B. FOUR-GROUP CLASSIFICATION					
100, 200 Food, beverages, • tobacco	0.4	0.1	0.3	0.2	0.2
300 Rents, light and fuel	− 0.5	− 0.2	1.6	2.1	1.5
500 Clothing and footwear	− 0.1	− 0.1	− 0.9	− 1.4	− 1.2
400, 600, 700, 800, 900, 000 Other	− 0.1	− 0.0	− 0.3	0.2	− 0.1

The numerical results are given in Table 10. The figures in column 3 represent the price effects that follow indirectly, because of (8.2), from an increase of one per cent in total per capita expenditure. The assumed price changes have a rather strong demand-reducing effect on real housing expenditures (rent, light and fuel), on entertainment, etc. (group 800) and on two groups dominated by personal services (group 600 and 900). Demand-stimulating effects are found particularly for transport etc. (group 700) and for typical manufactured goods (groups 400 and 500). A comparison of figures in columns 2 and 3 shows the relative importance of price effects and total expenditure effects.

Projections 1960–1970 comparable with those presented in section 6 are found in columns 5 and 6.

TABLE 10 – Projections of *private consumption* in 1970, National Accounts groups. *Per capita* figures at constant (1955) prices. Assumptions: a) Relative prices change as specified in the text; b) Total private *per capita* consumption expenditure (at 1955-prices) increases by 3 per cent annually; i.e. by 34.4 per cent in 10 years.

	Budget proportions in 1960 (at 1955-prices)	Expenditure elasticities (from table 5, col.2)	Price effect coeff.[a] $\Sigma_j e_{ij} \varepsilon_j$	Combined effect coeff. (columns 2 + 3)	Group expenditure in 1970. 1960 = 100 (at 1955-prices)	Ratios: budg. prop. 1970/ budg. prop. 1960
	1	2	3	4	5	6
A. TEN-GROUP CLASSIFICATION						
100 Food	0.299	0.68	−0.09	0.59	119	0.89
200 Beverages and tobacco	0.074	0.53	0.08	0.61	120	0.89
300 Rents, light and fuel	0.100	1.17	−0.51	0.66	122	0.91
400 Durable household goods, household operation	0.089	1.17	0.31	1.48	155	1.15
500 Clothing and footwear	0.154	0.83	0.36	1.19	142	1.06
600 Personal hygiene and medical care	0.051	1.18	−0.23	0.95	132	0.98
700 Travel and transportation	0.070	2.26	0.44	2.70	222	1.64
800 Education, literature, entertainment	0.064	1.47	−0.38	1.09	138	1.03
900 Hotel and restaurant services, etc.	0.025	1.08	−0.19	0.89	130	0.97
000 Other	0.074	0.94	0.07	1.01	135	1.00
Total	1.000	1.00	—	—	—	—
B. FOUR-GROUP CLASSIFICATION						
100, 200 Food, beverages, tobacco	0.373	0.65	−0.05	0.60	119	0.89
300 Rents, light and fuel	0.100	1.17	−0.47	0.70	123	0.92
500 Clothing and footwear	0.154	0.83	0.40	1.23	144	1.07
400, 600, 700, 800, 900, 000 Other	0.373	1.37	0.00	1.37	150	1.12
Total	1.000	1.00	—	—	—	—

[a] Price elasticities e_{ij} from Table 8 and elasticities ε_j from Table 9.

10. CONCLUDING REMARK

No branch of econometric research has been more successful than the study of consumption. It is now common knowledge that expenditure elasticities reflect basic regularities in the pattern of consumer demand. For many groups of goods and services an approximate value can be given to their elasticities and such estimates have many practical applications. It is a fact that the statistical agencies responsible for the collection and processing of consumption data have played little part in this development. Their main contribution has been to produce the tables of data from which others have derived elasticities etc. However, further systematic spadework in this field should start from the basic data and not from summary aggregates. Statistical agencies will have to face this challenge in the years to come.

CHAPTER 7

FUTURE CONSUMPTION IN SWEDEN

BY

RAGNAR BENTZEL

Industrial Institute for Economic and Social Research, Stockholm, Sweden

Introductory

The development of consumption in Sweden has been analysed in a series
of different studies at the Industrial Institute for Economic and Social
Research[1]. Most of these studies have ended with forecasts of the future
consumption pattern, although a few have been limited to analysis of past
development. The forecasts presented in this paper are a sequel to this
series of investigations. They are to a large extent based on the experiences
and results of the earlier studies and the same general principles of forecasting have been adopted.

This paper is divided into 5 sections. In order to give a general background to the forecasts, the first section gives a short description of the
development in Swedish consumption patterns during the last three decades. Section 2 is concerned with the methods used in the study. The
general assumptions underlying the forecasts are described in section 3.

---

[1]) R. BENTZEL *et al.*, Den privata konsumtionen i Sverige 1931–1965. (The Private
Consumption in Sweden 1931–1965), Stockholm, 1957.

R. BENTZEL, The Private Consumption in Sweden. Skandinaviska Banken, Quar-
terly Review 1957, 4.

J. EKSTRÖM, Den textila konsumtionen. (The Consumption of Textiles), Stockholm
1958.

J. WALLANDER, Studier i bilismens ekonomi. (Studies in the Economic Effects of
Motoring), Stockholm 1958.

G. ALBINSSON *et al.*, IUI's konsumtionsprognos för år 1965. En granskning och
revidering. (IUI's Consumption Forecast for 1965. A checking and an adjustment),
Stockholm 1960.

Å. SUNDSTRÖM-J. EKSTRÖM, Dryckeskonsumtionen i Sverige. (The Consumption of
Beverages in Sweden), Stockholm 1962.

G. ALBINSSON, Svensk populärpress 1931–1961 (Popular Magazines in Sweden
1931–1961), Stockholm 1962.

A detailed description of the calculations, commodity by commodity, is given in section 4. The last section is devoted to a summing-up of the forecasts.

1. THE DEVELOPMENT OF CONSUMPTION 1931–1960

During the last three decades Sweden has undergone a thorough economic and social transformation. At the close of the 1920's the country was still comparatively poor with a standard of living considerably lower than that of the more advanced western European states. Since then, however, there has been a rapid and steady economic growth and now Sweden is considered to have the highest standard of living in Europe. The complex causes behind this favourable development are not of concern here, although it should be remembered, that the country had the immense advantage of avoiding destruction during the second world war.

Growth in the Swedish economy has been combined with a growth in the share of national income devoted to capital formation. The investment ratio increased from 19 per cent in 1931 to 35 per cent in 1960. Even public consumption has come to claim an increasing share; as a result the share of income going to private consumption has been considerably reduced. Whereas in the beginning of the 1930's the share of private consumption amounted to 74 per cent, by 1960 it was under 55 per cent.

The increase in the volume of private consumption between 1931 and 1960 was about 110 per cent. As the population of the country climbed during this period from 6.2 to 7.5 million, the growth in consumption per head was somewhat less, about 73 per cent. This implies, if the war years are disregarded, an average yearly increase of about 2.4 per cent.

A rising standard of living is usually accompanied by several changes in the pattern of consumption. What has happened in Sweden is shown, roughly, in the diagram below, which illustrates the growth in the volume of consumption per head of certain traditional groups of goods and services: food, beverages, housing, etc. In order to make the diagram easy to read only the years 1931, 1938, 1946, 1954 and 1960 have been considered; these are spaced along the horizontal axis not according to a time scale, but to one, which represents the volume per head of total private consumption.

During the period under investigation the consumption of *food* in-

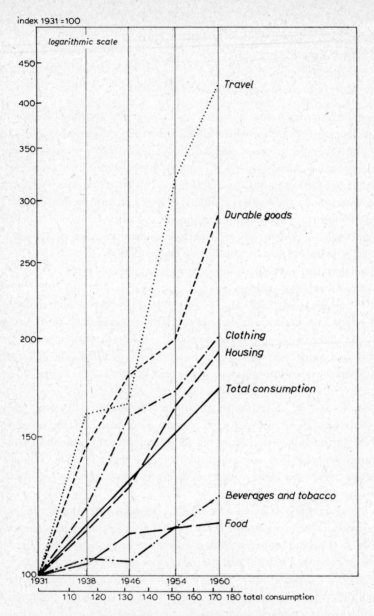

FIG. 1. Volume of consumption *per capita* for different goods and services 1931 to 1960. Index 1931 = 100; logarithmic scale.

creased by about 50 per cent – i.e., considerably less than total private consumption. Despite this limited growth in volume, the share of consumer spending devoted to food decreased only moderately, from 30 to 26 per cent; this reflects the fact that food prices have risen more than the average.

Within the food category, consumption of cereals and vegetables has grown more rapidly than consumption of animal foods. The growth in the former of these groups is accounted for, in large part, by a sharp increase in purchases of bread and pastries, together with vegetables and fruits, partly offset by a reduction in purchases of flour and potatoes. Within the animal group there has been a less clearly differentiated development. Most of the items have increased moderately. However, among meats and fish, there has been a marked switch from fresh, raw foods to tinned, frozen and ready-cooked food[2]).

An increase in the volume of food consumed does not mean that the calorie intake has also increased. In fact, it has decreased since the 1930's. The growth in volume must be seen, instead, as the result of changes in the distribution of food purchases.

For beverages and tobacco there was a moderate growth in volume, of 53 per cent from 1931 to 1960. Moreover, the price of these goods rose considerably. This is particularly true of the prices of alcoholic drinks which have been burdened with successively higher taxes. It must also be mentioned that, until 1955, spirits were subject to rationing.

The volume of consumption of housing (including fuel and light) increased during the first part of the observed period rather slowly. It gained speed, however, during the latter part of the period, and the total growth in volume from 1931 to 1960 amounted to 133 per cent. Since 1942 rent has been subject to control. This rent policy has led to an extensive housing shortage that still prevails.

The consumption of clothing increased quite rapidly until 1948. Then there was a period of stagnation that lasted until the middle of the 1950's. Since then consumption has gone up at its 'normal' pace. The total growth in volume between 1931 and 1960 amounts to 144 per cent.

Within the clothing group, strong structural changes have taken place. Purchases of ready-made clothing and knitted goods have expanded exceedingly fast; in volume terms these items have nearly quadrupled.This

---

[2]) This transfer is probably somewhat underestimated in the available statistical material.

increase has, obviously, been at the expense of purchases of yarn, cloth and tailored articles. The growth in the volume of the last group has been quite moderate – only about 50 per cent.

Purchases of durable goods (other than transport equipment) have quadrupled during the period under investigation. But development has been rather irregular and three sub-periods can be distinguished when the underlying rising trend was broken: during the depression of the thirties; during the war, and during the first half of the 1950's.

The durable-goods category is a heterogeneous one and it is not surprising that development has differed from item to item. Purchases of some goods, e.g. musical instruments, more simple kitchen equipment, chinaware, have grown comparatively little; by contrast furniture, household textiles, toys, and sports goods have grown rapidly. But the most rapid expansion has been in the group of electrical goods such as radios, vacuum cleaners, washing machines etc.

Television was introduced rather late in Sweden; regular transmissions started in 1956. After this, however, television ownership spread very rapidly, especially during 1958, 1959 and 1960. At the present time, 1962, more than one out of two Swedish households owns a television set.

Travel is another rapidly expanding category: the volume has grown fivefold. This development is, of course, mainly due to the expansion of motoring. The number of passenger cars in Sweden amounted to 1.2 million at the end of 1960 against only 100 thousand at the beginning of the 1930's. Sweden has now more passenger cars in relation to its population than any other country in Europe. At the end of 1961 there were 174 cars per 1000 inhabitants.

Public transport services grew quite fast until the beginning of the 1950's. Then began a stagnation, which, after the middle of the 1950's, became a downturn.

The Swedish sickness and health services have been strongly subsidized during the observed period. In 1955 a compulsory sick insurance was introduced which entitled the sick to a refund amounting to the larger part of their expenses for hospital care, doctors' fees and medicine. The contributions which are paid by individuals for this insurance do not cover costs, however; the principal part of the costs is financed from taxes.

It is evident that the concept of volume, where care of the sick is concerned, is difficult to define – it is even, perhaps, meaningless. This is why no volume curve for medical care has been included in the diagram above. It may be sufficient to mention that private expenditures for sick and medical care increased from 1.8 per cent of the private consumer's total outlay at the beginning of the 1930's to 3.1 per cent. In 1960 the total expenditure in Sweden for sick and health care was approximately three times as large as the amount paid by private consumers.

The remaining goods and services form a set of completely dissimilar items which, as a group, increased in volume by 95 per cent from 1931 to 1960. Within the group, personal services – such as those performed by maids, restaurant personnel and barbers – were either static or decreased.

The changes in consumption since the beginning of the 1930's can, for a large part, be described as a switch from necessities to more dispensable items. This change has shown itself in a relatively small growth in the consumption of most foodstuffs, shoes, underware, simpler kitchenware, etc., and in a rapid growth in purchases of vehicles, sports goods, electrical equipment, entertainment, etc. In the main, these changes are a normal consequence of the growth in real income. The same types of shifts can be observed from budget statistics which compare the consumption of different income classes. To a large extent these shifts have meant a transfer from non-durable to durable goods.

Another dominating feature has been the changes associated with the efforts of consumers to make domestic work easier. In food-buying this is evident in the switch from flour to bread, from fresh foods to tinned, frozen or ready-made products. In clothing one can distinguish the same feature in the transfer from tailor-made to ready-to-wear and from wool to knitted goods. It is again evident in the strongly increased demand for electrical household machines.

As with the change from necessities to luxurious, the desire to lessen domestic work is a natural consequence of an increase in income. But the tendency has doubtless been accentuated by many other conditions, among them the facts that the pay of domestic help has increased sharply relative to the price of electrical home equipment and that the price difference between 'raw-materials' and finished products has become considerably less. Further, both the growth in income and the desire to diminish the work of housewives in the home can be seen, in the past, as a consequence of one and the same phenomenon viz. the increase in the number of housewives gainfully employed.

During the period under discussion, consumption of personal services showed a special change. The number of maids, shoe-makers, and tailors has decreased sharply. Further, during the post-war period the quantity of services provided by restaurants and barbers has remained static. There are many reasons for this development; the dominating one has probably been the movement of prices. The price of non-subsidized personal services has, as a rule, risen considerably more than other prices, and this must be regarded as a natural phenomenon in a growing economy. For obvious reasons the increases in productivity, which have occurred in most other sectors of the economy and have tended to keep prices down, have been less pronounced in the service sector.

The period since 1930 has been one in which a host of new articles have found their way on to the Swedish market - radio and television sets, electrical household equipment, clothes made from artificial fibres, scooters, frozen food, juices etc. To begin with, new goods have mostly expanded at a rapid pace but, after a time, the growth rate has levelled off. Such expansions have often brought about a corresponding decrease in the purchases of one or several *other goods*. It is easy to find examples of this; artificial fibres have rapidly won ground at the expense of cotton and wool; and the expansion of television has led to a decrease in cinema going, etc.

The four general features just described have to a great extent, dominated the Swedish development of consumption. They are not, however, peculiar to Sweden. On the contrary, they can be found in all growing societies and seem to be necessary consequences of growth.

2. SOME METHODOLOGICAL REMARKS

The main part of the forecasts has been carried out with traditional single-equation regression methods applied to time-series. The reasoning underlying these methods is well-known and need not be enlarged on here. As a rule, logarithmic linear functions have been used, but there are some exceptions to this rule. In order to test the reasonableness of the observed income- and price-elasticities, these have, as far as possible, been checked against corresponding elasticities obtained from other sources: Swedish cross-section data, foreign experience and international comparisons between countries with different standards of living.

Forecasts based on time-series analysis always include an assumption that observed historical relationships are valid in the future. Such an assumption is obviously not always realistic. There are a lot of reasons for this; the framework of consumption may change in some respects, for example. Therefore it is necessary in each separate case to examine the assumption that the observed relationship will prevail in the future. It is, especially, very important to know to what extent the supply side in the past has been actively working by introducing new goods and qualities and to get an idea of what is to be expected from this side in the future. It is obvious that to a great extent this is a matter of personal judgment and that such judgment introduces an element of subjectivity into the calculations. This seems, however, to be unavoidable if we want to make reasonable forecasts.

A precondition for the possibility of using the regression method is, evidently, that one has access to a statistical material on the relationship between consumption and the explanatory variables, and also that one can predict the future development of the explanatory variables. This condition, however, considerably limits the choice of explanatory variables. As a rule only three types of such variables are used in this study, namely, demographic data, the average income, and real prices[3]).

In this context it must be remembered that the introduction of further variables does not necessarily give better forecast possibilities, even if we should get a better fit between historical data and the corresponding 'theoretical' values. By itself the introduction of one more explanatory variable means a new factor of uncertainty – the forecast for this new variable. Whether or not a new variable should be introduced must therefore rest on a judgment of the importance of this variable together with the degree of uncertainty about its future development.

As a rule the time-series analysis is based on statistical data covering the period 1931–1960. War years have, however, been excluded because consumption was then limited by an extensive system of regulations and cannot be identified with demand.

Although the above described time-series analysis often proved satisfactory, there were, however, several cases where a model of this simple type did not yield satisfactory results. This is particularly true in the case of those goods which were introduced during the period covered by the analysis. As typical examples we could take radio and television sets, and other electrical apparatus. Other goods for which the simple regression model does not function properly are those which have been forced from the market by the competition from newly introduced goods.

In situations where models with constant elasticities have not shown themselves to be adequate, other methods have been adopted. In some

---

[3]) The real price of a good is here defined as the quotient between the price index of the good and the general price index of consumer goods.

cases income elasticities from cross-section data were used, in other cases forecasts were made on the basis of simple time trends; and in still other cases foreign experiences provided a basis for the calculations. The methods used in the separate cases will be reviewed in section 4.

As already described, the income elasticities obtained from time-series analysis, have been compared with corresponding elasticities calculated from cross-section material. More often than not, discrepancies have appeared between these two types of elasticities. This should not, however, be interpreted as indicating an error in one – or both – of the elasticities but, rather, that elasticities from time-series contain effects that do not appear in cross-section analysis. During periods of rising prosperity the growth in income, as a rule, is accompanied by several other changes influencing consumption. The effects of such changes appear in the development of time-series, but not in cross-section analysis. Examples of such changes which, as well as changes in price relativities, have been of considerable importance in the Swedish development, are the introduction of new goods, the equalization of income distribution and the migration from the countryside. Such factors could be considered by explicitly including them in the relationships, but to consider more than a few of all such structural changes influencing consumption is practically impossible.

This dissimilarity between the two types of elasticities is evidently of great importance. Elasticities computed on the basis of time-series are, in themselves, not pure, but a sort of hybrid. They include some of the essential characteristics of the growth process. This is, however, an advantage rather than a disadvantage. As long as there is no reason to believe that the interaction between growth in income and its accompanying consequences shall be broken this is beyond doubt just the sort of relationship we need for a forecast. The use of cross-section data can easily lead to the wrong track, and must, therefore, be used with the greatest care. The ceteris-paribus assumptions that must be made when cross-section elasticities are applied to a development in time are often inconsistent with an assumption about rising income level. It is, for instance, not reasonable to combine an assumption about increasing real income with an assumption about unchanged price relativities, or with an assumption that no new goods will appear.

As stated at the outset, the forecasts presented in this paper are based on earlier analysis of consumption. This study started by an investigation of how the models used in earlier forecasts fitted to actuality during the years after the forecasts were made. If a good agreement between forecast and actuality was found, we accepted the model – unless obvious reasons indicated that a change ought to be made. In those cases where the models did not predict with desired accuracy, we have either made minor adjustments, or quite new calculations. Thereby we have, in all sorts of ways, attempted to learn from the earlier failures.

As already described the forecasts, with the exception of a few cases, were carried out from the demand side. The exceptions are the two groups housing and health. During the post-war years, supply and demand have never been in equilibrium in these fields. There has been an extensive shortage of housing as well as of doctors, nurses and hospital space. The available statistical data concerning consumption do not, therefore, reflect demand. To judge the extent of excess demand with any degree of accuracy has not been possible. Therefore we have not been able to carry out the necessary calculations for a forecast from the demand side. To add to the difficulty, residential construction in Sweden and medical care, are dependent to a considerable degree upon political decisions; consumption is strongly subsidized. How consumption in these fields develops, therefore, is dependent on political factors rather than on consumers' reactions.

3. THE GENERAL ASSUMPTIONS FOR THE FORECASTS

The forecasts presented in the next section are based on three types of fundamental assumptions. The first of these concerns the development of prosperity, the second the development of prices and the third the population development.

As long as peace in Europe is maintained, there is reason to believe that Sweden's economic growth will continue. To predict the rate of this growth is, however, not easy. There we stand on rather uncertain ground.

As mentioned earlier, the volume of private consumption per head has – during the last three decades – increased by about 2.4 per cent per year. According to a recently published report of a Royal Commission on the long-term planning of the Swedish economy, there is, however, reason to expect a more rapid growth in consumption during the first half of the 1960's[4]. In this report, the annual rate of growth of consumption was predicted to be $3^1/_2$ per cent per head. No calculations for the rate of development after 1965 were made, but there seems little reason to be-

---

[4] Svensk ekonomi 1960–1965, Statens offentliga utredningar 1962, 10.

lieve that the rate of growth during this period will be lower than in the first part of the decade. In this study, therefore, the above-mentioned rate of growth, $3^1/_2$ per cent, is assumed for the entire 1960's.

During an economic growth process, the price system, as a rule, undergoes certain characteristic changes. Goods acquiring large gains in productivity will become relatively cheaper – and vice versa. Experience shows us that it is industrial goods – in particular those of a more complicated technical nature – that become cheaper, while personal services tend to become more expensive. Such price shifts accompanying economic growth cannot, naturally, be neglected in a forecast.

It has not, in the present investigation, been possible to make a statistically supported forecast of future price movements. Instead, the simplified process of introducing schematic assumptions concerning price development has been adopted. These assumptions are based on general judgments concerning the probable development of productivity, competitive conditions within various branches of industry, the import situation etc. The judgments have been made commodity by commodity, so the result combines a number of differentiated assumptions about future prices.

It must be admitted that a considerable element of arbitrariness has been introduced into the final forecasts by this technique. This is, however, inescapable, and it should be emphasized that we do not avoid this arbitrariness by making less differentiated assumptions. Further, it has to be stressed that an assumption of unchanged relative prices during economic growth is in our opinion not only arbitrary, but also absurd.

Concerning the development of population, a forecast made within the Swedish Central Statistical Bureau has been accepted. According to this, the Swedish population will grow from 7.5 million at present to 8.0 million by 1970. Simultaneously, there will be a change in the age distribution which will increase the proportion of population at ages 20–30 and over 50.

4. THE FORECAST IN DETAIL

Food

The group *flour and grain* is a typical 'inferior goods', which has been declining strongly during the entire post-war period. We have, on the basis of time-series analysis, calculated an income elasticity of -1.1. The real price has been assumed to remain unchanged.

For *bread and pastries*, time-series analysis gives an income elasticity that is considerably larger than 1, and also a large price elasticity. These values are, however, evidently influenced by the large shift from home-baked to purchased bread. Obviously there is a limit to this shift. It must become less important in future. The experience of the past few years indicates that the elasticity is now lower than before. We have therefore chosen an income elasticity of 1.0 and a price elasticity of − 0.5. The real price is assumed to rise 10 per cent.

Milk and products occupies a central place in Sweden as milk is the great meal-time beverage. However, *per capita* consumption decreased gradually during the 1950's. In the case of milk this development can partly be seen as a resumption of the 'normal' pre-war level. Regression analysis resulted in estimates of the income elasticity just above zero and the price elasticity = − 0.4. With a projected rise in real prices of 15 per cent these elasticities forecast a further decline in *per capita* consumption and only a slight increase of the total volume. Milk is the only item with an over all decrease, while ice-cream consumption experiences the largest growth (doubling).

For *edible-fats*, time-series analysis shows an income elasticity of 0.3. This value, however, disagrees badly with the experience of the last few years. It seems quite clear that the elasticity has successively fallen, and is now below rather than above, zero. We have calculated that edible-fats consumption *per capita* will be unchanged, and that the real price will also be unchanged.

For *meat, pork and eggs*, the time-series show an income elasticity of 0.5 and a price elasticity of − 0.3. There has been no cause to question these values. The real price is assumed to increase by 10 per cent. The income elasticity for *fish* has been estimated to 0.4, while price elasticity seems to be − 0.2. Real prices will rise by about 10 per cent.

Potatoes and root crops are inferior goods. The time-series show − 0.7, as their income elasticity, and 0 as their price elasticity. These values are accepted for the forecast. It is supposed that real prices will fall by 10 per cent.

For the group *vegetables and fruits* time-series show an income elasticity of 1.0 and a price elasticity − 0.4. It is assumed that real prices will fall by 10 per cent.

The time-series for *sugar, chocolate and spices* show an income elasticity of 0.6 and a price elasticity of − 0.4. Real prices are assumed to fall by about 10 per cent.

TABLE 1 – Consumption volume and value: *food*

	Millions of kronor			Volume change in per cent	% Share	
	Volume[a])		Value 1970		1960	1970
	1960	1970				
Flour, bread etc.	*1433*	*1663*	*1815*	*+16*	*3.8*	*3.2*
Flour, grain	201	148	148	−27	0.5	0.3
Bread, pastries	1232	1515	1667	+23	3.3	2.9
Milk and fats	*2269*	*2360*	*2590*	*+4*	*6.0*	*4.6*
Milk, cream, cheese	1486	1530	1760	+3	3.9	3.1
Edible-fats	782	830	830	+6	2.1	1.5
Meat, fish, eggs	*3183*	*3969*	*4197*	*+25*	*8.4*	*7.4*
Meat, pork, eggs	2702	3378	3547	+25	7.2	6.3
Fish	481	591	650	+23	1.2	1.1
Potatoes, vegetables, fruits	*1662*	*2305*	*2075*	*+39*	*4.4*	*3.7*
Potatoes, root-crops	390	320	290	−18	1.0	0.5
Vegetables, fruits	1272	1985	1785	+56	3.4	3.2
Sugar, chocolate, spices[b])	*1093*	*1485*	*1337*	*+35*	*2.9*	*2.4*
Total	9640	11782	12044	+22	25.5	21.3

[a]) 1960 prices.
[b]) Canned foods included under meat, fish, vegetables etc.

The above calculations and judgments have resulted in the following forecast of food consumption (Table 1).

Food consumption in total is thus forecasted to increase by 22% (15% *per capita*), implying an over all income elasticity of 0.4. It should be stressed, however, that this growth does not mean a rising *per capita* consumption of calories. The rising volume merely reflects a changing composition of consumption: the trend from less to more processed foods and to higher qualities.

Tobacco

For this commodity the time-series show an income elasticity of 0.7 and a price elasticity of − 0.3. The fit between model and reality is, however, not very satisfactory. As it is difficult to find a better model, and the value 0.7 of the income elasticity corresponds quite well with experiences from cross-section material, we have, with a certain doubt, accepted these time-series elasticities. A five per cent rise in the real price is assumed (Table 2).

TABLE 2 – Consumption volume and value: *tobacco*

	Millions of kronor			Volume change in per cent	% Share	
	Volume[a])		Value 1970		1960	1970
	1960	1970				
Tobacco	1 252	1 653	1 735	+ 32	3.4	3.1

[a]) 1960 prices.

Beverages

For *beer and soft drinks* a fairly strong sensitivity to temperature can be observed. Very warm summers – e.g. 1955 and 1959 – have resulted in increases of 5–6 per cent over normal consumption. After allowing for this factor we get from time-series analysis an income elasticity of 0.8, and a price elasticity of − 0.7. These values have been accepted. Real prices are predicted to fall by 15 per cent. It should be noticed that consumption of beer as well as soft drinks is, internationally speaking, quite low in Sweden.

As mentioned in section 1 the rationing of alcoholic drinks was cancelled in 1955. At the same time large price increases were introduced. The reactions of consumers to price changes have become more marked than before. A time-series analysis of *spirits and wine,* adjusted with respect to the higher price elasticity of recent years, gives an income elasticity of 1.1 and a price elasticity of − 0.8. For the period up to 1970 we have assumed a rise in the real price of twenty per cent. The main part of the growth in volume will fall on wine. The consumption of wine in 1970 will probably be almost twice as high as in 1960. The level of wine consumption in Sweden is still quite low – about four litres per inhabitant a year. The growth in the consumption of spirits will be quite moderate, from 5 to 10 per cent. It must be noted here that Swedish alcohol consumption – on international standards – is rather heavily concentrated on strong spirits.

The hot beverages: *coffee, tea, and cocoa,* are less sensitive to price and income changes than either alcoholic or soft drinks. Coffee is regarded as a 'necessary good' in Sweden, comparable to tea in England. We have here chosen 0.4 for income as well as for price elasticity. Taking into consideration the present situation in the coffee market, we have calculated a real price decrease of 20 per cent by 1970.

For beverages our calculations have given the following result (Table 3):

TABLE 3 – Consumption volume and value: *beverages*

| | Millions of kronor | | | Volume change in per cent | % Share | |
| | Volume^a) | | Value 1970 | | | |
	1960	1970			1960	1970
Beer and soft drinks	656	1 023	818	+ 56	1.7	1.4
Spirits and wine	1 633	2 155	2 585	+ 28	4.3	4.6
Coffee, tea, cocoa	669	895	716	+ 34	1.8	1.3
Total	2958	4073	4119	+ 38	7.8	7.3

^a) 1960 prices.

Housing, fuel, and light

As mentioned in the previous section, the forecast for housing stems from the supply side. On the basis of plans for construction and the capacity of the building industry, the Royal Commision for long-range planning estimated the rate of growth of housing supply during the period 1960–1965 at 5 per cent per year. This growth, however, was considered insufficient to bring about equilibrium at present market prices.

Plans for residential construction for the years after 1965 do not exist at present. As far as can be seen, however, building activity will tend to successively increase. In 1960, 70 thousand apartments were constructed; the goal for 1965 is 85 thousand, and it seems reasonable to expect a little more than 100 thousand in 1970. These figures, together with a reasonable assumption about quality improvement, imply a growth rate of 6 per cent a year in the volume of housing during the second half of the 1960's.

There is reason to expect rent control to be cancelled later in this decade. The question arises, then, as to how rent will be affected. In the light fo the present excess demand, along with the expected sharp increase in family formation and an income elasticity for housing well over unity, it seems probable that the projected growth in supply will not be sufficient to create an equilibrium at present prices. We have predicted the necessary real rent increase to be 20 per cent.

For *fuel* and *light* we have, on the basis of previous experience, calculated a rate of growth that is half as large as the growth in the consumption of housing. Real prices ought to continue to decrease; we have calculated a fall until 1970 of 15 per cent.

The final results are shown in Table 4.

TABLE 4 – Consumption volume and value: *housing, fuel and light*

	Millions of kronor			Volume change in per cent	% Share	
	Volume[a])		Value 1970			
	1960	1970			1960	1970
Housing	3700	6290	7550	+70	9.8	13.3
Fuel and light	1830	2560	2175	+40	4.9	3.8
Total	5530	8850	9725	+60	14.7	17.1

[a]) 1960 prices.

Clothing

The development of consumption in the clothing field has been largely influenced by innovations. During the 1930's and 1940's there was an extensive expansion of the ready-to-wear industry, and the assortment of goods available was widened very much, especially in men's heavier wear. In the 1940's there was a corresponding development in women's clothing. After the war new fibre materials with new qualities were introduced, strongly competitive with raditional fabrics. During the 1950's, and especially during the latter part of the decade, the most important technical progress took place in the production of knitted goods. Largely through the development of new production methods, outer jersey garments now compete successfully with traditional garments. During the latter half of the 1950's, the purchase of knitted goods increased 80 per cent. Under these circumstances it is quite obvious that income and price elasticities from time-series data must be used with the greatest care in the case of ready-to-wear and knitted goods.

The real price of *knitted goods* fell 26 per cent between 1955 and 1961. To reckon with as rapid a price fall during the future seems unrealistic. The rapid technical development in this field, however, makes a fall probable. We have calculated that the real price will have decreased 15 per cent by 1970.

Where knitted goods are concerned it seems quite obvious that the innovation process will continue and be a dominating factor in the future. However, it is only possible to guess the speed of the development. We have reckoned with an income elasticity of 1.2 – which is substantially higher than the long-term value. We also use a price elasticity of – 0.6. and a cross elasticity with respect to ready-to-wear goods of 1.0.

TABLE 5 – Consumption volume and value: *clothing*

	Millions of kronor			Volume change in per cent	% Share	
	Volume[a])		Value 1970		1960	1970
	1960	1970				
Shoes [b])	738	1050	945	+ 42	2.0	1.7
Knitted goods	763	1395	1185	+ 83	2.0	2.1
Ready-to-wear	1845	3135	2820	+ 70	4.9	5.0
Yarn, cloth, tailoring	734	822	740	+ 12	1.9	1.3
Other	463	865	780	+ 87	1.2	1.4
Total	4543	7267	6470	+ 60	12.0	11.4

[a]) 1960 prices.
[b]) Including shoe-repairs.

Doubtless the *ready-to-wear* sector still has a rather high income elasticity. The course of innovations in light ready-to-wear clothing is evidently not over. As the 'industrialization' of the 1930's, 1940's and 1950's – when uneconomic handicraft and home products were 'out-competed' by manufactured goods – now seems to have covered the entire field, the income elasticity, 1.7, obtained by time-series analysis ought to be adjusted downwards. Cross-section analysis gives an income elasticity of 1.25. We have here taken a middle course and reckoned with the value of 1.4. We have chosen a price elasticity of – 0.4 and a cross elasticity against knitted wear of 0.4. We assume a fall in the real price of 10 per cent.

For the group *yarn, cloth, and tailoring* there is nothing in the development that would indicate an income elasticity larger than 0. We must expext a fall in prices and for the whole group this is assumed to be 10 per cent. The price elasticity is assumed to be – 0.5.

For *shoes* the time-series analysis has given an income elasticity of 0.6 and a price elasticity of – 0.25. There are no special reasons to doubt these values. It has been assumed that there will be a 10 per cent fall in price.

The subgroup *remaining clothing* constitutes a small, heterogeneous group. Two of the items (furs and leather wear) are near substitutes for ready-to-wear goods, and the remaining (hats, caps and handbags) are supplements. It seems justifiable to expect a high income elasticity. A time-series analysis has given an income elasticity of 1.5 and a price elasticity of − 0.5. The real price is assumed to decrease by 10 per cent.

The results of the calculations described above are shown in Table 5.

The figures in this table imply an income elasticity for the group as a whole of about 1. An income elasticity of this magnitude is in agreement not only with earlier findings in Sweden but also with the experience of several other countries.

Durable goods

For *furniture* the time-series give an income elasticity of 1.65. There is no reason to reject this figure. The real price is assumed to remain unchanged.

For *hardware* we have accepted the results of the time-series analysis: the income elasticity is 1.2, and the elasticity with regard to marriage rate is 0.5. It is assumed that the real price will remain unchanged.

The statistical material concerning *electrical equipment* is incomplete. Complete time-series data are available for four articles only: vacuum cleaners, sewing machines, radio and television sets. For the host of other electrical equipment, washing-machines, deep freezers, mixers, razors etc., time-series data are sporadic. Further, it should be mentioned that Swedish statistics in this field are not comparable with those of most other countries. Refrigerators and washing machines (except the very small ones) are usually installed in Sweden during the construction of houses, and accordingly regarded as integral parts of the apartment. Therefore, they are not treated as separate items in consumption statistics.

Purchases of *vacuum cleaners* and *sewing machines* increased rapidly during the 1930's and 40's. There was, however, a clear sign of stagnation in this field during the 1950's. As far as we can see, the introduction period is over for both these articles, and a further growth in ownership is not to be expected. More important innovations in these two fields seem unlikely. We have, therefore, reckoned with an unchanged volume per head in the future.

By the beginning of the 1950's the introduction period of *radios* was evidently over. There was, however, an important revival in the market, when, in the latter part of the 1950's, one more programme was introduced on ultra-short wave length, which could not be listened to on old sets, and portable transistors appeared. The dynamic force of these latest innovations is not yet completely exhausted, but it is falling off. For our forecast we have calculated a small growth, 20 per cent.

At the present time, *television* can reach practically every Swedish household. The widening of the transmission net can, consequently, have only a limited effect on the future development of television ownership.

The forecast for TV is based on a calculation of the development of the number of licence holders. For this purpose the country has been divided into a number of zones according to the particular point of time at which TV reached the area. For every zone the spread in licences is assumed to follow a logistic curve, with the saturation point at a licence ownership of 80 per 100 households. By 1970 this point will probably have been reached in almost all zones. By then the number of licences should amount to 2.4 million, which would correspond to an increase of 50000 licences in 1970.

The number of new TV sets bought during any year is approximately equal to the increase in the licences plus the number of discarded sets plus the growth in the number of sets belonging to households with more than one set. The mean length of life for a television set has been estimated to be about 7 years. A calculation with regard to the age structure of sets existing in 1970 indicates that about 300000 receivers will be discarded that year. As to the growth in multiple TV-ownership we have assumed that during 1970, it will amount to 100000. The total purchase of new TV receivers should thus amount to 450000 sets by 1970.

It is assumed that the average quality of a television set will increase by 15 per cent. This is motivated by the fact, that sets allowing for a second programme which probably will appear within the decade are about 15 per cent more expensive than the sets usually bought to-day. No allowance has been made for colour TV, as it seems most unlikely that regular transmission will be performed in Sweden during the forecast period.

The purchases of *other electrical household equipment* amounted in 1960 to about 300 million crowns. This group of goods is, obviously, expanding fast. How strong the future increase will be, however, is difficult to say, but it will probably be dominated by innovations. From the experience during 1955–1961 we have reckoned with an increase in volume terms of 162% by 1970. This is, it must be admitted, not much more than a guess.

For the entire group of electrical equipments we have assumed a 25 per cent fall in real prices.

For *household textiles* (blankets, carpets, draperies, etc.) and *glass and chinaware*, time-series analysis has given income elasticities of 1.5 and 1.3. Consumption of household textiles has been found to depend on the marriage rate with an elasticity of 0.3. The price elasticity of glass and chinaware is − 1.8. Real prices are assumed to be unchanged.

TABLE 6 – Consumption volume and value: *durable consumption goods*

	Millions of kronor			Volume change in per cent	% Share	
	Volume[a])		Value 1970		1960	1970
	1960	1970				
Furniture	535	1002	1002	+ 87	1.42	1.77
Hardware	195	320	320	+ 64	0.52	0.57
Electrical equipment	1202	1853	1390	+ 54	3.18	2.46
of which:						
Vaccuum cleaners	52	55	41	+ 7	0.14	0.07
Sewing machines	114	121	91	+ 7	0.30	0.16
Radio-sets	186	223	167	+ 20	0.49	0.30
TV-sets	548	668	501	+ 22	1.45	0.89
Other electr.						
equipment	300	786	590	+162	0.80	1.04
Household textiles	663	1215	1215	+ 83	1.76	2.15
Glass and chinaware	235	324	324	+ 38	0.62	0.57
Musical instruments	62	95	95	+ 53	0.16	0.17
Watches and jewellery	279	582	582	+109	0.74	1.03
Sports goods	195	359	323	+ 84	0.52	0.57
Photographic equipment	138	270	243	+ 96	0.36	0.43
Total	3502	6020	5504	+72	9,28	9,72

[a]) 1960 prices.

The results of the time-series analysis have also been used for the two groups, *watches and jewellery* and *musical instruments*. The income elasticities are 2.0 and 1.0. It has been assumed that real prices are unchanged.

According to available data, purchases of *sports goods, travel necessities and toys* increased quite strongly during the 1930's and 40's. They have, however, failed to continue this development during the late 1950's. Long-run trends indicate, anyhow, an income elasticity of 1.6.

Photographic equipment showed a faster development in the last decade than during earlier periods. The income elasticity of 1.8 based on the development during the fifties, is assumed to be valid in the future.

A summary of the forecast for the entire durable goods group shows a continued expansion and transformation during the 1960's. The predicted volume increase of 72 per cent is, however, not especially large in relation to earlier expansion (Table 6).

Travel

In the analysis of motoring we meet three strategic variables, the stock of cars, purchases of new cars and scrappage. By definition these variables satisfy the following identity: increase in stock = purchases of new cars – scrappage. When forecasting these three variables we have, because of this identity, only two degrees of freedom. One of the variables has to be regarded as a residual. The problem then arises which should be chosen. There are different opinions about the correct answer to this question.

The most widespread view is probably as follows: consumers' demand concerns the services provided by cars and the volume of such services is approximately proportionate to the stock of cars. Therefore this latter is the primary variable in a demand analysis. As, further, the extent of the scrappage is mainly determined by technical factors in combination with the age structure of the stock, this implies that purchasing of new cars is the residual variable.

This way of looking at the problem has been severely critized on the following grounds: the buyers of new cars are to be found within a rather limited group of people and the yearly inflow of new cars into the stock is determined by the number of these people and the average time they have their cars before selling them. This implies that the inflow of new cars into the stock is determined independently of the size of the stock and also independently of scrappage. Thus the stock is the residual variable.

It seems quite obvious that this latter view is the more realistic in the *short* run; there is much empirical evidence to support it. It is also fairly realistic in the *long* run. This does not, however, contradict the view that in the long run the other theory may also be justified. We may assume that there exists an equilibrium stock of cars corresponding to every income level in the society. The size of this equilibrium stock may very well be determined by the income level, regardless of whether the inflow of new cars is determined in the way described above or not. Further, it must be remembered that there is a regulator in the mechanism; the price structure of cars of different ages. Scrappage, too, must to some extent depend on this structure.

According to the above reasoning, it should, in principle, be possible to choose either the stock or the purchases of new cars as the primary variable in an analysis. In this study we have tried both. Our procedure has been as follows:

1. *The stock approach*

Regression analysis applied to time-series has for the size of the stock given an income elasticity of about 2. The fit is, however, not very good, and the elasticity value does not seem very reliable. Attempts to calculate income elasticities from cross-section data have given results which are obviously unrealistic.

Several years ago, it was found that the car density in Sweden during the 1950's followed the US development during the 1920's, i.e. during the time when the density in US was of the same magnitude as in Sweden during the 1950's. As is seen from Table 7 this similarity has continued in a remarkable way.

During the last 8 years a number of forecasts have been made on the basis of the assumption that the similarity in the development of car density in Sweden and the US continues. It is seen from the table that these forecasts up to now have given excellent results. To use the same procedure in this study is, however, not possible, because the development in

TABLE 7

Year	Sweden	1950	1952	1954	1956	1957	1958	1959	1960	1961
	USA	1916	1918	1920	1922	1923	1924	1925	1926	1927
Number of cars per 1000 inhabitants	Sweden	36	49	74	100	117	131	146	159	174
	USA	33	54	77	97	118	135	150	164	169

the US was interrupted by the great depression in the beginning of the thirties. It would be inconsistent with the general assumptions in this paper to assume that such a depression would occur in Sweden during the sixties.

As can be seen from a graph, the growth of car density in Sweden has been almost linear during the last eight years. If we extend this trend until 1970 we get a car density of 300 per 1000 inhabitants, which corresponds to a stock of 2.4 million cars. Such a development would be consistent with an income elasticity of 2.0 i.e. the value found by regression analysis[5]). All this seems to be in favour of a preliminary forecast of a growth in the stock up to 2.4 million in 1970.

In order to estimate scrappage a survival table for cars (Table 8) has been constructed on the basis of Swedish data.

TABLE 8 – Survival probabilities for passenger cars
(per cent)

Age	Probability	Age	Probability
0	100	7	86.1
1	99.4	8	79.6
2	99.5	9	66.5
3	98.5	10	62.7
4	96.6	11	60.0
5	96.3	12	56.4
6	86.2		

A combination of the above-mentioned preliminary stock forecast and the corresponding scrappage figures, calculated on the basis of this table implies an inflow of 290 thousand new cars in 1970. Consequently, if we accept the stock forecast and the scrappage table, we must also accept the figure 290 thousand as a forecast of purchases of new cars in 1970.

2. *The flow approach*

The number of new cars bought each year has increased from 128 thousand in 1955 to 180 thousand in 1961. We must doubtless reckon with much higher figures in the future. To make an independent forecast of purchases of new cars is, however, very difficult. A number of investigations including elasticity calculations have certainly been done in the US, but the results seem to be too unreliable to use as a basis for a forecast. It is more reasonable to rely on a comparison with the United States. According to the stock forecast above, Sweden would by 1970, have reached the US car density of 1954. That year the number of purchases of new cars amounted to 34 cars per 1000 inhabitants. Applying the same figure for Sweden would yield 270 thousand purchases of new cars in 1970.

---

[5]) R. BENTZEL *et al.*, Den privata konsumtionen i Sverige 1931–1965, Stockholm 1957, pp. 304–313.

In this way we have tried to estimate the future development with two different methods. Concerning purcases of new cars in 1970 the two methods give rather similar results, 290 and 270 thousand, which seems to be an indication of their reasonableness. As a definite forecast we have chosen the former figure.

As to the purchases of new cars, we have assumed a small increase, 15 per cent, in quality. Statistically this is treated as an increase in volume. Further we have assumed an unchanged proportion between personal and business use of car services.

The expenses for petrol, oil, repairs etc. have been assumed to vary in proportion to the number of cars.

No time-series analysis has been done on the consumption of *motor cycles* and *bicycles*. During the last 5–6 years heavy motor cycles have to a great extent been replaced by cars and bicycles by light motor cycles. In according with existing trends a rise in light motor cycle purchases and a decrease in heavy motor cycle and bicycle purchases are assumed during the 1960's. Petrol, repair and maintenance are assumed to be proportional to the forecast stock of cycles.

With regard to *recreational boating* no reliable data about sales, maintenance and fuel costs are available; the amount of 200 million Sw. kr. in 1960 is only a very rough measure of expenditure. For 1970 we have forecast an expenditure of 500 million Sw. kr. The real price has been assumed to remain unchanged.

We have accepted the results of time-series analysis for consumption of *public transport services* (excluding air travel). Besides an income elasticity of 1.9 it has been found that demand for public transport services varies in proportion to the factor $10^{-0.00174x}$, where x is passenger car density[6]).

During the late 1950's, there was a rapid growth of *air travel* and in 1960 total expenditures amounted to 60 million Sw. kr., divided between domestic regular lines (12 million Sw. kr.) and charter traffic (48 million Sw. kr.). Owing to lack of data, this amount, however, does not include international traffic on regular lines. The resulting underestimation is probably not too serious, as international air travel is mostly business travel.

Air travel will doubtless be among the most expanding items during the 1960's. In this case, the introductory process itself will probably be a

---

[6]) R. BENTZEL, Den privata konsumtionen i Sverige 1931–1965, Stockholm 1957, pp. 314.

TABLE 9 – Consumption volume and value: *travel*

	Millions of kronor			Volume change in per cent	% Share	
	Volume[a])		Value 1970		1960	1970
	1960	1970				
Transport equipment	3 442	6 878	6 266	+100	9.1	11.1
New purchases	1 457	2 867	2 436	+ 97	3.9	4.3
Passenger cars	1 281	2 674	2 272	+109	3.4	4.0
Motor cycles	83	114	97	+ 37	0.2	0.2
Cycles	93	79	67	+ 15	0.3	0.1
Petrol, maintenance	1 785	3 511	3 330	+ 97	4.7	5.9
Passenger cars	1 664	3 426	3 250	+106	4.4	5.7
Motor cycles	121	85	80	− 30	0.3	0.1
Recreation boats[b])	200	500	500	+150	0.5	0.9
Public transport	1 345	1 764	1 676	+ 30	3.6	2.9
of which:						
Air travel	60	350	246	+480	0.2	0.5
Total	4 787	8 642	7 942	+ 81	12.7	14.0

[a]) 1960 prices.
[b]) Including new purchases and petrol, maintenance.

more important determinant of the development than price and income changes. Accordingly, we have not used the traditional income-price model for the forecast.

The development pattern for domestic air travel in Sweden is similar to the US development, with a lag of a little less than twenty years: while the number of passenger kilometres per inhabitant in the US rose from 2.3 in 1933 to 19.6 in 1943, Sweden experienced the same development 17 years later (from 2.4 in 1950 to 20.7 in 1960). The expansion in the United States continued with undiminished speed up to 1953. The application of the same rate of growth to the Swedish development during the 1960's results in an expenditure of 120 million Sw. kr. in 1970. We have accepted this forecast.

Charter flights to Southern Europe have already become very popular in Sweden. Accordingly, foreign air travel cannot be expected to grow as much as domestic travel. The expenditure forecast in 1970 for charter flights abroad – five times the amount in 1960 – is to be regarded as a mere guess.

The total expenditure for air travel is put at 350 million Sw. kr. in 1970 (in prices of 1960). In accordance with recent experience, the real price is assumed to decline by 30 per cent (Table 9).

Health

In 1960 total expenditures on sickness and health services amounted to about 2700 million Sw. kr. Of this sum, consumers paid about 40 per cent directly and another 20 per cent in the form of contributions to the compulsory insurance. In the calculations we have included only the former of these two items. The contributions to the compulsory insurance have been regarded as taxes.

TABLE 10 – Consumption volume and value: *health care*

	Millions of kronor			Volume change in per cent	% Share	
	Volume[a])		Value 1970		1960	1970
	1960	1970				
Health care	1173	2050	2460	+75	3.1	4.4

a) 1960 prices.

The total expenditure in this group consists of costs for medicine, eyeglasses, doctors' fees, dentists' fees and hospital fees. The first two items are forecast on the basis of time-series analysis. The forecasts of the fees to doctors, dentists and hospitals are, however, as was said in section 3, calculated from the supply side. We have used the current plans for the future development of the Swedish sick and health care where data concerning the planned number of doctors, nurses, hospital places etc. are given for 1970.

For the whole group, our forecast gives an increase in total expenditure of 75 per cent. As this group consists mainly of services, we must expect that the real price – disregarding subsidies – will rise. In fact, we have assumed a price rise of 20 per cent (Table 10).

Other goods and services

This group is very heterogeneous. It includes restaurant services, different kind of household services (domestic services, laundry, telephone, telegraph, radio- and television licences and postage fees), some cultural and recreational items, hairdressing, funeral costs and toilet requisites. As the group is a residual, all forms of consumption not treated in the previous sections should be included here. Unfortunately, this has not been possible, as there are consumption items which enter neither in this residual group nor elsewhere. Among these are banking, insurance and education services.

The time-series analysis for *hotel and restaurant services* has given an income elasticity of 1.6 and a price elasticity of − 1.9. These figures have

TABLE 11 – Consumption volume and value: *other goods and services*

| | Millions of kronor | | | Volume change in per cent | % Share | |
| | Volume[a]) | | Value 1970 | | | |
	1960	1970			1960	1970
Hotel and restaurant services	640	783	980	+ 23	1.7	1.7
Household services [b])	998	1433	1429	+ 44	2.6	2.5
Household and toilet requisites	641	1055	900	+ 65	1.7	1.6
Recreation	1724	2637	2900	+ 53	4.6	5.1
Hairdressing	270	270	325	± 0	0.7	0.6
Undertaking	73	85	97	+ 20	0.2	0.2
Total	4346	6263	6631	+ 44	11.5	11.7

[a]) 1960 prices.
[b]) Including domestic services, laundry services, telecommunications, radio and TV licenses.

been accepted for the forecast. The real price is assumed to increase by 25 per cent.

During the 1950's *telephone* calls increased by 75 per cent. The number of telephones per 1000 inhabitants is now very large in Sweden, so we cannot expect the same rapid expansion in the future. As to the number of calls we have reckoned with a growth of 60 per cent. Outlays for *radio* licences are assumed to increase only slightly more than population. The forecast for *television* licences has been described above.

Laundry services are assumed to increase by 10 per cent in accordance with earlier trends, while the demand for *domestic services* will continue to decrease; this decades, however, not as fast as in the fifties. The real price probably will be some 30% higher 1970.

Recreation includes books, newspapers, magazines, admissions to cinemas, theatres and sporting events, photo services, flowers and legal

gambling. This group was expanding fast up to 1957. Since the introduction of TV, however, the situation has changed, and during the last years
consumption has been declining. The main problem for the forecast is
therefore to project the future impact of TV on expenditures for recreation. We believe that the importance of TV in this respect is already
on the decline. Therefore, we have assumed that in the very near
future recreation expenditures will resume the earlier (pre-TV) rate of
growth.

Hairdressing and *funeral services* are rather unimportant items. Hairdressing has been assumed to remain unchanged and funeral services to
develop in accordance with the projected number of deaths. Real prices
are assumed to increase by 30 per cent.

For *household and toilet requisites,* time-series analysis has given an
income elasticity of 0.8 and a price elasticity of − 0.9. The real price is
assumed to decrease by 10 per cent (Table 11).

There is little doubt that expenditure on tourism abroad will be one of
the fastest expanding items in the household budget during the 1960's.
This does not, however, appear in the table as there is no reliable statistical material about it. Although it is known that expenditure on tourism
abroad amounts to about 600 million crowns and this is about the same
as expenditure by foreign tourists in Sweden, there is no evidence as to
how these sums are distributed among different kinds of goods and services. In this study, therefore, we have ignored tourism abroad.

5. SUMMARY

Broadly speaking, the forecasts described in the previous section indicate
that consumption in Sweden will continue the trends of the last three
decades. Thus a further shift in spending away from necessities to more
luxurious items can be expected, mainly from food to durables and motoring. A continued stagnation or decrease in the use of many personal
services seems probable, while the desire to lighten housework will bring a
large increase in demand for household equipment and will still further
reduce spending on such items as flour and cloth in favour of the finished
articles, bread and ready-made clothing. Moreover, at the same time a
lot of new consumer goods will appear.

After classification according to the categories proposed by the editor
of this volume, the forecasts are summarized in Table 12.

A few features of the table require comment.

Since purchases of durables have risen much faster than total consumption during the last three decades, and especially in the 1950's, it
may seem surprising that the rise forecast for this decade is no more than
72 per cent. But it must be borne in mind that television only started in

TABLE 12 – Private consumption 1960 and 1970

	Millions of kronor			Volume change in per cent	% Share	
	Volume[a])		Value 1970		1960	1970
	1960	1970				
Flour, bread etc.	1433	1663	1815	+ 16	3.8	3.2
Milk and fats	2269	2360	2590	+ 4	6.0	4.6
Meat, fish, eggs	3183	3969	4197	+ 25	8.4	7.4
Potatoes, vegetables, fruits	1662	2305	2075	+ 39	4.4	3.7
Sugar, chocolate, spices	1093	1485	1337	+ 35	2.9	2.4
Tobacco	1252	1653	1735	+ 32	3.4	3.1
Beverages	2958	4073	4119	+ 38	7.8	7.3
Housing	3700	6290	7550	+ 70	9.8	13.3
Fuel and light	1830	2560	2175	+ 40	4.9	3.8
Clothing	4543	7267	6470	+ 60	12.0	11.4
Durable goods	3502	6020	5504	+ 72	9.3	9.7
Public transport	1345	1764	1676	+ 30	3.6	2.9
Transport equipment, purchases	1657	3367	2936	+ 103	4.4	5.2
Transport equipment, maintenance, petrol	1785	3511	3330	+ 97	4.7	5.9
Health care	1173	2050	2460	+ 75	3.1	4.4
Other goods and services	4346	6263	6631	+ 43	11.5	11.7
Total	37731	56600	56600	+ 50	100.0	100.0

[a]) 1960 prices.

Sweden in 1956 and the consequent rush to buy TV sets gave a somewhat
artificial boost to the growth in purchases of durable goods as a whole.
With TV purchases in 1960 at a peak, expenditure on durables was ex-
ceptionally high that year; compared with this high level, therefore, the
increase forecast by 1970 is comparatively moderate.

Despite the rapid expansion of private motoring in the 1950's and the
consequent stability in public transport services, it is predicted that the
latter will increase as much as 30 per cent over this decade, mainly because of a rapid growth in air travel.

The relatively high forecasts for housing and health services reflect the present shortage. They are based on the assumptions that the excess demand for housing will be met by a combination of a high activity in residential construction and an abandonment of rent control; and that the sickness and health services will be built up rapidly. The large increase in the proportion of total expenditure devoted to housing reflects not only better housing conditions, but also the opinion that rents must rise if there is to be equilibrium in the housing market with the stock of houses predicted in 1970.

CHAPTER 8

DEMAND ANALYSIS AND PROJECTIONS
FOR BRITAIN: 1900–1970

A Study in Method

BY

RICHARD STONE and ALAN BROWN

Department of Applied Economics, Cambridge

AND

D. A. ROWE

National Institute of Economic and Social Research, London, England

1. INTRODUCTION

The main purpose of this paper is to analyse the composition of British private consumption in 1970 on different assumptions about the state of the economy at that date. Although a great many calculations are given in this paper the whole picture is still far from complete; for this reason we have entitled the paper 'a study in method'.

Our work at present is based entirely on the analysis of time series; its main ingredients can be outlined as follows.

(1) We possess annual estimates of consumers' expenditure per head of the population, divided into thirty categories, and the corresponding price index-numbers from the beginning of this century. For the purpose of this paper we have grouped these categories into eight main classes. The sources of this information are set out in section 2.

(2) We use a model which enables a complete set of demand equations to be analysed simultaneously. In this model each class of expenditure is a homogeneous linear function of total expenditure and of the price index of each of the classes. The parameters of this system are not constants but linear functions of time. Thus each demand not only depends on total expenditure and the price structure but does so in a way which gradually changes over time. These changes can be extrapolated to yield a system

of demand equations for 1970 and the projections are based on these extrapolated coefficients. Thus shifts associated with changes in tastes and new commodities form an integral part of the model. Various forms of the model are described in section 3.

(3) We use a two-stage iterative computing program to estimate the parameters in the model. We stop the calculations when the change made by the latest cycle to the values of a particular set of parameters is, in some sense, small. Experience shows that convergence is difficult to achieve and depends, in part at least, on adopting a suitable set of starting values. Since there appears to be very little mathematical theory of convergent processes except in the simple case of two variables, there is evidently ground here for mathematical exploration. The computing sequence is described in section 4.

(4) The combination of (1), (2) and (3) gives us a consistent system of quantitative demand equations and the next thing to do is to see how well they describe the past. This is done in section 5 which also contains some comments on the changing pattern of demand which emerges from the analysis.

(5) When we come to 1970, the combination of (1), (2) and (3) gives a 'current' set of demand equations. We also need a 'current' set of determining variables: total expenditure per head and a price vector for the commodity groups analysed. The demand system forms part of a more general model of economic growth which starts by assuming, among other things, a level of expenditure per head in 1970 and calculates, among other things, a set of relative prices. At the moment, this particular part of the model has not been set up and so the estimates for 1970 have been made to depend on an extrapolation of past relative prices and on a level of total expenditure which is an assumed level and has not even the status of a target. The projections that we can make at present for 1970 are described in section 6.

As can be seen, the paper is a report of work in progress. It ends with some conclusions to be drawn from this work and a list of works cited.

We should like to express our thanks to Dr. L. J. Slater and to Gilbert Warren, of the Department of Applied Economics, who have been responsible for programming and for executing the calculations described in this paper.

2. THE SOURCES OF INFORMATION

The data on prices, quantities and expenditures used in this paper are based on four main sources depending on the period covered: for 1900 to 1919, the work of PREST and ADAMS [6]; for 1920 to 1938, the work of STONE, ROWE and others [12, 13]; for 1939 to 1945, the official publication [14]; and for 1946 to 1960, the official Blue Books on national income and expenditure [15]. The first two of these sources belong to a series which has as its purpose the carrying back of the Blue Book picture of the British economy to the beginning of this century. As we work backwards, the available information becomes, on the whole, less complete and less reliable. We have however succeeded in building up reasonably comparable series for thirty categories of expenditure which for the purpose of the present paper we have grouped into eight main classes. These categories and classes are set out in the Appendix.

In order to obtain series of expenditure at constant prices we have constructed index-numbers with 1938 as a base. We are now moving over to a postwar base, but the calculations with this new material will not be ready for some time.

3. THE MODEL

The linear expenditure system, which is the basic form of the model used here, has already been described on a number of occasions [3, 8, 10, 11] but a little must be said about it here if this paper is to be reasonably self-contained. In matrix form, the system of equations can be written as

$$\hat{p}e = b\mu + (I - bi')\hat{c}p$$

$$= \hat{p}c + b(\mu - p'c) \tag{3.1}$$

In (3.1): p denotes the price vector of the commodities or groups of commodities we are studying and $\hat{p}$ denotes a diagonal matrix formed from p; e denotes a vector of the quantities bought and so $\hat{p}e$ denotes a vector of expenditures; μ denotes total expenditure and so $\mu \equiv p'e$, where the prime denotes transposition; I and i denote respectively the unit matrix and the unit vector; and b and c denote vectors of parameters restricted by the fact that $i'b \equiv 1$.

From the first row of (3.1) we see that each element of $\hat{p}e$, that is each expenditure, is a linear function of total expenditure μ and of each of the prices, the elements of p. This system of equations is free from money illusion and is additive. The particular form of the matrix $(I - bi')\hat{c}$ which multiplies the price vector p is dictated by the fact that a plausible way to keep the number of parameters small is to impose on the system the Slutsky condition, that is the condition that the matrix of elasticities of substitution be symmetric. With n commodity classes and these restrictions there are only $2n - 1$ independent parameters to be estimated.

From the second row of (3.1) we can give a simple interpretation of the consumers' behaviour which the model represents. The total expenditure on a commodity class, an element of $\hat{p}e$, is made up of two parts. First, the average consumer buys a fixed quantity, an element of c, at whatever prices happen to be ruling, and the total cost of these purchases is $p'c$ which we call committed expenditure. Second, the average consumer looks to see how much money he has left and distributes this over the commodity classes in proportion to the elements of b, which sum to 1. The amount of money left over after committed expenditures have been paid for, $\mu - p'c$, we call supernumerary income.

We shall now summarize a number of properties of the model, some of which are advantageous, others restrictive.

(i) As has been shown by SAMUELSON [7] and GEARY [4] the preference field (or utility function), v say, is given by

$$\log v = b'[\log (e - c)] \tag{3.2}$$

or by any monotonic transformation of this expression. Thus the utility level can be calculated for any given set of purchases but the discovery that $v_1 > v_0$ could only tell us that the utility level in period 1 was greater than the utility level of period 0; it could not tell us by how much it was greater.

(ii) As has been shown by KLEIN and RUBIN [5] the system enables a constant-utility index-number of the cost of living to be constructed. This index is measured by the ratio μ_1^*/μ_0 where

$$\mu_1^* = p_1'c + (\mu_0 - p_0'c)\pi_b. \tag{3.3}$$

In (3.3) π_b denotes a geometric index of the price ratios (period 1 divided by period 0) with the elements of b as weights. Thus the minimum amount of money needed in period 1 to enable the average consumer to remain on the same indifference surface as in period 0 is equal to committed expenditure at the prices of period 1 plus the supernumerary income of period 0 changed by a geometric index of the price ratios.

(iii) The system can only describe a world of substitutes from which complementary and inferior classes of commodity are excluded. This can be seen by deriving the elasticity of substitution, s_{jk} say, between commodities j and k. This elasticity takes the form

$$s_{jk} = \frac{(b_j - \delta_{jk})b_k\mu}{p_j e_j p_k e_k}\ (\mu - p'c) \tag{3.4}$$

where $\delta_{jk} = 1$ if $j = k$ and is zero in other cases. Assuming that supernumerary income is positive, the fact that all own-elasticities s_{jj} must in theory be negative means that $0 < b_j < 1$. This rules out inferior goods. In this case $b_j b_k$ is necessarily positive and so all s_{jk}, $j \neq k$, must be positive. This rules out complementary goods.

(iv) The Engel curves of the system, that is the relationships between e_j and μ for fixed p, are linear. The slope of the line is b_j/p_j and so varies with p_j; the intercept is $c_j - b_j(p'c)/p_j$.

(v) The ordinary price-quantity demand curves of the system, that is the relationships between e_j and p_j for fixed μ and for fixed values of the remaining elements of p, are hyperbolae. With positive c_j they cannot be elastic.

(vi) The price-quantity demand curves calculated on the assumption that real income is held constant can be derived as follows. Writing p_{j1} for the price of commodity j in period 1, suppose $p_{j1} = p_{j0}$ for $j = 2, 3, ..., n$. Then (3.3) implies that

$$\mu_1^* = p_1'c + (\mu_0 - p_0'c)\,(p_{11}/p_{10})^{b_1}. \tag{3.5}$$

From (3.1) it follows that in this case

$$e_{11} = (1 - b_1)c_1 + b_1(\mu_1^* - \sum_{j=2}^{n} p_{j1}c_j)/p_{11}. \tag{3.6}$$

If a substitution is made for μ_1^* from (3.5) into (3.6), it follows that

$$e_{11} = c_1 + b_1(\mu_0 - p_0'c)/p_{10}^{b_1}p_{11}^{(1-b_1)} \tag{3.7}$$

which gives e_{11} as a function of p_{11} when real income is held constant.

The model which has just been described can be generalised so as to remove two fairly obvious defects. In the first place, the vectors b and c are constant and this implies that the average consumer never changes the quantities he feels committed to buying and never changes the way he allocates his expenditure out of supernumerary income. But, as the standard of living rises, one would expect committed quantities to rise and allocations to change. We can allow for these possibilities by making b and c depend on any variables which take preassigned values and, as was indicated in [8, 9], this change in the model will not destroy its basic properties. In this paper we shall make use only of the simplest possibility, namely that b and c are linear functions of time, Thus at time θ, $\theta = 1$, $2, \ldots, t$,

$$b_\theta = b^* + b^{**}\theta \tag{3.8}$$

and

$$c_\theta = c^* + c^{**}\theta. \tag{3.9}$$

With this generalisation, it is necessary that $i'b^* \equiv 1$ and $i'b^{**} \equiv 0$ and so in place of the original $2n - 1$ independent parameters we now have $2(2n - 1)$.

In the second place, the model implies that adjustments are instantaneous: if total expenditure changes, the components immediately assume new equilibrium values. But in many cases one would expect that adjustment would take time because, for example, the average consumer may be faced with a financing problem in the case of such durable goods as cars, washing machines and television sets, or he may at first not know what to think of a new product that is put on the market and so take some time to make up his mind about it. A dynamic form of the model which takes account of such considerations is described in [3, 10, 11]. We shall not discuss it here because, while dynamic adjustments are certainly important, we shall ignore them in this paper and concentrate on the kind of changes that can be reflected in the changing parameters described in the preceding paragraph.

4. THE COMPUTING SEQUENCE

An important feature of the models that have just been described is that we can estimate the parameters in them by reasonably plausible and efficient methods. In doing so we have ignored the complication of supply equations and adopted an iterative two-stage method based on the assumption that we are justified in minimizing the sum of the disturbances in each equation at each period of time. This assumption enables us to use the method of least squares with the usual scalar variance matrix for the disturbances. This is not ideal partly because the commodity groups vary greatly in size and partly because the expenditures at current prices on these commodity groups vary greatly over time. One might expect our method to give better results for large commodity groups and for recent years, in which prices have been much higher, than for small groups and for the early part of the century. To some extent this seems to be true; that the effect is not more marked is perhaps an indication that the use of a scalar variance matrix is not a serious source of error.

For the static model, with systematically varying parameters as in (3.8) and (3.9), the method is as follows. We begin by guessing values of b^* and b^{**}, which we shall denote by b_0^* and b_0^{**}. We then form a vector, y_θ say, of type $n \times 1$ as follows

$$y_\theta \equiv \hat{p}_\theta e_\theta - (b_0^* + \theta b_0^{**})\mu_\theta. \tag{4.1}$$

We also form a matrix, Y_θ, say, of order n, where

$$Y_\theta = [I - (b_0^* + \theta b_0^{**})i']\hat{p}_\theta. \tag{4.2}$$

Apart from a random element, y_θ and Y_θ are connected by the relationship

$$y_\theta = [Y_\theta \vdots \theta Y_\theta]\begin{bmatrix} c^* \\ \hline c^{**} \end{bmatrix}. \tag{4.3}$$

If we now define

$$y \equiv \{y_1, y_2, \ldots, y_t\} \tag{4.4}$$

and

$$Y \equiv \{Y_1, Y_2, \ldots, Y_t\} \tag{4.5}$$

we can write, apart from a random element,

$$y = Xg \tag{4.6}$$

where $X \equiv [Y \vdots \theta Y]$ and $g \equiv \{c^* \vdots c^{**}\}$. The least-squares estimator, g_1, of g is

$$g_1 = (X'X)^{-1}X'y. \tag{4.7}$$

Given g_1, we can form a vector, w_θ say, of type $n \times 1$, where

$$w_\theta \equiv \hat{p}_\theta[e_\theta - (c_1^* + \theta c_1^{**})] \tag{4.8}$$

and a matrix, W_θ say, of order n, where

$$W_\theta \equiv [\mu_\theta - p_\theta'(c_1^* + \theta c_1^{**})]I. \tag{4.9}$$

Apart from a random element, w_θ and W_θ are connected by the relationship

$$w_\theta = [W_\theta \vdots \theta W_\theta] \begin{bmatrix} b^* \\ \hline b^{**} \end{bmatrix}. \tag{4.10}$$

If we now define

$$w \equiv \{w_1, w_2, ..., w_t\} \tag{4.11}$$

and

$$W \equiv \{W_1, W_2, ..., W_t\} \tag{4.12}$$

we can write apart from a random element,

$$w = Zh \tag{4.13}$$

where $Z \equiv [W \vdots \theta W]$ and $h \equiv \{b^* \vdots b^{**}\}$. The least-squares estimator, h_1, of h is

$$h_1 = (Z'Z)^{-1}Z'w.$$

Given h_1 we can return to (4.3), replace b_0^* and b_0^{**} by b_1^* and b_1^{**} and calculate the next approximation $g_2 \equiv \{c_2^* \vdots c_2^{**}\}$ to g. If we continue in this way until the estimates cease to change, we shall have reached a solution.

We can see from (4.9) that W_θ is a scalar matrix and so, in estimating h, the system of equations breaks down into a set of single equations. From (4.2) we can see that Y_θ is not a scalar matrix and so in estimating g we are in effect obtaining average values derived from all the equations. From (3.1) we can see that $b\mu$ appears as a separate term on the right-hand side and so, since $p'e \equiv \mu$, it follows from the adding-up theorem that the constraint $i'b = 1$ is automatically satisfied by least-squares estimates. This result carries through when b is replaced by the more complicated form in (3.8).

As can be readily imagined it is not easy to obtain complete convergence in a case like this nor even to be certain that a unique limit of convergence exists independently of the initial values b_0^* and b_0^{**}. In the apparent absence of a mathematical theory of such convergent processes, we have stopped our calculations when the sum of the absolute values of the changes of the elements of c from one cycle to another falls below the level of one part in ten thousand. In the present case this required twelve cycles and the same number of minutes on the computer EDSAC 2 which, on this program, operates at the relatively slow speed of about one million multiplications a minute. These figures give some idea of the size of the computing task needed to yield the thirty independent parameters set out in the following section.

Even with a computer as powerful as EDSAC 2, there is a limit to the number of commodity groups that can be analysed simultaneously: at present this limit is ten, though we shall soon be able to increase it substantially. If therefore total expenditure is divided into a larger number of groups a different method is needed. Such a method can be based on the fact that the model is decomposable so that the constituent elements of main groups can be analysed separately and then put together to form a consistent system. We shall not describe this method here because we are not going to use it in this paper, but it can be found in section 3 of chapter V of [3].

The dynamic model with unchanging coefficients contains $3n - 1$ independent parameters because it contains a vector of adjustment rates as well as b and c. These parameters can be estimated by a modification of the method outlined above. The only complication is that the adding-up theorem no longer assures that least-squares estimates will automatically provide the identity $i'b \equiv 1$; accordingly we must introduce an undetermined multiplier and fit the equations subject to this constraint.

5. AN APPLICATION OF THE MODEL

The application discussed in this section relates to the eight commodity groups set out in the Appendix. The period covered is 1900 to 1960 and, in estimating the parameters, the years 1914 through 1919 and 1940 through 1947 were left out because of the abnormal conditions of war periods. We thus have $n(t - 14) = 376$ observations from which to determine $2(2n - 1) = 30$ independent parameters.

If we let θ range from -60 to 0 so that $\theta = 0$ in 1960, the estimates of the parameters are as shown in table 1.

In this table the elements of b^* and c^* relate to 1960 and all are subject to fairly considerable trends: those shown in the column b^{**} are equally divided between positive and negative; while those shown in the column c^{**} are all positive. Thus, for example, the proportion of supernumerary income spent on food fell at the rate of 0.39 per cent each year until in 1960 it was as low as 8.05 per cent. At the same time committed purchases per head of food measured in 1938 prices rose each year by £ 0.332 until in 1960 they reached £ 33.73. In 1960 supernumerary income was £ 38.32 per head and committed expenditure on food at 1960 prices was £ 93.1

TABLE 1 – Parameters for eight consumption groups, 1900–1960

	b^*	b^{**}	c^*	c^{**}
1. Food	0.0805	− 0.0039	33.73	0.332
2. Clothing	0.1569	0.0021	9.26	0.043
3. Household	0.2263	0.0021	24.59	0.154
4. Communications	0.0023	− 0.0004	1.13	0.026
5. Transport	0.2342	0.0016	8.97	0.165
6. Drink and tobacco	0.0956	− 0.0019	10.20	0.058
7. Entertainment	− 0.0143	− 0.0008	5.05	0.075
8. Other	0.2186	0.0012	9.99	0.064
Total	1.0001	0.0000	102.92	0.917

per head. Thus, according to the model, food expenditure per head in 1960 should have been £ [93.1 + (38.32 × 0.0805)] = 96.2 compared with the observed value of £ 95.8. In this case the error is rather less than one half of one per cent.

The performance of the model over the sixty-one years is shown in the diagram. For comparative purposes the different series are drawn on a common logarithmic scale, though it must be remembered that the model is a linear one and that it is the sum of the absolute discrepancies that is being minimised. The general impression is that on the whole the fit is reasonably good. The postwar years appear to come out particularly well, but this is due to the use of a logarithmic scale. Let us now look at the series one by one.

Food. This is the largest commodity group and the fit is good throughout. Although the two war periods were left out in estimating the parameters, the series shown in the diagram (pp. 212–213) include all the years. The effect of food rationing in the second war in holding expenditure below the level given by the model is clearly shown. This is not, of course, the whole effect of rationing since μ represents total expenditure, not disposable income.

Clothing. In this case the fit is also good, though not quite as good as for food. In particular, through the 1950's the model reproduces the trend of the observations well but does not fully reproduce their sinuosities.

Household. Here it seems just possible to detect some systematic errors due to the assumption of trends in the parameters which are common to all periods. Before the first war these trends seem slightly too strong and in the interwar period they seem not quite strong enough. But on the whole the discrepancies are small and in the 1950's the fit is distinctly good.

Communications. This is a very small group which rises particularly rapidly. The fit is good, however, in the 1950's.

Transport. This is a heterogeneous series made up of public and private transport of all kinds and includes expenditure on private vehicles. Here the use of a common trend in all periods has well-marked bad effects: what is required is an accelerating trend. This is not surprising because the series is dominated by the rise of the motorcar. In the 1900's cars were a novelty, during the interwar period they became generally accepted by the middle classes and since the last war they have begun to appeal to a mass market. A revised program which allows the trends to be parabolic rather than linear would probably remove most of the systematic discrepancies in the earlier part of the period. It would not however enable the halt in 1956 to be reproduced but that could hardly be expected since it was due to the effects of the Suez crisis, a specific event that cannot be reflected in a general model.

Drink and tobacco. Although the fit is good in the 1900's and the 1950's, the course of expenditure in the years between the wars is badly reproduced. It is not very easy to see why this should be so since the analysis for the interwar years alone given in [13] was reasonably successful. In the war periods we can see the opposite of a rationing effect, namely expenditure well in excess of the level given by the model.

Entertainment. This is a small and heterogeneous group which is made up of expenditure on public entertainment, reading matter and sports and travel goods. As with transport, there seems to be a case here for an accelerating trend.

Other. Here there seems to be a case for a decelerating trend or, at least, for smaller trends in the 1900's and in the 1920's and 30's than in the postwar period.

Our conclusion from this survey of the individual series is that the model is usable for projections to 1970 but could be significantly improved by introducing parabolic in place of linear trends.

Another way to assess the model is to examine some of its implications for consumers' behaviour over the last six decades. Let us look at two examples.

First, it is well-known that the proportion of total expenditure devoted to food has remained remarkably constant over the last half century and that at the same time budget studies show total expenditure elasticities for

TABLE 2 – Total expenditure elasticities for food

	$b_{j\theta}$	$\dfrac{p_{j\theta}\, e_{j\theta}}{\mu_\theta}$	Elasticities from	
			Model	Budgets
1900	0.314	0.327	0.96	—
1938	0.166	0.292	0.57	0.59
1955	0.100	0.343	0.29	0.30
1960	0.080	0.309	0.26	0.25

food which tend to fall through time. This appears paradoxical but it follows from the model provided that the element of b for food has a negative trend. In fact it has, and furthermore the elasticities derived from the model at different times are in close agreement with those obtained from budget studies.

The elasticity at time θ of expenditure on commodity j with respect to total expenditure is, from (3.1):

$$\frac{\partial (p_{j\theta} e_{j\theta})}{\partial \mu_\theta} \cdot \frac{\mu_\theta}{p_{j\theta} e_{j\theta}} = \frac{b_{j\theta}\mu_\theta}{p_{j\theta} e_{j\theta}} = \frac{\partial e_{j\theta}}{\partial \mu_\theta} \cdot \frac{\mu_\theta}{e_{j\theta}}. \tag{5.1}$$

From the first row of (5.1) we see that his elasticity is equal to the proportion of supernumerary income spent on j at time θ divided by the proportion of total expenditure devoted to j at time θ, and from the second row we see that the expenditure elasticity is equal to the corresponding quantity elasticity. The value of this elasticity at selected dates is shown in Table 2 together with similar estimates derived from budgets.

The similarity of the figures in the last two columns is striking and, further, the information derived from budgets taken in the early years of the century suggests an elasticity of about one. The same budget estimates for 1938, reached by different methods, can be found in [1, 13]. The budget estimates for 1955 and 1960 are taken from [16]. The latter are strictly *income* elasticities and are restricted to total food consumed at home. For both these reasons they are probably a little on the low side but, as the compilers note, they are in themselves probably a little on the high side because 'the tendency to understate incomes, common to all budget surveys, is relatively greater among households with higher incomes'. Accordingly, we have not attempted any adjustment of the published figures.

A falling income elasticity can be given an interesting interpretation in the light of the log-normal-integral Engel curves developed in [1, 2].

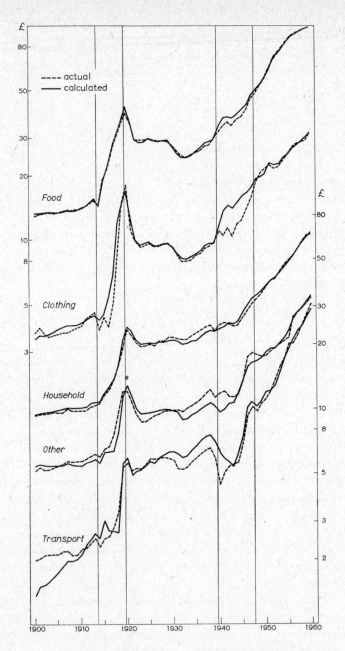

FIG. 1. Expenditure per head in Britain at current prices.

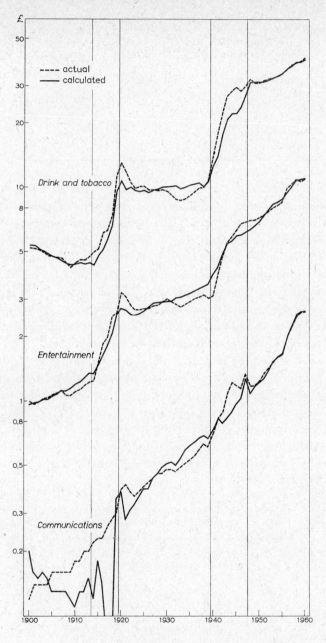

FIG. 1

TABLE 3 – Food saturation in £ 1938 per head

	Observed food expenditure	Per cent of saturation	Implied saturation
1900	21.3	0.39	54.7
1913	21.7	0.51	42.6
1924	23.9	0.59	40.5
1938	27.4	0.65	42.2
1950	31.5	0.78	40.7
1960	34.7	0.86	40.4

These Engel curves imply a relationship between the elasticity and the saturation level so that if we know the actual level of expenditure at constant prices associated with a given elasticity we can calculate the corresponding saturation level. This is done for selected years in Table 3.

The implication of this table is that in the early years of this century the level of food consumption aimed at by the average consumer fell by about 20 per cent and after that remained practically constant. From a casual knowledge of the history of food habits a fall in the saturation level between the nineteenth and twentieth centuries seems plausible and so does a constancy of the saturation level over the last generation.

We conclude that the success of the comparison of food elasticities, and the general attitude to food implied, provide additional reasons for accepting the model in spite of the limitations to which we drew attention in section 3 above.

The second implication, which we shall now discuss, is less conclusive though equally interesting. It concerns the history of committed expenditure in relation to total expenditure. This relationship is set out for selected years in Table 4.

TABLE 4 – Committed expenditure in relation to total expenditure (£ current per head and ratios)

	Committed expenditure	Total expenditure	Ratio
1900	23.9	39.5	0.61
1913	35.7	45.1	0.79
1924	76.9	85.6	0.90
1938	82.8	93.8	0.88
1950	179.2	182.2	0.98
1960	271.9	310.2	0.88

This Table shows that at all dates the proportion of expenditure committed has been higher than 50 per cent and that in the last generation it has normally been as high as 85 to 90 per cent. During war time it has usually risen to, and even above, 100 per cent only to fall again as more normal conditions return. Its very high level since the 1920's implies that for the broad groups of commodities considered here, the pattern of purchases is dominated by the gradual increases in committed purchases which reflect a basic standard of living that has been achieved and is not lightly to be given up. This picture of the consumer, hemmed in by his aspirations and achievements, and incapable of altering his consumption pattern radically in response to price movements seems to us very convincing, especially in a world which exploits far more than it used to the persuasive powers of advertising and the financing easements of hire purchase.

So, again, this implication of the model seems to us to tell in its favour, though such a conclusion is bound to be highly speculative in the present state of knowledge. It is, of course, a conclusion that relates to broad groups of consumption and not to its fine structure. If we wanted to include different brands of orange juice as separate commodities, we should have to modify the model. In fact, as was pointed out in [8], it is possible to replace $\hat{c}$ by $\hat{p}D$ where D is a symmetric matrix; but for our purposes we did not think it necessary to consider this generalization.

6. DEMAND PROJECTIONS FOR 1970

We shall now show how the model can be used to make demand projections for 1970. The five steps involved are as follows.

(i) We calculate b_θ and c_θ for $\theta = 10$.

(ii) We calculate p_θ for $\theta = 10$. As we explained in the introduction, the general model of which this demand system forms a part enables us to calculate future shadow prices. This part of the model is not yet working and so, for the purpose of this paper, we have estimated the price vector in 1970, p_{10}, from exponential trends fitted to the eleven years 1950 through 1960.

(iii) We calculate μ^* from

$$\mu^*_{10} = p'_{10}c_{10} + (\mu_0 - p'_0c_{10})\,\pi_{10\,b_{10}}/\pi_{0\,b_{10}}. \qquad (6.1)$$

Equation (6.1) is the same as (3.3) with μ and p equal to their 1960 values and b and c equal to their 1970 values. The amount of money

μ_{10}^{*} is therefore the amount which would be required by the average consumer of 1970, faced initially with the total expenditure and price structure of 1960, to feel equally well off under the price conditions of 1970. We are thus looking at the comparison from the point of view of the 1970 consumer because it is his value of b and c which will be used in estimating the composition of total consumption. We can see, however, from (6.1) that by replacing b_{10} and c_{10} by b_0 and c_0 we could make this comparison from the point of view of the 1960 consumer.

(iv) We calculate $\mu_{10} = \mu_{10}^{*} e^{10\varrho}$ where ϱ denotes the instantaneous rate of growth in real consumption per head that we wish to consider between 1960 and 1970.

(v) We calculate e_{10} from (3.1), replacing b, c, p and μ by b_{10}, c_{10}, p_{10} and μ_{10}. The values of b_{10}, c_{10} and p_{10} are set out in Table 5.

TABLE 5 – Estimates of b, c and p for 1970

	b	c	p
Food	0.0415	37.05	4.476
Clothing	0.1779	9.69	3.112
Household	0.2473	26.13	3.517
Communications	− 0.0017	1.39	4.158
Transport	0.2502	10.62	3.477
Drink and tobacco	0.0766	10.78	4.042
Entertainment	− 0.0223	5.80	3.468
Other	0.2306	10.63	3.356

TABLE 6 – Projected consumption levels in 1970 and actual levels in 1960
(£ 1938 per head)

	e_0	e_{10} for different values of ϱ				
		0.020	0.025	0.030	0.035	0.040
Food	34.7	38.2	38.4	38.7	39.0	39.3
Clothing	11.5	16.5	18.2	19.9	21.6	23.5
Household	27.7	34.6	36.5	38.6	40.8	43.1
Communications	1.2	1.3	1.3	1.3	1.3	1.3
Transport	13.6	19.2	21.3	23.4	25.7	28.0
Drink and tobacco	11.5	13.1	13.6	14.1	14.7	15.4
Entertainment	4.8	5.0·	4.9	4.7	4.5	4.3
Other	13.1	18.9	20.8	22.8	25.0	27.2
Total	118.0	146.8	155.0	163.5	172.6	192.1

TABLE 7 – Projected consumption levels in 1970, related to observed levels of 1.00 in 1960

	$\hat{e}_0^{-1}/e_{10}$ for different values of ϱ				
	0.020	0.025	0.030	0.035	0.040
Food	1.10	1.11	1.11	1.12	1.13
Clothing	1.43	1.57	1.72	1.88	2.04
Household	1.25	1.32	1.40	1.48	1.56
Communications	1.16	1.15	1.14	1.12	1.11
Transport	1.42	1.57	1.72	1.89	2.06
Drink and tobacco	1.14	1.18	1.23	1.29	1.34
Entertainment	1.05	1.02	0.98	0.93	0.89
Other	1.44	1.59	1.74	1.90	2.07
Total	1.24	1.31	1.39	1.46	1.54

TABLE 8 – Percentage distribution of consumption in 1960 and 1970

	$100 e_0/i' e_0$	$100 e_{10}/i' e_{10}$ for different values of ϱ				
		0.020	0.025	0.030	0.035	0.040
Food	29.4	26.0	24.8	23.7	22.6	21.6
Clothing	9.8	11.3	11.7	12.1	12.5	12.9
Household	23.4	23.6	23.6	23.6	23.7	23.7
Communications	1.0	0.9	0.9	0.8	0.8	0.7
Transport	11.5	13.1	13.7	14.3	14.9	15.4
Drink and tobacco	9.7	8.9	8.8	8.7	8.5	8.4
Entertainment	4.0	3.4	3.1	2.9	2.6	2.3
Other	11.1	12.9	13.4	14.0	14.5	15.0
Total	100.0	100.0	100.0	100.0	100.0	100.0

From these values we find, using steps (iii) and (iv) that $\mu_{10} = 550, 578, 608, 639$ and 672 for $\varrho = 0.020, 0.025, 0.030, 0.035,$ and 0.040. Using step (v) we can now compile Table 6 in which e_0 is compared with the different values of e_{10} obtained by taking different values of ϱ.

For comparative purposes, the results set out in Table 6 can be presented differently. First, in Table 7, each of the estimates is related to the corresponding observed value in 1960.

Second, in Table 8, the observed values for 1960 and the various estimates for 1970 are expressed as proportions of their respective totals.

Finally, in addition to a distribution of consumption, that is expenditure at base-year (1938) prices, it is useful to have a distribution of expenditure at current prices. This is provided in Table 9.

TABLE 9 – Percentage distribution of expenditure in 1960 and 1970

	$100\hat{p}_0 e_0/p_0' e_0$	$100\hat{p}_{10} e_{10}/p'_{10} e_{10}$ for different values of ϱ				
		0.020	0.025	0.030	0.035	0.040
Food	30.9	31.0	29.8	28.5	27.3	26.2
Clothing	10.0	9.4	9.8	10.1	10.5	10.9
Household	21.0	22.1	22.2	22.4	22.5	22.6
Communications	0.8	1.0	1.0	0.9	0.8	0.8
Transport	9.9	12.2	12.8	13.4	14.0	14.5
Drink and tobacco	13.2	9.6	9.5	9.4	9.3	9.2
Entertainment	3.5	3.2	2.9	2.7	2.4	2.2
Other	10.7	11.5	12.1	12.6	13.1	13.6
Total	100.0	100.0	100.0	100.0	100.0	100.0

Our projections for 1970 are contained in Tables 5 through Table 9: let us now comment on them.

First, we can see from Table 5 that by 1970 the elements of b for the two small groups, communications and entertainment, have become negative: indeed the element of b for entertainment had already become negative by 1960. This is unacceptable theoretically though, for such small groups, it may not lead to serious error in the general picture for 1970. It arises from the extrapolation of linear trends which, when negative, will inevitably lead to this result in due course. These results show the practical need to improve the form of the trends we have introduced into the coefficients. We have mentioned the possibility of parabolic trends which would almost certainly lead to an improvement. But, with their single point of inflection, parabolas also have their dangers, and we ought, perhaps, to base the trends on the past history of the consumption series themselves. For the moment, we simply mention this problem; we shall not do anything about it in this paper.

Second, we can also see from Table 5 that the projected prices in 1970 show very different levels relative to 1938: for example, food prices are estimated to rise to 4.5 times and clothing prices to only 3.1 times the level of 1938. These results are partly the result of observed changes to 1960 and partly the result of extrapolation based on price trends in the 1950's. This extrapolation is of considerable importance in arriving at the estimates for 1970: for example by 1960 food prices were about 2.8 and clothing prices about 2.7 times the level in 1938. Since we are not in a position to calculate shadow prices for 1970 from our general model, we do not want to defend the price projections we have made; they were introduced simply to illustrate the method and could, of course, be replaced by any other set of 1970 prices which a more detailed study of probably future movements in prices might suggest. We mention this point because in so far as relative prices are important, our high relative price for food and low relative price for clothing will tend to depress food consumption and stimulate the consumption of clothing in 1970.

Third, if we turn to Tables 6 and 7 we see that projected food consumption is only some 11 per cent above the 1960 level and that the increase only varies over the range 10 to 13 per cent for increases in total consumption between 24 and 54 per cent. This result is partly due to the changing demand patterns and partly to the high relative price of food. The implied elasticity of food consumption in 1970 with respect to total expenditure is in the neighbourhood of 0.15 compared with 0.26 in 1960 and 0.57 in 1938.

For the smallest rate of growth in total consumption, $\varrho = 0.02$, drink and tobacco combined show an increase of 14 per cent in consumption, a value similar to food. But they show a much greater rise as ϱ increases, until for $\varrho = 0.04$ their increase is 34 per cent over the level of 1960. The level of household consumption, which includes accomodation, fuel and light, and running expenses including household durables, is both higher and more steeply rising than that of drink and tobacco: the range is from 25 to 56 per cent above the 1960 level.

A the top of the scale, we find clothing, transport and other which range from some 43 per cent above the 1960 level for $\varrho = 0.02$ to some 106 per cent above it for $\varrho = 0.04$.

Fourth, these very different increases naturally bring about considerable changes in the pattern of consumption, particularly for growth rates in total consumption which are much larger than have been experienced in the past. The proportions represented by food and by drink and tobacco tend to fall; that represented by household is approximately constant; and those represented by clothing, transport and other tend to rise. These changes can be seen in Table 8.

Fifth, when we turn to Table 9 we can see that the changes in the pattern of expenditure are smaller. Thus, for example, for small values of ϱ, the proportion of total expenditure devoted to food in 1970 is the same as in 1960, and the proportion devoted to clothing in 1970 is actually less than in 1960. The main exceptions to the general proposition of this paragraph are transport whose proportion of total expenditure is substantially larger and drink and tobacco whose proportion of total expenditure is substantially smaller in 1970 than in 1960.

Finally, we think that the picture of future consumption which emerges from our analysis is on the whole a plausible one which could usefully be taken as a basis for discussion. But, as we have said, this paper is mainly a study in method and the results obtained are certainly not the best that the model is capable of. In the light of our general model the next steps would seem to be as follows.

(i) Try to correct the faults in the model which are apparent in this paper: in particular the use of only linear trends in the coefficients.
(ii) Try to improve the price projections. The use of shadow prices from the general model is the ideal.
(iii) Try to distinguish more commodity groups. This is partly a question of computing and partly a question of suitable aggregation. Progress in this direction may well entail the use of the dynamic version of the model and also of committed purchases which depend on relative prices.
(iv) Try to narrow down the range of growth rates in total consumption which are worth serious consideration, avoiding those which are unnecessarily low or impossibly high. The main object of our general model is to do just this.

These developments are all foreshadowed in our Programme for Growth: it only remains to do the work.

7. CONCLUSIONS

In this section we shall bring together a number of comments on the model and its use which are scattered through the earlier sections. We can set out our conclusions under a number of heads, as follows.

(1) The main strength of the model is that it enables us to analyse the demand for all groups of commodities over a comparatively long period within a single conceptual framework. We do not have to consider commodity groups one at a time nor do we have to treat postwar demand functions as though they were unrelated to the demand functions of earlier periods. From the point of view of projections this is a great advantage because it means that we are getting a consistent picture based on a considerable span of the past rather than a series of partial pictures based on only a short span.

(2) Since this is the first analysis of its kind, it is naturally not in a very finished form. We have seen that, for some commodity groups, the assumption of linear trends introduced avoidable errors and that there were groups which could have been better approximated by accelerating or decelerating trends. On the assumption that all growth is fundamentally sigmoid in character, this is very much what one would expect. The simple thing to do to meet this difficulty is to replace linear trends by parabolic ones, and this we propose to do. We do not, however, feel very easy about parabolic trends and we hope eventually to be able to introduce sigmoid trends into the model or to make the trends dependent on the past values of consumption. This last possibility is particularly important when projections are based on abnormally high growth rates and when, as a consequence, consumers' behaviour may be expected to undergo unusually rapid change.

(3) We attach importance to the results obtained from the model conforming with other independent results such as those obtained from budget studies. In the case of food we have shown that they do conform, and we intend to see what happens with other commodity groups.

(4) We intend to experiment with the dynamic version of the model because it allows for the fact that consumers' adjustments take time. This is particularly important in the case of durable goods which are becoming of much greater importance than they were in the past. First, however, we must solve the computing problems of introducing trends in the parameters of the dynamic model.

(5) We intend to use the decomposable property of the model to subdivide the small number of commodity groups analysed in this paper. As we make our groups smaller we shall have to pay more attention to the nature of these groups than we did here, because we must avoid groups that are complementary or inferior to the others. When we do this we may have to consider the version of the model in which committed purchases are a function of the price structure.

(6) From a statistical point of view the chief weakness of the model probably lies in the assumption of a scalar variance matrix. We should, therefore, try to replace this assumption by something more realistic.

(7) We have seen that the model gives rise to considerable computing difficulties largely because of the problem of choosing initial values which will ensure convergence. In view of the more sophisticated models now being proposed in econometrics this problem seems to provide a useful field for research in applied mathematics.

(8) As far as projections are concerned, all the work we have described is a beginning rather than an end. It represents our best attempt to learn the lessons of history about the gradual changes in consumers' behaviour. But before our future year is reached there will be some more history, as yet unknown, which may have a radical effect on consumers. This is perhaps unlikely as far as broad commodity groups are concerned but it is highly likely when we come to their constituents. If we had been writing in 1938 about 1960 we might have detected that a considerable rise was likely even for the small group 'entertainment' but we could not have learnt from history that by 1960 television would have largely replaced the cinema as a medium of popular entertainment. The only way in which we can hope to learn about such developments is by discussing our projections with those who are trying to bring the developments about and those whose subject is the relationship of man to the society in which he lives. This means that we must bring technical and business experts as well as sociologists and social psychologists into the picture and try to adjust our view of the future in the light of their reactions. Econometrics provides an agenda; it does not, by itself, provide the probable facts of our future. But the econometrician can be of good heart because without an agenda discussion would degenerate into noise and we should be as far away as ever from the solution of our problems.

REFERENCES

[1] AITCHISON, J. and J. A. C. BROWN, 'A synthesis of Engel curve theory', The Review of Economic Studies, vol. XXII (1954–1955) pp. 35–46.

[2] AITCHISON, J. and J. A. C. BROWN, 'The Lognormal Distribution', Cambridge University Press (1957).

[3] CAMBRIDGE, DEPARTMENT of APPLIED ECONOMICS, 'A Computable Model of Economic Growth', Chapman and Hall (London 1962).

[4] GEARY, R. C., A note on 'A constant-utility index of the cost of living', The Review of Economic Studies, vol. XVIII, no. 45 (1949–1950) pp. 65–66.

[5] KLEIN, L. R. and H. RUBIN, 'A constant-utility index of the cost of living', The Review of Economic Studies, vol. XV, no. 38 (1947–1948) pp. 84–87.

[6] PREST, A. R., assisted by A. A. ADAMS, 'Consumers' Expenditure in the United Kingdom, 1900–1919', Cambridge University Press (1954).

[7] SAMUELSON, PAUL A., 'Some implications of "linearity"', The Review of Economic Studies, vol. XV, no. 38 (1947–1948) pp. 88–90.

[8] STONE, RICHARD, Linear expenditure systems and demand analysis: 'An application to the pattern of British demand', The Economic Journal, vol. LXIV, no. 255 (1954) pp. 511–527.

[9] STONE, RICHARD, 'Transaction models with an example based on the British national accounts', Accounting Research, vol. VI, no. 3 (1955) pp. 202–226.

[10] STONE, RICHARD, 'Input-Output and National Accounts', O.E.E.C. (Paris, 1961).

[11] STONE, RICHARD and GIOVANNA CROFT-MURRAY, 'Social Accounting and Economic Models', Bowes and Bowes (London, 1959).

[12] STONE, RICHARD and D.A.ROWE, 'The Measurement of Consumers' Expenditure and Behaviour in the United Kingdom, 1920–1938', Vol.II, Cambridge University Press (forthcoming).

[13] STONE, RICHARD et al., 'The Measurement of Consumers' Expenditure and Behaviour in the United Kingdom, 1920–1938', Vol.I, Cambridge University Press (1954).

[14] U.K. CENTRAL STATISTICAL OFFICE, 'Statistical Digest of the War', H.M.S.O. and Longmans Green (London, 1951).

[15] U.K. CENTRAL STATISTICAL OFFICE, 'National Income and Expenditure: 1961', H.M.S.O. (London, 1961 and annually).

[16] U.K. MINISTRY of AGRICULTURE, FISHERIES AND FOOD, 'Domestic Food Consumption and Expenditure: 1960', H.M.S.O. (London, 1962).

The Classes of Consumers' Expenditure and their Component Categories

1. Food
   1.1. Bread and cereals
   1.2. Meat, bacon, fish
   1.3. Dairy products, oils, fats
   1.4. Fruit, potatoes, other vegetables
   1.5. Other foods
   1.6. Beverages
2. Clothing
   2.1. Footwear
   2.2. Other clothing
3. Household
   3.1. Rent, rates, water charges
   3.2. Coal
   3.3. Electricity
   3.4. Gas
   3.5. Other fuel
   3.6. Furniture and furnishings
   3.7. Hardware, radio and electrical goods
   3.8. Domestic servants, polishes, matches
4. Communications
   4.1. Postal services
   4.2. Telephone and telegraph services
5. Transport
   5.1. Motor vehicles
   5.2. Pedal cycles
   5.3. Running costs of vehicles
   5.4. Railway travel
   5.5. Other travel
6. Drink and tobacco
   6.1. Beer
   6.2. Wines and spirits
   6.3. Tobacco

7. Entertainment
    7.1. Entertainments, sport and travel goods
    7.2. Books, newspapers, magazines
8. Other
    8.1. Other goods
    8.2. Other services

GROSS NATIONAL PRODUCT AND PRIVATE CONSUMPTION IN THE FEDERAL REPUBLIC OF GERMANY IN 1960 AND 1970

BY

GERHARD GEHRIG

Ifo-Institut für Wirtschaftsforschung, München, Germany

I. SUMMARY

The long range projections of both gross national product and private consumption are based on a macro-economic model involving a production function, a consumption function and two definition equations. The parameters are estimated from data obtained in the observation periods 1925 to 1938 and 1950 to 1957.

The projection of gross national product and private consumption to 1970 is possible on the assumptions that the parameters remain as constant as in the past and that the random variables will take a value which is most likely: one or zero respectively. In addition, the projections require forecasts for the exogenous variables. Thus, the projections of the endogenous variables depend not only on the accuracy of the two assumptions above but also on the exact forecast of the exogenous variables.

Assuming correct forecasts for the exogenous variables (Table 2) 'capital', 'labour', 'imports', 'imports other than capital goods', the most likely value of GNP in 1970 is 385.8 bill. of 1954 DM and of private consumption 231.8 bill. of 1954 DM. These figures imply an average annual increase between 1960 and 1970 of 4.9 per cent for GNP and 5.0 per cent for private consumption. Consumption per head would rise by 4.2 per cent a year in the same period reaching 4005 DM in 1970 when the population is expected to be 57.9 millions.

If a forecast is made instead of a projection one would expect a not wholly utilized stock of equipment in 1970 so that the actual values are likely to be smaller than the computed ones. Thus, in spite of full employment real GNP could be about 6 per cent lower than the projected values and real private consumption about 3 per cent lower.

Of course, these forecasts and projections are made only for a normal economy under a reasonably free market policy. Major disturbances such as war or large-scale inflation, would influence the results considerably. As far as possible allowance is made for the effects of the Common Market.

II. THE MODEL

1. PRODUCTION FUNCTION

The following production function (Fig. 1) was derived by time series analysis of the determining factors of production in the periods 1925 to 1938 and 1950 to 1957[1]):

$$\log Q = \log 0.1695 + 0.3508 \log K^{m^*} + 0.7304 \log L + 0.2487 \log M^* +$$
$$ (0.0565) \phantom{\log K^{m^*} +} (0.0700) (0.0163)$$

$$+ 0.0200 \, T \log e + \log \check{u}_Q. \tag{1}$$
$$(0.0006)$$

$$D = 2.4595; \quad R^2 = 0.9921; \quad V^* = \pm 0.34\%;$$

$$s^* = \pm 0.0075; \quad V = \pm 1.53\%; \quad s = \pm 2.48 \text{ bill. of DM.}$$

Domestic production (Q) is explained in terms of the stock of fixed capital in use at the middle of the period (K^{m^*}), labour (L), the imports of goods other than capital goods (M^*), a time trend (T) representing technical progress and a random disturbance $(u_Q)^2)$. Table 1 shows time series for the variables of the production function. The data apply to the changing territory of Germany. All values are given in constant DM. The standard errors of the parameters are in parenthesis below the parameters. D represents the ratio of the mean square successive difference to the variance; R^2 is the coefficient of determination, V^* the coefficient of variation and s^* is the standard error of the function. Standard error s and coefficient of variation V are calculated from antilogarithms[3]). The estimates are derived by ordinary least squares.

---

[1]) For further details see G. GEHRIG and K. C. KUHLO, 'Eine ökonometrische Analyse des Produktionsprozesses'. Ifo-Studien, 7. Jg. 1961, p. 175–237.
[2]) For details about these variables see section III.
[3]) Footnote see p. 229.

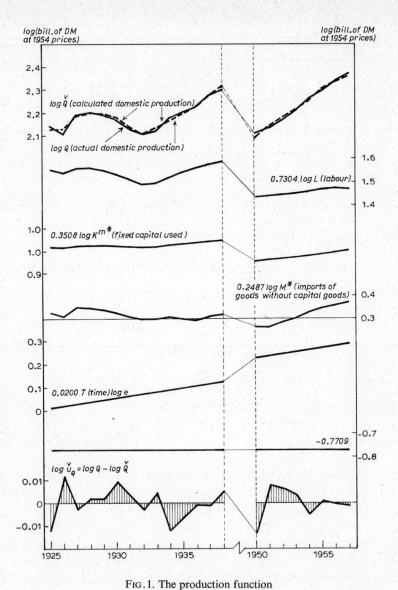

FIG. 1. The production function

$$\log Q = -0.7709 + 0.3508 \log K^{m*} + 0.7304 \log L + 0.2487 \log M^* +$$
$$+ 0.0200 \, T \log e + \log \hat{u}_q.$$

According to Fig. 1 all time series for the variables of the production function show a break between 1938 and 1950, as the post-war series refer to a smaller area than the pre-war series. Curiously no production function of type (1) could be calculated either for the pre-war period (1925 to 1938) or for the post-war period (1950 to 1957). The results were strongly influenced by multicollinearity within the exogenous variables. Basing the calculations on the whole period of observation, however, the disturbing influence of multicollinearity seems to disappear completely according to various tests:

All the parameters are significant to the 99.9 per cent level[4]). Using the 5 per cent significance level for the D-ratio no significant autocorrelation can be determined. The coefficient of variation indicates with a probability of 67 per cent a standard error of only ± 0.34 per cent with respect to the mean of the logarithms of the endogenous variables. The coefficient of determination is high and the actual values of Q are well described (Fig. 1).

Thus, there is some evidence to support the use of function (1) for purposes of long range projections.

2. CONSUMPTION FUNCTION

The consumption function of the model (Fig. 3) is calculated from data for the period 1950 to 1957:

$$C = 12.2826 + 0.4533 Q + \hat{u}_C \qquad (2)$$
$$(2.2596) \quad (0.0127)$$

$$D = 2.7962; \quad R^2 = 0.9954; \quad V = \pm 1.38\%;$$

$$s = \pm 1.27 \text{ bill. of DM.}$$

---

[3]) The formulae for s and V are in general:

$$s^2 = \sum_{t}^{T} (X_t - \check{X}_t)^2 / T - G; \quad V = \pm s/\overline{X}$$

$T =$ size of the sample
$G =$ number of the variables involved in the equation
$X =$ actual value of the endogenous variable X
$\check{X} =$ computed value of the endogenous variable X
$\overline{X} = 1/T \sum_{t}^{T} X_t.$

[4]) This fact is no exact proof for the lack of multicollinearity as shown by K. A. Fox and J. F. Cooney, 'Effects of Intercorrelation upon Multiple Correlation and Regression Measures'. US Department of Agricultural Marketing Service, Washington 25, D.C., April 1954.

TABLE 1 – Time series for the variables of the model

No.	Year[a)]	Labour Man-hours 1954 = 100 L	Billions of DM at 1954 prices						
			Imports of goods excluding capital goods M*	Fixed capital used K^{m*}	Domestic production Q	Imports of goods M^w	Gross national product Y	Private consumption C	Q − C = R
0	1	2	3	4	5	6	7	8	9
1	1925	135.8	20.5	789.0	133.5				
2	1926	130.0	17.6	778.1	133.7				
3	1927	138.2	25.8	805.1	153.6				
4	1928	138.5	25.1	823.7	158.7				
5	1929	134.0	23.7	837.2	156.7				
6	1930	127.9	21.0	826.5	151.9				
7	1931	119.9	17.5	806.7	138.2				
8	1932	110.8	16.3	786.6	127.8				
9	1933	112.5	16.3	800.6	134.9				
10	1934	123.1	17.5	838.5	146.4				
11	1935	131.2	16.0	863.4	156.7				
12	1936	137.9	15.6	891.0	168.6				
13	1937	145.5	18.1	922.2	187.8				
14	1938	151.8	19.5	954.6	206.6				
15	1950	92.4	11.7	522.3	125.1	12.0	113.1	69.2	55.9
16	1951	94.2	11.5	540.3	136.8	11.8	125.0	73.8	63.0
17	1952	95.6	14.2	559.6	150.1	14.7	135.4	79.3	70.8
18	1953	97.6	16.6	580.9	162.8	17.2	145.6	88.2	74.6

TABLE 1 – (continued)

No.	Year[a]	Man-hours 1954 = 100	Billions of DM at 1954 prices						
		Labour	Imports of goods excluding capital goods	Fixed capital used	Domestic production	Imports of goods	Gross national product	Private consumption	$Q - C$
		L	M^*	K^{m*}	Q	M^w	Y	C	$= R$
0	1	2	3	4	5	6	7	8	9
19	1954	100.0	21.0	605.9	178.1	21.7	156.4	92.8	85.3
20	1955	103.3	25.1	636.5	200.7	26.3	174.4	101.5	99.2
21	1956	104.8	27.7	672.3	215.6	29.2	186.4	110.5	105.1
22	1957	104.1	31.4	710.1	229.8	33.3	196.5	117.1	112.7
23	1958	103.4	34.3	748.6	239.9	37.0	202.9	122.6	117.3
24	1959	104.3	41.0	789.1	260.7	44.2	216.5	129.7	131.0
25	1960	106.0	48.7	837.8	292.1[p]	52.7	239.4[p]	141.7[p]	150.4[p]

p = preliminary.
[a] = 1960 with the Saarland included.

Private consumption (C) is explained in terms of domestic production (Q) and random disturbance (u_C). The variables are measured in constant DM. Using definition (3) the parameters could be estimated by the method of maximum likelihood[5]).

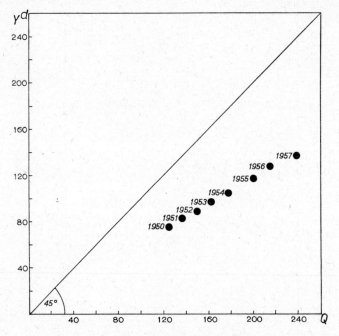

FIG. 2. Domestic production (Q) and disposable income (Y^d) from 1950 to 1957 (bill. of DM at 1954 prices).

Function (2) represents a consumption function as well as a function closing the model. Consumption could be better explained theoretically and statistically by disposable income instead of domestic production. However, there are considerable difficulties in projecting disposable income. Analysing the statistical relationship between the variables, the scatter diagram (Fig. 2) indicates a strong positive correlation which makes the substitution of domestic production for disposable income in function (2) look reasonable. As a consequence of this substitution R^2

[5]) The standard errors of the parameters of the consumption function are derived from those of the reduced form equations by means of Klein's approximate formula (6.2.12). See L. R. KLEIN, 'A Textbook of Econometrics', Evanston and White Plains 1956, Second Printing, p. 258.

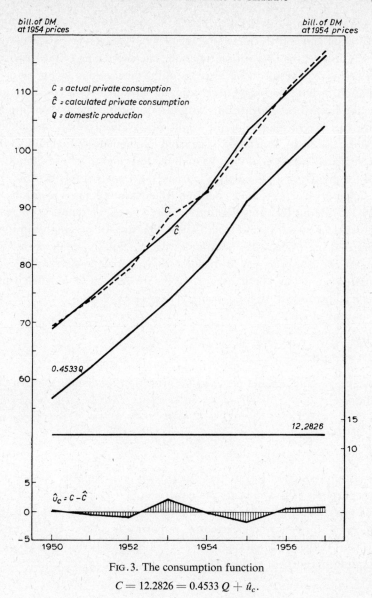

FIG. 3. The consumption function

$$C = 12.2826 = 0.4533\, Q + \hat{u}_c.$$

decreases slightly from 0.9968 to 0.9954 and V increases from ± 1.16 per cent to ± 1.38 per cent. The D-ratio changes from 2.3108 to 2.7962. This value is still within the 5 per cent significance levels indicating no significant serial correlation of the residuals.

The observation period is limited to the post-war years 1950 to 1957 and does not include the pre-war years 1925 to 1938 as is the case with the observations of the production function. The shortening of the observation period is a result of an analysis of the determining factor for consumption in both periods[6]). According to this analysis a consumption function linear in the logarithms with disposable income as determining factor can be calculated for the whole observation period only if the variables are either undeflated or deflated by population. Functions with price-deflated variables do not pass all the tests and therefore cannot be used for predictive and analytical purposes. Probably this is because the consumer price index is not a good enough deflator for a period as long as 1925–1957. However, consumption functions based on data for the relatively short post-war period from 1950 to 1957 are still acceptable in spite of introducing price-deflated variables. In general, the analysis showed that for the post-war period disposable income alone determines consumption no matter whether the variables are deflated or undeflated and whether logarithms are used or not. Thus, we can try to insert function (2) into the model.

3. DEFINITIONS

Besides a production and consumption function the model has two definitions:

$$Q = C + R. \tag{3}$$

$$Y = Q - M^w. \tag{4}$$

Domestic production (Q) is used for private consumption (C) and for other purposes (R), as indicated in equation (3). The variable R contains gross investment, government consumption and balance on goods and services of foreign trade excluding imports of goods. According to equation (4), the gross national product (Y) is equal to domestic production minus imports of goods (M^w).

---

[6]) G. GEHRIG, 'Eine ökonometrische Analyse des Konsums von 1925 bis 1938 und 1950 bis 1957'. 'Schriftenreihe des Ifo-Instituts für Wirtschaftsforschung', Nr. 52, Berlin 1962.

III. FORECAST OF THE EXOGENOUS VARIABLES

1. STOCK OF FIXED CAPITAL IN USE[7])

The following formula shows some components of the stock of fixed capital in use:

$$K_t^{m*} = \alpha_t^m K_t^{m,\,A} + K_t^{m,\,B}; \quad 0 \leq \alpha_t^m \leq 1. \tag{5}$$

K^{m*} represents the sum of the stock of equipment in variable use over time $(\alpha^m K^{m,\,A})$ and the stock of buildings used completely $(K^{m,\,B})$. All variables of equation (5) refer to the middle (m) of the year t, and α stands for the degree of utilization.

The stocks of equipment (K^A) and buildings (K^B) at the end of year t are calculated by

$$K_t^i = I_t^{b,\,i} - I_t^{e,\,i} + K_{t-1}^i; \quad i = A,\, B. \tag{6}$$

Net investment, consisting of the difference between gross investment (I^b) and capital consumption (I^e), is added to the stock of capital in the preceding year in order to obtain the stock of capital for the present year. Basing the calculations on the middle of the year can be done by formula

$$K_t^{m,\,i} = \tfrac{1}{2}(K_t^i + K_{t-1}^i) = \tfrac{1}{2}(I_t^{b,\,i} - I_t^{e,\,i}) + K_{t-1}^i. \tag{7}$$

Equation (7) shows that the calculation of the capital stock variable for 1970 depends on gross investment and on replacement in all the years prior to 1970.

a) Gross Investment[8])

Gross investment in equipment and building from 1960 to 1970 is given in Table 3. The following assumptions were made: the rate of growth of investment in equipment will be consistently greater than that of gross national product whereas the rate of growth of investment in buildings will slightly decrease. Investment in housing will tend to slow down in the coming years. Underground structure will increase considerably as will factory building. Publicly financed construction of all types except underground structure is expected to develop normally.

---

[7]) For further details on this subject see: G. GEHRIG, 'Eine Zeitreihe für den Sachkapitalbestand (1925/38 und 1950/57)', Ifo-Studien, 7. Jg. 1961, p. 7–60.

[8]) The forecasts up to 1970 have been performed in the Ifo-Institut under the direction of Dr. H. Hahn.

b) Replacement

Replacement of equipment and buildings is calculated separately:

$$I_t^e = I_t^{e,A} + I_t^{e,B}. \tag{8}$$

Estimates for replacement of buildings can be derived from the formula

$$I_t^{e,B} = b K_{t-1}^B. \tag{9}$$

A value of 0.0032 for b was found in the past. Lack of further information makes it necessary to apply this value to the projections.

Capital consumption in equipment can be estimated from the equation

$$I_t^{e,A} = a_t d_{t-l} I_{t-l}^{b,A}. \tag{10}$$

The following assumption underlies equation (10): replacement in year t is equal to gross investment in year $t - l$ as there is no capital consumption during the lifetime (l) of equipment. Replacement is assumed to take place at the very end of the lifetime. The coefficient a_t represents loss of equipment during the Second World War. As some equipment has been destroyed during the war, replacement will be lower.

$$a_t = 0.63 \quad \text{for} \quad t = 1945, \ldots, 1970$$

$$a_t = 1.00 \quad \text{for} \quad t \lessgtr 1945, \ldots, 1970. \tag{11}$$

Moreover, due consideration has to be given to the change in territory when using this method of estimating replacement. This is done by coefficient d which is important when replacement equals gross investment in the war and pre-war periods.

$$d_{t-l} = 0.60 \quad \text{for} \quad t - l = 1919, \ldots, 1944$$

$$d_{t-l} = 1.00 \quad \text{for} \quad t - l \gtrless 1919, \ldots, 1944. \tag{12}$$

From 1958 to 1970 the constant average lifetime (l) will be 22 years. Special investigations indicate a 1.5 year decrease of the equipment's lifetime within a decade. In spite of this it is still possible to apply a constant lifetime to calculations of replacement as a good approximation because a slightly varying lifetime has not much effect on the stock variable.

The figures for expected replacement in equipment and buildings from 1960 to 1970, calculated by means of the formulae (8) to (12), are shown in Table 3.

c) Degree of Utilization

The degree of utilization is assumed to be unity in 1970. This implies that capital (K^m) is completely used. Hence, it is equal to the stock of fixed capital in use

$$K_t^{m*} = K_t^m. \tag{13}$$

Considering equations (5) to (13) the following expression for K_t^m can be derived:

$$K_t^m = \tfrac{1}{2} I_t^b - \tfrac{1}{2}(a_t d_{t-l} I_{t-l}^{b,A} + b K_{t-1}^B) + K_{t-1}. \tag{14}$$

Table 2 and 3 indicate the value of the capital stock at the middle of 1970.

2. LABOUR, IMPORTS AND TECHNICAL PROGRESS[9])

Labour (L) is defined as a product of the number of persons employed (E) and the corresponding labour time (H)

$$L = EH. \tag{15}$$

As E and H are indices L is also an index; it represents the working hours per year in the whole economy. The index number of labour for 1970 is listed in Table 2.

The forecast of employed persons was mainly done by applying from past experience, the proportions of men and women of different ages in the labour force, to a population projection, subdivided in age and sex from the Federal Statistical Office[10]). In addition a migration surplus of 100000 up to 1965 and of 80000 employed persons up to 1970 seems to be likely. Assuming the present degree of full employment 200000 persons will be unemployed in 1970. Moreover, the labour force will, by 1970, decrease by 400000 persons as a result of introducing an additional obligatory school year throughout the Federal Republic. Thus, the total number of employed persons in 1970 is expected to be 26525 millions which corresponds to an index number of 120.6 based on 1954.

Hours worked are mainly determined by a decreasing trend. In 1970 the working week is assumed to be 40 hours for employees in all branches of the economy except agriculture. This implies that the index number of working hours per employed person will be 82.1 in 1970.

---

[9]) See footnote 8.

[10]) 'Die voraussichtliche Bevölkerungsentwicklung bis 1975 nach Geschlecht und Alter'. Statistischer Bericht VIII/7/80 des Statistischen Bundesamtes vom 26.3.1959 in connection with a supplementary paper of Division VIII of the Federal Statistical Office from August 8, 1960.

TABLE 2 – Some figures for the variables of the model in 1950 and 1960 and 1970

No.	Symbols	Variables	Bill. of DM at 1954 prices, index for L — Values			Rates of growth %				Percentage errors between actual and calculated values[b] %	
			actual		projected	1950–1960		1960–1970			
			1950	1960	1970	total	per annum[a]	total	per annum[a]	1950	1960
0	1	2	3	4	5	6	7	8	9	10	11
		Endogenous:									
1	Q	Domestic production	125.1	292.1	484.3	133.5	8.9	65.8	5.2	– 3.0	– 0.3
2	Y	Gross national product	113.1	239.4	385.8	111.7	7.8	61.2	4.9	– 3.4	– 0.3
3	C	Private consumption	69.2	141.7	231.8	104.8	7.4	63.6	5.0	– 2.2	– 2.3
4	R	$Q - C$	55.9	150.4	252.5	169.1	10.4	67.9	5.3	– 4.1	1.7
		Exogenous:									
5	L	Labour	92.4	106.0	99.0	14.7	1.4	– 6.6	– 0.7		
6	K^{m*}	Stock of capital used	522.3	837.8	1519.9	60.4	4.8	81.4	6.1		
7	M^*	Special imports	11.7	48.7	86.7	316.2	15.3	78.0	5.9		
8	M^w	Imports of goods	12.0	52.7	98.5	339.2	16.0	86.9	6.5		

Symbols: z = percentage change per annum
f = percentage error
Z = actual value
$\hat{Z}$ = calculated value

k = variable
b = beginning of the period
e = end of the period

a) $z_k = \left(\dfrac{Z_{k,e}}{Z_{k,b}}\right)^{\frac{1}{e-b}} - 1$

b) $f_k = 100\,\dfrac{Z_k - \hat{Z}_k}{Z_k}$

Table 2 also shows the expected values of total imports of goods in 1970 and of this total less capital goods. Imports of capital goods are assumed to be not more than a fifth of gross fixed investment in equipment. A further assumption is that the rates of exchange in 1970 will be equal to those of 1961.

Technical progress (T) is considered to be a trend and its calculation is based on

$$T = t - 1924,   (16)$$

where t stands for the calendar year.

IV. RESULTS

1. INTERPRETATION OF THE RESULTS

Table 2 (column 5, rows 1 to 4) lists the results of the projections for the endogenous variables in 1970. The same table shows that all endogenous variables are expected to grow less from 1960 to 1970 than they did in the preceeding decade. Moreover, contrary to post-war development, the predicted average rate of growth per annum of private consumption (5%) is slightly higher than that of GNP (4.9%). The increase in the variable R will be especially slow compared to its growth from 1950 to 1960. In spite of a reduced average consumption growth rate, consumption per head will still increase from 2654 DM in 1960 to 4005 DM in 1970 representing an annual growth rate of 4.2 per cent. Between 1950 and 1960 this percentage increase was 6.1. The following figures supplement these conclusions:[11]

Year	Population in millions at the middle of the year	Real private consumption per head in DM
1950	46.9	1475
1960	53.4	2654
1970	57.9	4005

All projections are point estimates and have an upper and lower confidence limit. The standard error of projection[12] for 1970 based on

[11] Population in 1970 is projected by the Federal Statistical Office (see footnote 10).
[12] See A. HOTELLING, 'Problems of Prediction', The American Journal of Sociology, XLVIII (1942–1943), p. 68.

logarithms of the domestic production is $\pm\,0.03234$. Hence, there is a confidence range of projected domestic production between $+\,7.7$ and $-\,7.2$ per cent according to a 67.8 per cent probability level. The standard error of private consumption for 1970 amounts to 4.14 bill. of DM indicating a confidence interval of $\pm\,1.8$ per cent at the same probability level if domestic production is correctly projected.

The average percentage increase of GNP between 1960 and 1970 of 4.9 per cent is near the lower limit of Krengel's expected 5 to 6 per cent[13]). Taking the upper probability limit the growth rate of GNP of 5.8 per cent would be well within Krengel's tolerance interval. However, since complete utilization of the equipment stock is assumed, actual domestic production and GNP will probably be smaller and are expected to lie in the lower part of the confidence interval rather than in the upper part.

Again it should be emphasized that the endogenous variables of the model can be projected correctly only if the exogenous variables are free of errors. Their values for 1970 are given in Table 2. The forecasts imply that the average growth rates of all the exogenous variables except net investment will slow down from 1960 to 1970. The amount of labour will decrease as a consequence of reductions in working hours and the slow increase in persons employed. At the same time, net investment grows more (6.1%) from 1960 to 1970 than in the preceeding decade (4.8%) as a result of relatively little replacement of equipment in the second half of the decade. After 1970 replacement will rise faster. Compared with Krengel's estimates cited by Geary[14]) the replacement figures shown in Table 3 are essentially lower. Yet, they seem to coincide with Krengel's assumptions concerning development over time. The difference in level between the two kinds of estimates is most likely the result of using different methods of computation.

2. ACCURACY OF THE PROJECTIONS

It is possible to make some tests of the goodness of fit for projections done with the model; one of these is an ex post-projection. Values of the exogenous variables for a year in the past which is outside the model's observation period are inserted into the model in order to compute values for the endogenous variables. These figures can be compared with actual

---

[13]) See 'Europe's future in figures', edited by R.C.Geary, Amsterdam 1962, p.328.
[14]) Op. cit. p.326.

TABLE 3 – Capital formation and stock of capital from 1960 to 1970

Billions of DM at 1954 prices

No.	Year[a]	Gross fixed investment			Replacement			Stock of capital		
		equipment $I^{b,A}$	buildings $I^{b,B}$	total I^b	equipment $I^{e,A}$	buildings $I^{e,B}$	total I^e	equipment $K^{m,A}$	buildings $K^{m,B}$	total K^m
0	1	2	3	4	5	6	7	8	9	10
1	1960	30.5	26.1	56.6	6.7	1.7	8.4	292.9	544.9	837.8
2	1961	34.2	27.7	61.9	8.1	1.8	9.9	319.1	572.3	891.4
3	1962	36.6	28.8	65.4	8.5	1.9	10.4	346.2	598.7	944.9
4	1963	39.2	30.0	69.2	9.5	2.0	11.5	375.1	626.1	1001.2
5	1964	41.5	30.7	72.2	9.7	2.0	11.7	405.8	654.5	1060.3
6	1965	43.8	31.3	75.1	8.5	2.1	10.6	439.4	683.4	1122.8
7	1966	46.5	32.1	78.6	6.0	2.2	8.2	477.3	713.0	1190.3
8	1967	49.5	33.2	82.7	1.4	2.3	3.7	521.6	743.4	1265.0
9	1968	52.7	34.3	87.0	1.5	2.4	3.9	571.2	774.8	1346.0
10	1969	56.2	35.5	91.7	2.0	2.5	4.5	623.9	807.2	1431.1
11	1970	60.1	36.9	97.0	4.1	2.6	6.7	679.0	840.9	1519.9

[a] with the Saarland included.

values for the dependent variables to find the accuracy of the ex post-projection. As there are no errors in the independent variables the resulting differences are due only to the system.

The relative errors in the endogenous variables of the ex post-projection for 1960 are shown in Table 2, column 11. The result is surprisingly good especially compared with that of the same test for the year 1950 which lies within the model's observation period (Table 2, column 10).

Looking for a single expression of all errors in the endogenous variables of the model at a given time, formula (17) can be recommended provided that large deviations are weighted independently of scale more than small ones if the absolute values of the corresponding variables are high as well:

$$
F_t = \left[\frac{\sum\limits_{n}^{N} \left(\frac{Z_{n,t} - \hat{Z}_{n,t}}{Z_{n,t}} \right)^2 Z_{n,t}}{\sum\limits_{n}^{N} Z_{n,t}} \right]^{\frac{1}{2}}
\tag{17}
$$

F_t is a measure for the average error of projection in time t based on relative deviations between actual (Z) and computed ($\hat{Z}$) values of N endogenous variables weighted in a special way.

According to equation (17) the error in 1950 is 3.2 per cent and in 1960 the error of the ex post-projection amounts only to 1.2 per cent. This may demonstrate the model's usefulness in establishing long range projections.

Further tests of the accuracy of the projections are given by the standard error and the coefficient of variation of the production function and consumption function. These statistical tests show relatively good results for the data on which the model is based. However, in making a projection it is necessary to include the projected data into the calculation of the standard error. This error of projection increases with the rising future values of the exogenous variables and therefore the confidence limits expand as well.

The values of the standard errors of projection for 1970 have been given in section IV. 1. The confidence interval seems to be large indicating about ± 7 per cent of GNP. In spite of this the point estimates in Table 2 for 1970 are still most likely. The ex post-projection for 1960 demonstrates that nearly all point estimates are even better than those of 1950 although the tolerance limits have increased.

It is possible to enlarge the model by introducing additional functions and thus to improve eventually the accuracy of the projections. First of all an investment function should be considered. We succeeded in deriving the following investment function from annual data for the period 1950 to 1957 by means of least squares:

$$I^b = -7.0729 + 0.2231\, Q + \check{u}_{I^b}, \tag{18}$$
$$(2.5851)\quad(0.0145)$$

$$D = 1.6247;\ \ R^2 = 0.9753;\ \ V = \pm 4.55\%;$$

$$s = \pm 1.45 \text{ bill. of DM.}$$

Work is in progress to introduce this function into the model.[15] Meanwhile function (18) was used to test whether there were inconsistencies between the forecast of gross fixed investment (I^b) shown in Table 3 and the projected domestic production ($\check{Q}$) up to 1970. No disturbing discrepancies emerged. Computed investment was continuously higher than the values predicted according to the least squares estimates which are biased and due to the assumption of complete utilization of the equipment stock.

---

[15] Meanwhile a model involving the investment function is established and will be published in the 'Schriftenreihe des Ifo-Instituts'.

Symbols

Q = Domestic production

K_t^{m*} = Stock of fixed capital in use at the middle (m) of the year t

K_t^m = Stock of fixed capital at the middle of the year t

K_t = Stock of fixed capital at the end of the year t

α = Degree of utilization

A = Equipment

B = Buildings (including construction)

I^b = Gross fixed capital formation

I^e = Replacement of fixed capital (capital consumption)

l = Lifetime

a, b, d = Constants

L = Labour

E = Persons employed

H = Working time

M^w = Imports of goods

M^* = Imports of goods other than capital goods

T = Trend variable

t = Calendar year

Y = Gross national product (GNP)

C = Private consumption

R = Variable containing gross investment, government consumption, balance on goods and services of foreign commerce excluding imports of goods

u = Random variable

$\vee$ = Least squares estimate

$\wedge$ = Maximum likelihood estimate

D = Ratio of the mean square successive difference to the variance

R^2 = Coefficient of determination

V = Coefficient of variation

s = Standard error of the function

The standard errors of the parameters are shown in parenthesis below the parameters.

CHAPTER 10

CRITIQUES DES METHODES DE PREVISION DE LA CONSOMMATION ET SUGGESTIONS PRATIQUES

PAR

VERA CAO-PINNA

Professeur agrégée à l'Université de Rome, Italie

Introduction

L'utilité d'un ensemble de prévisions cohérentes de l'évolution probable de la demande de biens de consommation, non seulement dans une économie de marché, mais aussi dans une économie à planification plus ou moins souple, est tellement évidente, qu'il est presque superflu d'en énumérer tous les avantages.

Même si l'on néglige le fait que la valeur totale des transactions en biens de consommation représente de 50 à 60 pourcent du chiffre d'affaire global des transactions en biens et services finaux des pays industrialisés[1]), il suffit de rappeler que l'inflation, plus ou moins cachée, qui accompagne toujours le processus de la croissance économique, trouve souvent son origine dans les déséquilibres, temporaires ou systématiques, entre l'offre et la demande des biens de consommation.

En fait, ces déséquilibres sont provoqués, non seulement par l'intervention de facteurs exogènes, mais aussi par l'ignorance, ou par une connaissance très imparfaite, soit des dimensions actuelles et futures de la demande globale des divers groupes de produits, soit de leur localisation géographique, compte tenu des possibilités, ou des difficultés, d'accroître le volume des échanges inter-régionaux.

Bien qu'un effort de programmation ou de controle rigide de la localisation des investissements et des niveaux d'activité des secteurs producteurs de biens de consommation (en particulier des biens de consom-

---

[1]) Voir, par exemple, les rapports entre ces valeurs qui ressortent des Tableaux input-output publiés en annexe à: «Information Statistiques» n⁰ 6, 1960 de l'Office Statistique des Communautés Européennes.

mation non durables) ne soit, ni désirable, ni techniquement concevable,
à cause de la dispersion et des difficultés d'association des petites et
moyennes entreprises opérant dans ces vastes secteurs du système économique, il est évident que des informations systématiques sur les perspectives de la demande des divers biens de consommation faciliteraient beaucoup l'action d'équilibre des mécanismes du marché, auxquels on accorde
encore trop de confiance dans les économies libérales ou partiellement
controlées.

On peut voir une preuve du besoin croissant d'informations sur les
dimensions et la localisation probable de la demande de biens de consommation dans la prolifération des études de marché que les grandes
entreprises industrielles des pays occidentaux utilisent pour programmer
leurs investissements et pour en réduire les risques. Les inconvénients de
ces travaux sont toutefois bien connus, car ce sont les mêmes qui caractérisent toute analyse partielle des phénomènes économiques: non-dif-
fusion des résultats des enquêtes, difficulté de mesurer l'importance relative de la demande des produits d'entreprises particulières par rapport à
la demande totale des produits similaires, difficulté d'évaluer l'expansion
du pouvoir d'achat de leur propres clients, etc.

Il est, d'autre part, évident que, même dans une économie planifiée, la
détermination des tendances qui se manifestent spontanément, par rapport
aux objectifs poursuivis en matière d'évolution de la structure de la consommation privée, constitue un stade préliminaire, mais essentiel, des
travaux visant à éclairer les décisions sur l'opportunité de maintenir, ou
de modifier ces objectifs dans l'avenir.

Les initiatives prises récemment, à l'échelle nationale et internationale,
d'organiser des études systématiques sur les perspectives de la demande
de biens de consommation représentent donc une étape très importante
vers l'établissement de services nationaux chargés de fournir couramment, aux gouvernements et aux entreprises privées et publiques, des
informations cohérentes et assez détaillées sur les dimensions futures de
la demande nationale et régionale de ces biens.

La réalisation d'un tel objectif implique, toutefois, que les efforts de la
recherche soient intensifiés et poussés, non seulement dans le domaine de
la récolte et de l'amélioration des données de base, mais aussi dans le
domaine scientifique, à la mise au point de méthodes d'exploitation des
matériaux statistiques utilisables pour les prévisions à moyen et à long
terme de la demande de biens de consommation.

Le but de cet article est précisement celui de rappeler les faiblesses des données et des méthodes actuellement utilisées pour les prévisions de la consommation privée et d'attirer l'attention des institutions, nationales et internationales, actuellement engagées dans ces recherches sur la possibilité de simplifier beaucoup et de réduire dans une mesure appreciable le coût de ces projections.

Faiblesses des données de base utilisables pour les prévisions de la consommation

1. Pour évaluer le fondement empirique des prévisions de la demande de biens de consommation, il est peut-être utile de rappeler, d'abord, que le but de ces travaux est celui d'anticiper l'évolution spontanée de la *structure* d'un agrégat macroscopique très complexe – la consommation privée – et que, comme tout effort prévisionnel, ces recherches doivent nécessairement reposer sur un cadre d'hypothèses, générales et spécifiques, dont la plus importante est celle de la non-intervention, au cours de la période de prévision, de facteurs exogènes très importants et capables de modifier profondément le régime politique, économique et monétaire du pays à l'étude [2]).

La valeur empirique de toute prévision économique dépend, toutefois de la mesure où les tendances anticipées sont *justifiés* et *expliquées*, en raison de l'influence exercée par les facteurs étroitement liés à leur évolution.

La finalité même de ces recherches exclue, donc, que l'on se limite à l'usage de la méthode de la simple extrapolation des trends de la consommation de chaque groupe de biens et services et suggère, de plus, l'opportunité de n'avoir recours aux consultations des experts de marché et aux comparaisons internationales que pour raffiner, plûtot que pour établir, les prévisions relatives à des produits particuliers.

La meilleure méthode utilisable en ce domaine est, en fait, celle des modèles économétriques, permettant d'expliciter les relations fonction-

---

[2]) Dans le cadre de cette hypothèse générale, un véritable effort de prévision, prétendant dépasser le but d'un simple exercice de projection, doit, toutefois, tenir compte de l'influence permanente de certains facteurs exogènes qui caractérisent l'évolution «normale» d'un système économique moderne (taux d'inflation controlée et altération tolérable du système des prix relatifs, nationaux et internationaux; amélioration des techniques de production, commercialisation et publicité, apparition de nouveaux produits et substitution d'autres produits, intervention des pouvoirs publics visant à modifier la distribution du revenu, ou à orienter les préférences des consommateurs, suivant les objectifs à long terme de la politique économique.

nelles, plus ou moins complexes, existant entre les dimensions, actuelles et probables, de la demande d'un produit donné et le niveau, actuel et futur, d'une ou de plusieurs variables dont l'évolution est dirigée par des facteurs bien plus complexes que la demande du produit à l'étude et qui peuvent, donc, être considérées comme des variables indépendantes.

Ces relations, pas nécessairement linéaires, peuvent être interprétées par des «lois» différentes, décrivant le degré d'intensité des variations marginales de la consommation de chaque produit, par rapport aux variations marginales des facteurs considérés comme déterminants, pourvu que la somme des valeurs monétaires assignées aux prévisions détaillées ne s'écarte pas trop du montant indépendamment estimé pour l'agrégat macroscopique de la consommation privée[3]).

Le choix des relations fonctionnelles et des variables «explicatives» utilisables pour établir un corps assez détaillé de prévisions sur la demande des divers groupes de produits dépend, toutefois, de la quantité et de la qualité des matériaux statistiques disponibles; c'est à dire, de la possibilité d'axer les prévisions:

a) sur les résultats d'une *analyse dynamique* des variations annuelles enregistrées dans les séries chronologiques de la consommation moyenne par tête de chaque produit, ou de chaque catégorie de dépenses, de même que pour les niveaux moyens des facteurs généralement censés expliquer en grande partie les variations de longue période dans le standard de vie moyen;

b) ou bien sur les résultats d'une *analyse statique* des variations enregistrées, au cours d'une annee donnée, dans les structures de la consommation totale d'un échantillon d'unités ménagères assez représentatif de la stratification démographique, géographique et socioprofessionelle de l'ensemble à étudier.

---

[3]) Il peut, en effet, arriver que, pour des raisons de cohérence avec les estimations (ou les objectifs poursuivis à l'égard) des autres composantes de la demande finale (consommation publique, investissements, exportations), on juge nécessaire d'attribuer un caractère définitif à la valeur indépendamment prévue, ou programmée, pour l'agrégat de la consommation privée et que, donc, il soit nécessaire d'éliminer la différence qui résulte normalement de la confrontation entre cette valeur globale et la somme des valeurs monétaires assignées aux prévisions détaillées de la consommation de chaque groupe de biens et services. Cette différence peut être facilement éliminée par une répartition, entre toutes les rubriques de consommation, qui ressemble suffisamment les élasticités de chaque rubrique par rapport à la consommation totale. Cependant si son ordre de grandeur était supérieur à un pourcent, il faudrait en chercher les causes et refaire les projections relatives à quelques catégories de dépenses, en particulier celles dont la relation avec le pouvoir d'achat total est plutôt faible.

Le débat classique sur la supériorité ou les faiblesses de l'une ou de l'autre méthode, en tant qu'instrument de prévision, ne trouve, en effet, son fondement et ne peut trouver sa solution que sur le plan *statistique*, plutôt que sur le plan méthodologique, car personne n'oserait nier les avantages d'une analyse dynamique de séries chronologiques assez longues et soigneusement établies (recouvrant plus de facteurs que ceux actuellement disponibles pour expliquer l'évolution de la structure de la consommation moyenne de chaque produit), par rapport aux limitations de l'analyse cross-section d'une représentation instantanée et partielle de la variabilité des phénomènes étudiés.

C'est pourquoi il nous paraît utile de passer, d'abord, rapidement en revue les sources principales des imperfections dont sont normalement affectées les données de base utilisables pour l'analyse de la demande de biens de consommation, dans les pays où l'urgence d'aborder les écueils de la prévision a dépassé celle d'organiser ou de perfectionner, avant tout, les instruments d'une analyse si complexe.

2. La méfiance souvent manifestée à l'égard des prévisions de la demande de biens de consommation dégagées du traitement mathématique des séries chronologiques trouve son origine dans le fait que, dans la plupart des pays, les estimations macroscopiques de la consommation «apparente» et des dépenses globales pour chaque groupe de biens et services sont encore un sous-produit des travaux effectués pour établir les comptes nationaux.

Il suffit de rappeler que (sauf dans quelques pays) les séries de ces estimations sont rarement établies à l'aide de tableaux «input-output» périodiques, permettant seuls de vérifier la cohérence intime des estimations de l'offre et de la demande intermédiaire et finale de chaque groupe de produits; de controler les bases bien fragiles, voir tout à fait conventionnelles, sur lesquelles reposent encore, dans la plupart des pays, les estimations ou les imputations relatives à la consommation privée de certaines catégories de produits (automobiles et carburants, loyers fictifs, auto-consommation des ménages agricoles, prix payés par les ménages des catégories commerciales); sans parler des méthodes, plus ou moins rudimentaires, utilisées pour la détermination des variations des stocks et pour la déflation des séries à prix courants du revenu et de la consommation privée.

Il nous semble par conséquent légitime d'affirmer que les estimations annuelles de la consommation des divers groupes de biens et services ne

fourniront que des indications grossières sur les changements de la
structure de la demande intérieure de biens de consommation, jusqu'à ce
que la valeur statistique des séries de base de la consommation privée soit
systématiquement contrôlée à l'aide d'informations *directes* sur la consommation intermédiaire et finale de chaque groupe de produits: c'est à
dire: jusqu'à ce que l'analyse dynamique trouve des bases statistiques
plus solides, à savoir: d'une part, les enquêtes *périodiques* sur la technologie et la structure des coûts d'exploitation de chaque branche de
production et, d'autre part, les enquêtes *périodiques* sur les budgets de
famille de chaque catégorie sociale, source primaire aussi digne de foi
que celles permettant d'établir la production et la consommation intermédiaire des divers groupes de biens et de services[4]).

Parmi les avantages de cette dernière source d'information, par rapport à des séries chronologiques de la consommation «apparente»,
établies sur la base de sources statistiques non primaires, on évoque
souvent le fait que les résultats d'une enquête instantanée peuvent être
utilisées immédiatement pour la prévision, tandis que, pour l'utilisation
des séries chronologiques, il faut attendre que l'accumulation des données
recouvre une période assez longue pour en éliminer l'influence des fluctuations cycliques et transitoires. Le défaut de séries assez longues et non
affectées par des évènements exceptionnels est, en effet, un des handicaps
typiques de la méthode dynamique.

Tout en appréciant cet avantage pratique des enquêtes instantanées sur
les budgets familiaux, il ne faut pas, toutefois, oublier qu'elles aussi
présentent de nombreux inconvénients qui minent la valeur statistique et
prévisionnelle des élaborations auxquelles les données élémentaires
peuvent être soumises: surtout lorsqu'elles ne sont que le résultat d'enquêtes sporadiques et relatives à des périodes assez éloignées du moment
où elles sont utilisées pour la prévision.

3. La première raison qui justifie les doutes sur la valeur *statistique* des
niveaux moyens de la consommation de chaque produit dégagés des enquêtes sur les budgets de famille réside dans les difficultés auxquelles se

---

[4]) Il n'y a pas, en effet, de raisons valables pour supposer que les erreurs, volon-
taires et involontaires, contenues dans les annotations des dépenses effectuées par les
échantillons de ménages soumis à ces enquêtes soient plus importantes que celles qui
affectent les données couramment fournies aux services nationaux de statistique par
les entreprises qui ne tiennent pas une comptabilité régulière de leurs propres transactions.

heurtent la formation et la stratification d'un échantillon de ménages qui soit assez représentatif de l'ensemble des consommateurs et de leur standard de vie.

Ces difficultés trouvent leur origine dans le conflit entre l'essence même de la statistique qui réside dans la recherche des homogénéités parmi les anomalies apparentes de l'ensemble étudié et dans les aspérités auxquelles se heurte, en pratique, la recherche de l'homogénéité dans un domaine économique marqué par l'individualité de la nature humaine et par la variabilité extrême de toutes ses manifestations.

L'impossibilité de disposer d'un «bench-mark» complet des caractéristiques individuelles de l'univers des consommateurs, recouvrant aussi les facteurs bio-physiques et psychologiques, (qui sont les moteurs fondamentaux des besoins humains) et la difficulté d'attribuer des valeurs numériques aux facteurs qualitatifs, expliquent le recours si fréquent qu'on est obligé de faire à l'hypothèse selon laquelle toutes les caractéristiques de cet univers qui ne sont pas susceptibles d'être mesurées par les méthodes statistiques sont distribuées de manière «normale» et que, donc, leur influence sur le comportement et les préférences des consommateurs peut être négligée, sans inconvénients sérieux.

Mais, ce qui est le plus ennuyeux c'est que les informations sur les caractéristiques mesurables (du moins en principe) et dont on sait à priori que leur distribution *n'est pas du tout «normale»* sont, elles aussi, très limitées.

Des exemples typiques de facteurs dont la distribution ne peut être connue qu'après avoir effectué des enquêtes ad hoc et qui ne peuvent, donc, être considérés dans la formation de l'échantillon, sont la variable «pouvoir d'achat disponible pour la consommation» et (lorsque les statistiques fiscales ne sont pas bonnes) la variable «revenu». Et, puisque ces variables sont justement les plus souvent utilisées pour expliquer les variations du standard de vie, il est évident que la préparation d'un échantillon de ménages est une opération extrèmement délicate et aléatoire, car on doit se contenter d'une stratification des ménages basée sur des indicateurs très indirects de la différentiation du pouvoir d'achat (tels que, par exemple, la catégorie professionnelle, ou non-professionnelle, du chef de ménage) et dont la correspondance avec la stratification effective de cette variable fondamentale ne peut pas être vérifiée à l'échelle nationale.

Mais un autre inconvénient surgit au stade du traitement statistique des résultats de ces enquêtes, à cause de la nécessité de réduire le volume

des calculs impliqués par une analyse de regression recouvrant une masse
de données normalement très vaste et, donc, de l'opportunité de *regrouper* et d'échelonner les ménages observés, suivant l'intensité (croissante) des caractéristiques considérées comme facteurs explicatifs de leur
comportement (niveau du revenu ou de la dépense totale par tête).

En effet: même si la disponibilité de calculateurs électroniques de
grande capacité permettrait désormais de développer l'analyse sur la
totalité des observations individuelles, les résultats resteraient tout de
même affectés par les imperfections et la variabilité des données élémentaires: de manière qu'il semble être encore préférable d'atténuer l'influence de leurs anomalies par des regroupements permettant de saisir
immédiatement de dessin et le rythme des relations tendancielles entre la
consommation de chaque produit et le niveau de la variable «explicative».

Ces regroupements devraient être, en principe, effectués de manière à
obtenir une différentiation maxima entre les strates successives des ménages et une variabilité minima à l'intérieur de chaque strate. Mais il est,
en pratique, difficile de respecter parfaitement cette deuxième condition:
à cause surtout du faible degré de représentativité des enquêtes à l'égard
des familles très pauvres et des familles très riches et de la variabilité très
élevée de leur comportement que l'on peut attribuer à l'importance que
les recettes occasionnelles et les profits transitoires ont dans ces milieux[5]).
Il en résulte que la discontinuité des relations fonctionnelles entre la
consommation de plusieurs produits et le niveau du revenu persiste,
malgré le regroupement des ménages, et que les paramètres de ces relations perdent souvent beaucoup de leur efficacité interprétative.

Nous réservant de retourner plus avant sur cet aspect critique de
l'analyse cross-section, nous nous limiterons, pour l'instant, à rappeler
que l'impossibilité de stratifier ex-ante les échantillons des ménages qui
doivent être soumis à l'enquête, suivant les facteurs qui influencent directement la structure de leur consommation et les difficultés de les regrouper
suivant des critères rigoureux, empêchent de considérer les valeurs *moyennes* des variables à l'étude comme des véritables données *statistiques* utilisables pour rapporter à l'ensemble, les résultats des enquêtes sur les budgets de famille.

Ceci explique pourquoi les résultats de ces enquêtes (surtout lors-

---

[5]) Voir, par exemple: les résultats de l'étude de H. P. MILLER: 'Income of the American People', Dissertation, American University, 1953.

qu'elles ne sont pas effectuées périodiquement) se prêtent mieux à être utilisés, en termes *relatifs* et comparatifs, plutôt qu'en termes *absolus*, et qu'ils ne peuvent fournir que des *indications*, plus ou moins grossières, de la distribution du pouvoir d'achat et de la consommation parmi les diverses classes de la stratification démographique, économique et sociale du pays, ou de la région étudiée.

Les limitations de la méthode dynamique

4. La nature défectueuse des séries chronologiques de la consommation privée et des données cross-section résultant d'enquêtes sporadiques sur les budgets de famille n'est, toutefois, qu'une des faiblesses d'ordre *statistique* qui minent la valeur prévisionnelle des deux méthodes alternativement ou simultanément utilisables en ce domaine.

Un autre inconvénient, commun à l'analyse dynamique et à l'analyse statique, consiste, en effet, dans le nombre, généralement limité, des variables utilisables pour «expliquer» les variations dans la structure de la consommation privée. Les deux méthodes sont, toutefois, handicapées par cette limitation d'une manière différente: ce qui rend encore plus difficile la comparaison des résultats des deux types d'analyse.

Les séries chronologiques généralement disponibles pour effectuer une analyse dynamique de la consommation moyenne de chaque groupe de produits sont celles (normalement utilisées sous forme de nombres indices) du revenu national, ou de la consommation totale par tête (calculés à prix constants); des prix moyens d'un certain nombre de produits (surtout alimentaires) et du niveau général des prix, parfois remplacé par l'index du coût de la vie, ou par l'index des salaires réels.

Le protagoniste abstrait d'une analyse dynamique basée sur les séries chronologiques des variables macroscopiques reste, toutefois, le «*consommateur moyen*», ce qui empêche de considérer *explicitement* l'influence exercée par les facteurs stucturels, tels que: la structure démographique et professionnelle, la distribution du revenu, le facteur agglomération et, très souvent, aussi le facteur régional qui joue, dans certains pays et au cours de certaines périodes, un rôle important dans l'évolution de la structure de la consommation privée.

Cette limitation de l'analyse dynamique est due à la centralisation des services de statistique et aux difficultés d'établir des séries régionales de la disponibilité et de la consommation effective des divers groupes de produits.

Le coût des efforts (déjà entrepris en quelques pays)[6]) pour fractionner le système statistique national est, en effet, très élevé et, puisqu'il y a des raisons de croire que l'ère d'une «photo électronique» capable de représenter et de classer immédiatement et perpétuellement tout les détails de l'univers économique est encore lointaine, il est plus probable que les analystes de la demande de biens de consommation devront continuer à limiter l'application de la méthode dynamique dans le domaine abstrait des valeurs moyennes.

L'expédient d'introduire le facteur *temps* comme variable explicative additionnelle ne fait d'autre part qu'aggraver, plutôt que réduire, la faiblesse d'une analyse dynamique basée sur les séries chronologiques de la consommation privée.

En effet, dans une analyse dynamique où il n'est pas possible d'introduire explicitement les facteurs structurels comme variables indépendantes, le facteur temps ne peut pas être censé représenter seulement l'évolution normale et graduelle des facteurs exogènes (tels que goûts, habitudes, innovations, progrès commercial et publicitaire) car, dans le cas d'une expansion «normale» du système économique, le niveau moyen des autres variables explicatives (revenu, prix, coût de la vie) évolue, aussi plus ou moins régulièrement dans le temps, lequel devient donc une variable «omnibus» fictivement représentative de tous les facteurs qui agissent sur la structure et sur l'évolution des variables considérées comme indépendantes. Cette inter-corrélation entre les variables ainsi dites indépendantes donne, pour cette raison, lieu à des phénomènes de collinéarité qui contribuent à accroître la marge d'erreur des paramètres des fonctions de consommation et, surtout, à réduire leur signification économique.

Les avantages et les inconvénients de la méthode statique

5. *L'analyse cross-section* présente, par contre, l'avantage de permettre la prise en considération de facteurs structurels, pour expliquer les différences existantes – à un instant donné – dans le standard de vie des diverses catégories de ménages.

---

[6]) En Italie, par exemple, on a déjà procédé à la désaggrégation des séries de la comptabilité nationale (à partir de 1951) en trois grandes zones géographiques (Nord-Ouest, Sud et le reste d'Italie) et les premières tentatives de programmation économique ont déjà montré la nécessité de procéder à une régionalisation et désaggrégation plus poussée de ces séries.

Les informations rassemblées par les enquêtes sur les budgets de famille sont en effet très nombreuses : taille et composition démographique des ménages, catégorie et position professionnelle de leurs chefs, degré d'activité de leurs membres, zone géographique et degré d'agglomération des centres de résidence, revenu et (ou) consommation totale, stock de biens durables, structure détaillée des dépenses de chaque ménage soumis à l'enquête et, parfois, quantité et prix unitaires payés pour un nombre de produits et d'articles spécifiques. L'ensemble de ces informations offre ainsi un matériel précieux pour l'analyse économétrique des interrelations entre les variables observées.

Cependant, l'ampleur même de cette documentation soulève des problèmes sérieux, non seulement au stade préliminaire de la vérification du degré de véracité et de cohérence des données élémentaires et de leur classification, mais aussi au stade du traitement statistique et mathématique de ces données. En effet, la complexité des calculs nécessaires pour développer une analyse de *régression multiple* sur la totalité des observations individuelles, visant à isoler l'influence de chaque facteur sur le niveau de la consommation de chaque produit est telle que, malgré la disponibilité de calculateurs électroniques, on se contente encore d'exploiter, de la meilleure manière possible, les avantages de la *régression simple* entre les valeurs *moyennes* de la consommation, ou des dépenses effectuées par chaque strate de ménages et les valeurs *moyennes* respectives du facteur considéré comme la variable explicative *principale* des différences entre leur standard de vie (revenu ou dépense totale par tête).

Par conséquent, l'analyse cross-section à deux seules variables n'a pas pour protagoniste l'abstraction d'un seul consommateur moyen, ni la foule réelle des membres des ménages observés, mais une succession de *consommateurs «moyens»*, échelonnés suivant le pouvoir d'achat respectif, mais dont le degré de représentativité statistique est inévitablement affecté par les difficultés d'une stratification rigoureuse, surtout dans les sections extrêmes de leur distribution.

Le but d'une analyse cross-section, élaborée ad hoc comme instrument de prévision, est tout de même celui de vérifier si la succession des valeurs moyennes décrivant les structures de la consommation de chaque strate des ménages observés à un instant donné est, plus ou moins intensément, mais surtout, étroitement liée à la succession des valeurs moyennes du pouvoir d'achat, de sorte que (en admettant l'hypothèse peu réaliste d'une distribution «normale», tant des erreurs d'échantillonage, que de l'influence des facteurs non considérés) les relations entre ces succesions de valeurs peuvent être supposées valables à n'importe quel niveau inter-médiaire de la consommation des ménages compris en chaque strate.

La disponibilité des données élémentaires permet, toutefois, d'atténuer l'arbitraire de cette supposition et d'approfondir l'analyse, car si les di-mensions de l'échantillon le permettent, il est possible de différentier ul-térieurement la succession des consommateurs «moyens», par la prise en considération d'autres facteurs non distribués normalement.

Le recours à l'expédient de fractionner l'analyse de régression simple, pour étudier séparément l'influence du facteur revenu sur la structure de la consommation des diverses catégories sociales, en particulier des caté-gories agricoles et non-agricoles, ou dans les diverses régions du terri-toire national, est, en effet, justifié par les résultats de nombreuses études qui ont démenti la validité de l'hypothèse d'homogénéité du comporte-ment des consommateurs, par rapport aux variations du pouvoir d'achat respectif et, par conséquent, la possibilité d'utiliser une équation de régression *unique* pour «expliquer» la «loi générale» de la demande d'un produit donné[7]).

Il faut, en outre, rappeler que les inconvénients du regroupement de données hétérogènes sont accentués par le fait que les relations fonc-tionelles revenu-consommation sont rarement linéaires, même à l'inté-rieur de catégories de consommateurs assez homogènes, et que donc le fractionnement de l'analyse de régression simple, par catégorie sociale et par région, présente des avantages remarquables, car il permet d'utiliser facilement des ajustements curvilinéaires (par exemple, semi-logarith-miques ou bi-logarithmiques) et d'en atténuer les erreurs dues au re-groupement des données élémentaires.

En effet, if faut rappeler que l'utilisation de fonctions linéaires (ou linéarisables) implique que l'on juge acceptable l'hypothèse d'accroisse-ments constants ou, dans le cas de fonctions exponentielles, d'élasticités constantes de la consommation de chaque produit, par rapport à la variable indépendante (revenu ou dépense totale). Mais, puisque cette hypothèse se fonde sur la condition «ceteris paribus» de la combinaison de tous les autres facteurs qui influencent la consommation de chaque produit, il en résulte que si des variations importantes, mais d'intensité différente,

---

[7]) Voir, par exemple, les résultats des analyses effectuées par F. GIUSTI et R. GUARI-NO sur un échantillon de ménages urbains collectés en 1953–1954 par l'Institut Italien de Statistique et publiés dans le volume 'Indagine statistica sui bilanci di famiglie non-agricole negli anni 1953–1954': Annali de Statistica; Année 89 Série VIII, Vol. II – Institut Central de Statistique, Rome, 1960.

sont prévues pour les divers facteurs (surtout à l'égard de la structure socio-professionnelle et de l'apport régional à la formation du P.N.B.), l'hypo-thèse de constance des accroissements, ou des élasticités, de la consomma-tion moyenne de chaque produit n'est plus théoriquement admissible.

Le problème des revenus extrêmes et l'opportunité d'éliminer leur influence dans l'élaboration des courbes d'Engel

6. Les avantages que l'analyse cross-section présente, par rapport à l'analyse dynamique des séries chronologiques, sont, toutefois, sérieuse-ment atténuées par le caractère arbitraire des hypothèses fondamentales sur lesquelles normalement repose son utilisation pour la prévision.

Ces hypothèses concernent:
1) la stabilité, au cours de la période de prévision, de la distribution du pouvoir d'achat (c'est à dire, des poids relatifs de chaque strate de ménages);
2) la stabilité de la structure des prix relatifs des divers groupes de biens et services et des autres facteurs qui influencent le comportement des consommateurs, tels que les goûts, les techniques commerciales et publicitaires, etc. ...;
3) l'automatisme de l'évolution du comportement des consommateurs, lorsqu'ils passent d'une classe à l'autre du revenu.

La rigidité de ces hypothèses est, en général, due à la rareté d'enquêtes systématiques et périodiques sur les budgets de famille, qui seules pour-raient fournir des informations précieuses, soit sur les modifications de la distribution du pouvoir d'achat, à l'échelle nationale et régionale, soit sur l'évolution du comportement des divers strates de ménages vis à vis des variations des prix relatifs, ou d'autres phénomènes, tels que l'apparition ou une diffusion plus large de produits et de services nouveaux.

Et, comme les marges d'erreur dues à la non-considération, dans la prévision, de l'influence exercée par tous ces facteurs sur la structure et la répartition régionale de l'agrégat consommation privée sont sûrement plus importantes que celles dues à une faible représentativité de quelques catégories sociales[8]), on peut s'interroger sur l'utilité que peuvent présen-

---

[8]) Par exemple: d'après un document (non publié) du Départment de l'Agriculture des Etats Unis d'Amérique, il résulte que les modifications dans la distribution du revenu (enregistrées par les deux enquêtes sur les budgets des familles urbaines effec-tuées au printemps des années 1942 et 1955) auraient contribué pour le 45% à l'augmen-tation de la dépense par tête pour l'alimentation, enregistrés entre les deux années.

ter, pour la prévision, des enquêtes très vastes, mais effectuées occasion-
nellement et sans leur assigner le but précis d'éclairer le rôle joué par les
divers facteurs dans l'évolution de la structure de la consommation privée.

Nous pensons, en effet, que les enquêtes sur les budgets de famille
devraient essentiellement viser à enrichir et à améliorer la documentation
nécessaire pour *dynamiser l'analyse statique de la consommation effective*
et pour en rendre les résultats plus comparables avec ceux dégagés de
l'analyse des séries chronologiques de la consommation «apparente»
établies sur la base des statistiques de l'offre des divers groupes de biens
et de services.

Notre analyse critique des données et des inconvénients des méthodes,
encore trop mécaniquement utilisées pour la prévision de la consommation, n'avait en fait nullement pour but de décourager les initiatives en
ce domaine, mais justement au contraire, celui de montrer (si jamais il
y'en avait besoin) la nécessité d'intensifier la récolte et l'exploitation des
budgets familiaux, comme source fondamentale pour l'anticipation des
tendances, spontanées ou conditionnées, qui domineront les marchés des
biens de consommation, dans le futur.

7. Ce sont, toutefois, les inconvénients mentionnées à l'égard de la difficulté de stratifier correctement les échantillons des ménages, suivant le
pouvoir d'achat respectif, et de la variabilité extrême que l'on constate
souvent dans le comportement des ménages appartenant aux classes
«pauvres» et «riches», qui nous suggère l'opportunité de proposer que
ces classes soient négligées dans l'organisation des enquêtes périodiques
sur les budgets de famille, autant que dans l'élaboration des courbes
d'Engel pour les prévisions de la consommation.

En effet: sans nier l'exigeance d'essayer, de temps en temps, d'évaluer
l'importance relative des sections extrêmes de la distribution du revenu et
de faire des sondages sur la ventilation, par catégories de dépense, du
pouvoir d'achat dont disposent des ménages typiquement (même si tran-
sitoirement) très «pauvres» ou très «riches», is nous paraît pertinent de
poser la question de l'utilité que peuvent présenter, pour la prévision, les
informations concernant le comportement de ces catégories.

Sans compter la difficulté d'obtenir des informations véridiques sur
leur propre standard de vie, il faut tenir compte du fait que les dépenses
effectuées par les membres des familles très «pauvres» ou très «riches»
sont si souvent imposées, ou stimulées, par des circonstances accidentelles et dépourvues de toute logique d'administration budgétaire, qu'il

est bien difficile d'identifier des relations assez stables entre les échelles de leur propres besoins et le pouvoir d'achat dont ils disposent. Il en résulte que la prise en considération de ces catégories dans l'analyse cross-section ne fait qu'accentuer la nature erratique des paramètres des courbes d'Engel et, donc, affaiblir leur efficacité prévisionnelle.

Tout en nous rendant compte que la limitation des enquêtes aux budgets de familles appartenant aux classes «*moyennes*» (identifiables dans les catégories des *travailleurs*, dépendants et indépendants, ou, en général, dans les familles caractérisées par un rapport normal entre unités productives et unités de consommation) équivaudrait à limiter le champ d'application du modèle Engelien aux biens de grande consommation et de qualité moyenne, nous pensons qu'il soit préférable de concentrer les efforts de la recherche sur le comportement de ces catégories, au lieu de pousser l'exercice de la prévision jusqu'aux détails insaisissables des biens demandés par les sections périphériques d'une collectivité nationale ou régionale.

Les considérations sur lesquelles repose notre proposition sont les suivantes:

a) dans une économie en expansion, le rôle joué par les classes «moyennes» dans l'évolution de la structure de la consommation privée devient de plus en plus prépondérant;

b) la distribution du revenu à l'intérieur des classes «moyennes» est peu asymétrique et les variations de cette distribution sont moins profondes que celles de la distribution du revenu parmi toutes les catégories sociales;

c) l'adaptation des goûts et des standards de vie de ces catégories de ménages est, lors du passage d'une classe de revenu à la suivante, plus rapide que celle des classes inférieures et supérieures et, pourtant, les variations de la structure de la consommation des catégories moyennes suivent, plus ou moins étroitement, mais en tout cas plus régulièrement, les variations du pouvoir d'achat respectif;

d) les effets des facteurs autres que le revenu (surtout les variations des prix relatifs et l'apparition de nouveaux produits) ont une diffusion très rapide et générale parmi les classes moyennes; de telle sorte qu'il serait possible d'en tenir compte plus facilement dans la prévision des niveaux moyens de la consommation des divers groupes de biens et services.

8. Dans la mesure où toutes ces considérations peuvent être acceptées comme assez réalistes, ou moins grossières que les hypothèses sur les-

quelles reposent les projections fondées sur l'analyse statique du comportement de tous les ménages observés par des enquêtes sporadiques
prétendant recouvrir la totalité de l'univers des consommateurs, il nous
semble légitime d'affirmer que la limitation des enquêtes aux classes
moyennes serait justifiée, non seulement en raison des économies réalisables dans l'opération, très coûteuse, de la récolte des données élémentaires et de la vérification de leur véracité, mais aussi en raison des
possibilités qu'elle offre d'intensifier les enquêtes et, donc, d'étudier l'influence sur la structure de la consommation des facteurs autres que le
revenu, ou la dépense totale, par tête, en particulier: les variations des
prix relatifs et des goûts, le stock de biens durables et leur forme de
paiement, la propriété des logements, la nature permanente ou transitoire
des revenus, etc. ...

Notre proposition équivaut, d'ailleurs, à suggérer une application plus
radicale de l'expédient couramment recommandé pour réduire les inconvénients de la variabilité de certains groupes d'observations qui consiste à
pondérer les niveaux moyens de la consommation des divers groupes de
produits de chaque strate de ménages en proportions inverses à la variabilité des niveaux du revenu des ménages classifiés en chaque strate[9]).

Nous nous promettants de nouveau de retourner sur ce sujet dans un
autre article qui sera dédié à l'illustration des résultats d'une expérience
concrète qui vient de nous confirmer le rôle joué par la variabilité des
revenus extrêmes sur la nature erratique des paramètres des courbes
d'Engel et, donc, sur leur validité prévisionnelle, nous nous limiterons à
rappeler que l'analyse cross-section ne peut être utilisée comme instrument de prévision que si l'ajustment entre les successions des valeurs
moyennes de la consommation *effective* des divers groupes de produits et
celles des valeurs *calculées* (à l'aide des fonctions de consommation) est
assez satisfaisant, du moins en correspondance des niveaux de revenu (ou
de dépense totale par tête) compris dans le champ de variation prévu pour
cette variable. Rappelons en outre que, si les ajustements obtenus par
l'utilisation de courbes d'Engel dégagées d'une distribution de ménages
recouvrant une échelle de revenus suffisamment large, mais tranchée à

---

[9]) En effet: suivant une suggestion de J. A. C. Brown, le test de l'homogénéité des
divers groupes d'observations peut être limité à l'égard de la variable indépendante, en
considération de l'étroite relation existant entre la variabilité des standards de vie des
ménages classeés en chaque strate et la variabilité des niveaux de revenus respectifs.
Voir: S. J. PRAIS et J. ATCHINSON: 'The Grouping of Observations in Regression
Analysis', in Revue de l'Institut International de Statistique, Vol. 22, La Haye, 1954.

l'égard des classes très «pauvres» et très «riches», donneraient des résultats systématiquement meilleurs que les ajustements obtenus par l'utilisation de courbes d'Engel dégagées d'une distribution plus ou moins représentative de toutes les catégories sociales, on pourrait conclure que *la prise en considération des revenus extrêmes est nuisible, plutôt qu'utile, pour la mise au point d'un instrument de prévision.*

Bien que de nombreuses expériences devront être faites avant de démontrer le fondement empirique de cette conclusion, nous n'avons pas voulu manquer la chance d'attirer l'attention des organisations et des experts engagés dans les travaux de prévision de la demande de biens de consommation sur la possibilité de réduire les coûts de la récolte et de l'exploitation des budgets familiaux, sans préjuger l'éfficacité de leur utilisation pour la prévision.

SUMMARY

Forecasts of consumption that are more than simple extrapolations are based on relationships between consumption and certain determinant factors. These relationships can be derived from time-series and from budget studies. They can take several forms, provided some care is taken that the total of the forecasts of all individual consumption items is reasonably close to the forecast of total consumption obtained independently. Usually, this condition is easy to fulfil.

Statistically, time series leave much to be desired; they are rare, short, and often little related to independent data on output and foreign trade. Regression analysis of time series rarely provides opportunity to estimate the influence of determinant factors other than income and prices.

Budget studies have their own weaknesses. As they are essentially sample observations, which cannot be properly stratified by income brackets, their average consumption pattern may be far from representative. They do, however, allow the analysis of the impact of a number of different factors on consumption, and it is possible to introduce fairly complicated functions of income.

The erratic consumer behaviour encountered in both the highest and the lowest income brackets of a budget enquiry often affects the Engel relationships that could be derived from the observations. It is suggested that projections of average consumption patterns could be better based on relationships derived from the middle portion only of the income distribution.

CHAPTER 11

PROJECTIONS DE LA DEMANDE DES PRODUITS AGRICOLES EN EUROPE OCCIDENTALE EN 1970*)

PAR

L. M. GOREUX

Organisation des Nations Unies pour l'Alimentation et l'Agriculture, Rome, Italie

Dans une étude publiée récemment par la FAO[1]), nous avons procédé à une analyse des tendances mondiales de la demande, de la production et du commerce des produits agricoles, les moyennes triennales 1957–1959 et 1969–1971 correspondant respectivement à la base et au terme de la période de projections. Le but de cette étude était d'abord de prévoir la nature et la gravité des problèmes qui risqueraient de se poser dans le domaine de l'agriculture et de l'alimentation au cours de la prochaine décennie si les politiques demeuraient inchangées. C'était ensuite d'analyser comment ces politiques devraient être modifiées pour faciliter la résolution des problèmes prévus.

L'Europe de l'Est et la Chine Continentale avaient été considérées séparément en raison des problèmes particuliers des économies fortement planifiées; le reste du monde avait été divisé en deux groupes: le groupe des pays riches et le groupe des pays pauvres, l'accent étant placé sur les relations entre le groupe des riches et le groupe des pauvres.

Dans cet article, nous nous limiterons aux projections de la demande des produits agricoles dans le groupe des riches. Les résultats, pays par pays, figurent dans les tableaux contenus dans l'annexe statistique, mais ces résultats doivent être interprétés avec prudence car notre objet était d'étudier les problèmes par grands groupes de pays et non point les problèmes particuliers de tel ou tel pays. On insistera, dans le texte, sur les problèmes d'ordre méthodologique tout en essayant d'établir une distinc-

---

*) Pour l'Annexe voir p. 357.

[1]) «Produits Agricoles – Projections pour 1970», E/CN 13/48 – CCP 62/5 Rome, 1962.

tion entre ce qui nous paraît solide et ce qui nous paraît fragile dans l'établissement de ces projections. Tenant compte de la marge d'erreur probable des résultats, nous nous efforcerons pour conclure d'analyser dans quelle mesure les résultats déjà obtenus peuvent contribuer à la formulation des politiques économiques.

1. PROJECTIONS DU VOLUME DE LA DEMANDE AU NIVEAU DE LA FERME ET NON PAS DE LA DÉPENSE DES PARTICULIERS AU NIVEAU DU DÉTAIL

Les objectifs poursuivis conditionnent évidemment dans une large mesure les méthodes adoptées. Ce que nous recherchions n'était point de déterminer l'évolution des dépenses des particuliers entre les différents postes de leur budget, telles les dépenses de restaurant, de pâtisserie ou d'habillement, c'était de déterminer l'évolution de la demande en termes de produits agricoles de base tels le blé, le sucre ou le coton, et ceci afin de permettre une confrontation entre projections de la demande et projections de la production agricole. Aussi, plutôt que de partir des dépenses finales des consommateurs, de projeter ces dépenses, puis d'en déduire la demande intermédiaire en termes de produits de base, a-t-il paru à la fois plus simple et plus sûr de partir de la demande en termes de produits de base telle qu'elle apparaît dans les bilans alimentaires publiés par la FAO et de projeter directement l'évolution de cette demande pour chaque type d'utilisation. Les raisons qui nous ont enclins à ce choix sont de plusieurs ordres :

(i) En partant des bilans alimentaires, on peut facilement analyser l'évolution de la ration en termes d'éléments nutritionnels. Or, dans les pays à revenu élevé, l'évolution de cette ration en termes de calories, de graisses et de protéines, peut être projetée avec plus de précision que l'évolution de la dépense alimentaire au niveau du détail. Aussi est-il essentiel de compléter l'approche économétrique basée sur la théorie des choix par des considérations d'ordre nutritionnel. Cette nécessité est encore plus pressante dans les pays à revenu faible, car dans ces pays l'amélioration du niveau nutritionnel est un des objectifs même du plan.

(ii) Dans les pays à revenu élevé, l'élasticité de la demande par rapport aux prix est, par grands groupes de produits agricoles, généralement plus voisine de zéro que de l'unité. Si le coefficient d'élasticité quantité-prix est égal à $-0,25$, une baisse des prix de 20 pourcent entraînerait une réduction de 5 pourcent dans les quantités demandées mais une augmentation de 15 pourcent dans les dépenses. Comme il est fort difficile d'introduire d'une façon satisfaisante les variations des prix dans un modèle de projection, on diminue la marge d'erreur en réduisant l'influence des prix, c'est-à-dire en établissant les projections en termes de quantités de produits de base plutôt qu'en termes de dépenses.

(iii) Le passage de la nomenclature des dépenses de consommation à la nomenclature des produits agricoles pose des problèmes délicats car, même pour la période de base, on ne dispose en général pas d'une matrice «input-output» suffisamment détaillée. Ces problèmes sont évidemment aggravés lorsqu'on ne considère plus la période de base mais le terme de la projection. Par exemple, si à une dépense au détail de 100 correspond une valeur à la ferme de 50 en 1958, et si la dépense au détail devient 140 en 1970, il n'est pas du tout certain que la valeur à la ferme augmente proportionnellement, c'est-à-dire passe de 50 en 1958 à 70 en 1970. Il est probable que la valeur à la ferme augmente moins vite que la marge entre valeur au détail et valeur à la ferme. En effet, la demande se portera sur des produits ayant subi un processus de transformation de plus en plus poussé, tels que les légumes surgelés, tandis que le coût de distribution augmentera vraisemblablement plus rapidement que le coût de production à la ferme. Il est fort difficile de mesurer l'influence respective de ces deux facteurs, amélioration des services de transformation et de distribution d'une part, modification des coûts relatifs d'autre part. Aussi pensons-nous que, même dans le cas où l'on veut procéder à la fois à la projection des dépenses des particuliers et à la projection des débouchés du secteur agricole, il ne serait pas indiqué de partir des dépenses pour arriver au secteur agricole après avoir formulé certaines hypothèses quant à l'évolution des secteurs de transformation et de distribution. Nous pensons qu'il serait préférable de partir simultanément des projections des dépenses et des projections des produits agricoles de base et, ensuite, sur la base d'une étude économique des secteurs de transformation et de distribution, d'arriver par approximations successives à des projections cohérentes des dépenses au niveau du détail et des quantités au niveau de la ferme. Aussi nous proposons-nous de suivre cette approche dans la préparation de notre prochaine étude.

2. LE CADRE DU DÉVELOPPEMENT ÉCONOMIQUE

Pour projeter la demande, le premier problème était d'établir un cadre du développement économique. Ce cadre est schématisé dans le Tableau I en Annexe, qui comporte une seule hypothèse d'accroissement démographique mais deux hypothèses d'accroissement du revenu. Ces deux hypothèses ont été choisies afin de pouvoir apprécier l'influence d'un rythme plus ou moins rapide d'expansion économique sur la demande des produits agricoles et aussi afin de souligner qu'il s'agissait bien de projections conditionnelles, et non de simples prévisions. Ces hypothèses ont été retenues en automne 1961. Depuis lors, le Secrétariat de l'OCDE a procédé à un travail en profondeur dans le cadre de l'objectif de croissance de 50 pourcent; aussi peut-on, aujourd'hui, comparer nos hypothèses avec les résultats encore provisoires de l'étude faite par l'OCDE pour les cinq principaux pays de cette organisation[2]). On constate que les hypothèses démographiques sont peu différentes, que notre hypothèse de revenu élevé correspond aux objectifs de l'OCDE pour les Etats-Unis, le Royaume-Uni et la France, tandis que pour l'Allemagne et l'Italie les objectifs de l'OCDE sont plus voisins de notre hypothèse faible que de notre hypothèse forte.

Il eut été important d'établir une distinction entre le taux d'accroissement du Produit National Brut, du revenu disponible des particuliers et de la consommation privée. Dans les six pays du Marché Commun où une telle distinction a pu être faite, on a basé les projections de la demande sur les taux d'accroissement de la consommation totale des particuliers. Pour les autres pays, une telle distinction n'a pu être opérée faute de temps et on a donc supposé que PNB et consommation privée augmenteraient au même rythme. Il n'a pas été possible de tenir compte de l'influence d'une modification de la distribution du revenu sur la demande globale car la distribution actuelle est généralement mal connue et il est fort difficile de prévoir comment cette distribution se modifiera au cours des dix prochaines années.

On a admis dans cette étude que la demande alimentaire augmenterait, ceteris paribus, proportionnellement à l'accroissement démographique. Il n'a pas été tenu compte ni de l'influence de la modification de la structure de la population par âge, ni de l'influence de l'urbanisation, mais il semble qu'à l'échelon national les effets spécifiques de ces deux facteurs soient généralement relativement peu importants. Aussi, le réel problème était-il de projeter l'évolution de la demande individuelle. Pour la facilité de l'exposition on mettra l'accent, dans ce qui suit, sur la demande alimentaire en étudiant l'influence du revenu, des facteurs nutritionnels et des

---

[2]) OCDE, «Note du Secrétariat sur les projections de la demande en produits alimentaires dans les pays de l'OCDE pour 1970», AGR/WP 1 (62) 7, Paris, 1962.

prix. On examinera ensuite les problèmes particuliers posés par la projection de la demande non-alimentaire en l'illustrant par deux exemples : les besoins d'alimentation du bétail et la demande de fibres textiles.

3. REVENU ET CONSOMMATION

Le premier problème consistait dans le choix d'une fonction caractérisant les relations entre consommation par personne et revenu par personne. Un certain nombre de fonctions de consommation ont été expérimentées, en particulier celles indiquées dans le Tableau 1 ; leur choix a été basé sur trois critères : la précision statistique de l'ajustement, la vraisemblance de la fonction dans le cadre de la théorie de la consommation, et la simplicité du mode d'estimation des paramètres.

La courbe représentative de l'équation (4) (Tableau 1), représentée sur le graphique 1, semble pouvoir traduire d'une façon assez satisfaisante l'évolution des quantités consommées d'un produit donné lorsque le revenu passe d'un niveau très faible à un niveau très élevé. Le premier segment AB de la courbe catactérise un produit de luxe dont la consommation augmente rapidement en fonction du revenu ; le segment BC caractérise un bien de nécessité, le taux d'accroissement de la consommation diminuant progressivement lorsque le revenu augmente ; le segment CD caractérise un bien inférieur dont la consommation diminue lorsque le revenu augmente. Cette fonction est bien adaptée à l'étude de la consommation des céréales ou plus généralement des carbohydrates lorsqu'on dispose d'un éventail de revenu très ouvert allant, par exemple, de l'Inde aux Etats-Unis. Les pays très pauvres sont dans la portion BC de la courbe, voire – pour certains groupes particulièrement démunis – à l'extrêmité supérieure de la section AB. La zone du maximum C correspond à des pays comme le Portugal et la Turquie, tandis que tous les pays riches sont situés sur la section descendante CD. Il est toutefois assez exceptionnel de disposer de données statistiques couvrant l'ensemble de la courbe AD, et donc de pouvoir déterminer avec précision les trois paramètres de la fonction (4). Aussi, cette fonction n'a-t-elle été retenue que lorsqu'il s'agissait de projeter la demande de céréales dans les pays en voie de développement pour lesquels le niveau de consommation au cours de la période de base se situe le long du segment BC de la courbe représentée sur le Graphique 1. Pour l'Europe occidentale et l'Amérique du Nord, on a utilisé les fonctions (2) et (3) impliquant toutes deux une diminution du coefficient d'élasticité lorsque le revenu augmente, cette

TABLEAU 1 – Fonctions de consommation

Fonction		Propension marginale à consommer	Coefficient d'élasticité
(1) Logarithmique	$\log y = a + b \log x + u$	$b \dfrac{y}{x}$	b
(2) Semi-logarithmique*	$y = a + b \log x + u$	$\dfrac{b}{x}$	$\dfrac{b}{y} = \dfrac{b}{a + b \log x}$
(3) Log-inverse*	$\log y = a - \dfrac{b}{x} + u$	$b \dfrac{y}{x^2}$	$\dfrac{b}{x}$
(4) Log-log-inverse*	$\log y = a - \dfrac{b}{x} - c \log x + u$	$\dfrac{y(b - cx)}{x^2}$	$\dfrac{b - cx}{x}$
(5) Log normal* a)	$y = y_\infty \, P(\log x / \mu, \sigma^2) + u$	$\dfrac{y}{x} \dfrac{1}{\sigma} \dfrac{Z(t)}{P(t)}$	$\dfrac{1}{\sigma} \dfrac{Z(t)}{P(t)}$

* Toutes les formules se rapportent aux logarithmes népériens. L'utilisation des logarithmes décimaux entraîne l'utilisation d'un facteur de correction; ainsi le coefficient d'élasticité peut s'écrire: $0,4343 \dfrac{b}{y}$ pour la fonction (2), $2,3026 \dfrac{b}{x}$ pour la fonction (3), $- c + 2,3026 \dfrac{b}{x}$ pour la fonction (4).

a) P représente l'intégrale de la fonction normale d'écart-type σ et de moyenne μ, Z est l'ordonnée de la distribution normale et t est la variable réduite $t = - \dfrac{\mu}{\sigma} + \dfrac{1}{\sigma} \log x$.

diminution étant plus marquée pour la fonction log-inverse que pour la fonction semi-logarithmique. La courbe représentative de la fonction log-inverse est une sigmoïde présentant un point d'inflexion pour un niveau de revenu faible et une asymptote horizontale lorsque le revenu tend vers l'infini. La forme de cette courbe est assez voisine de celle de l'intégrale de la distribution log-normale proposée par Brown et Aitchinson et représentée dans le Tableau 1 par l'équation (5); la fonction log-inverse est

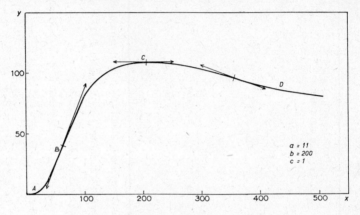

GRAPHIQUE 1. Courbe représentative de la fonction

$$\log_e y = a - \frac{b}{x} - c \log_e x.$$

moins souple que la fonction log-normale car elle dépend seulement de deux paramètres au lieu de trois, mais son ajustement statistique est beaucoup plus aisé.

Les fonctions de consommation ont été ajustées sur une documentation statistique très abondante: les niveaux moyens de consommation annuelle par pays pour une vingtaine de produits tels qu'ils apparaissent dans les bilans alimentaires publiés par la FAO au cours des dix dernières années d'une part, et une centaine d'enquêtes de consommation effectuées un peu partout de par le monde au cours de la dernière décennie, d'autre part. On indiquera ici seulement une des caractéristiques de la méthode de calcul utilisée: la stratification des données avec analyse de covariance entre strates.

Dans les enquêtes de consommation on a procédé à une stratification des ménages en fonction de leur composition ou de leur lieu de résidence (grandes villes, petites villes, campagne), ou de la période de l'enquête en cas d'enquêtes permanentes ou semi-permanentes. A l'intérieur de chaque strate on a ajusté une équation de regression entre consommation par tête et revenu par tête et on a testé la significativité des regressions ainsi obtenues. Dans le cas où les regressions calculées à l'intérieur de chaque strate étaient significatives, on a testé la significativité des différences entre les coefficients de regression relatives à chacune des strates. Si les pentes des droites de regression n'étaient pas significativement différentes entre strates, tandis que les niveaux de ces droites étaient significativement différents, on a retenu comme estimateur le plus efficient de la regression entre consommation et revenu la moyenne pondérée des coefficients de regression par strate, la pondération étant basée sur la valeur de la variance à l'intérieur de chaque strate. Si ni les pentes ni les niveaux des droites de regression par strate n'étaient significativement différents, on a retenu comme estimateur le plus efficient le coefficient de regression calculé pour l'ensemble de la population non-stratifiée.

Une méthode analogue a été utilisée pour analyser dans le temps et dans l'espace l'évolution de la consommation moyenne annuelle par pays. Par exemple, pour étudier la demande de sucre, on a groupé les statistiques de base dans trois tableaux dont les colonnes correspondaient aux années et les lignes aux pays. Le premier tableau se rapportait au revenu exprimé en dollars à des prix constants par tête et par an, le second à la consommation de sucre en kilogs par tête et par an, et le troisième aux prix réels du sucre en cents par kilog. Ces trois tableaux ont tout d'abord été analysés ligne par ligne, ce qui correspond à l'analyse classique des séries chronologiques par pays; la significativité des différences obtenues entre les coefficients de regression par pays a été testée par l'analyse de covariance en suivant la méthode exposée plus haut dans le cas d'un échantillon de ménage stratifié. Ensuite on a procédé à une analyse par colonne, en d'autres termes, on a comparé les niveaux de consommation dans des pays différents au cours d'une même année. On a combiné comme précédemment les résultats obtenus année par année et ceci afin de retenir l'estimateur le plus efficient. Finalement, on a combiné les résultats obtenus pour l'ensemble des lignes et pour l'ensemble des colonnes et on a testé la significativité des différences enregistrées dans l'analyse des séries chronologiques et dans les comparaisons entre pays[3]). En pratique, l'en-

---

[3]) De tels calculs ont été exécutés il y a environ deux années pour une vingtaine de pays et une quinzaine de produits au cours d'une période de 5 à 8 ans. On procède actuellement à une révision de ces calculs en intégrant aux séries les nouvelles statistiques disponibles.

semble des calculs est opéré en une seule étape sur machine électronique. L'avantage est de présenter les résultats d'une façon systématique année par année, pour l'ensemble des années, pays par pays, pour l'ensemble des pays, et pour l'ensemble des années et des pays, tout en offrant un test objectif de la significativité des différences obtenues. Il est particulièrement intéressant de pouvoir baser l'estimation des paramètres sur la combinaison de séries chronologiques relatives à plusieurs pays, car le faible nombre des degrés de liberté est un des écueils essentiels de l'analyse des séries chronologiques dans un pays donné.

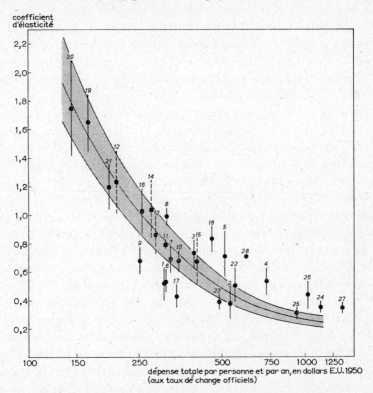

GRAPHIQUE 2. Variation de l'élasticité-revenu selon le niveau de revenu : toutes viandes – Comparaison des résultats provenant d'enquêtes sur les ménages, de séries chronologiques et de comparaisons internationales (voir l'annexe au graphique).
La zone hachurée correspond à l'estimation (au seuil de probabilité de 95 pourcent) résultant de l'analyse de covariance des séries chronologiques. Les croix correspondent à la valeur du coefficient d'élasticité au point moyen à partir d'enquêtes de consommation, les segments de part et d'autre de ces croix à la marge d'estimation au seuil de 95 pourcent.

TABLEAU 2 – Equation utilisé pour projeter l'influence de l'effet revenu sur la demande

Fonction	Coefficient d'élasticité	Accroissement de la demande
(1) Semi-logarithmique $y = a + b \log_e x$	$\eta = \dfrac{b}{y}$	$\dfrac{y'}{y} - 1 = 2{,}3026\, \eta \log_{10} \dfrac{x'}{x}$
(2) Log-inverse $\quad \log_e y = a - \dfrac{b}{x}$	$\eta = \dfrac{b}{x}$	$\log_{10} \dfrac{y'}{y} = 0{,}4343\, \eta \left(1 - \dfrac{x}{x'}\right)$
(3) Log log-inverse $\quad \log_e y = a - \dfrac{b}{x} - c \log_e x$	$\eta = \dfrac{b}{x} - c$	$\log_{10}\dfrac{y'}{y} = \dfrac{\eta}{1 - \dfrac{x}{x_M}}\left[0{,}4343\left(1-\dfrac{x}{x'}\right) - \dfrac{x}{x_M}\log_{10}\dfrac{x'}{x}\right]$

x, y et η représentent respectivement le revenu par habitant, la demande par habitant et le coefficient d'élasticité durant la période de base ; x' et y' désignent le revenu et la demande à la fin de la période de projection. Dans la fonction (3) intervient un paramètre supplémentaire x_M, qui représente le niveau de revenu auquel la consommation atteint son maximum. Le coefficient 0,4343 (ou son inverse 2,3026) correspond à la transformation des logarithmes décimaux en logarithmes naturels.

Pour les pays à revenus élevés (Japon et Afrique de Sud exclus) la fonction (2) a été utilisée pour tous les produits sauf les viandes, les produits laitiers dans les pays de l'Europe Méditerranéenne, le poisson, les légumes et fruits, le café et le cacao, pour lesquels on a utilisé la fonction (1). La fonction (3) n'a été utilisée que pour les céréales en Asie.

Entre les séries chronologiques, les comparaisons entre pays et surtout les enquêtes de consommation, nous nous sommes trouvés devant plus de 5000 fonctions de consommation et le problème était de faire un choix. Le principe fut de non point se baser sur un seul type d'analyse aussi précis fut-il, mais de choisir une fonction quelque peu subjectivement, après avoir comparé les résultats émanant d'analyses diverses. Pour faciliter une telle comparaison, on a souvent eu recours à des méthodes graphiques, comme illustré sur la Fig. 2; mais il faut admettre que de tels résultats ne sont jamais tout à fait comparables: peu d'enquêtes de consommation sont représentatives de l'ensemble de la population du pays et ces enquêtes se rapportent généralement aux dépenses par produit mais non aux quantités consommées comme dans les séries chronologiques et les comparaisons entre pays.

Pour projeter la demande dans les pays à revenu élevé on a utilisé seulement des fonctions à deux paramètres. Ces fonctions étaient donc parfaitement déterminées (1) par la forme de leur équation, (2) par le point ayant pour coordonnées les valeurs du revenu et de la consommation lors de la période de base (1957–1959) et (3) par le coefficient d'élasticité lors de cette même période. Aussi, après avoir choisi la forme de la fonction et la valeur du coefficient d'élasticité en 1957–1959 (Tableau III en Annexe), a-t-on pu calculer l'éffet revenu en appliquant aux taux d'accroissement du revenu contenus dans le Tableau I en Annexe les formules indiquées dans le Tableau 2.

4. MODIFICATION DU NIVEAU NUTRITIONNEL DE LA RATION ALIMENTAIRE

Après avoir ainsi calculé les indices caractérisant l'évolution de la demande individuelle pour chacun des dix groupes de produits alimentaires, les résultats dérivés de l'étude purement économique furent analysés du point de vue nutritionnel en opérant la transformation figurée dans l'équation (1):

$$Y'B = N \tag{1}$$

$$Y = \begin{bmatrix} \dfrac{y'_i}{y_i} \\[2mm] \dfrac{y'_i}{y_i} \\[2mm] \dfrac{y'_{10}}{y_{10}} \end{bmatrix} \qquad B = \begin{bmatrix} C_1 & P_1 & G_1 \\ C_i & P_i & G_i \\ C_{10} & P_{10} & G_{10} \end{bmatrix} \qquad N = [C', P', G']$$

y_i'/y_i = rapport entre la consommation individuelle du produit i projetée en 1970 et la consommation enregistrée en 1957 – 1959.

C_i, P_i et G_i = nombre de calories, grammes de protéines et graisses fournies par le produit i dans la ration journalière moyenne, lors de la période de base 1957–1959

C', P', G' = composition de la ration globale projetée pour 1970 en calories, protéines et graisses.

La matrice B fut établie sur la base des bilans alimentaires publiés par la FAO, les calculs furent donc effectués seulement en termes de calories, protéines et graisses. D'autres éléments nutritionnels pourraient être pris en considération si l'on disposait des informations statistiques; il suffirait d'ajouter des colonnes supplémentaires dans la matrice B. Le vecteur N indique quelle serait, en 1970, la composition de la ration en termes d'éléments nutritionnels si la consommation évoluait suivant les lois économiques analysées dans la section précédente, les résultats de cette analyse étant résumés dans le vecteur Y.

Dans les pays où il n'existe pas de rationnement alimentaire c'est, nous semble-t-il, à ce stade que doit intervenir le dialogue entre l'économiste et le nutritioniste. S'il n'existe pas de graves carences alimentaires, le libre choix des consommateurs constitue l'élément essentiel et les considérations d'ordre nutritionnel interviennent surtout à titre de test de cohérence. Ce test est important car, comme il a été noté précédemment, la demande alimentaire globale en termes de calories peut généralement être projetée avec plus de précision que la demande de tel ou tel produit. Aussi a-t-on ajusté les indices y_i'/y_i caractérisant l'évolution de la demande par produit en procédant par approximations successives jusqu'à obtenir dans le vecteur N des résultats satisfaisants du point de vue nutritionnel.

Par exemple, dans le cas des Etats-Unis, l'approche économique par produit avait conduit initialement à une très légère augmentation du contenu calorique de la ration au cours de la période de projection. Comme les nutritionistes pensent que le contenu calorique devrait très légèrement diminuer, on a réduit quelque peu la valeur des coefficients d'élasticité pour les produits apportant une forte contribution calorique à la ration. En d'autres termes, la projection de la demande de céréales fut obtenue comme un élément résiduel de la ration; cette méthode reflète d'ailleurs assez bien le comportement du consommateur déjà riche qui compense tout accroissement ultérieur de sa consommation de produits chers en réduisant sa consommation de pain et de féculents pour conserver sa «ligne». Dans le cas du Japon, l'accroissement de 10% projeté pour le contenu calorique de la ration traduit en partie l'augmentation des besoins résultant d'une augmentation de la taille moyenne[4]) et du développement corporel associés à l'accroissement et à la diversification de la consommation protéïque.

Comme il eut été trop long de reproduire tous les calculs intermédiaires, les coefficients d'élasticité et les taux d'accroissement de la demande individuelle figurant dans les Tableaux III et IV en Annexe, sont ceux finalement retenus après application du test de cohérence nutritionnel. Pour apprécier ce que cette demande alimentaire représenterait quant aux débouchés de l'agriculture, les indices d'accroissement par produits furent pondérés en fonction de la part respective de ces produits dans le revenu brut de l'agriculture après avoir opéré divers ajustements relatifs au commerce international et aux utilisations non-alimentaires. Cette opération fut effectuée en ajoutant une colonne supplémentaire à la matrice B de l'équation (1); l'élément f_i de cette colonne pour la ligne i, indique la part du produit i dans le produit agricole brut, $f_i = y_i p_i / \Sigma_i y_i p_i$, p_i et y_i représentant respectivement quantités consommées et prix du produit i au niveau de la ferme. L'élément supplémentaire introduit dans le vecteur N indique l'augmentation f'/f du coût de la ration individuelle aux prix de la ferme.

Dans le cas des pays à revenu faible où il existe des carences nutritionnelles prononcées, le dialogue entre le nutritioniste et l'économiste prend beaucoup plus d'importance et peut devenir la base de l'élaboration d'une politique nutritionnelle. Il nous semble toutefois que, là encore, la première étape consiste à déterminer le vecteur de gauche de l'équation (1), c'est-à-dire à calculer quelle serait l'évolution de la consommation par groupes de produits si les consommateurs pouvaient effectuer librement leur choix. Souvent la valeur du coefficient d'élasticité par rapport au revenu est élevée pour les aliments dits «protecteurs», en particulier pour les produits animaux et les fruits. Mais cette valeur ne correspond pas toujours aux désirs du nutritioniste: dans beaucoup de pays en voie de développement, l'élasticité de la demande est élevée pour le sucre, mais faible pour les légumineuses et surtout pour la farine de poisson. Par contre, le sucre raffiné ne fournit que des calories et des calories souvent chères, tandis que légumineuses et farine de poisson apportent à bon

---

[4]) La taille moyenne du garçon japonais de 14 ans est passée de 1,449 mètre en 1948 à 1,545 m en 1961 et l'on prévoit qu'elle atteindra 1,584 m en 1970 ('Nutrition in Japan 1962', Ministry of Health and Welfare, Tokyo, Oct. 1962).

marché des acides aminés essentiels. Aussi est-il souvent nécessaire pour le planificateur de prendre des mesures destinées à modifier l'évolution spontanée résultant des préférences individuelles des consommateurs.

On peut certes éduquer le consommateur en matières nutritionnelles; ceci revient à modifier les paramètres de la fonction de demande en organisant des cours et des démonstrations culinaires auprès des ménagères. Toutefois, même informé, le consommateur peut s'obstiner à consacrer une part importante de l'accroissement de son revenu à l'achat de sucreries plutôt qu'à celui de farine de poisson ou de légumineuses. Pour résoudre le conflit entre le choix spontané du consommateur et le choix raisonné du planificateur, il est nécessaire de s'adresser à l'homme politique car il s'agit de prendre des mesures qui peuvent être impopulaires mais doivent rester politiquement acceptables; par exemple, taxer plus lourdement la vente de sucre ou de coca cola et subventionner la vente de farine de poisson et de légumineuses, voire même décréter l'incorporation obligatoire d'un pourcentage donné de ces produits dans des aliments de consommation courante, tel le pain.

Même dans le cas où le gouvernement est décidé à imposer une politique nutritionnelle stricte, nous pensons qu'il est préférable de partir de l'étude économique, c'est-à-dire de l'établissement du vecteur Y, quitte à le modifier ultérieurement par des mesures fiscales ou des décrets, plutôt que de fixer a priori des objectifs nutritionnels N indépendamment des conditions économiques. Certes, il serait séduisant d'appliquer les techniques de la programmation linéaire consistant à atteindre un certain nombre d'objectifs nutritionnels au coût minimum; toutefois, l'utilisation pratique d'une telle méthode requiert l'introduction d'une série de conditions réintroduisant les facteurs revenu, goûts et habitudes de consommation; aussi retombe-t-on finalement sur une approche très voisine de celle proposée ci-dessus.

5. L'INFLUENCE DES PRIX

Dans une première étape, on a projetè la quantité qui serait demandée en 1970 aux prix de 1958. Dans une seconde étape, on s'est efforcé, pour certains produits du moins, de construire un segment de la courbe de demande quantité-prix et ceci en associant aux points projetés à des prix constants une valeur du coefficient d'élasticité de la demande par rapport aux prix. Ainsi nous avons projeté la demande de fèves de cacao en 1970 pour trois niveaux de prix correspondant à 18, 24 et 30 cents par livre.

Nous disposions d'assez bonnes statistiques relatives aux broyages, et il avait été possible de mesurer l'élasticité de la demande de fèves par rapport aux prix d'importation de ces fèves. Mais, pour la plupart des autres produits, les seules estimations des coefficients d'élasticité de la demande par rapport aux prix dont nous disposions se rapportaient au marché du détail. Même à ce niveau, les estimations étaient souvent rares et nous nous sommes efforcés de les contrôler en utilisant la règle suivante comme garde-fou: dans le cas où il n'existe pas de substitut pour le produit considéré, ce qui est le cas pour le sucre, le coefficient d'élasticité par rapport aux prix est du même ordre de grandeur que le coefficient d'élasticité par rapport au revenu mais de signe contraire; par contre, le coefficient d'élasticité-prix est supérieur en valeur absolue au coefficient d'élasticité-revenu, et la différence est d'autant plus grande qu'il existe des substituts plus voisins.

Notre but, toutefois, n'était pas d'établir la courbe de la demande quantités/prix au niveau du détail mais au niveau du marché des produits de base et ceci afin de pouvoir la confronter avec la courbe de l'offre au stade de la ferme ou de l'exportation des produits de base. Il était donc nécessaire d'émettre certaines hypothèses sur l'importance des marges de transformation et de distribution et sur la rigidité de ces marges. Dans le cas des produits tropicaux, ce problème avait une importance particulière car nous devions estimer l'influence d'une réduction des droits de douane et des taxes intérieures sur la demande d'importation de ces produits. Aussi avons-nous classé les composantes du prix de détail sous trois rubriques: prix à l'importation, droits de douane et taxes intérieures, marge de transformation et de distribution. Les résultats de cette étude pour 12 pays européens sont indiqués dans le Tableau VII. Il est frappant de constater que, même pour le café, le prix d'importation représente en moyenne dans les 12 pays considérés seulement 37 pourcent du prix au détail. Dans de telles conditions, l'influence d'une réduction des taxes et des droits de douane dépend étroitement des hypothèses faites sur l'évolution des marges de transformation et de distribution. Dans cette étude, deux hypothèses avaient été émises: a) ces marges restent constantes en termes de dollars, ce qui implique une légère augmentation du profit des secteurs de transformation et de distribution; b) ces marges sont constantes en termes de pourcentages, ce qui implique une réduction du profit des secteurs de transformation et de distribution puisque le coefficient d'élasticité par rapport aux prix au détail est généralement inférieur à l'unité.

On aurait pu évidemment faire beaucoup d'autres hypothèses; la réaction des industries de transformation et des organismes de vente dépend largement de leurs structures, du degré de concurrence et aussi de la demande des consommateurs. Pour retenir l'hypothèse la mieux adaptée au pays considéré, il serait donc nécessaire de procéder à une étude économique détaillée des secteurs de transformation et de distribution. Ce problème, que nous avons effleuré dans le cas des produits tropicaux, se retrouve évidemment dans le cas de tous les produits agricoles et il faut reconnaître que l'introduction de prix variables dans le modèle de projection exigerait une étude sur l'ensemble de secteurs de transformation et de distribution. On pourrait alors établir le pont entre la dépense alimentaire des consommateurs et les débouchés que cette dépense représente pour les agriculteurs, pont que nous n'avons pas essayé d'établir dans cette étude mais dont nous reconnaissons la nécessité.

En fait, le niveau de la demande individuelle est influencé par d'autres facteurs que le revenu, les considérations nutritionnelles et les prix; mais l'influence de ces autres facteurs, la modification des goûts en particulier, est fort difficile à mesurer. Par exemple, de l'ensemble des analyses économétriques faites sur la demande de thé il apparaît que dans les pays à revenu élevé cette demande n'est guère influencée ni par les modifications du revenu individuel ni par celles des prix. Dans ces pays, la consommation de thé est surtout influencée par des facteurs d'ordre sociologique tel l'institution du «tea break», par des facteurs techniques tel l'introduction de produits nouveaux (thé en sachets, thé soluble, café soluble, café espresso, etc.). L'analyse des séries chronologiques peut révéler l'amplitude de l'effet combiné de ces facteurs sous forme d'une tendance résiduelle; c'est sur cette analyse que nous nous sommes basés pour projeter la demande de thé dans les pays à revenu élevé, mais il faut bien reconnaître que l'extrapolation de cette tendance reste entachée d'un facteur largement subjectif.

6. PROJECTION DE LA DEMANDE DE MATIÈRES PREMIÈRES AGRICOLES

Eu égard à l'importance du processus de transformation, la projection de la demande des céréales pour l'alimentation du bétail ou de la demande d'importation des fibres textiles pose des problèmes délicats.

Dans le cas de l'alimentation du bétail on a projeté les besoins séparément pour chaque type des spéculation animale. Par exemple, on est parti de la quantité de céréales secondaires consommée par les porcs en

1957–1959; on a multiplié cette quantité par l'indice caractérisant l'accroissement de la demande de porcs entre 1957–1959 et 1970; le produit ainsi
obtenu a alors été ajusté en le multipliant par un coefficient caractérisant les modifications prévisibles entre 1958 et 1970 du nombre de kilos de
céréales utilisés pour produire un kilo de porc. Le point le plus faible de
cette estimation est précisément l'hypothèse faite quant à ce dernier coefficient qui reflète l'effet combiné d'un facteur physiologique caractérisant
l'amélioration du coefficient de transformation animale résultant par
exemple de l'amélioration des races, et d'un facteur économique caractérisant la substitution entre céréales et autres produits d'alimentation.
L'importance de cette hypothèse peut être illustrée par le fait qu'une
réduction moyenne de 5 pourcent sur le coefficient retenu diminuerait de
4 millions de tonnes, c'est à dire d'environ 20 pourcent, les besoins d'importation en céréales secondaires de l'Europe occidentale en 1970.

L'importance d'une telle marge d'erreur montre qu'il est essentiel
d'améliorer nos méthodes d'estimation dans ce domaine et pour ce faire
nous pensons qu'il est nécessaire d'établir un bilan fourrager complet. Ce
bilan pourrait se présenter sous la forme d'un tableau à double entrée
dont les lignes correspondraient aux divers produits utilisés pour l'alimentation animale et les colonnes aux divers types de spéculation animale.
Il serait d'ailleurs utile d'établir une distinction entre les besoins alimentaires couvrant la ration d'entretien et ceux couvrant la ration de production; par exemple, d'établir une distinction entre le nombre d'unités
fourragères nécessaires à la ration d'entretien d'une vache laitière et le
nombre d'unités fourragères nécessaire à la production d'un kg de lait
par cette vache. Il faudrait alors projeter en 1970 non seulement le flux de
production en termes de tonnes de lait ou de tonnes de viande par an,
mais également le stock du cheptel nécessaire pour assurer ce flux. On
pourrait ainsi saisir d'une façon beaucoup plus précise les deux facteurs
mentionnées précédemment: a) la réduction du nombre d'unités fourragères nécessaires à la production d'une tonne de lait résultant soit d'un
accroissement du rendement laitier par vache, ce qui réduirait la ration
d'entretien par rapport à la ration de production, soit d'une meilleure
transformation des unités fourragères en protéïnes animales; b) les possibilités de substitution entre céréales et autres aliments du bétail prenant
en considération les disponibilités des divers types d'aliments, le niveau de
leurs prix relatifs et les modifications structurelles de l'exploitation, telle
la réduction de la main d'oeuvre, susceptibles d'influencer le choix de telle
ou telle ration.

Il existe une certaine similitude entre les problèmes qui viennent d'être exposés quant à la projection de la demande de céréales pour l'alimentation du bétail et les projections de la demande des fibres textiles. Dans un cas comme dans l'autre il faut tenir compte d'un certain nombre de ressources qui peuvent entrer en concurrence pour satisfaire un certain nombre de besoins. Dans cette étude, les besoins ont été classés en trois grandes catégories (habillement H, tissus de ménage M, usages industriels I) et les ressources en quatre groupes (coton C, laine L, rayonne R et fibres synthétiques non-cellulosiques S).

La première étape était donc de construire pour la période de base le tableau des besoins et ressources[5] schématisé ci-dessous :

Besoins \ Ressources	Coton	Laine	Rayonne	Synthétiques	Toutes fibres
Habillement	H_C	H_L	H_R	H_S	H
Tissus de ménage	M_C	M_L	M_R	M_S	M
Usages industriels	I_C	I_L	I_R	I_S	I
Tout usage	C	L	R	S	T

La seconde étape consistait à projeter les taux d'accroissement de la demande par type de besoins. Pour l'habillement et les tissus, de ménage, ces taux ont été calculés suivant une méthode voisine de celle utilisée pour la demande alimentaire. La demande par tête a été projetée en utilisant une fonction de demande semi-logarithmique et en partant de la valeur estimée du coefficient d'élasticité de la demande pour la période de base. En multipliant les indices d'accroissement de la demande individuelle par l'indice d'accroissement démographique, on a obtenu les indices d'accroissement de la demande totale caractérisées par H'/H et M'/M pour l'habillement et les tissus de ménage respectivement. Pour les usages industriels, l'indice de la demande totale I'/I a été lié directement à l'indice de la production industrielle en donnant une pondération plus lourde aux industries grosses consommatrices de fibres textiles. On a ainsi obtenu le vecteur Y figurant dans l'équation (2).

---

[5] Dans notre étude ce tableau a été exprimé en poids net de fibres ce qui sous-estime l'importance des fibres synthétiques par rapport au coton. Afin de mieux pouvoir analyser le phénomène de substitution entre fibres il serait utile d'exprimer les quantités utilisées de chaque fibre en équivalent coton, le coefficient d'équivalence entre fibres synthétiques et coton étant basé sur les possibilités d'utilisation respectives par kilo de produit.

La troisième étape qui était la plus délicate, consistait à émettre des hypothèses sur les phénomènes de substitution entre fibres susceptibles de se produire entre 1957–1959 et 1970 pour chaque type de besoin. Dans le cas du coton utilisé dans l'habillement par exemple, ce phénomène de substitution fut catactérisé par le coefficient

$$\frac{h_c'}{h_c} = \frac{H_c'}{H'} \bigg/ \frac{H_c}{H}.$$

Le coefficient h_c était connu, c'était la part du coton par rapport à l'ensemble des fibres textiles utilisées dans l'habillement au cours de la période de base 1957–1959. Le problème était donc d'émettre une hypothèse sur ce qui pourrait devenir cette part h_c' en 1970. Ces hypothèses furent largement basées sur l'analyse des modifications du pourcentage d'utilisation des diverses fibres par type de besoin enrégistrées au cours de la dernière décennie. Des statistiques fort détaillées étaient disponibles pour les Etats-Unis, des statistiques moins détaillées existaient pour le Japon, mais il existait fort peu d'information pour l'Europe occidentale. Certes, il eût été souhaitable d'établir une distinction entre l'influence des prix relatifs et celle des modifications d'ordre technologique. Malheureusement, on connaît mal la valeur des élasticités de substitution par rapport aux prix, car l'analyse statistique en est rendue difficile par la forte correlation enrégistrée au cours des dernières années entre les variations des prix des divers fibres. En ce qui concerne la technologie, il est important de tenir compte de l'opinion des techniciens quant aux chances d'introduction de nouvelles fibres ou de fibres améliorées, quant à l'évolution des coûts de production et quant aux projets d'installation de nouvelles usines. Il faut néanmoins reconnaître que les hypothèses faites sur l'évolution de la part des synthétiques par type de besoins restent largement subjectives.

La dernière étape consiste à projeter la demande totale de chaque fibre en multipliant le transposé du vecteur Y caractérisant les taux d'accroissement par types de besoins (2ème étape) par la matrice M caractérisant les besoins et ressources lors de la période de base (1ère étape) et modifié par les hypothèses retenues quant à la substitution inter-fibres (3éme étape). Si on disposait des statistiques adéquates, il faudrait diviser chacun des groupes de besoins en sous-groupes, c'est-à-dire augmenter le nombre de lignes figurant dans Y et M. Il faut souligner que pour améliorer les projections par fibres, il est indispensable de procéder à un travail statistique de base, car les données par fibres et par utilisation finale sont actuellement fragmentaires et peu précises en Europe occidentale.

$$Y'M = D \tag{2}$$

$$Y = \begin{bmatrix} \dfrac{H'}{H} \\[2mm] \dfrac{M'}{M} \\[2mm] \dfrac{I'}{I} \end{bmatrix} \qquad M = \begin{bmatrix} \dfrac{h'_C}{h_C} H_C, & \dfrac{h'_L}{h_L} H_L, & \dfrac{h'_R}{h_R} H_R, & \dfrac{h'_S}{h_S} H_S \\[3mm] \dfrac{m'_C}{m_C} M_C, & \dfrac{m'_L}{m_L} M_L, & \dfrac{m'_R}{m_R} M_R, & \dfrac{m'_S}{m_S} M_S \\[3mm] \dfrac{i'_C}{i_C} I_C, & \dfrac{i'_L}{i_L} I_L, & \dfrac{i'_R}{i_R} I_R, & \dfrac{i'_S}{i_S} I_S \end{bmatrix}$$

$$D = [C', L', R', S']$$

7. LES PROJECTIONS DE LA DEMANDE ET LEURS IMPLICATIONS QUANT AUX POLITIQUES ÉCONOMIQUES

Les projections de la demande telles qu'elles apparaissent dans le Tableau VI en Annexe sont évidemment fonction des hypothèses retenues quant au rythme de croissance de la population et du revenu. Pour l'ensemble de l'Europe occidentale, dans l'hypothèse d'une expansion économique rapide, les deux tiers de l'accroissement de la demande alimentaire mesurée aux prix à la ferme, seraient dus à l'accroissement du revenu par tête et un tiers seulement à l'accroissement démographique. Par contre, dans la plupart des autres régions, l'effet démographique jouera le rôle prédominant: dans les pays en voie de développement, même si l'objectif de la décennie de développement était réalisé (5 pourcent d'accroissement annuel du PNB), l'effet population dépasserait d'un tiers l'effet revenu. Aux Etats-Unis, même dans l'hypothèse d'un accroissement rapide du revenu, l'effet démographique serait 4 ou 5 fois supérieur à l'effet revenu.

L'accroissement démographique peut être considéré comme une donnée sur laquelle les politiques ne peuvent rien ou presque, en Europe occidentale du moins. L'accroissement du revenu individuel est un objectif de politique générale laissant une bien faible marge de manoeuvre au planificateur, car presque tous les gouvernements s'efforcent d'atteindre le taux d'expansion maximum. Les projections de la demande intérieure ne peuvent donc être modifiées par des choix politiques que dans une marge relativement étroite, en exerçant par exemple une pression sur le niveau des prix au détail. Par contre, la production indigène et les échanges internationaux peuvent être fortement influencés par les politiques et

le niveau des prix, surtout en ce qui concerne les produits pris indivi-
duellement, car il existe à long terme de larges possibilités de substitution
entre les différentes spéculations. Les projections de la demande, ou du
moins du segment de la courbe reliant les quantités demandées aux prix,
peuvent donc être considérées dans une large mesure comme des données
qui, si elles sont suffisamment solides, peuvent servir de base à l'orientation des politiques de production et d'exportation.

En ce qui concerne la demande alimentaire, les projections établies par
grands groupes de produits semblent fournir un ordre de grandeur suffisamment valable. Par exemple, entre 1957–1959 et 1970, la demande de
céréales pour l'alimentation humaine diminuerait dans l'ensemble de
l'Europe occidentale d'environ 10 pourcent, et une modification du niveau
des prix n'aurait pratiquement pas d'effet sur la demande; la réduction
prévue serait légèrement supérieure à l'augmentation de la population,
mais en tenant compte d'un remplacement de certaines céréales secondaires par le blé et de la réduction du taux de blûtage dans certains pays,
les besoins en blé pourraient rester sensiblement constants. Pour les huiles
et les graisses, la demande par tête augmentera fort peu sauf dans l'Europe
méditerranéenne, Italie incluse. Dans le Nord-ouest de l'Europe, une diminution des prix aurait peu d'effet sur la demande totale d'huiles et de
graisses, mais une modification des prix relatifs pourrait largement stimuler la consommation de telle graisse ou de telle huile. Dans le Nord-
Ouest de l'Europe, il ne semble pas que, même avec une baisse des prix du
beurre à la consommation, la demande effective puisse augmenter aussi
rapidement que la production laitière, dans le cas où les politiques lai-
tières demeureraient inchangées. En d'autres termes, il paraît indispensable de modifier ces politiques en décourageant la production de lait à
forte teneur en matières grasses et en stimulant la production de viande
bovine aux dépens de celle du lait.

Pour l'ensemble de la demande alimentaire évaluée aux prix à la ferme,
les projections indiquent pour l'ensemble de l'Europe occidentale un taux
d'accroissement annuel de 1,7 à 2 pourcent, suivant l'hypothèse de revenu
retenue. Par contre, au cours de la dernière décennie, la production agricole européenne a augmenté annuellement d'environ 2,7 pourcent dont le
plus clair était dû à l'amélioration des rendements. Il semble bien qu'en
poursuivant les politiques agricoles actuelles, la production pourrait augmenter presque aussi rapidement que par le passé, ce qui résulterait en
une aggravation des problèmes de surplus sur les marchés commerciaux
mondiaux.

Certes, le problème n'est pas le même dans toute l'Europe : dans les pays méditerranéens, il semble que l'accroissement de la production agricole pourrait être absorbé par la demande intérieure sans grande difficulté, spécialement en tenant compte des possibilités d'accroissement encore considérables de la consommation des produits animaux, accroissement qui pourrait être stimulé par une baisse des prix de ces produits. C'est donc essentiellement dans l'Europe du Nord-Ouest, et en particulier en France, que le rythme d'accroissement de la demande semble nettement inférieur à celui de la croissance potentielle du secteur agricole. Cette situation, qui se retrouve d'ailleurs dans nombre de pays développés hors d'Europe, est en contraste flagrant avec la situation des pays en voie de développement.

Dans l'Europe du Nord-ouest, même en tenant compte d'une certaine réduction des importations nettes, il ne semble pas que les débouchés de l'agriculture, et par suite le revenu brut agricole, puissent augmenter de beaucoup plus de 2 pourcent par an au cours de la prochaine décennie. Comme la part des dépenses d'exploitation dans ce revenu continuera à croître, le revenu agricole net progressera vraisemblablement peu si les niveaux des prix et le volume des subventions à l'agriculture restent ce qu'ils sont aujourd'hui. Comme, pour des raisons éthiques et sociales, l'écart entre les revenus du travail dans l'agriculture et dans les autres secteurs économiques ne doit point s'élargir, une réduction de la main d'oeuvre paraît indispensable. Les politiques doivent donc être adaptées à la résolution des modifications structurelles de l'agriculture requises.

En ce qui concerne la demande d'importation des produits tropicaux en Europe occidentale, les perspectives ouvertes aux pays en voie de développement sont peu brillantes. A prix constants, les importations nettes de l'Europe occidentale pourraient augmenter de 1,5 à 2 pourcent par an, au maximum. Certes, les importations de café, de cacao, de fruits et de bois tropicaux pourraient augmenter très rapidement en Europe de l'Est et dans l'Union Soviétique ; néanmoins à prix constants, même dans l'hypothèse la plus favorable, la valeur globale des importations de produits tropicaux de l'ensemble des pays à revenu élevé ne semble pas devoir augmenter de plus de 2,5 pourcent par an. En d'autres termes, le volume des exportations des produits tropicaux vers les pays à revenu élevé pourrait au mieux croître au même rythme que celui de la population des pays en voie de développement et donc à un rythme inférieur à celui requis pour les investissements de biens d'équipement, dans le cadre de la décennie du developpement des Nations-Unies.

Une réduction des droits de douane et des taxes intérieures pourrait stimuler la demande d'importation. D'après les calculs effectués pour douze pays européens, une réduction complète de ces droits et taxes pour le café, le cacao, le thé, les agrumes et les bananes, pourrait créer une demande supplémentaire de quelque 150 millions de dollars; ce serait utile et cela constituerait une preuve de bonne volonté de la part des pays importateurs, mais ceci ne suffirait certes pas à couvrir les besoins d'importation des pays en voie de développement.

Le problème de l'équilibre de la balance commerciale entre pays industriels et non-industriels est encore aggravé par l'évolution des termes de l'échange car les prix des produits agricoles par rapport à ceux des produits manufacturés se sont dégradés de façon continue depuis 1954. Dans l'étude des moyens à mettre en oeuvre pour influencer cette évolution, une distinction doit être faite entre les produits dont la demande d'importation est élastique par rapport aux cours internationaux, et ceux dont la demande est inélastique. Le caoutchouc naturel et la plupart des fibres textiles entrent dans la première catégorie car il existe dans le long-terme de larges possibilités de substitution entre matières premières agricoles et synthétiques. L'évolution du coût de production de ces dernières est alors l'élément dominant et la politique des pays exportateurs de produits naturels doit être centrée sur l'accroissement de la productivité en vue d'améliorer dans toute la mesure du possible la position concurrentielle des produits naturels. Par contre, pour la plupart des produits alimentaires, en particulier les céréales, le café, le thé, la demande d'importation est peu élastique par rapport aux variations des cours mondiaux. Il est alors indispensable d'harmoniser demande et offre sur le plan mondial. Aussi les projections de la demande des produits de base sont-elles appelées à jouer un rôle essentiel dans la discussion et la formulation des accords internationaux par produits.

SUMMARY

In a study recently published by FAO, trends in demand, production and trade were analysed for the major agricultural commodities. Projections were made for the period 1957–1959 through 1969–1971 on the basis of two alternative assumptions as to income growth and one as to population. The main purpose of the study was to identify the problems likely to emerge for the principal agricultural commodities during the sixties if policies remain unchanged, and to examine how those policies should be modified so as to facilitate solutions of the problems foreseen. The world was divided into three major groups: (1) Eastern Europe and Mainland China, (2) other high-income countries, (3) other low-income countries.

The present paper is limited to the projection of demand for agricultural commodities in the high-income countries of Group (2). Details on the projections by individual countries are given in the statistical Appendix, but these country projections should be used cautiously since the basic purpose of the original study was to analyse the problems of food and agriculture for broad groups of countries and not for any single one. It should also be noted that the projections refer to demand for agricultural commodities valued at the farm level and not to food or clothing expenditure at retail. The study therefore deals with the prospects for the farm industry and only indirectly with those for the processing and marketing sectors.

The body of the present paper is, however, mainly concerned with the methodological problems arising from the preparation of these projections. Particular attention is devoted to the link between total living expenditure per caput and the consumption per caput of major food groups. The statistical material used comprised about 100 household surveys and a variety of ten year time-series covering much of the world. A number of demand functions, shown in Table 1, were investigated. The three- parameter function (4) represented in Figure 1 corresponds fairly well to the expected variations in the consumption of most food items over a very wide income range. However, in most cases within the recorded income range, a two-parameter function is precise enough. In the high-income countries, the projections were based on the two-parameter functions given under number (2) and (3) in Table 1; function (4) was used only for projecting the demand for cereals in developing countries. In the process of statistical fitting, frequent use of covariance analysis was made for selecting the most efficient estimator in a stratified population.

Household survey data were thus stratified according to type of family, level of urbanization, time-periods, etc. Regressions were fitted (1) separately within each stratum, thus allowing for a difference in the slopes and the levels of the individual regression lines, (2) within all strata, allowing for a difference in levels but not in slopes, (3) between strata averages, (4) for all data together, ignoring stratification. On the basis of the analysis of the variances, the most efficient unbiased estimator of the regression coefficient was then selected. Similarly, time-series were combined for a number of countries and the data analysed with a two-way stratification (by country and by year). It was then possible to test the significance of the differences recorded both in the levels and in the slopes of the regression lines fitted within countries and within years, and subsequently to select the most efficient estimator of the slope, which was often a weighted average of the slopes within each country. The advantage of such a method is to increase the number of degrees of freedom left for the estimation of the parameters; this is of particular interest since the low number of degrees of freedom is one of the major shortcomings in time-series analysis for a single country.

The results of the statistical analysis based both on budget data and time-series show that, for broad commodity groups, there is a great deal of similarity between consumers' reactions in different countries when these consumers are in a similar economic environment. In countries lacking the appropriate statistical data, it therefore seems possible to roughly estimate the parameters of the demand function by analogy with the results known for other countries with similar economic conditions. The values of the parameters used in the projections were not systematically derived from one particular method, say cross section, rather than from another, say time series; the selection was made on the basis of the various results obtained for the country concerned and also of those available for other countries at similar stages of development. Some subjective element, or 'intuition', was therefore introduced in the last stage of the selection of the coefficients used.

The results of the projections for the various food items, as derived from the demand functions, were then analysed in terms of overall nutritional intakes and adjustments were made, where necessary, to arrive at a consistent pattern of nutritional intake. Reference is made in the text to possible ways of modifying the initial demand projections into targets, so as to improve nutritional levels in countries with pronounced nutritional deficiencies more rapidly.

The projections of demand for food and beverages were generally computed on the basis of expected population and income growth. Price effects were introduced later at the reconciliation stage between the projections of demand and supply. In some cases, an overall general trend factor was also introduced to take account of the effects of factors other than population, income and price.

The problems raised in the projection of intermediate demand are illustrated by two examples: the demand for feed and for textile fibres. Attention is drawn to the need for improving basic data as regards feed balance sheets and the end-uses of fibres, and for studying more thoroughly likely changes in the values of technological coefficients of transformation.

The last section of the paper refers to the possible utilization of demand projections for policy decisions. In high-income countries, policy decisions can influence domestic demand for food to only a small extent, and certainly much less than it can domestic production or trade. Projections of demand, or of the quantity-price demand schedule, if precise enough, can therefore provide a basis for the formulation of production and trade policies.

As regards domestic food production, there is a serious danger of oversupply during the sixties in the high-income countries. In Western Europe, demand at farm prices is unlikely to rise by more than 2 percent a year during the sixties as against an increase in food production which reached 2.7 percent a year during the fifties. The value added by the farm sector is likely to increase less rapidly than gross agricultural output; most of the rise in per caput farm income in the developed countries during the sixties will therefore have to result from a reduction in the size of the farm labour force, the key to the long-term problem of farm income parity. The likely problems by commodities are also briefly referred to in the text and the danger of milk surpluses in the EEC is emphasized.

As regards the import demand for tropical commodities, prospects do not appear very bright for the developing countries. At best, these imports, valued at constant prices, could rise by 2.5 percent a year; in other words, the export proceeds of low-income countries derived from agricultural commodities are unlikely, on a per caput basis, to increase during the sixties. Since for the low-income countries as a whole (excluding the few oil-exporting countries) agricultural commodities accounted for 72 per cent of total export earnings in 1958–1960, the slow growth in import demand envisaged for tropical commodities will constitute one of the major world trade problems of the sixties.

Various ways of stimulating import demand for tropical commodities are briefly referred to: the complete abolition of tariffs and internal taxes on coffee, cocoa, tea, citrus and bananas would for example stimulate the total import demand of 12 European countries by about 150 million dollars a year. International commodity agreements could also help check the downward trend in the terms of trade for those commodities with a price-inelastic import demand. This would require a closer harmonization of less-developed countries' export targets which should be based on realistic projections of overall world import demand.

CHAPTER 12

AN ATTEMPT AT FORECASTING THE DEMAND FOR HIGHER EDUCATION IN THE NETHERLANDS*)

BY

HANS LINNEMANN

Netherlands Economic Institute, Rotterdam, Netherlands

1. INTRODUCTION

For a number of years the study of the 'economics of education' has been a fashionable subject for theoretical and research economists. The interest in the role played by education in the process of economic growth is the result of several factors. On the theoretical side, the inadequacy of the production functions of the Cobb-Douglas type in explaining past growth trends has induced research on education as a third factor in the production process. In addition, practical questions of more immediate importance have acted as catalysts; the Western countries are facing the challenge of a high rate of growth in the USSR (where output of scientific and technical manpower is relatively larger than in Western societies), and the developing countries are trying to build up their education system in accordance with the needs of development plans.

Most of the analytical work of recent years has been confined to the study of the interrelations between production and human skill. From production forecasts or targets for the national economy or for specific branches of it, targets for the output of qualified manpower are derived, and these targets of skill production can be transformed again into targets for the education system at its various levels and in different specializations. In this way the *demand* for human skill can be estimated fairly accurately, if the relevant statistical information is available. Less work has been done on the factors governing the *supply* of human skill. The supply of skill is largely determined by the actual number of students leaving the education system at the various levels of education. Thus, the

---

*) The author is indebted to Mr. P. A. Cornelisse for his comments and for performing the necessary calculations.

supply of skill depends on the earlier, preceding demand for education services. The present article concentrates on an analysis of the demand for education, more particularly the demand for higher education. Empirical exercises focus on the Netherlands.

2. THE DEMAND FOR EDUCATION

In the preceding section the demand for education was linked to the supply of productive skill. It is obvious that the latter is impossible without the former; yet it would be wrong to assume that education is demanded only for the purpose of future participation in the production process. In most countries primary education, and often also a part of secondary education, are considered a precondition for human happiness and for the proper functioning of social and political institutions. Usually school attendance for these types of education is compulsory; in Western Europe and North America the age limits for compulsory education are from 6 or 7 years till 14 or 15 years. The demand for education of this age group can be estimated directly from demographic data. This is a case of forced or compulsory consumption for which the forecasting of future demand is a fairly simple matter, not requiring economic analysis.

For other types and levels of education services, notably technical and vocational secondary education and higher education, the situation is more complicated. Here demand is not only a function of demographic conditions, but is also dependent on economic and social factors. At these levels of education the objective of future participation in the production process in a certain expertise or capacity becomes an important element in the decisions on the demand side. An interesting question is whether demand for these more advanced levels of education is to be considered as consumptive demand or as investment. It is obvious that the explanatory variables entering in the demand function are likely to be different in these two cases.

From a national-economic point of view by far the greater part of the cost of education is seen as investment: it is a sacrifice made today in order to obtain a higher production volume or a higher 'level of well-being' during a number of years in the future. For the individual the investment aspect is less pronounced, although it is certainly not completely lacking. On the individual level, there is often a strong desire to satisfy intellectual needs or to develop latent skill. According to the limited evidence available, there is no clear relationship between the demand for education in a given specialization and the income to be received from it[1]). Thus, it would seem as if the demand for education at the individual level is to a large extent a function of the individual's subjective preferences (given his economic, social and intellectual conditions) rather than a function of his interest in maximizing future income. In other words, the individual behaviour equation will have to describe a psychic process rather than a behaviour based on calculated aims. It would seem to be appropriate, therefore, to conceive of the individual demand function for education services as a consumption function (psychic behaviour) and not as an investment function (calculated behaviour).

After attaining a given level of education, the benefits of this education will be obtained over a long period of time. Education is a durable asset, and the demand for it might be compared with the demand for durables. However, education is not subject to large fluctuations in demand such as may occur in the case of durable consumer goods. This stability is due to the fact that the services of the (traditional) educational system are demanded usually only once in a life time (there is no demand for 're-placement', except in very rare cases), and, moreover, this demand is generally concentrated in a well-defined age group (demand cannot easily be postponed).

After these brief remarks of a theoretical nature, we now turn to the more empirical aspects of the matter. In the following sections the discussion is confined to the demand for higher education. The reasons for this choice are (i) compulsory education does not present major problems in estimating future demand, and (ii) non-compulsory secondary education is more heterogeneous and statistically less well-described than higher education. It is true, of course, that the demand for the various levels of education is interrelated. For higher education this means that the number of students entering the university for the first time cannot surpass the number of secondary school graduates of that year; usually it will not be more than a certain proportion of the latter number. We will assume for the time being that the secondary school graduates are relatively abundant in comparison with the number of students entering the university; we will take up this point again later (section 6).

---

[1]) See H. CORREA, The Economics of Human Resources, The Hague, 1962, pp. 83 and 84.

3. THE FACTORS DETERMINING THE DEMAND FOR HIGHER EDUCATION

Total or aggregate demand for higher education in a country, measured in terms of the total number of students enrolled at institutions of higher education, depends on the intensity of demand at the individual level and on the size and structure of the population. In the subsequent discussion we analyze demand at the individual or micro-level; aggregation to demand at the national or macro-level will simply require multiplication of the demand intensity at the micro-level by the appropriate population number.

Individual demand for higher education is a function of a number of factors, of which the following seem to be the most outstanding[2]):

1. intellectual capacity
2. educational level of parents
3. income
4. price of education.

The last two factors are of course quite familiar to the economist. The first two factors are responsible for systematic differences in individual preferences concerning higher education at equal income and price levels. For a detailed discussion of the influence and significance of these and other factors the reader is referred to the study of H. Correa, already quoted.

We will now try to quantify the importance of the four abovementioned explanatory variables, confining the empirical analysis to the Netherlands. Several attempts have been made to estimate certain elements of the demand function for higher education on the basis of international (European) cross-section analyses. None of these attempts, however, has been successful, largely because of differences in the definition of higher education or in the measurement of the size of student bodies.

In the Netherlands two earlier studies were made in which regional differences in the demand for higher education were analyzed along the lines of the present approach. In 1954 the Netherlands Economic Institute published a study in which the regional differences in student enrolment ratios were analyzed[3]). Three explanatory variables were introduced:

---

[2]) *op. cit.*, Ch. VII.

[3]) Onderzoek naar de behoefte aan universitair onderwijs in de gemeente Rotterdam. Rotterdam, 1954. See Appendix III of the report.

   (i) the relative number of male university[4]) graduates between 40 and
       65 years of age;
  (ii) an index of the regional income level, and
(iii) a weighted index of the distance to the various universities.

Of these three factors the one indicating the relative number of university
graduates was by far the most important. The other two factors hardly
contributed to the explanation of regional differences in demand. The
multiple correlation coefficient was high (0.94).

A similar study was undertaken by the Netherlands Central Bureau of
Statistics in 1958[5]).

In this analysis the 1954/1955 enrolment ratios of university students
younger than 35 years from 76 regions were first 'explained' with the help
of three variables:

   (i) a combined index of regional income level and regional intelligence
      level (supposed to be intercorrelated, with $r = 0.25$),
  (ii) the relative number of male university graduates between 40 and
      65 years of age, and
(iii) an index of the degree of urbanization of the region.

The income index referred to in (i) has been corrected for regional differences in the average distance to the universities. The variables (i) and
(ii) were equally important in explaining the differences in enrolment
ratios; the influence of the degree of urbanization was almost negligible.
The multiple correlation coefficient was 0.93.

In a second exercise only two explanatory variables were used:

   (i) an index of regional intelligence level, and
  (ii) the relative number of male university graduates (the same variable as
      in (ii) in the preceding paragraph).

Again, the significance of these two factors was about the same; the correlation coefficient was 0.94. A third calculation revealed that the introduction, in addition to the two above factors, of three other variables

---

    [4]) The word university refers, throughout this article, to all institutions of higher
education having academic status, including those that are usually called a School
(like the Netherlands School of Economics).
    [5]) 'Analyse van de interregionale verschillen in deelneming aan hoger onderwijs',
Statistische en Econometrische Onderzoekingen, 1958, Den Haag, 1958, p. 14 ff.

(income, distance, and degree of urbanization) did not make a significant contribution to the explanation of the regional differences because of the high intercorrelation between these five explanatory variables.

The results of these cross-section studies would seem to show that the most important factors determining the demand for higher education are:

(i) the stimulating influence exerted by those that had academic training themselves,

(ii) the intelligence level, and

(iii) the income level.

Except for differences in distance to the universities, there are no regional differences in the price of education; the impact of this factor, therefore, could not be estimated. A shortcoming of both studies under discussion is that insufficient attention was given to the intercorrelation between the explanatory variables. While in the study of the Central Bureau of Statistics the variables representing the intelligence level and the income level were not introduced separately because they were supposed to be intercorrelated, the intercorrelation between the relative number of graduates and the income level was even higher ($r = 0.53$). The same objection applies to the 1954 study of the Netherlands Economic Institute.[6])

In spite of their shortcomings, the studies discussed in this section have shown that the four factors listed play a preponderant part in determining the demand for higher education. In the next section a simple time series analysis is made of the demand for higher education in the Netherlands as a whole. In such an analysis it is impossible, however, to introduce intellectual capacity as an explanatory variable. First of all, no reliable information is available; second, on *a priori* grounds it seems likely that the average intellectual level of a country changes only very slowly; and third, even if a slowly rising trend in intellectual capactiy were assumed, multicolinearity would obscure the measurement of the effect of this factor. In the subsequent analysis, therefore, the variable 'intellectual capacity' will not appear.

---

[6]) The regional differences in the demand for higher education were analyzed also by R. RUITER and M. EISMA in their study 'De invloed van de spreiding van het wetenschappelijk onderwijs op het aantal studenten in Nederland', Economische en Statistische Berichten, 20 September 1961, pp. 820. Their approach to the problem is somewhat different, however, and their conclusion that the differences in university enrolment are mainly due to differences in secondary school enrolment seems to be of limited value as long as the latter differences in enrolment are not explained through the introduction of what seem to be the more fundamental or basic variables.

4. THE DEVELOPMENT OVER TIME OF THE DEMAND FOR HIGHER EDUCATION
   IN THE NETHERLANDS

We now analyze the demand for higher education in the Netherlands on
the basis of time series starting at the beginning of this century. As there
were no restrictive factors on the supply side of higher education, the
actual size of the student body in the various years may be supposed to be
determined by demand factors only. Therefore, it is possible to estimate
the demand function directly from the actual development over time,
except of course for the years in and immediately after the Second World
War when the special conditions that prevailed disrupted the normal
pattern of behaviour.

Apart from the purely demographic factors the two most important
variables determining the changes in the demand for higher education
were the income level and the number of people having an academic
degree. The importance of the price factor is limited only. In the Netherlands admission fees for the university and other direct costs of academic
study constitute only a small fraction of the total price of higher education. The bulk of the cost consists of the living expenses of the student,
which depend obviously on the general level of the cost of living. The relative price of higher education has therefore changed little in the course
of time. This also holds if the income foregone by the student is included
in the price of education. This statement has to be modified somewhat,
however, in view of the large increase in the number of student loans and
grants, particularly in the post-war period. The effect of this increase in
financial assistance has been to lower – at least from the private point of
view – the price of higher education. This will be exemplified later.

Because of the intercorrelation, already discussed, between income and
the number of academic graduates, the relation between the number of
students and these two variables has been studied for each of the explanatory variables separately. First, the number of students per 1000 inhabitants has been related to the income per head of the population.
Since for a majority of the students studying at a given moment of time
the initial decision to go to the university was taken several years earlier,
an average time lag of three years between the number of students and the
income level has been assumed. The relationship is shown in Graph 1.

Probably the most striking feature of the graph is the break in the
relationship caused by the Second World War. Because of postponed
demand the number of students was unusually high in the immediate

post-war years, until in 1951 or 1952 the more 'normal' relationship was restored. However, the demand for higher education persisted on a substantially higher level than before the war, at comparable income levels. This might be due to a number of factors, of which in the purely economic sphere the following two seem the most relevant:

(i) the lowering of the price of education through a more generous scholarship system, and
(ii) a more equable income distribution.

It is likely that changes in the pre-war social patterns have been at least as important as these economic factors (e.g. the phenomenon of the 'working student'), as well as the lengthening of the study period.

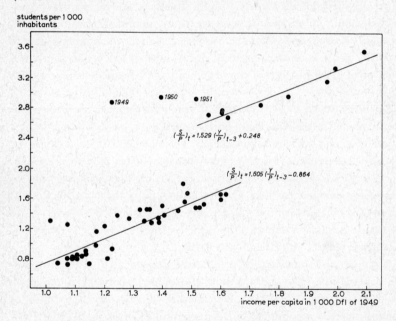

GRAPH 1. The relative number of university students in relation to the national income per head, 1903–1960.

Through the least squares method, regression lines have been fitted to the observations of the pre-war and the post-war period separately. The equations are

$$\left(\frac{S}{P}\right)_t = \frac{1.605}{(0.147)} \left(\frac{Y}{P}\right)_{t-3} - 0.864 \qquad (4.1)$$

for the pre-war period, and

$$\left(\frac{S}{P}\right)_t = \frac{1.529}{(0.153)}\left(\frac{Y}{P}\right)_{t-3} + 0.248 \qquad (4.2)$$

for the post-war years 1952 to 1960 inclusive. In these formulae,

S = number of students at universities
P = total population (in 1000)
Y = national income at prices of 1949 (in millions Dfl.)

The correlation coefficients were 0.87 and 0.97, respectively. The figures in brackets below the regression coefficients indicate the standard errors. The regression coefficients do not differ significantly. The income elasticity of demand corresponding with the first equation varies at different points of the curve; it is between 1.5 and 2.0 along the stretch shown in Graph 1. Because of the relatively small value of the constant term in equation (4.2), this equation implies an almost constant elasticity with a value of about 0.9.

For statistical reasons it would have been advisable to correlate changes in student ratios with changes in income level, as both series show a pronounced and fairly continuous upward movement which might cause spurious correlation. This procedure was impossible, however, as other investigations have shown that short-term income fluctuations do not influence the demand for (higher) education[7]. It is the usual or normal income level that determines the demand for these services. Moreover, on theoretical grounds a relationship of the type of the above equations was to be expected and is perfectly acceptable.

A similar but somewhat more refined approach was followed in a second calculation. Instead of the number of students per 1000 inhabitants, the variable to be explained was defined in this case as the number of students per 100 inhabitants in the age group from 18 to 24 years. This variable was correlated with income per head, just as in the first exercise. Graph 2 illustrates the relationship. The regression equation for the pre-war years runs as follows:

$$\left(\frac{S}{P_s}\right)_t = \frac{1.243}{(0.124)}\left(\frac{Y}{P}\right)_{t-3} - 0.627 \qquad (4.3)$$

---

[7] See e.g. H. CORREA, op. cit., p. 82.

while for the post-war years 1951 to 1960 (inclusive) the equation is

$$\left(\frac{S}{P_s}\right)_t = \underset{(0.197)}{1.727} \left(\frac{Y}{P}\right)_{t-3} - 0.159 \tag{4.4}$$

The correlation coefficients were 0.85 and 0.95, respectively. The more accurate elimination of demographic factors in the last calculation has

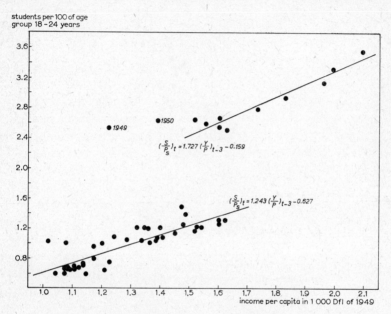

students per 100 of age group 18–24 years

$(\frac{S}{P_s})_t = 1.727 \, (\frac{Y}{P})_{t-3} - 0.159$

$(\frac{S}{P_s})_t = 1.243 \, (\frac{Y}{P})_{t-3} - 0.627$

income per capita in 1 000 Dfl of 1949

GRAPH 2. The relative number of university students in relation to the national income per head, 1903–1960.

improved the results, in comparison with the first computation. Along the range of the curve that is shown in Graph 2, the income elasticity as calculated from equation (4.3) varies again between 1.5 and 2.0. Equation (4.4) reveals an almost constant elasticity of around 1.05.

Having studied the significance of the first important explanatory variable, income, we now turn to the second one: the number of graduated people. We assume that the number of graduated people of a given generation determines the number of students in the next generation. This does not mean that only youngsters of whom the father or mother completed academic studies will go to the university. The assumption implies that the 'inducement' or 'spread' effect of an academic graduate through his social contacts with the younger generation is constant over time. If this assumption holds, we would find a relationship between the number of graduates of a given year and the student population of, say, 20 or 25 years later.

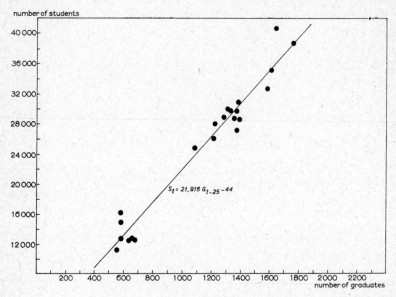

GRAPH 3. The number of university students in relation to the number of graduates of the previous generation, 1935–1960.

The assumption has been tested on the basis of the available data, covering the period 1910 to 1960. The war years 1942 to 1945 were dropped. The least squares procedure led to the following results:

$$S_t = 19.210\,G_{t-20} - 49 \qquad (4.5)$$
$$(1.341)$$

and

$$S_t = 21.916\,G_{t-25} - 44 \qquad (4.6)$$
$$(1.027)$$

in which G stands for the number of academic graduates and S for the number of students. The correlation coefficients were 0.94 and 0.98, respectively. The latter of these two relationships is illustrated by Graph 3.

The functional relationship between S_t and G_{t-25} seems to be clearly established. Yet this approach is not really satisfactory. First, a break between the pre-war and post-war relationship was to be expected. As Graph 3 shows, the data are rather inconclusive in this respect, largely because the pre-war observations are very few in number. Also it is remarkable that the data for the years immediately following the Second World War fit well into the pattern – which they should not do. For various reasons it seems that the causal interrelationship is fairly illusory. Actually the close correlation between S_t and G_{t-20} or G_{t-25} might be explained in the following way. There is an almost constant relationship of a 'technical' character between the number of students in a given year and the number graduating in the same year: $G_t = \alpha \cdot S_t$. Also, the number of graduates has shown a regular long-term growth, which implies that

$$G_t = \beta \cdot G_{t-\theta}.$$

In this equation the value of β is fairly stable, at least for values of θ like the ones used here. Thus, the fraction β/α in

$$S_t = \frac{\beta}{\alpha} G_{t-\theta}$$

is stable too. Equations (4.5) and (4.6) are therefore not necessarily the expression of a causal relationship. They will not be used for forecasting purposes.

5. A FORECAST OF THE DEMAND FOR HIGHER EDUCATION IN THE NETHERLANDS

The analysis of the preceding section showed that income per head is the only factor the long-term influence of which on the demand for higher education could be established reasonably well. On the basis of this relationship a forecast of future demand has been made. It is assumed that the relative price of education will not change during the period of the forecast. For obvious reasons, it is also assumed that consumer preferences will remain unchanged. The influence exerted by the number of graduates of the previous generation – one of the factors behind these preferences – could not be isolated in a way that would allow the explicit introduction of this variable in the demand function.

A forecast of the total demand in the Netherlands for higher education – i.e. a forecast of total student enrolment – has been made for three future years: 1965, 1970 and 1975. The character and quality of the demand equation as found in the preceding section do not permit forecasting still further ahead. Moreover, the demand forecasts have to be based on forecasts of income which will also become less reliable the further ahead they are taken. The same is true, although to a lesser extent, of demographic forecasts underlying demand predictions.

The future growth rates of income used for the present study were taken from two sources. In the first ASEPELT volume, J. Sandee estimates the future annual growth of the GNP of the Netherlands at 4.4 per cent for the period until 1965, and at 5.1 per cent for the years 1966–1970[8]).

TABLE 1 – Forecasts of the total number of university students in the Netherlands

	Using equation (4.2)		Using equation (4.4)	
	Case A	Case B	Case A	Case B
1965	48000	48000	57000	56000
1970	60000	59000	78000	76000
1975	76000	74000	90000	87000

A study of the Netherlands Economic Institute mentions somewhat lower figures for the same two periods: 4.0 per cent and 4.9 per cent, respectively[9]). We assume that the growth rates of national income will be identical with one or other of these two sets of figures. For the years 1971 and 1972 the same growth rates are applied as those for the period 1966 to 1970. The high alternative (the ASEPELT figures) will be referred to as case A, the low alternative (the NEI estimate) as case B. The forecasts of the total population were taken from a study of the Central Bureau of Statistics on demographic trends[10]); the size of the population in the age bracket 18 to 24 years was partly taken from the same source, partly estimated from observations of the past. Inserting these data in the equations (4.2) and (4.4) the following results are obtained.

The difference between the results of equation (4.2) and equation (4.4) is rather large. This is due, first of all, to a higher income elasticity of demand implied in equation (4.4). It should be remarked here that over the

[8]) J. SANDEE, 'Possible Economic Growth in the Netherlands', Europe's Future in Figures, ed. by R. C. Geary, North-Holland Publishing Company, Amsterdam, 1962, pp. 162 ff.

[9]) Income and Consumption Trends in Western Europe, Rotterdam, 1962.

[10]) Maandschrift van het Centraal Bureau voor de Statistiek, W. DE HAAN, Zeist, July 1961, pp. 657 ff.

period 1951 to 1960 – on which the equations (4.2) and (4.4) are based – the growth of P has consistently been somewhat faster than that of P_s, thus leading to a lower income elasticity in equation (4.2) than in equation (4.4). As it seems to be more significant to explain the enrolment ratio for the age group concerned (instead of the ratio for the population as a whole), equation (4.4) is preferred to (4.2). A second reason for the difference between the results of the two calculations lies in the more accurate treatment of demographic factors in equation (4.4). In the calculations based on the latter equation the influence of changes in the age structure can be easily seen. The post-war birth wave reaches higher education in 1966 or 1967 and following years. Therefore, the increase in the total student body will be much larger between 1965 and 1970 than between 1970 and 1975. This is borne out by the figures resulting from equation (4.4), not by those of equation (4.2). The results from equation (4.4) should be considered as the better forecast.

It may be advisable at this point to add a few words reminding the reader of the various elements of uncertainty inherent in the forecast. Even if there are no changes in tastes or preferences *vis-à-vis* education services or in the relative price of education, the forecasts of the numbers of students may still be proved wrong because of the remaining inaccuracies in the estimation of the demand relations. The standard errors of the regression coefficients of equations (4.2) and (4.4) have a magnitude of 10 per cent and 14 per cent, respectively, of the value of these coefficients. As the value of the constant term in both equations is relatively very small, it follows that – at the 2σ or 95 per cent probability level – the future number of students could well deviate, for statistical reasons, by 20 per cent (eq. (4.2)) or 28 per cent (eq. (4.4)) from the number given in the above forecast. This means that the figures of the forecast, e. g., in the case of equation (4.4), should actually be read as follows:

TABLE 2

	Case A	Case B
1965	57000 ± 16000	56000 ± 16000
1970	78000 ± 22000	76000 ± 21000
1975	90000 ± 25000	87000 ± 24000

These possible deviations are indeed substantial. In this light, the distinction between Case A and Case B is hardly significant.

6. A COMPARISON WITH OTHER FORECASTS

Other forecasts of future student enrolment have been made, of which the more recent ones may be mentioned briefly. In 1956 the Netherlands Central Bureau of Statistics published an estimate of the future number of students up to 1970[11]); this estimate is considerably lower than ours. Three years later another estimate was made by the Statistics Committee of the Interuniversitair Contactorgaan (chairman Professor J.J.J.Dalmulder)[12]). These figures, too, are lower than the present estimates, but

TABLE 3 – A comparison of forecasts of total student enrolment in the Netherlands

	Central Bureau of Statistics (1956)	Statistics Committee (1959)	Present estimate
1965	47200	49300–53400	56000–57000
1970	55900	59100–64500	76000–78000
1975	—	59900–66400	87000–90000

higher than the 1956 CBS estimates. Both projections are based mainly on demographic factors; no analysis is made of the interrelation between income and demand. The various estimates are compared in the table below.

An interesting question is whether the high level of demand as given in the present estimate will not be restricted by the number of secondary school graduates having the required qualifications for university enrolment. On theoretical grounds this would seem to be impossible, because demand for these two levels of education is complementary. Still, we might have overestimated the income elasticity of the demand for higher education, so that the number of qualified secondary school graduates would not be large enough to supply the projected number of university students. This, however, is not the case. Let us see what the situation will be in the year 1970, which is in a sense a peak year in our estimates.

According to our forecast, the total student body of 1970 will correspond to 4.76 to 4.87 per cent of the total population of the age group 18

---

[11]) Berekeningen omtrent de toekomstige omvang van het Nederlandse Hoger Onderwijs en de aantallen afstuderenden 1956–1970, W. DE HAAN, Zeist, 1956.

[12]) De ontwikkeling van het aantal academici tot 1980 – aanbod en behoefte, W. DE HAAN, Zeist, 1959.

to 24 years. This implies an increase in the enrolment ratio since the base year 1958 – in which year this ratio was 3.13 – of 52 to 56 per cent. In a recent OECD report[13]) Professor I. Svennilson proposes a coherent set of targets for 1970 for the various education levels, classified according to age groups. For the age group of 20 to 24 years Professor Svennilson proposes for the Netherlands an increase over the 1958 enrolment ratio of 50 per cent, a figure which comes close to ours (neglecting some differences in the coverage of the figures). This increase is consistent, according to Professor Svennilson, with an increase in the enrolment ratio for the 15 to 19 years age group (including the secondary school graduates) of 37 per cent, also between 1958 and 1970. This latter figure is certainly not very high; other authors predicted an increase in the enrolment ratio in this age group of 60 per cent between 1955 and 1970[14]). It may be concluded, therefore, that the number of secondary school graduates will be sufficiently large in relation to the future number of (new) university students implied by the present demand forecast, so as not to form a limiting factor.

---

[13]) I. SVENNILSON (in association with F. Edding and L. Elvin), Targets of Education in Europe in 1970, Policy Conference on Economic Growth and Investment in Education, Vol. II, OECD, Paris, 1962, p. 94.

[14]) J. F. DEWHURST, J. O. COPPOCK, P. L. YATES, and associates, Europe's Needs and Resources, Twentieth Century Fund, New York, 1961, p. 1019.

CHAPTER 13

EVOLUTION DE L'ALIMENTATION BELGE PAR NATURE ET ORIGINE DES PRODUITS

PAR

JACQUELINE POELMANS

Directeur du Centre Interuniversitaire pour les Etudes de la Consommation Privée, Bruxelles, Belgique

INTRODUCTION

Objet de cet article

Quel que soit le pays pris en considération, les dépenses de consommation alimentaire[1]) représentent une part importante du total du budget des ménages puisque, même pour les pays dont le niveau de vie est le plus élevé, ces dépenses atteignent encore 25 à 30% du total des dépenses de consommation privée.

Pour la Belgique ces dépenses atteignaient en 1960 un montant légèrement supérieur à 117 milliards de francs belges soit 28% des montants dépensés à titre de consommation et un cinquième environ de Produit National brut pour la même année.

Tout exercice de prévision des dépenses des particuliers implique donc qu'un soin tout particulier soit apporté aux calculs relatifs à l'évolution future des dépenses de consommation alimentaire. Dans ce domaine, la nécessité de pouvoir effectuer, dans le cadre d'hypothèses données, des projections correctes est d'autant plus impérieuse que la consommation de produits alimentaires est étroitement liée à la production agricole laquelle pose à son tour à la plupart des gouvernements des problèmes particulièrement difficiles à résoudre.

Qui dit projection, dit implicitement connaissance approfondie du passé; en matière de consommation alimentaire, le terrain n'est certes pas vierge et, à côté des remarquables apports de l'Organisation des Nations Unies pour l'Alimentation et l'Agriculture (O.A.A.), les travaux effectués par les instituts de recherches nationaux ne se comptent plus.

---

[1]) Il ne sera question ici que de produits alimentaires à l'exclusion des boissons (eaux – vins – alcools – bières – jus de fruits – limonades).

La plupart de ces études ont principalement visé à mettre en évidence les facteurs qui influencent soit le niveau soit l'évolution de la consommation alimentaire; elles ont surtout mis l'accent sur le rôle joué par l'évolution des revenus et les mouvements de prix.

Les multiples enquêtes budgétaires existant dans de nombreux pays ont d'ailleurs largement contribué à la connaissance de ces phénomènes.

Le but de cet article est de fournir aux économistes-prévisionnistes des éléments supplémentaires d'appréciation et notamment ceux résultant d'analyses parallèle de la consommation alimentaire et des productions destinées à la satisfaire.

Le choix de plus en plus étendu de produits sans cesse plus élaborés qui ont été mis à la disposition des consommateurs en Europe Occidentale depuis la fin de la dernière guerre, nous a conduite à penser qu'une étude approfondie de la structure de la consommation alimentaire en Belgique au cours de la décennie 1950–1960 pourrait constituer un bon exemple de l'évolution des réactions des consommateurs devant d'évolution de la structure de l'offre et contribuer dans une certaine mesure à améliorer la formulation de prévisions dans ce domaine.

Méthode et plan

Si l'on excepte l'effet revenu et l'influence des prix, les facteurs principaux qui guident les ménagères dans le choix des produits alimentaires sont les qualités nutritionnelles des aliments, la facilité dans l'utilisation des produits achetés, les préférences manifestées par les divers membres du ménage. L'ensemble de ces comportements se concrétise, sous forme d'habitudes alimentaires qui résultent de l'éducation, des connaissances et des préjugés des familles, auxquels viennent se superposer les effets de la publicité.

Partant de ces quelques considérations, nous avons adopté, pour cet article, le plan suivant:

I. *examen des modifications de la structure de la consommation alimentaire vue sous l'angle nutritionnel et diététique*

— les chiffres belges décèlent un accroissement important de la part des dépenses consacrées à la viande (sous toutes ses formes) et aux produits laitiers pour lesquels les dépenses se sont accrues respectivement de 56 et de 48% en 10 ans et une expansion significative mais moindre des achats de fruits et légumes (40%);

— par contre, la part des dépenses relative aux œufs, aux céréales et féculents, aux huiles et graisses et aux produits à base de sucre va en diminuant: ceci résulte dans les trois derniers cas de phénomènes de saturation et dans le premier de la substitution œufs/viande.

II. *mesure de l'influence exercée par l'évolution des techniques de production sur la composition de la consommation alimentaire*

Les produits alimentaires mis sur le marché se présentent principalement sous deux formes: frais à l'état naturel ou transformés, notamment en vue de leur conservation.

Depuis la fin de la dernière guerre on a assisté en Europe Occidentale à une diversification considérable des modes de transformation des aliments et à une multiplication à l'infini des produits présentés au consommateur par les industries alimentaires, suivant en cela les voies tracées par les Etats-Unis. Il n'est pas sans intérêt de voir comment le consommateur a réagi à cette offensive de la production et jusqu'à quel point il s'est laissé tenter par des fabrications nouvelles, des emballages séduisants ou des présentations plus pratiques.

De cette deuxième partie, il ressort que les dépenses correspondant à l'achat de produits non transformés (produits agricoles ou de la pêche acquis tels quels) par les consommateurs, ont augmenté deux fois *plus* vite que celles des produits transformés (mis sur le marché par les industries alimentaires); parmi ces derniers, ceux qui ont fait l'objet de l'expansion la plus spectaculaire, sont la margarine, certains produits laitiers, les aliments de régime, les confitures et les fruits conservés; on peut avancer avec une assez grande certitude qu'il s'agit là du résultat combiné de l'amélioration de la qualité des produits et d'une modification de la mentalité des consommateurs.

La divergence de tendance constatée est plus grande encore quand la comparaison porte sur les évolutions en quantité; en effet, les quantités consommées de produits naturels se sont accrues de 51% en 10 ans tandis que celles des produits transformés n'ont augmenté que de 14%; ceci résulte d'une hausse des prix relatifs des produits transformés.

Ces divers mouvements ont eu pour conséquence de faire tomber la part des dépenses consacrée à l'achat de produits des industries alimentaires de 60% à 55,5% du total des dépenses de consommation alimentaire (voir tableau 3).

III. *mesure de l'influence exercée sur la production agricole par les modifications de structure de la consommation alimentaire*

Qu'il s'agisse de l'application de critères diététiques ou de décisions prises en faveur de produits naturels plutôt qu'au profit de produits transformés, le comportement du consommateur entraîne des modifications au niveau de la production.

Nous avons tenté de mesurer ces incidences tant en valeur qu'en termes quantitatifs. L'analyse en valeur a conduit à la décomposition des dépenses alimentaires belges en cinq parts: Agriculture et Pêche, Industries alimentaires, Distribution, Etat, Importations; elle révèle une diminution des parts de l'Agriculture et des Importations résultant d'un accroissement de celles des Industries alimentaires et de la Distribution – la part de l'Etat est restée relativement stable.

Les chiffres ainsi calculés étant fortement influencés par l'existence d'une politique agricole belge assez protectionniste, les conclusions qu'on peut en tirer sont difficiles à extrapoler et à généraliser, sauf pour le cas particulier de la Belgique.

Ces données ont néanmoins permis de dégager que la part des produits de l'agriculture et de la pêche (exprimée en valeur-production), dans les dépenses totales d'alimentation, avait diminué de 13% entre 1950 et 1960. Les revenus des agriculteurs qui dépendent en même temps des quantités vendues et des prix unitaires qui leur sont payés ont donc diminué, par rapport aux dépenses des consommateurs, d'un peu plus de 1% par an.

L'analyse en quantité, qui complète cette analyse en valeur, indique que pour une augmentation des dépenses (à prix constants) de 25% l'accroissement des quantités de produits agricoles de base n'a été que de 21%. Cet écart doit être considéré comme un minimum. Pour l'avenir, il ira vraisemblablement en grandissant pour deux raisons:

– la diffusion des produits des industries alimentaires va en s'accélérant spécialement pour la Belgique qui, pour des raisons psychologiques et commerciales[2]), a un certain retard à ce sujet par rapport à d'autres pays européens
– l'accroissement relatif de la consommation de viande fraîche sera moins rapide.

---

[2]) Il existe notamment des réglementations rendant difficile la vente de viande sans cellophane par les épiceries.

Une mesure de l'accroissement de l'écart n'était pas possible au stade actuel des travaux, de même qu'une appréciation de la même nature par catégories de produits.

Considérations statistiques

Pour effectuer les travaux dont les résultats viennent d'être brièvement commentés, nous disposions des séries chronologiques publiées dans les Cahiers Economiques de Bruxelles pour 39 espèces de produits alimentaires[3]); ces séries qui étaient les meilleures à l'époque présentaient néanmoins certaines imperfections d'ampleur variable suivant les produits, qu'il s'agisse de l'appréciation des quantités consommées ou des prix unitaires moyens payés; nous avons signalé dans le texte celles de ces imperfections qui étaient susceptibles de biaiser les résultats obtenus. Les calculs couvrent la décennie 1950–1960 et ont porté sur 4 années, 1950–1953–1957 et 1960; les années intermédiaires ayant surtout pour objet de contrôler les tendances dégagées.

Il convient de signaler ici que les statistiques disponibles n'ont pas permis de pousser aussi loin qu'on l'aurait voulu l'étude sur l'évolution de la transformation et la commercialisation des produits alimentaires qui fait l'objet de la deuxième partie. Ainsi nous savions, en ce qui concerne l'aspect quantitatif, que les chiffres de poisson frais comprenaient aussi le poisson surgelé et que la rubrique légumes frais couvre aussi les légumes épluchés et emballés sous cellophane. Pour l'aspect prix, nous savions aussi que les prix unitaires moyens ne tiennent pas toujours compte de l'évolution des conditionnements, comme la vente des confitures en rations individuelles, du thé en sachets prévus pour une tasse, du lait en tube, etc. ...

Ces remarques portent à croire que les chiffres sont de ce fait sous-estimés et que dès lors cette sous-estimation se répercute dans les résultats obtenus, elle conduit notamment à exagérer légèrement les tendances à l'expansion des produits naturels (2me partie) et l'importance des produits agricoles (3me partie).

Nous tenons à remercier chaleureusement ici M.G.Labeau et Mme N.Lambilliotte-Ghysen qui ont avec une patience inlassable procédé aux calculs analytiques, à la recherche et au regroupement d'une documentation souvent difficile à recueillir.

---

[3]) Les chiffres ont été publiés dans le numéro 9 pour les années 1950 à 1959 et dans le numéro 14 pour l'année 1960.

PREMIERE PARTIE

CHANGEMENTS DANS LA STRUCTURE DIETETIQUE
DE LA CONSOMMATION ALIMENTAIRE

Les dépenses de consommation alimentaire se sont accrues en valeur de 42% entre 1950 et 1960.

Une analyse de la structure de ces dépenses indique – comme il fallait s'y attendre d'ailleurs – que les consommateurs n'ont pas pour autant réparti également cet accroissement sur toutes les catégories de produits qui composent leur alimentation.

Le Système Normalisé de Comptabilité Nationale[4]) suggère une dé-composition des dépenses en denrées alimentaires par catégories de produits; c'est de cette présentation que la subdivision en 39 rubriques adoptée par la Belgique s'est inspirée[5]).

Les critères retenus par les auteurs du Système Normalisé sont principalement diététiques, certains regroupements résultent cependant de raisons purement statistiques: nature des statistiques de production (ex.: les pommes de terre qui sont dans la même catégorie que les fruits et les légumes).

Le détail de la classification belge permet l'établissement de catégories basées uniquement sur les qualités diététiques des produits consommés; pour ce faire il a été fait usage de la «liste de groupes d'aliments» préconisée par l'Organisation des Nations Unies pour l'Alimentation et l'Agriculture[6]).

Le tableau ci-dessous donne l'évolution relative de chacun de ces groupes.

On constate ainsi que la part des dépenses consacrée à la viande et aux produits laitiers (laits et fromages) se sont fortement accrues, respectivement de 17% et 11%; en contrepartie, des diminutions importants se sont produites pour les corps gras (huiles et graisses) 17% et pour les œufs 14%.

Parmi les autres groupes, notons le poisson dont la part est restée stationnaire, les légumes et les fruits dont l'importance relative est en légère augmentation: 3%, les céréales, féculents et légumineuses ainsi que le sucre et les produits sucrés dont la part va légèrement en diminuant.

---

[4]) A Standardised System of National Accounts (OECE – 1952 – p. 23 – Table VII).

[5]) Voir dans l'introduction la référence relative à la source des chiffres (note 3).

[6]) Voir en annexe I le contenu des groupes d'aliments.

TABLEAU 1 – Changements dans la structure diététique de la consommation alimentaire entre 1950 à 1960 (en pourcentage des dépenses totales d'alimentation exprimées à prix courants)

	Groupes d'aliments[a])	1950	1953	1957	1960
1	Céréales Féculents et amidons légumineuses, noix et graines	15,9	15,7	15,0	15,3
2	Sucre et sirops	6,0	5,9	5,8	5,7
3	Légumes et fruits	12,6	11,3	13,7	13,0
4	Viandes, abats et charcuterie	29,3	32,1	32,8	34,4
5	Œufs	5,0	4,9	4,6	4,3
6	Poissons, crustacés et mollusques	3,1	2,9	3,0	3,1
7	Laits et fromages	7,9	8,2	8,5	8,8
8	Huiles et graisses	12,8	13,1	11,2	10,6
9	Divers	7,4	5,9	5,4	4,8

[a]) Tables de composition des aliments (minéraux et vitamines) pour l'usage international par Charlotte CHATFIELD, publié par l'Organisation des Nations Unies pour
l'Alimentation et l'Agriculture (FAO) en décembre 1954.

Si l'on groupe les viandes, les poissons et les œufs dont le rôle dans
l'alimentation des pays occidentaux est assez similaire et qui se substituent
les uns aux autres (notamment en raison de variations de prix) on remarque que la part des dépenses alimentaires consacrées à ces produits a
augmenté de 12% en 10 ans, passant de 37,4% à 41,8% du total.

L'évolution ainsi caractérisée n'a pas toujours été continue ; les chiffres
annuels pour toute la période montrent que si la hausse pour les viandes
et la baisse pour les œufs et les produits à base de sucre ont été ininter-
rompues, l'évolution des parts de dépenses pour les autres produits ne
s'est pas faite sans à-coups.

Ces évolutions erratiques ont deux causes principales ; d'une part les
mouvements de prix relatifs des produits consommés et d'autre part le fait
que contrairement à l'économiste le consommateur ne raisonne pas en
parts des dépenses alimentaires mais plutôt en parts des dépenses totales
de consommation.

Ceci conduit à examiner quelle a été dans l'évolution ressortant du
Tableau 1 l'incidence respective des mouvements de prix et de quantités ;
en effet, un changement dans la structure des dépenses peut résulter soit
de modifications dans la composition des achats alimentaires, soit de
modifications plus ou moins substantielles dans les prix relatifs des
catégories de produits alimentaires les unes par rapport aux autres ; en
d'autres termes, l'accroissement de la part relative d'une denrée dans

l'ensemble ne signifie pas nécessairement que sa consommation ait augmenté; cet accroissement peut être le résultat d'une hausse de prix non accompagnée d'une augmentation de la quantité consommée. Notons qu'une modification dans les qualités achetées peut, en raison des prix unitaire payés, entrainer aussi une modification de la structure des dépenses.

TABLEAU 2 – Influence des variations de prix et de quantité sur la consommation alimentaire par tête (pourcentage de variation de 1950 à 1960)

Groupes d'aliments[a]	Variation en valeur	Variation en quantité[b]	Variation des prix[b]
Légumes et fruits	40	35	4
Viandes, abats et charcuterie	56	33	17
Poissons, crustacés, mollusques	32	24	6
Laits et fromages	48	24	19
Œufs	16	15	1
Sucres et sirops	25	5	19
Huiles et graisses	13	4	8
Céréales, féculents, légumineuses	28	0	28
Divers	− 11	− 19	9
Total de la consommation alimentaire	35	18	14

[a]) Les groupes ont été classés par ordre décroissant des variations de quantité.
[b]) Les variations de quantités ont été calculées par le truchement d'indices de Laspeyres et les variations de prix grâce aux indices de Paasche.

Il a déjà été dit que les dépenses totales d'alimentation se sont accrues en valeur de 42% entre 1950 et 1960; ce mouvement résulte pour $^2/_3$ environ soit 25% d'une augmentation des quantités consommées et pour $^1/_3$ environ – 14% – d'une majoration de prix; ceci correspond à une hausse de 18% de la consommation alimentaire par tête.

Le Tableau 2 peut être examiné sous deux angles:

1) *influence des mouvements de prix sur les quantités consommées*

On aurait pu croire qu'il existerait une corrélation inverse entre l'évolution des quantités vendues et celle des prix payés; en fait, il n'en est rien et les données réunies dans le Tableau 2 indiquent qu'en ce qui concerne les groupes d'aliments pris dans leur ensemble et pour la période considérée, il n'existe aucune corrélation entre les variations de prix et de quantités.

Ceci revient à dire que même si les hausses de prix ont été importantes l'expansion de la consommation n'en a pas été entravée (ex. viande) et que même si les prix ne montent que dans des proportions modestes il ne s'en suit pas pour autant un accroissement significatif des quantités consommées (ex. huiles et graisses).

Notons, que ce raisonnement reste vrai si l'on pousse l'analyse plus loin en subdivisant les dépenses alimentaires en 39 rubriques (suivant la classification belge) plutôt qu'en 9 groupes (voir Graphique 1).

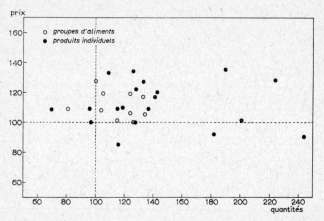

GRAPHIQUE 1. Relation entre les variations de prix et de quantités.

Notons aussi qu'il n'en serait sans doute plus de même si l'on pouvait étudier comment jouent les substitutions à l'intérieur de chacune des rubriques distinguant les produits de luxe des produits ordinaires et les qualités les unes des autres. Le matériel statistique disponible ne permet pas actuellement une telle analyse au niveau national.

2) *analyse des variations quantitatives de consommation:*

Si les prix n'ont joué qu'un rôle effacé dans le développement de la consommation alimentaire, vu sous un angle diététique, la question se pose de savoir quels facteurs plus déterminants ont influencé cette évolution; dans ce but, examinons tour à tour, chacun des groupes d'aliments.

— *les fruits et légumes* viennent en tête; il s'agit d'une tendance générale à l'accroissement de la consommation de produits riches en vitamines facilitée par l'augmentation·des revenus;

— le développement de la consommation de *viandes* a été continu et fort important malgré une hausse substantielle des prix; il résulte par le truchement de l'expansion des revenus d'une diffusion sans cesse grandissante des ventes de viande dans toutes les classes de la population ainsi que de la diminution de la population agricole. La viande sous toutes ses formes, est en effet considérée actuellement comme un aliment hautement désirable notamment en raison de la haute valeur nutritionnelle des protéïnes qu'elle contient;

— malgré une hausse de prix très limitée et des qualités nutritives comparables, la consommation de *poisson* n'a pas connu la même expansion que celle de la viande; on peut invoquer comme justification: le prix absolu élevé du poisson, la difficulté de conservation, la difficulté d'approvisionnement de certaines régions du pays et sans doute surtout une réticence naturelle des consommateurs;

— le groupe *laits-fromages* s'est développé à peine plus que la moyenne malgré la valeur diététique reconnue des produits qui le compose; il est vraisemblable qu'ici la hausse des prix a joué un certain rôle; ajoutons cependant que les habitudes de la population ne la porte pas naturellement à accroître fortement sa consommation de lait: la qualité médiocre des produits mis sur le marché y est sans nul doute pour beaucoup;

— il est curieux de constater que malgré une stabilité des prix et un pouvoir nutritif complet la consommation *d'œufs* par tête n'a cru que très modérément; c'est un résultat direct de la préférence marquée par le consommateur pour la viande;

— trois groupes: les *produits sucrés*, les *corps gras* et les *produits à base de céréales et féculents* indiquent un plafonnement de la consommation par tête; dans les deux premiers cas il s'agit de saturation; dans le dernier on assiste à un remplacement de certains aliments par d'autres dont les caractéristiques diététiques sont considérées comme meilleures, on assiste donc à un changement des habitudes de consommation comme corollaire à l'élévation du niveau de vie (contraction de la demande de pain et de pommes de terre);

— la catégorie «autres produits» ne mérite pas d'être commentée, elle est la somme d'une série d'évaluations statistiques de valeur douteuse; elle n'intervient d'ailleurs en 1960 que pour moins de 5% du total des dépenses de consommation alimentaire.

Que faut-il retenir de cette analyse si l'on veut procéder à des prévisions?

1. La tendance générale est à l'augmentation de la consommation de viandes, de légumes et de fruits. L'accroissement des quantités consommées se réalise même dans un climat de hausse des prix relatifs étant donné l'importance que les ménagères attachent à un meilleur équilibrage de l'alimentation de leur famille par un accroissement des rations protéines et vitamines.

Cette tendance sera d'autant plus rapide qu'elle se réalisera dans un contexte d'accroissement des revenus ou de mouvements limités des prix relatifs.

2. Ni une expansion des revenus, ni un mouvement baissier des prix relatifs ne sont susceptibles d'entraîner une augmentation sensible des ventes par tête pour les produits à base de sucre, les corps gras ou les féculents; tout au plus peut-on s'attendre à l'intérieur de ces catégories à des substitutions résultant soit de mouvement des revenus ou de modifications dans la répartition de ceux-ci soit d'appréciations diététiques.

3. Pour l'avenir, les produits laitiers et les fromages sont une grande inconnue; les achats de ces produits restent étroitement liés à l'évolution des revenus mais ils dépendent aussi très directement de la qualité des produits mis sur le marché, qualité qui, à son tour, peut entraîner des modifications du comportement des consommateurs, qui peut se produire d'autant plus rapidement que les générations d'après-guerre qui depuis 1960 apparaissent comme parties prenantes sur le marché sont d'avance acquises à des habitudes alimentaires, qui ont cours depuis longtemps aux Etats-Unis.

4. Les facteurs ainsi énumérés – qui ne sont pas les mêmes dans tous les cas – peuvent par leur juxtaposition entraîner des modifications inattendues dans le montant total des dépenses d'alimentation et partant dans le rapport dépenses alimentaires à dépenses totales de consommation; il n'est, en effet, pas prouvé que les consommateurs raisonnent plutôt en termes de l'un que de l'autre.

DEUXIEME PARTIE

CHANGEMENTS DANS LE DEGRE DE TRANSFORMATION DES PRODUITS ALIMENTAIRES CONSOMMES

Un schema évolutif, simpliste, montre l'homme passant de la nourriture à l'état naturel à l'optimisation diététique adéquate, équilibrant exactement les vitamines et les calories, la gastronomie et le temps disponible à la préparation des repas; entre la pomme d'Eve et le comprimé quotidien du «Meilleur des Mondes» se trouve, quelque part sur le chemin de l'histoire la période actuelle que nous nous proposons d'analyser et de situer.

La transformation des produits agricoles sous leur forme naturelle en produits alimentaires s'est pendant de siècles effectuée au niveau des ménages ou dans le cadre d'entités économique fermées; suivant les cas, la fabrication à l'échelle industrielle en dehors de ces entités s'est développée plus ou moins rapidement; ainsi, le sucre qu'il fut extrait des betteraves sucrières ou des cannes à sucre était au XVIIe siècle déjà produit presqu'exclusivement par de petites usines; quant au pain, s'il existait à la fin du XIXe siècle de multiples boulangeries dans les villes, il n'en restait pas moins de nombreux ménages, même citadins, qui boulangeaient chez eux une fois par semaine; plus récemment encore, avant la guerre 1940–1944, la confection des confitures était dans la majorité de familles belges l'objet des soins les plus attentifs, actuellement l'achat de confitures industrielles est très généralement répandu.

Depuis 1945, les industries alimentaires et les commerçants en alimentation ont rivalisé d'ingéniosité pour mettre sur le marché des produits alimentaires de plus en plus élaborés, présentés dans des emballages toujours plus séduisants et plus pratiques à utiliser.

Comment les consommateurs ont-ils répondu à cette offensive de l'«offre»? Comment ont-ils opéré leur choix dans la gamme de produits qui est actuellement mise à leur disposition? Quels sont les facteurs qui ont agi sur leur détermination?

Si l'augmentation des revenus a facilité l'acquisition des produits transformés, d'autres influences ont aussi joué du côté de la «demande»: amélioration de la qualité, évolution sociale provenant notamment de la diminution du nombre de ménages agricoles, diffusion des habitudes ayant cours aux Etats-Unis, augmentation du nombre des femmes ayant une occupation professionnelle, évolution de la mentalité féminine au sujet des produits qualifiés de «conserves».

S'il ne paraît pas possible actuellement, d'évaluer l'incidence respective de ces divers facteurs, on peut cependant tenter de mesurer quelles ont été dans l'ensemble les réactions des consommateurs à cet égard et les répercussions qu'ils ont eues sur la composition de la consommation alimentaire.

En bref, voyons si les progrès réalisés dans l'industrialisation et la présentation des produits alimentaires ont eu pour conséquence en Belgique entre 1950 et 1960 de modifier l'allure du «pattern of consumption».

Deux comparaisons ont été faites dans ce but :

— la première consiste à comparer l'évolution de la valeur au prix de
  détail des produits alimentaires consommés à l'état naturel ou non
  transformé avec celle des autres produits alimentaires, c'est-à-dire de
  ceux qui ont subi une transformation quelle qu'elle soit ;
— la seconde vise à déceler quelles sont les espèces de produits alimentaires transformés dont la consommation s'est développée le plus
  rapidement.

Evolution de la consommation de produits non transformés

Les produits non transformés sont ceux qui sont livrés au consommateur
sous la forme sous laquelle ils ont été produits à la ferme (en Belgique
ou à l'étranger) : il s'agit des œufs, des pommes de terre, des fruits et des
légumes frais, du lait de ferme, de la volaille ; sont à y ajouter le poisson
frais y compris les mollusques et les crustacés.

Un problème de classement se pose pour la viande ; il va sans dire que –
sauf dans le cas d'abattage à domicile dans les fermes – la viande n'est pas
livrée par l'agriculture aux ménages sans avoir subi, sinon des transformations fondamentales, tout au moins une série d'aménagements assez
importants dans les abattoirs et les boucheries ; faut-il pour autant classer
la viande parmi les produits alimentaires transformés ?

Le Groupe d'études de la Comptabilité Nationale[7]) et les auteurs de
l'input-output de la Belgique pour 1953[8]) ont pour leur part considéré que
les abattoirs et les boucheries étaient des industries alimentaires (c'est
d'ailleurs la position que nous avons aussi adoptée dans la 3me partie de
cet article) ; sans mettre en doute la valeur de leurs arguments, vus dans
le cadre dans lequel ils s'inscrivent, il paraît plus opportun pour l'analyse
qui nous occupe de classer la viande parmi les produits non transformés ;
en effet, la viande est considérée par le consommateur comme un produit
frais n'ayant pas subi de manipulation en dehors du découpage, de
plus elle entre directement en concurrence avec la charcuterie et les
conserves de viande qui sont considérées elles, comme des produits
transformés.

---

[7]) Premiers Eléments d'une Comptabilité Nationale de la Belgique–1948–1951 par le
Groupe d'Etudes de la Comptabilité Nationale (page 42, Tableau 4), publié en 1953.
[8]) E.S. KIRSCHEN et R. DE FALLEUR «Analyse input-output de l'économie belge en
1953».

Notons que les produits dits non transformés ont néanmoins subi une série d'opérations en cours de distribution, opérations qui se perfectionnent au cours des temps et qui accroissent la valeur du produit mis sur le marché; il s'agit du classement par qualité, du triage et de la présentation finale (exemples: sélection des légumes, triage des œufs, présentation des fruits en caisses, boîtes ou cageots).

TABLEAU 3 – Evolution de la part des dépenses relatives à l'achat de produits transformés et non transformés

Années	Produits non transformés		Produits transformés
		dont viande	
	en pourcentage des dépenses totales à prix courants		
1950	40,0	14,0	60,0
1951	40,6	15,3	59,4
1952	41,4	15,3	58,6
1953	41,5	15,7	58,5
1954	41,4	15,9	58,6
1955	42,3	16,0	57,3
1956	42,8	15,8	57,2
1957	43,9	16,2	56,1
1958	43,3	16,6	56,7
1959	45,1	16,5	54,9
1960	44,5	16,8	55,5

Ainsi et contrairement à ce qu'on avait tendance à penser, les produits non transformés ont gagné du terrain entre 1950 et 1960; au début de la période, ils constituaient 40% des dépenses alimentaires totales, en 1960 ils atteignaient près de 45%; cette tendance a été quasi continue, le Tableau 3 n'indiquant en effet que d'infimes reculs en 1954 et 1958; cette évolution qui peut, à première vue, paraître surprenante, résulte surtout de l'accroissement important des dépenses de viande fraîche qui, en 1960, représentaient $1/3$ environ de la consommation de produits non transformés; l'augmentation des achats de fruits et de légumes frais a aussi joué un rôle déterminant.

Le même calcul effectué en considérant la viande comme un produit transformé donne en 1950, 26% pour les produits non transformés et 74% pour les autres; en 1960 le rapport s'établit à 27,7% pour les premiers et 72,3% pour les seconds; vue sous cet angle, la structure de la consommation alimentaire (exprimée à prix courants) se serait donc à peine modifiée au cours de la décennie étudiée.

Ceci conduit à rechercher si sur le plan quantitatif les tendances évolutives sont les mêmes.

TABLEAU 4 – Evolution de la consommation des produits transformés et non transformés

Années	Dépenses à prix courants		Dépenses aux prix de 1953	
	Produits non transformés	Produits transformés	Produits non transformés	Produits transformés
1950	100,0	100	100,0	100,0
1951	107,5	104,8	110,0	99,0
1952	115,9	109,0	114,7	100,1
1953	118,2	111,5	119,0	102,0
1954	123,0	116,0	121,5	103,2
1955	129,0	117,6	130,8	106,1
1956	138,0	124,0	127,5	111,2
1957	145,5	125,0	131,4	110,1
1958	147,5	128,4	138,0	111,1
1959	157,5	128,4	148,2	112,1
1960	158,9	131,2	151,1	114,3

Le Tableau 4 confirme l'accroissement plus élevé des achats de produits non transformés; en effet, si les dépenses en valeur effectuées pour les achats de produits à l'état naturel ont augmenté de presque 60% pendant la même période, les achats de produits des industries alimentaires n'ont haussé que de 31,2%, soit à peine plus de la moitié; si la comparaison porte sur l'évolution en quantité – qui est la plus intéressante quand il s'agit de réunir des informations en vue de procéder à des prévisions – on constate que la différence est encore plus considérable puisque la première catégorie de produits augmente d'un peu plus de 50% et la seconde de près de 15% seulement, soit à un rythme inférieur au tiers du premier.

Evolution de la consommation des produits transformés

Les constatations qui viennent d'être faites entraînent automatiquement les questions suivantes:

— pourquoi la vente de produits transformés ne s'est-elle pas amplifiée dans une plus large mesure

— n'y a-t-il pas parmi les produits transformés des produits neufs à diffusion rapide et des produits plus traditionnels à diffusion plus lente ou même en régression?

Le Tableau 5 apporte une première réponse à ces questions.

Examinons tour à tour les raisons qui expliquent l'evolution de la consommation des trois catégories de produits distinguées dans le Tableau 5.

Les Tableaux 5 et 6 conduisent à diverses conclusions intéressantes:

1) les dépenses relatives aux produits dont la consommation s'est développée moins vite que la moyenne ne représentent que 30% du total pour les produits transformés

2) les dépenses correspondant aux produits en expansion très rapide, plus de 200% par tête en 10 ans, sont peu importantes: 2.204 millions de frs.b. soit 4% environ des produits vendus par les industries alimentaires

3) les raisons qui ont entraîné la régression de consommation par tête sont multiples:

effet prix et effet revenu, raisons diététiques qui entraînent soit des substitutions, soit la saturation.

Si l'on examine les 6 produits classés dans cette catégorie dans une perspective de prévision, on arrive à la conviction que seule une modification de la tendance des prix pourrait entraîner un changement de comportement pour le café et pour le beurre de ferme – pour ce dernier produit l'augmentation pourrait même être renforcée si les croyances actuelles concernant les qualités alimentaires de la margarine venaient à se modifier; les mouvements constatés pour les autres produits se maintiendront.

4) Si on compare les justifications des produits dont l'expansion est inférieure à la moyenne à ceux dont l'expansion dépasse ce niveau, on constate que pour les premiers, ces justifications sont disséminées alors que pour les seconds, il y a nette prédominance de l'influence de l'accroissement des revenus d'une part, de l'amélioration de la qualité et de la diversification des produits d'autre part.

Cette prédominance est d'autant plus grande que l'on descend dans le Tableau 6 vers les produits en expansion très rapide; ajoutons d'ailleurs que l'accroissement spectaculaire de ces derniers résulte principalement de modifications qui se sont réalisées dans les habitudes de consommation résultant en même temps de l'évolution des concepts alimentaires et de l'allègement du travail ménager.

TABLEAU 5 – Evolution des dépenses de consommation de produits transformés

Produits alimentaires (classés par ordre croissant de l'indice)	Montant absolu des dépenses en 1960 (en millions de frs. b.)	Variation des dépenses par tête – indice calculé sur base 1950 = 100
Produits en régression		
Lait conservé	427	72
Café et chicorée	4 160	82
Beurre de ferme	3 246	83
Compotes et similaires	63	85
Sucre	1 889	96
Thé	62	99
Produits dont l'expansion est inférieure à la moyenne		
Huile	806	107
Beurre de laiterie	5 280	109
Fruits secs	225	117
Conserves de poisson	1 610	119
Patisserie	861	120
Produits dont l'expansion est supérieure à la moyenne		
Légumes conservés	1 090	126
Pain et produits de la boulangerie	9 954	130
Chocolat	2 606	130
Divers	1 089	130
Pâtes alimentaires	494	136
Légumes secs	72	136
Biscuits et biscottes	1 891	140
Confiserie	1 441	141
Lait de laiterie	2 938	143
Charcuterie	10 328	144
Fromages	3 245	155
Margarine	2 942	189
Crême fraîche	275	220
Aliments de régime	480	227
Confitures	512	243
Fruits conservés	435	270
Yoghourt	112	322
Laits spéciaux	247	1 165 [a]
Laits au chocolat	143	1 953 [a]

[a]) de 1953 à 1960.

TABLEAU 6 – Justification de l'évolution de la consommation de produits transformés

	Diététique ou hygiénique	Effet revenu	Effet prix	Modification qualité et diversification des produits	Substitution	Saturation	Modification des habitudes ou facilité
Produits en régression							
Lait conservé	X						
Café et chicorée	X		X				
Beurre de ferme	X	X	X		lait		
Compotes et similaires					confitures	X	
Sucre						X	
Thé						X	
Produits dont l'expansion est inférieure à la moyenne							
Huile	X						
Beurre de laiterie			X		margarine		
Fruits secs			X				
Conserves de poisson		X					
Pâtisserie	X						
Produits dont l'expansion est supérieure à la moyenne							
Légumes conservés	X	X		X			
Pain et produits boulangerie		X					
Chocolat		X		X			
Divers		X		X			X
Pâtes alimentaires				X			X
Biscuits et biscottes	X	X					
Confiserie		X		X			

TABLEAU 6 – *(suite)*

	Diététique ou hygiénique	Effet revenu	Effet prix	Modification qualité et diversification des produits	Substitution	Saturation	Modifications des habitude ou facilité
Lait de laiterie	×	×		×			×
Charcuterie	×	×					×
Fromages		×		×			
Margarine	×		×		beurre		
Crème fraîche		×		×			
Aliments de régime		×		×			
Confitures		×		×			×
Fruits conservés		×		×			×
Yoghourt	×	×		×			×
Laits spéciaux	×	×		×			×
Laits au chocolat							×

TROISIEME PARTIE

MODIFICATIONS DANS LA STRUCTURE
DE LA PRODUCTION

Il a été tenté jusqu'ici de mesurer l'influence du comportement des consommateurs sur la structure de la consommation alimentaire, qu'il s'agisse de la nature diététique des produits achetés ou de la forme sous laquelle les ménagères se les procurent.

N'ayant en vue que la satisfaction de ses besoins, le consommateur se préoccupe peu de connaître quelles répercussions les choix qu'il opère ont sur la structure et l'évolution de la production agricole, quelles modifications ils entraînent dans l'activité des industries alimentaires et de la distribution.

La connaissance des relations qui existent entre le niveau des dépenses de consommation alimentaire d'une part, la valeur des produits agricoles consommés correspondants et l'apport ultérieur des industries alimentaires et de la distribution, d'autre part, peut notamment donner des indications précieuses pour l'établissement de prévisions de production agricole.

Dans ce domaine, aucune étude systématique sur l'ensemble de la consommation alimentaire n'a, à notre connaissance, été entreprise jusqu'ici; le problème de l'évaluation de l'accroissement de la production agricole qui peut résulter d'un accroissement déterminé de la consommation des produits alimentaires est pourtant au centre des préoccupations des économistes et des organismes internationaux qui se préoccupent tant de l'agriculture des pays développés que de l'avenir des pays sous-développés dont l'économie dépend principalement de la vente des produits de leur agriculture.

Les statistiques agricoles générales réunies depuis plusieurs années par les offices de statistiques internationaux ont conduit sur ce point, à la formulation d'idées générales; ainsi, GOREUX, qui a depuis longtemps attiré l'attention sur ce problème dit, dans un autre article publié dans cet ouvrage[9]:

«Il est probable que la valeur à la ferme augmente moins vite que la marge entre valeur au détail et valeur à la ferme. En effet, la demande portera sur des produits ayant subi un processus de transformation de

---

[9] Page 262.

plus en plus poussé tels que les légumes surgelés tandis que le coût de la distribution augmentera vraisemblablement plus rapidement que le coût de production à la ferme».

Il nous a paru que des progrès sensibles dans la prévision de la consommation de produits agricoles ne pourraient être faits que si l'on essayait de préciser l'idée avancée par GOREUX. En d'autres termes, il faudrait, à partir de prévision de consommation exprimées en dépenses pouvoir déduire des prévisions de consommation de produits agricoles.

A titre de première contribution à la connaissance de ce phénomène, une analyse a été faite pour la Belgique concernant la décennie 1950–1960; elle permet de mettre en évidence pour ce pays et pour la période considérée:

1) quelles sont les parts des dépenses alimentaires qui ont servi à rémunérer l'agriculture, les industries alimentaires et la distribution;
2) quelles sont les conséquences du comportement des consommateurs sur la consommation des produits agricoles de base.

1. Décomposition des dépenses de consommation alimentaires

Toute dépense effectuée par les consommateurs – qu'il s'agisse des ménages ou des collectivités – au titre de la consommation privée correspond à la somme des valeurs ajoutées par certains secteurs de production plus les importations et les montants versés à l'Etat à divers titres, au cours des processus de production et de distribution.

Dans le cas des denrées alimentaires, les secteurs de production les plus importants sont l'agriculture[10]) et la pêche, les industries alimentaires et le commerce; les autres secteurs n'interviennent qu'à tire subsidiaire et le total de leurs valeurs ajoutées est minime par rapport aux autres branche d'activité, il s'agit, entre autres, des transports, des assurances, des communications; l'Input–Output de la Belgique pour 1953, publié en 1958, sur la base des données statistiques disponibles à cette époque, permet de déduire que l'ensemble de ces branches représente moins de 5% du montant total de la consommation alimentaire pour cette année.

Partant de ces constatations, il est possible de procéder à une décomposition des dépenses de consommation alimentaire en utilisant un schéma simplifié inspiré de l'analyse input–output.

---

[10]) Produits végétaux et élevage à l'exclusion de la sylviculture.

Ce schéma distingue dans ces dépenses plusieurs parts qui correspondent:

1) au paiement des importations;
2) à la rémunération de l'agriculture et de la pêche belges;
3) à la contribution des secteurs «industries alimentaires» et «distribution»;
4) aux montants prélevés ou alloués par l'Etat au cours des processus de production ou de distribution.

La définition de ces parts – qui ne correspondent pas toujours, pour des raisons de simplification – aux définitions input–output est reprise en Annexe II.

Les calculs ont été effectués pour quatre années; couvrant une décennie qui débute alors que les problèmes d'approvisionnement de l'après-guerre ont disparu, mais qui est malheureusement entachée au départ des répercussions qu'ont pu avoir sur la consommation de certains produits, les évènements de Corée.

Les chiffres eux-mêmes résultent de l'analyse détaillé de données à prix courants relatives à 39 espèces de produits alimentaires. On trouvera, dans le tableau ci-dessous, une évaluation relative de la part de chacun des secteurs choisis exprimée en pourcentage de la dépense totale:

TABLEAU 7 – Décomposition des dépenses de consommation alimentaire en Belgique, de 1950 à 1960 (en pourcentage de la dépense totale)

Années (1)	Agriculture et Pêche (2)	Industries alimentaires (3)	Distribution (4)	Etat (5)	Importations (6)
1950	42,1	20,0	18,5	3,4	16,0
1953	44,2	21,6	17,6	2,9	13,7
1957	42,1	23,4	19,1	3,0	12,4
1960	39,8	25,5	20,1	3,1	11,5

Tel qu'il est conçu, ce tableau permet de dégager les faits suivants:

1) la part des importations a baissé dans des proportions importantes, tombant de 16% à 11,5%, soit de 30% en 10 ans; l'étude détaillée par produit démontre qu'il s'agit plus des résultats d'une politique de protectionnisme agricole que d'une conséquence naturelle du choix préférentiel de produits belges par le consommateur;

2) la part des industries alimentaires s'est accrue d'un quart, passant de 20 à 25,5% du total des dépenses; cette évolution peut avoir plusieurs causes:

   a) la consommation de produits frais est remplacée par la consommation de produits plus élaborés: par exemple, remplacement de poisson frais par du poisson surgelé;

   b) les éléments constitutifs de la part des industries alimentaires s'accroissent par rapport à la valeur des produits agricoles inclus, par ex., hausse des salaires ou augmentation du pourcentage de profit;

   c) remplacement des produits étrangers par des produits nationaux, par ex., confitures anglaises remplacées par confitures belges (ce dernier aspect sera étudié plus loin).

3) la part de la distribution a eu tendance à augmenter; cette évolution, moins forte que celle décelée pour d'autres secteurs, ne paraît pas avoir été continue;

4) la part de l'Etat est très peu importante et n'a guère varié dans le temps; notons néanmoins qu'il s'agit de la différence entre la somme des taxes perçues et des subsides accordés et que ces derniers avaient fortement augmenté à partir de 1957.

La deuxième colonne du Tableau 7 indique une tendance à la diminution de la part qui est échue au secteur «agriculture et pêche», notamment à partir de 1953; ce phénomène mérite d'être souligné car il s'est produit en même temps qu'un rétrécissement des importations.

Ces constatations nous ramènent automatiquement au problème central qui nous préoccupe, à savoir l'évolution comparée de la production agricole et de la consommation de produits alimentaires.

Le Tableau 7 caractérise une situation propre à la Belgique et n'est, à ce titre, que d'un enseignement limité pour des généralisations; un autre regroupement des chiffres permet cependant de mettre plus clairement en évidence l'évolution de l'importance des inputs agricoles.

Avant d'interpréter ces chiffres, une *remarque préliminaire* s'impose: Partant du tableau précédent, le Tableau 8 a été obtenu en subdivisant la colonne (6) importations, en produits agricoles de base (nouvelle colonne (3)) et produits transformés (nouvelle colonne 6)); théoriquement, le but à atteindre était de regrouper sous le total (4) la valeur à la ferme de tous les produits agricoles et de la pêche consommés par la population belge soit sous leur forme originelle, sous forme transformée, au cours des années étudiées; pour des raisons pratiques, deux entorses ont dû être faites à cette règle, elles concernent toutes deux les produits importés:

1) les produits agricoles ont été comptés au prix d'importation, ce qui tend à surévaluer les chiffres; l'incidence de ce facteur va d'ailleurs en diminuant;
2) les produits fournis par les industries alimentaires étrangères ont été comptés pour leur valeur pleine dans la colonne (6), alors que la partie correspondant à la valeur à la ferme des produits agricoles qu'ils contiennent devrait être rajoutée au total de la colonne (4) qui

TABLEAU 8 – Evolution des inputs agricoles (en pourcentage de la dépense totale)

Années	Produits agricoles et de la pêche			Industries alimentaires			Distri-bution	Etat
	indigè-nes	importés	total	indigè-nes	étran-gères	total		
(1)	(2)	(3)	(4)	(5)	(6)	(7)	(8)	(9)
1950	42,1	11,2	53,3	20,0	4,8	24,8	18,5	3,4
1953	44,1	9,6	53,8	21,6	4,1	25,7	17,6	2,9
1957	42,1	8,6	50,7	23,4	3,8	27,2	19,1	3,0
1960	39,8	7,6	46,4	25,5	3,9	29,4	20,1	3,1

est donc sous-évalué de ce chef; la correction à effectuer doit être inférieure à 1% du total des dépenses et va aussi en diminuant de 1950 à 1960.

Ces imperfections ne sont pas de nature à modifier *les constatations* auxquelles conduit un examen du Tableau 8:

1) Pour l'ensemble de la période, les produits agricoles représentent environ 50% des dépenses de consommation alimentaire; mais il importe de souligner que leur part a diminué de 13%; compte tenu des imperfections de calcul, on peut dire, qu'*en valeur, la part des produits agricoles et de la pêche a diminué d'un peu plus de 1% par an, en Belgique, entre 1950 et 1960.*
2) La part combinée des industries alimentaires et de la distribution augmente en compensation de 13%, passant de 43,3% à 49,5% du total; le point caractéristique de cette évolution est le *développement relativement plus rapide et moins hésitant de la part des industries alimentaires:* 19% contre 9% pour la distribution.

En conclusion, l'impression d'ensemble qui se dégage des chiffres – au niveau global – est qu'on a assisté en Belgique au cours de la dernière décennie à un renforcement du processus industrialisation – commercialisation dans le domaine de l'alimentation.

Les calculs étant faits en valeur, une utilisation à usage prospectif des résultats obtenus s'avère assez délicate; en effet, l'évolution de la part d'un secteur par rapport à un autre peut provenir en partie de mouvements relatifs de salaires et de profits; ceci est surtout vrai pour la distribution où l'accroissement de la marge peut provenir autant de l'amélioration du service rendu que du renchérissement de ceux-ci; dans ce domaine, seules des impressions peuvent être rassemblées, leur chiffrage et leur évaluation n'a pas été faite; on peut d'ailleurs se demander jusqu'à quel point elle

TABLEAU 9 – Evolution quantitative de la consommation de produits agricoles de base
(Indices calculés sur base 1950 = 100)

Produits agricoles de base	1953	1957	1960	1960
	pour la population totale par tête			
Produits à expansion rapide				
Légumes	135	171	200	189
Volaille	129	148	196	186
Graines oléagineuses	100	111	173	164
Viande sur pied	115	124	138	131
Poisson	114	133	136	129
Produits à expansion lente				
Œufs	99	117	116	110
Pommes de terre	101	104	108	102
Froment	103	107	107	101
Produits stationnaires ou en régression				
Betteraves	98	100	105	99
Lait	105	106	102	97
Fruits	113	85	96	91
Fèves de cacao	82	96	95	90
Gibier	97	94	91	86
Epices	66	87	88	83
Café[a]	75	77	79	75
Chicorée	85	70	72	67
Riz[a]	30	30	30	28
Total des produits agricoles de base	106	112	121	114

[a] En fait, il y a stabilité pour le riz et le café – l'évolution qui ressort du tableau dépend du chiffre de 1950 qui était anormalement élevé en raison des évènements de Corée.

peut l'être; ainsi, certains services se sont détériorés du fait de la fermeture obligatoire hebdomadaire des magasins, de la diminution du nombre de ceux qui acceptent de porter à domicile par contre, les points de vente sont mieux répartis et les formes les plus modernes de distribution se répandent rapidement; reste à savoir s'il s'agit là d'une amélioration ou non des services rendus: le point peut être discuté et reste très subjectif.

2. Evolution quantitative de la consommation de produits agricoles

Les imperfections des méthodes de calcul basées sur des évaluations en valeur, nous ont conduit à procéder à une approche quantitative; celle-ci consiste au premier stade à mesurer l'évolution – en quantités – de tous les produits de l'agriculture et de la pêche consommés par la population belge sous quelque forme que ce soit.

Les résultats de cette investigation ont été repris dans le tableau 9.

Quelques indications au sujet de la signification de ces chiffres et de leur mode de calcul paraissent indispensables:

— les calculs ont été effectués à partir d'une valorisation aux prix de 1953[11]) des quantités de produits agricoles de base (exprimées en quantités physiques) contenus dans les produits consommés, qu'ils soient belges ou étrangers;
— une série d'hypothèses ont dû être formulées pour permettre de mener les calculs à bien[12]).
a) la composition interne d'un produit ou d'une catégorie de produits a été considérée comme constante au cours de la période (par ex., le pourcentage de sucre contenu dans les biscuits);
b) la composition interne d'un produit ou d'une catégorie de produits a été considérée comme semblable, qu'il s'agisse de produits indigènes ou de produits importés (ex: le pourcentage de sucre contenu dans les confitures belges ou allemandes).

Il est difficile de dire jusqu'à quel point une telle simplification peut altérer les résultats; il est vraisemblable qu'en moyenne et sur 10 ans, les

---

[11]) Il s'agit des prix-producteurs de l'agriculture belge en 1953, à l'exception des produits exotiques valorisés au prix moyen à l'importation pour la même période.

[12]) Malgré l'adoption de ces hypothèses, les calculs présentaient une série de difficultés résultant de la détermination des prix – producteurs moyens et du choix de «clés de répartition» des diverses composantes des produits consommés (sur ce point, les avis des experts ne concordent pas toujours).

erreurs introduites sont minimes mais rien ne permet de dire qu'elles sont systématiques.

En bref, les chiffres qui ont servi de base au calcul des indices du Tableau 9 qui sont reproduits au Graphique 2, représentent la valeur aux

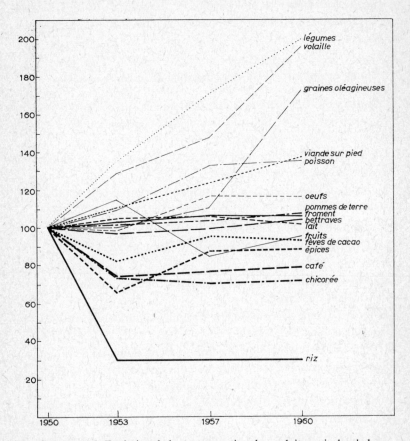

GRAPHIQUE 2. Evolution de la consommation de produits agricoles de base.

prix de 1953 de *tous*[13]) les produits agricoles qui ont été consommés par la population belge pour les années choisies, sous forme de produits alimentaires; leur interprétation doit se faire avec prudence.

Ainsi, *la consommation belge globale de produits agricoles et de la pêche s'est accrue quantitativement de 21% en 10 ans;* si l'on exclut la viande, qui

[13]) A ce point de vue, le calcul en quantité est donc meilleur que ceux ci-dessus effectués en valeur.

représente un tiers de dépenses et dont la demande a augmenté particulièrement rapidement au cours de la période étudiée, l'accroissement constaté n'est plus que de 12%.

Il est intéressant de constater que, sauf les graines oléagineuses qui entrent dans la fabrication de la margarine, tous les produits dont la demande a été en expansion rapide sont originaires des zones tempérées; les produits d'origine tropicale cultivés par les pays sous-développés n'ont fait l'objet que d'une demande stationnaire ou en régression.

TABLEAU 10 – Comparaison entre l'évolution quantitative des produits alimentaires de base et les dépenses de consommation alimentaire (Indices calculés sur base 1950 = 100)

	1953	1957	1960
1) Valeur à la production ou à l'importation des produits alimentaires de base (aux prix de 1953)	106	112	121
2) Dépenses de consommation alimentaire (aux prix de 1953)	106	115	125
3) Ecart: a) absolu	0	3	4
b) en pourcentage de l'accroissement de 2)	0	20	16

Cet accroissement global de 21% des quantités consommées de produits agricoles est à rapprocher de l'augmentation de 25% réalisée pendant la même période par les dépenses de consommation alimentaire exprimées en termes réels (aux prix de 1953); à noter que si l'on veut faire le même rapprochement, viande exclue, on a d'une part une hausse de 12% des produits agricoles de base et, d'autre part, un accroissement de 21% des dépenses à prix constants.

Le tableau ci-dessus indique quelle a été l'évolution de ces chiffres entre 1950 et 1960.

La divergence entre l'évolution des séries 1) et 2) du Tableau 10 concrétisées par l'écart figurant sous 3) représente l'évolution du processus d'industrialisation et de commercialisation des produits alimentaires consommés.

Un exemple simple permettra de comprendre exactement le contenu de cette notion et la signification de l'écart mesuré par la ligne 3a).

Imaginons que la consommation alimentaire se réduise exclusivement à l'achat de petits pois; ceux-ci peuvent être consommés sous trois formes: frais, surgelés ou conservés en boîte. Le poids total des petits pois consommés reste stable au cours de la période envisagée; par contre, les proportions de pois surgelés et en boîte augmentent pendant le même temps; les calculs se présentent comme suit:

(pour simplifier le raisonnement, on a considéré qu'il n'y avait pas d'importations).

	1950	1960
Valeur à la production (à prix constants)		
Consommation totale	*100*	*100*
dont consommés frais	80	60
destinés à la surgélation	—	5
destinés aux conserveries	20	35
Montants des dépenses (à prix constants)		
Consommés frais	160	120
(prix production × 2)		
Surgelés		
(prix production × 2) + 20%	—	12
Conservés		
(prix production × 2) + 30%	52	91
Dépenses totales	212	223
sur base 1950 = 100	*100*	*115*

L'augmentation relative des achats de produits surgelés et conservés se traduit donc dans les chiffres par un accroissement de 15% des dépenses de consommation en termes réels alors que la consommation de produits agricoles de base est restée inchangée; celui-ci représente l'accroissement du processus d'industrialisation et de commercialisation.

Notons cependant que tout le raisonnement ainsi échafaudé repose sur l'hypothèse que les produits plus élaborés ou qui sont présentés au consommateur sous une forme mieux utilisable voient leur prix majoré d'une somme équivalente au service rendu; l'échelle des prix présentée au consommateur irait donc en croissant depuis le produit acheté sous forme originelle, jusqu'au produit ayant subi le plus de transformations; or, si cette relation est exacte à un moment déterminé, il n'en est pas toujours de même si l'on prend des moyennes calculées sur un an car les usines de transformation s'approvisionnent sur le marché quand les prix sont les plus bas; en outre, il est possible que des produits d'industries alimentaires étrangères soient importés à des prix qui peuvent être égaux ou inférieurs aux produits frais indigènes correspondants.

Ces deux facteurs font que les accroissements relatifs ressortant du Tableau 10 sont certainement sous-évalués, ils n'en donnent pas moins une indication précieuse quant au rythme auquel se développe la demande de produits de base par rapport aux dépenses; celle-ci confirme d'ailleurs les conclusions auxquelles avait conduit l'analyse en valeur; remarquons que dans les deux cas, les chiffres laissent supposer que c'est seulement à partir de 1953 que les consommateurs ont accru relativement leurs ventes de produits mis sur le marché par les industries alimentaires.

De tout ceci, il faut retenir qu'en Belgique, entre 1950 et 1960:

1) *sur le plan global, les quantités consommées de produits alimentaires de base augmentent moins vite que les dépenses alimentaires exprimées en termes quantitatifs;*
2) *l'écart constaté varie entre 15 et 20% de l'accroissement des dépenses;* cet écart peut atteindre 40% si l'on exclut la viande des calculs;
3) il est possible que cet écart ira en croissant dans l'avenir; la période étudiée et la méthode utilisée (4 années pour une période de 10 ans) ne permettent pas de formuler des conclusions précises sur ce point;
4) il n'est pas possible de faire systématiquement un rapprochement du même genre par catégories de produits, un même produit agricole entrant dans la fabrication de plusieurs denrées alimentaires (ex. betterave) et une denrée alimentaire combinant plusieurs produits agricoles (ex. confiserie).

Sur ce dernier point, des indications précieuses peuvent néanmoins être extraites du Tableau 9:

a) si l'on considère seulement les postes significatifs, on constate que la consommation par tête diminue pour les fèves de cacao, les fruits et le lait; l'évolution marquée par la consommation de fruits peut paraître anormale, comme les statistiques de base sont fort imparfaites mieux vaut réserver son jugement sur ce point.

Par contre, le ralentissement de la demande de fèves de cacao s'explique par un phénomène de saturation et le remplacement de chocolat par des aliments aussi nourrisants et moins nocifs pour l'organisme; quant au lait, il s'agit surtout des répercussions de la diminution de la demande de beurre au profit de la margarine – aussi par souci diététique: il n'est pas certain que cette dernière tendance se prolonge dans l'avenir;

b) la consommation par tête est quasiment stationnaire pour les betteraves, le froment et les pommes de terre, trois produits dont la demande a atteint la saturation et qui, dans le futur, pourraient même
passer dans la catégorie «en régression»;

c) par contre, la consommation par tête s'est fortement développée pour
la viande, la volaille et le poisson; il s'agit là d'aliments considérés par
la population belge comme supérieurs; leur évolution relative dépend
principalement de substitution trouvant leur origine dans les mouvements de prix (c'est l'explication de la vogue de la volaille).

Les cas des graines «oléagineuses» est différent, il constitue le pendant du cas «lait»: son expansion est directement liée à la demande de
margarine.

Quant aux légumes, ils paraissent être par excellence un produit en
expansion; il faudrait néanmoins se garder d'un excès d'optimisme, la
qualité des statistiques de base utilisées incite, en effet, à la prudence
et il est possible que les accroissements indiqués soient exagérés.

ANNEXE I

Contenu des groupes d'aliments du Tableau I

Groupes d'aliments	Rubriques correspondantes de dépenses de consommation du GECN[a])
1. Céréales Féculents et amidons Légumineuses, noix et graines	Pain et produits de la boulangerie Pâtisserie Pâtes alimentaires Aliments de régime Riz Biscuits Biscottes Pommes de terre Fruits secs Légumes secs
2. Sucre	Sucre Confitures Compotes et produits similaires Confiserie Fruits confits Chocolat
3. Légumes et fruits	Fruits frais indigènes Fruits frais exotiques Fruits conservés Légumes frais Légumes conservés
4. Viande, abats, charcuterie	Viande fraîche, réfrigérée, congelée Charcuterie et conserves Volaille Gibier
5. Œufs	Œufs
6. Poissons	Poissons frais Poissons conservés
7. Lait et fromage	Lait frais Lait conservé Fromages
8. Huiles et graisses	Huile Beurre Margarine
9. Divers	Café Chicorée Thé Epices Divers

[a]) Voir dans l'introduction la référence relative à la source des chiffres.

335

Définition des Secteurs

1. L'AGRICULTURE

Les producteurs agricoles belges désignés dans cet article par le vocable «l'agriculture» comprennent aussi les pêcheurs; leur part correspond à la valeur aux prix production – c'est-à-dire aux prix auxquels ils sont vendus par les fermiers – des produits agricoles belges consommés par la population belge soit à l'état frais, soit sous forme transformée (ex., fruits contenus dans les confitures).

2. LES IMPORTATIONS

Le reste du monde désigné ici sous le vocable «importations» correspond aux importations:

a) de produits agricoles directement destinés à la consommation;
b) de produits agricoles incorporés aux produits alimentaires fabriqués et vendus en Belgique;
c) des produits alimentaires consommés en Belgique;

telles qu'elles ressortent des statistiques douanières établies par l'Institut National de Statistique.

3. LES INDUSTRIES ALIMENTAIRES

Les «Industries alimentaires» comprennent, en plus des industries classiques de ce secteur travaillant pour l'alimentation humaine, l'ensemble des bouchers, des charcutiers et des boulangers belges qui, dans la présente étude, ne sont considérés comme commerçants que pour les produits qui leur sont fournis par d'autres industries alimentaires. La part des industries alimentaires correspond ici à la différence entre la valeur au prix de vente de ces industries de leur production destinée au marché belge et la valeur au prix payé par ces industries des produits agricoles intervenant dans la fabrication – que ceux-ci soient indigènes ou importés.

Ces montants ne correspondent donc pas à la valeur ajoutée par ces industries, pour deux raisons:

— le calcul ne porte que sur la partie de la production destinée au marché intérieur;
— ces montants comprennent, en plus de la valeur ajoutée, le prix des matières premières non alimentaires, des biens et des services achetés à d'autre branches de la production.

4. LA DISTRIBUTION

Le commerce et la distribution à tous les stades et sous toutes les formes sont désignés ici sous le vocable «distribution»; celui-ci correspond:

1) à la différence entre la valeur à la production et à l'importation des produits agricoles indigènes ou importés, consommés frais, et la valeur de ces mêmes produits estimés au prix de détail (dans le cas d'auto-consommation, il n'y a pas de distribution), à l'exclusion des prélèvements opérés par l'Etat.
2) à la différence entre la valeur des produits des industries alimentaires belges ou importés au prix – production ou importation et la valeur des mêmes produits au prix de détail, à l'exclusion des prélèvements opérés par l'Etat.
   Il s'agit donc d'une notion différente de celle de marge commerciale.
3) aux marges qui pourraient être prélevées lors de l'achat par certaines industries alimentaires de produits en provenance d'autres industries alimentaires.

5. L'ETAT

La part de l'Etat comprend les prélèvements effectués à son profit tout au cours du processus de fabrication, de production ou de distribution: droits de douane, taxes à l'importation, taxe de transmission, droits d'accises, etc. ..., ces montants étant diminués des subsides accordés par l'Etat à certaines branches de production.

Pour l'analyse interne des dépenses de consommation alimentaire, il a été fait largement appel à la documentation existant aux Ministères des Affaires économiques, de l'Agriculture, des Finances et à l'Institut National de Statistique.

En ce qui concerne les marges de distribution, la documentation a été particulièrement difficile à rassembler; dans certains cas, les Ministères de l'Agriculture ou des Affaires économiques avaient, pour des raisons d'intérêt général, réuni les données adéquates; pour les autres cas, il n'existait pas de données officielles ni de statistiques systématiques, même de source privée; pour parer cette carence, des enquêtes ont été menées par nous auprès de grands organismes de distribution (grands magasins, coopératives, supermarchés) et auprès des institutions qui disposaient d'informations sur le petit commerce de détail; c'est l'ensemble des chiffres ainsi rassemblés qui a permis le calcul des «marges de distribution». Nous ne tenons pas à dissimuler que pour certains produits les chiffres retenus sont de qualité médiocre et pourraient donner lieu à discussion; les recoupements auxquels nous nous sommes livré nous portent cependant à croire que les tendances dégagées n'en seraient pas fondamentalement modifiées.

SUMMARY

An analysis of the reactions of Belgian consumers to structural changes in the supply of food between 1950 and 1960 may be of some use in forecasting food consumption.

Table 2 shows wide variations in *per capita* consumption increases (in volume) which bear little relation to price variations. Rising standards of living have stimulated consumption of vegetables and meat while the intake of starchy foods was virtually constant. But this breakdown by nutritional composition cannot do justice to the rise of packaged and prepared foods. If all foods are divided into 'unfabricated' and 'fabricated' products, one would expect the fabricated products to expand faster. Table 4, however, shows the reverse. This is largely due to the fast increase in consumption of (unfabricated) meat.

Tables 5 and 6 represent an attempt to analyse divergent expansion rates of fabricated products. Products with an expansion rate below the average comprised only 30% of the total. Prices were of little importance, and could only explain why certain products lagged behind. Almost all the fast growing products showed improvements in quality and variety, while rising incomes and changed attitudes towards packaged and prepared foods contributed largely to their expansion.

By means of a detailed analysis by products, the cost of food of the consumer can be divided up between Belgian and imported agricultural producers, Belgian and foreign food industries, and retail trade (Table 8). This table shows that the food industry took a growing share, at the expense of agriculture. Within agriculture, foreign products declined faster. To some extent this may be due to divergent price trends. Table 10 however, shows that the volume of basic food-stuffs consumed rose less than the volume (i.e. expenditure at constant prices) of food consumption as a whole. If meat is left out of the computations, the intake of basic food-stuffs even showed a 40 per cent less increase than food consumption in constant retail prices.

EXTRACT FROM THE STATUTES OF THE EUROPEAN SCIENTIFIC ASSOCIATION FOR MEDIUM AND LONG TERM FORECASTING[1])

Name and head office

1) The European Scientific Association for Medium and Long Term Forecasting (ASEPELT) is hereby founded as an International Scientific Association.
The head office of the Association is situated in a commune of Brussels and surroundings. The present address is 49, Rue du Châtelain, Brussels.

Purpose

2) The purpose of the Association is to organise and promote original scientific studies, either on methods of medium and long term economic forecasting and programming, or on the preparation of specific forecasts.
The Association will achieve its purpose:
a) through exchanges of information between members on their research programmes, the forecasting methods which they use, and the results obtained;
b) through publication of symposia or collective studies;
c) through organization of research on forecasting.

3) The Association is composed of associate and corresponding members.

4) New associate members will be chosen among persons:
— residing in Europe,
— of university or equivalent status,
— whose main employment is not in national or international official organizations, known for their publications in the field of activity of the Association.

5) Corresponding members may belong to two categories:
a) Those of category A are persons of the same scientific standing as associate members, but whose principal employment is either
— in official economic organizations located in Europe and engaged in medium and long term forecasting,
— or in international organizations concerned with European problems.
Members of category A engage in the activities of the organization in a personal capacity.
b) Members of category B are official economic organizations located in Europe and dealing with medium and long term forecasting or international organization concerned with European problems.

6) New associate and corresponding members will be elected by secret ballot and on a two thirds majority of associate members present.

7) Associate members alone have the right to vote at general assemblies. Each associate member has a single vote.

[1]) Unofficial English translation of the Statutes published in Annexe au Moniteur Belge, 3 août 1961.

Bureau of the Association

President: E.S. KIRSCHEN

Vice-Presidents: T. BARNA

V. CAO-PINNA

Representative of corresponding members: R. REGUL

Secretary: J. WAELBROECK

LIST OF MEMBERS OF THE EUROPEAN ASSOCIATION FOR MEDIUM AND LONG TERM ECONOMIC FORECASTING
(on April 1st 1963)

A. Associate Members

H. Aujac	Bureau d'Information et de Prévisions Economiques (BIPE), Paris
T. Barna	University of Sussex, Sussex
W. Bauer	Rheinisch-Westfälisches Institut für Wirtschaftsforschung, Essen
W. Beckerman	The National Institute of Economic and Social Research, London
J. Benard	Centre d'Etudes de la Prospection Economique à Moyen et Long Terme (CEPREL), Paris
R. Bentzel	Industriens Utredningsinstitut, Stockholm
G. Bombach	Wirtschaftswissenschaftliche Seminare der Universität Basel, Basel
V. Cao-Pinna	Università di Roma, Roma
E. Dassel	Centre Emile Bernheim pour l'Etude des Affaires, Bruxelles
B. M. Deakin	Economist Intelligence Unit, London
R. Frisch	Sosialøkonomisk Institutt, Oslo
R. C. Geary	The Economic Research Institute, Dublin
G. Gehrig	IFO-Institut für Wirtschaftsforschung, München
Z. Kenessey	Office Central Hongrois de Statistique, Budapest
E. S. Kirschen	Département d'Economie Appliquée de l'Université Libre de Bruxelles (DULBEA), Bruxelles
R. Krengel	Deutsches Institut für Wirtschaftsforschung, West-Berlin
J. Lasuen	Madrid
H. Linnemann	Nederlandsch Economisch Instituut, Rotterdam
A. Nataf	CERMAP, Arcueil (Seine)
N. Novacco	SVIMEZ, Roma
P. Nørregard Rasmussen	Institute of Economics, University of Copenhagen, Copenhagen
J. Piperoglou	Doxiadis Associates, Athens
G. Rottier	Secrétaire Général du Centre de Recherche et de Documentation sur la Consommation, Paris
R. Stone	Department of Applied Economics, Cambridge

B. Corresponding Members (Statutes, art. 5A)

L. M. Goreux	FAO, Roma
C. Gruson	Ministère des Finances, Paris
A. Kervyn de Lettenhove	Ministère des Affaires Economiques et de l'Energie, Bureau de Programmation Economique, Bruxelles

343

P. MILLET	Commission Economique pour l'Europe, Bruxelles
R. REGUL	CECA, Luxembourg
J. SANDEE	Centraal Planbureau, 's-Gravenhage
R. WAGENFUHR	Office Statistique des Communautés Européennes, Bruxelles

C. Corresponding Members (Statutes, art. 5B)

F. LE GUAY	OECD, Paris

APPENDICES

Appendix B

N. Novacco and F. Pilloton: Structural Changes in Italy's Private Consumption Expenditures Projections for the Next Ten Years

pp. 347–356

Annexe

L. M. Goreux: Projections de la Demande des Produits Agricoles en Europe Occidentale en 1970

pp. 357–363

BASIC DATA AND RELATED CALCULATIONS

Table I - Classifications of private consumption expenditures [a])

ASEPELT (recommended classification)	HOUSEHOLD BUDGETS (survey of 1 999 Italian household budgets)	ISTAT (national accounts)
1. *Food*	1. *Food*	1. *Food*
cereals and products (including also pastry)	cereal products (excluding pastry)	bread and cereals (excluding pastry)
meat, fish, eggs (including also poultry, frozen meat or fish, lard, smoked bacon; excluding tinned meat or fish, and sausages)	meat (including items of ASEPELT classification, plus tinned meat or fish, and sausages; excluding lard)	meat (including items of ASEPELT classification, plus tinned meat or fish, and sausages; excluding lard)
	fish (including frozen and tinned fish)	fish (including frozen and tinned fish)
	eggs (only for direct consumption)	
milk and products (including also ice cream)	milk and products (excluding ice cream)	milk, cheese and eggs (excluding ice cream)
potatoes, vegetables and fruits (including also citrus fruits, raisins, nuts; excluding tinned products)	potatoes	potatoes, vegetables and fruits (including also tomato products)
	fresh and dried fruits (including also citrus fruits, raisins and nuts)	
	olives	
	fresh, dried and preserved vegetables and legumes	
other foods (including also tinned products, sausages, salt, spices and vinegar)	animal and vegetable fats	oils and fats
	sugar (direct consumption)	sugar, jam, honey
	jam, preserved fruits and fruit juices	
	tomato products	
	candy and ice cream	
	salt	
	vinegar	
	other minor expenses (including food consumed outside of home)	other foods (including syrups, fruit juices, mineral and aerated water, salt, spices, coffee, tea, cocoa, etc)
2. *Beverages*	2. *Beverages*	2. *Alcoholic beverages*
alcoholic beverages	wine	
	beer	
	liquors and brandies	
	coffee	
	tea and spices	
	coffee substitutes	
	other non alcoholic beverages	
3. *Tobacco*	3. *Tobacco*	3. *Tobacco*
4. *Clothing and footwear* (including also leather products and repairs)	4. *Clothing and footwear*	4. *Clothing and footwear* (including suits and dresses, underwear, knitted goods, hosiery, yarns and sewing thread, ready-made clothing, shoes and other products, including also repairs)
	underwear	
	knitted goods and hosiery	
	yarns and sewing thread	
	ready-made clothing	
	shoes	
	cotton fabrics	
	woollen fabrics	
	fabrics of silk and other fibres	
	clothing accessories	
	clothing repairs	
5. *Household durables* (including also furniture, bedding, carpets, toys, records, watches, jewelry, repairs; excluding transport equipment)	5. *Household durables*	5. *Household durables* (including also furniture, sewing machines, radio and television sets, electric household appliances, crystal-ware, cutlery and fancy goods)
	furniture	
	electric household appliances	
	glassware and pottery	
	kitchen equipment	
	mattresses, carpets, curtains	
	non-electric heaters	
	other products of engineering industry	

[a]) The progressive numbers and names assigned to each group of expenditures in this table do not correspond to the numbers and names used in the original classifications.

Table I (continued)

ASEPELT	HOUSEHOLD BUDGETS	ISTAT
6. *Non durable household goods and miscellaneous personal services* (this item is grouped under Miscellaneous in the ASEPELT classification)	6. *Non durable household products and miscellaneous personal services* soap, detergents etc. wax and polish linen other household products	6. *Non durable household products and miscellaneous personal services* (including paid household services, kitchen soap and other detergents, electric lamps, linen, shoe repairs, dry cleaning services, matches)
7. *Fuel and electric power*	7. *Fuel and electric power*	7. *Fuel and electric power* (including electric power, coalgas, heating coke, natural gas, gas in containers, fuel oil, charcoal, firewood)
8. *Dwellings*	8. *Dwellings* rent, joint ownership costs, water rates and repairs	8. *Dwellings* (including rent, joint ownership costs, water rates)
9. *Health and hygiene* (including also drugs, voluntary and compulsory insurance; excluding cosmetics and toilet articles)	9. *Health and hygiene* toilet articles drugs and medical services	9. *Health and hygiene* (including barbers', hairdressers' and other services, shaving blades, toilet soap, doctors' fees, drugs)
10. *Communications* (including also postal and telecommunication expenses)	10. *Communications* public transport services telephone and radio charges	10. *Communications* communications (including regular mail, postal orders, cables and telephone services) other transport services (including railways, tramways, trolley-bus lines, bus lines, shipping lines, taxi-cabs, hired cars, luggage storage services)
11. *Private transport (purchase)* (excluding repairs)	11. *Private transport (purchase)* transport means	11. *Private transport (purchase)* purchase of transport means (including motor vehicles, motorcycles, motorscooters, bicycles)
12. *Private transport (operation)* (including petrol, tyres, repairs)	12. *Private transport (operation)* operation and maintenance of transport means	12. *Private transport (operation)* operation of private transport (including motor vehicles and motorcycles)
13. *Miscellaneous* (including cosmetics, flowers, papers and catering services)	13. *Miscellaneous* books, newspapers and magazines recreation toys other services and taxes charity	13. *Miscellaneous* hotels and public catering places (including hotels, restaurants and bars, with reference exclusively to service expenses) books and newspapers entertainment (including movies, theatre plays, sport events, etc.) other recreation (including lotteries, hunting and fishing, flowers, radio subscription fees, toys and photographs, matches and smoking accessories) miscellaneous expenses (including schools, jewelry etc., religious expenses, political expenses, labor union expenses, legal expenses, middlemen's fees for financial operations, life insurance, funeral expenses, other)

Table II - Material utilized in the SVIMEZ study - *Per capita* private consumption by annual expenditure class
(Survey of household budgets - Values in 1953 lire)

Expenditure item	Annual expenditure class										
	I (up to 75 000)	II (75 000- 125 000)	III (125 000- 175 000)	IV (175 000- 225 000)	V (225 000- 275 000)	VI (275 000- 325 000)	VII (325 000- 375 000)	VIII (375 000- 425 000)	IX (425 000- 525 000)	X (525 000- 725 000)	XI (more than 725 000)
1. *Food*	40 498	59 505	81 996	100 088	113 792	127 886	142 310	154 178	154 507	202 163	218 440
2. *Beverages*	2 260	4 867	7 804	9 871	10 937	12 721	13 906	15 214	17 125	18 874	20 276
3. *Tobacco*	1 587	3 060	3 996	5 495	6 606	8 395	7 700	10 565	9 936	13 264	14 867
4. *Clothing and footwear*											
underwear	7 489	13 735	21 696	30 499	43 869	50 720	58 882	63 796	80 929	114 269	247 086
knitted goods and hosiery	658	984	1 808	2 746	3 560	4 439	5 353	5 500	7 739	9 713	21 182
yarns and sewing thread	850	1 484	2 548	3 413	4 504	5 548	6 574	6 407	9 170	11 376	19 642
ready-made clothing	385	521	780	1 021	1 095	1 466	1 429	1 295	1 942	1 580	3 994
shoes	1 654	4 574	7 400	11 340	19 831	19 787	19 721	27 316	32 878	54 569	129 846
cotton fabrics	2 613	3 522	4 670	5 838	7 037	8 371	9 242	9 920	11 267	10 615	19 923
woollen fabrics	619	767	939	1 095	1 170	1 655	1 725	1 633	1 906	3 266	5 472
fabrics of silk and other fibres	360	1 069	1 880	2 649	2 989	4 477	7 466	5 620	7 404	10 394	14 476
clothing accessories	77	154	366	440	631	1 003	1 224	1 053	1 487	2 271	6 034
clothing repairs	238	494	969	1 447	2 260	3 204	4 733	3 900	5 573	8 285	19 328
	35	166	336	510	592	770	1 415	1 152	1 563	2 200	7 189
Household durables											
furniture	1 008	2 463	4 767	7 027	11 189	13 186	17 609	18 728	28 418	44 694	118 796
electric appliances	249	493	955	1 392	3 017	2 730	4 594	3 108	8 723	9 339	34 561
glassware and pottery	62	218	880	1 354	1 809	2 569	3 527	3 818	5 415	11 143	23 150
kitchen equipment	169	272	396	504	727	1 005	1 111	1 893	1 750	2 224	7 873
mattresses, carpets, curtains	157	194	381	496	611	900	1 390	832	1 341	2 169	6 371
non-electric heaters	66	186	277	373	721	935	985	917	2 145	4 042	10 607
other products of engineering industry	217	714	1 007	1 773	2 760	3 530	3 966	5 451	5 598	11 447	31 484
	88	386	871	1 135	1 544	1 517	2 036	2 709	3 446	4 330	4 750

Table II (continued)

Expenditure item	Annual expenditure class										
	I	II	III	IV	V	VI	VII	VIII	IX	X	XI
6. *Non durable household goods and miscellaneous personal services*	1 939	2 454	3 496	4 105	4 936	5 920	7 132	6 324	8 499	8 383	22 707
soap, detergents, etc.	967	1 161	1 506	1 868	2 008	2 280	2 344	2 538	2 926	2 619	3 465
wax and polish	155	215	274	339	438	617	699	856	947	904	1 558
linen	706	945	1 563	1 688	2 221	2 707	3 810	2 564	4 131	4 338	17 226
other household products	111	133	153	210	269	316	279	366	495	522	458
7. *Fuel and electric power*	2 703	4 721	7 078	9 257	10 973	12 887	15 228	16 881	17 026	21 826	33 373
8. *Dwellings*	1 534	2 183	3 852	4 713	8 798	11 176	12 107	19 224	16 072	23 983	35 460
9. *Health and hygiene*	960	2 441	4 001	5 473	6 718	7 746	10 578	10 593	15 430	14 093	22 827
toilet articles	346	815	1 416	2 079	2 814	3 949	3 958	4 522	5 587	6 658	10 078
drugs and medical services	614	1 626	2 585	3 394	3 904	3 797	6 620	6 071	9 843	7 435	12 749
10. *Communications*	307	871	1 327	2 677	4 072	5 265	6 637	7 750	8 783	10 877	26 917
telephone and radio charges	11	71	250	391	656	865	1 146	1 465	1 835	2 350	5 474
public transport services	296	800	1 077	2 286	3 416	4 400	5 491	6 285	6 948	8 527	21 443
11. *Private transport (purchase)*	272	783	1 451	2 969	3 852	7 071	7 526	15 213	19 181	25 459	146 805
12. *Private transport (operation)*	149	212	626	1 220	2 045	2 825	4 224	4 558	11 867	12 215	41 000
13. *Miscellaneous*	1 781	4 868	8 750	14 292	20 742	30 783	41 053	53 124	75 813	91 069	228 540
books, newspapers and magazines	324	866	1 570	2 582	3 358	4 621	5 108	8 332	6 854	8 280	14 576
recreation	232	679	1 514	2 121	2 834	4 642	5 514	6 612	7 754	9 504	19 837
toys	19	59	86	115	162	202	395	304	245	257	2 062
other services and taxes	1 198	3 009	5 485	9 094	13 690	20 267	29 005	35 946	57 695	70 139	176 387
charity	8	255	95	380	698	1 051	1 031	1 930	3 265	2 889	15 678
Total	62 487	102 163	150 840	197 686	248 529	296 581	344 892	396 148	463 586	601 169	1 177 094

Table III - Calculations used in the SVIMEZ study - *Per capita* private consumption as a function of aggregate expenditure - First method of analysis (Basic statistical source: household budget survey)

Expenditure item	$y = a + bx + cx^2$	Calculated *per capita* value [a] (1953 lire)		
		1958	1965	1970
1. *Food* [b]	$23\,873 + 366.73\ x - 0.17728\ x^2$	91 229	108 229	123 168
2. *Beverages*	$437 + 48.97\ x - 0.02751\ x^2$	9 272	11 435	13 302
3. *Tobacco*	$-\ 76 + 31.60\ x - 0.01607\ x^2$	5 695	7 138	8 398
4. *Clothing and footwear*	-	32 420	46 148	59 065
underwear	$-\ 926 + 18.70\ x$	2 885	4 004	5 065
knitted goods and hosiery	$31 + 17.23\ x$	3 542	4 573	5 551
yarns and sewing thread	$380 + 2.72\ x$	935	1 097	1 251
ready-made clothing	$-\ 11730 + 115.83\ x$	11 895	18 832	25 406
shoes	$1362 + 24.55\ x - 0.00795\ x^2$	6 055	7 281	8 411
cotton fabrics	$237 + 4.47\ x$	1 148	1 415	1 669
woollen fabrics	$-\ 1571 + 24.69\ x - 0.00938\ x^2$	3 070	4 286	5 376
fabrics of silk and other fibres	$-\ 586 + 5.36\ x$	505	827	1 131
clothing accessories	$-\ 2284 + 20.63\ x - 0.00099\ x^2$	1 880	3 086	4 224
clothing repairs	$-\ 44 + 2.08\ x + 0.00349\ x^2$	525	747	981
5. *Household durables*	-	8 838	12 735	16 805
furniture	$-\ 125 + 6.43\ x + 0.01994\ x^2$	2 013	2 956	3 982
electric appliances	$73 + 4.57\ x + 0.01401\ x^2$	1 586	2 251	2 975
glassware and pottery	$42 + 2.08\ x + 0.00392\ x^2$	628	863	1 111
kitchen equipment	$53 + 1.82\ x + 0.00306\ x^2$	554	745	950
mattresses, carpets, curtains	$-\ 156 + 2.88\ x + 0.00557\ x^2$	662	990	1 338
non-electric heaters	$-\ 687 + 11.31\ x - 0.00557\ x^2$	1 386	1 907	2 365
other products of engineering industry	$-\ 637 + 9.93\ x + 0.01500\ x^2$	2 009	3 023	4 084
6. *Non durable household goods and miscellaneous personal services*	-	4 274	4 984	5 710
soap, detergents, etc.	$929 + 4.65\ x - 0.00223\ x^2$	1 784	2 000	2 190
wax and polish	$172 + 1.29\ x$	435	512	585
linen	$1034 + 1.71\ x + 0.01029\ x^2$	1 810	2 200	2 638
other household products	$146 + 0.51\ x - 0.00012\ x^2$	245	272	297
7. *Fuel and electric power*	$443 + 46.82\ x - 0.01607\ x^2$	9 315	11 669	13 794
8. *Dwellings*	$-\ 3558 + 57.19\ x - 0.02030\ x^2$	7 251	10 108	12 681
9. *Health and hygiene*	-	5 878	7 746	9 416
toilet articles	$-\ 729 + 16.43\ x - 0.00614\ x^2$	2 363	3 176	3 905
drugs and medical services	$-\ 554 + 21.80\ x - 0.00896\ x^2$	3 515	4 570	5 511
10. *Communications*	-	3 130	4 574	5 943
telephone and radio charges	$-\ 489 + 5.08\ x$	546	850	1 139
public transport services	$-\ 1290 + 19.02\ x$	2 584	3 724	4 804
11. *Private transport (purchase)*	$-\ 186 + 5.41\ x + 0.07601\ x^2$	4 071	6 522	9 349
12. *Private transport (operation)*	$-\ 1634 + 12.86\ x + 0.02020\ x^2$	1 824	3 160	4 559
13. *Miscellaneous*	-	20 572	30 647	40 535
books, newspapers and magazines	$283 + 13.67\ x$	3 068	3 887	4 663
recreation	$-\ 901 + 18.01\ x$	2 768	3 847	4 869
toys	$-\ 259 + 1.93\ x - 0.00023\ x^2$	125	234	334
other services and taxes	$-\ 10088 + 110.61\ x + 0.04033\ x^2$	14 121	21 873	29 488
charity	$29 - 0.06\ x + 0.01141\ x^2$	490	806	1 181
Total		203 769	265 095	322 725
Differences	-	- 39	- 1478	- 2350
Aggregate expenditure	-	203 730	263 617	320 375

[a] The calculation was made attributing to the functions' independent variable the values of Lit. 203 730/1 000 for 1958, Lit. 263 617/1 000 for 1965, and Lit. 320 375/1 000 for 1970.

[b] The semi-logarithmic function relating to a total of about 50 items of food expenditures is:

$$y = -\ 180\,110.721 + 119\,149.380\ \log_{10} x\ .$$

This function produces the following values: 95 012 for 1958, 108 347 for 1965, and 118 437 for 1970.

Table IV- Calculations used in the SVIMEZ study - *Per capita* private consumption as a function of aggregate expenditure - Second method of analysis (Basic statistical source: household budget survey)

Expenditure item	$y = k \frac{1}{\sqrt{2\pi}} \int_{-\infty}^{+\xi} e^{-\frac{1}{2}t^2} dt$; for $\xi = a + b \log x$		Calculated *per capita* value [a]) (1953 lire)		
	k [b])	ξ	1958	1965	1970
1. *Food*	800 000	- 6.0328983 + 0.3993770 log x	99 940	117 884	132 856
2. *Beverages*	21 500	- 12.1091119 + 0.9836288 log x	10 024	12 191	13 777
3. *Tobacco*	20 000	- 9.7350111 + 0.7506166 log x	5 776	7 147	8 265
4. *Clothing and footwear*			32 560	44 503	56 022
underwear	1 000 000	- 7.8709812 + 0.4166188 log x	2 735	3 785	4 805
knitted goods and hosiery	150 000	- 7.9698693 + 0.4900736 log x	3 586	4 793	5 919
yarns and sewing thread	500 000	- 5.4725155 + 0.2110354 log x	955	1 135	1 290
ready-made clothing	1 000 000	- 9.1072622 + 0.5608324 log x	12 170	17 570	22 869
shoes	800 000	- 5.6555338 + 0.2637495 log x	6 020	7 248	8 317
cotton fabrics	2 500 000	- 5.6673392 + 0.1932414 log x	1 180	1 413	1 613
woollen fabrics	100 000	- 9.0410656 + 0.5825266 log x	2 742	3 838	4 885
fabrics of silk and other fibers	250 000	- 8.6997016 + 0.4764624 log x	505	740	978
clothing accessories	1 000 000	- 9.0139364 + 0.5039920 log x	2 165	3 235	4 340
clothing repairs	150 000	- 9.3082324 + 0.5391911 log x	494	746	1 006
5. *Household durables*			7 530	11 363	15 330
furniture	3 000 000	- 9.3150181 + 0.4953944 log x	1 680	2 610	3 615
electric appliances	200 000	- 10.9531136 + 0.6891148 log x	1 144	1 868	2 663
glassware and pottery	1 000 000	- 7.7240872 + 0.3673960 log x	610	850	1 085
kitchen equipment	1 000 000	- 7.7178519 + 0.3637792 log x	535	745	945
mattresses, carpets, curtains	500 000	- 9.2365484 + 0.5022816 log x	485	753	1 028
non-electric heaters	1 500 000	- 9.1203781 + 0.4990522 log x	1 898	2 880	3 908
other products of engineering industry	8 000	- 12.0467247 + 0.8997088 log x	1 178	1 657	2 086
6. *Non durable household goods and miscellaneous personal services*	-		4 314	5 234	6 064
soap, detergents, etc.	100 000	- 4.6543675 + 0.2090977 log x	1 793	2 046	2 255
wax and polish	50 000	- 6.5129277 + 0.3350809 log x	392	495	2 928
linen	2 000 000	- 6.5540752 + 0.2822171 log x	1 910	2 430	580
other household products	250 000	- 5.7297899 + 0.2126146 log x	219	263	301
7. *Fuel and electric power*	1 000 000	- 6.4127265 + 0.3316862 log x	9 155	11 530	13 640
8. *Dwellings*	3 000 000	- 8.0141110 + 0.4200676 log x	5 985	8 385	10 755
9. *Health and hygiene*	-		5 498	7 278	8 907
toilet articles	50 000	- 9.0193623 + 0.5973245 log x	2 148	2 950	3 699
drugs and medical services	70 000	- 7.6684743 + 0.4909998 log x	3 350	4 328	5 208
10. *Communications*	-		2 657	4 029	5 454
telephone and radio charges	10 000	- 14.2315835 + 1.0230353 log x	422	719	1 034
public transport services	1 000 000	- 8.9231824 + 0.4973496 log x	2 235	3 310	4 420
11. *Private transport (purchase)*	10 000 000	- 10.4740680 + 0.5775202 log x	3 200	5 500	8 100
12. *Private transport (operation)*	500 000	- 11.8358537 + 0.7407088 log x	1 355	2 398	3 613
13. *Miscellaneous*	-		16 024	25 034	34 522
books, newspapers and magazines	100 000	- 9.4381786 + 0.6124864 log x	2 555	3 651	4 713
recreation	100 000	- 10.3316861 + 0.6822665 log x	2 320	3 485	4 624
toys	100 000	- 7.8193735 + 0.3927966 log x	127	177	226
other services and taxes	2 500 000	- 10.4137669 + 0.6365432 log x	10 600	16 975	23 838
charity	100 000	- 12.1039797 + 0.7746621 log x	422	746	1 121
Total	-	-	204 018	262 476	317 305
Differences	-	-	- 288	1 141	3 070
Aggregate expenditure	-	-	203 730	263 617	320 375

[a]) The calculation was made attributing to the functions' independent variable the values of Lit. 203 730 for 1958, Lit. 263 617 for 1965, and Lit. 320 375 for 1970.

[b]) With regard to the values of parameter k, cf. explanations published in: SVIMEZ, *Stime sui Consumi Privati* e.c.c., *op.cit.* p. 26.

Table V - Material utilized in the SVIMEZ study - Aggregate private consumption from 1950 to 1958 at current prices (ISTAT data; billion lire)

Expenditure item	1950	1951	1952	1953	1954	1955	1956	1957	1958
1. *Food*	3 077	3 421	3 660	3 890	4 084	4 313	4 612	4 780	4 970
2. *Alcoholic beverages*	354	385	444	524	596	649	668	668	706
3. *Tobacco*	288	306	331	361	379	409	433	459	482
4. *Clothing and footwear*	794	997	1 012	1 061	1 006	1 004	1 068	1 132	1 140
5. *Household durables*	123	139	145	157	161	163	187	212	244
6. *Non durable household goods and miscellaneous personal services*	242	304	291	323	317	331	351	384	399
7. *Fuel and electric power*	125	138	174	215	224	235	255	280	296
8. *Dwellings*	95	141	175	189	207	236	276	322	369
9. *Health and hygiene*	210	217	251	280	287	317	339	377	397
10. *Communications*	201	211	242	272	301	327	357	371	382
communications	37	42	49	54	63	72	84	93	101
public transport services	164	169	193	218	238	255	273	278	281
11. *Private transport (purchase)*	76	100	105	133	134	138	133	127	134
12. *Private transport (operation)*	65	103	133	169	192	241	289	323	343
13. *Miscellaneous*	581	627	741	819	825	910	957	1 007	1 031
hotels and public catering places	156	164	183	214	219	248	268	288	300
books and newspapers	75	98	134	146	149	162	172	186	187
entertainment	126	137	166	182	196	213	215	218	218
other recreational expenses	106	108	113	127	119	131	137	146	151
other	118	120	145	150	142	156	165	169	175
Total	6 231	7 089	7 704	8 393	8 713	9 278	9 925	10 442	10 893

Table VI - Material utilized in the SVIMEZ study - Aggregate private consumption from 1950 to 1958 at 1954 prices (ISTAT data; billion lire)

Expenditure item	1950	1951	1952	1953	1954	1955	1956	1957	1958
1. *Food*	3 442	3 665	3 797	3 980	4 084	4 173	4 296	4 434	4 659
2. *Alcoholic beverages*	509	516	601	584	596	644	674	694	620
3. *Tobacco*	320	323	336	361	379	396	416	441	463
4. *Clothing and footwear*	906	936	892	1 074	1 006	1 008	1 073	1 110	1 116
5. *Household durables*	125	124	130	143	161	165	176	207	239
6. *Non durable household goods and miscellaneous personal services*	267	276	276	305	317	324	338	357	365
7. *Fuel and electric power*	147	156	180	209	224	231	245	275	295
8. *Dwellings*	197	198	201	203	207	210	216	223	230
9. *Health and hygiene*	282	284	287	293	287	311	324	362	376
10. *Communications*	239	245	260	285	301	343	367	372	375
communications	42	45	49	55	63	70	77	85	87
public transport services	197	200	211	230	238	273	290	287	288
11. *Private transport (purchase)*	71	89	96	125	134	144	142	137	145
12. *Private transport (operation)*	76	104	133	168	192	231	266	291	309
13. *Miscellaneous*	662	677	724	799	825	868	899	919	926
hotels and public catering places	176	183	199	208	219	237	248	258	266
books and newspapers	96	112	138	146	149	160	168	174	174
entertainment	151	151	154	178	196	200	206	202	197
other recreational expenses	112	109	109	121	119	119	121	126	129
other	127	122	124	146	142	152	156	159	160
Total	7 243	7 593	7 913	8 529	8 713	9 048	9 432	9 822	10 118

Table VII - Material utilized in the SVIMEZ study - *Per capita* private consumption from 1950 to 1958 at 1954 prices [a]) (Italian lire)

Expenditure item	1950	1951	1952	1953	1954	1955	1956	1957	1958
1. *Food*	73 598	77 610	80 087	83 517	85 190	86 604	88 810	91 248	95 305
2. *Alcoholic beverages*	10 884	10 927	12 676	12 255	12 432	13 365	13 933	14 282	12 683
3. *Tobacco*	6 842	6 840	7 087	7 575	7 906	8 218	8 600	9 075	9 471
4. *Clothing and footwear*	19 372	19 821	18 814	22 537	20 985	20 919	22 182	22 843	22 829
5. *Household durables*	2 673	2 626	2 742	3 001	3 358	3 424	3 638	4 260	4 889
6. *Non durable household goods and miscellaneous personal services*	5 709	5 845	5 821	6 400	6 612	6 724	6 987	7 347	7 467
7. *Fuel and electric power*	3 143	3 303	3 797	4 386	4 673	4 794	5 065	5 659	6 035
8. *Dwellings*	4 212	4 193	4 240	4 260	4 318	4 358	4 465	4 589	4 705
9. *Health and hygiene*	6 030	6 014	6 053	6 148	5 987	6 454	6 698	7 450	7 692
10. *Communications*	5 110	5 188	5 485	5 980	6 279	7 119	7 587	7 655	7 670
communications	898	953	1 034	1 154	1 314	1 453	1 592	1 749	1 779
public transport services	4 212	4 235	4 451	4 826	4 965	5 666	5 995	5 906	5 891
11. *Private transport (purchase)*	1 518	1 885	2 025	2 623	2 795	2 988	2 936	2 819	2 966
12. *Private transport (operation)*	1 625	2 202	2 805	3 525	4 005	4 794	5 499	5 989	6 321
13. *Miscellaneous*	14 156	14 336	15 270	16 767	17 208	18 015	18 585	18 912	18 942
hotels and public catering places	3 763	3 875	4 197	4 365	4 568	4 919	5 127	5 309	5 441
books and newspapers	2 053	2 372	2 911	3 064	3 108	3 320	3 473	3 581	3 559
entertainment	3 229	3 198	3 248	3 735	4 088	4 151	4 259	4 157	4 030
other recreational expenses	2 395	2 308	2 299	2 539	2 482	2 470	2 501	2 593	2 639
other	2 716	2 583	2 615	3 064	2 962	3 155	3 225	3 272	3 273
Total	154 872	160 790	166 902	178 974	181 748	187 776	194 985	202 128	206 975

[a]) *Per capita* values were calculated on the basis of the data of Table VI, considering the de facto population.

Table VIII - Calculations used in the SVIMEZ study - *Per capita* private consumption as a function of aggregate expenditure - Third method of analysis (Basic statistical source: historical private consumption series of Table VII)

Expenditure item	$y = f(x)$	Calculated *per capita* value [a]) (1954 lire)		
		1958	1965	1970
1. *Food*	$- 263\,230 + 154\,203.88 \log_{10} x$	93 922	110 738	123 398
2. *Beverages*	$5\,107 + 40.73\,x$	13 540	15 948	18 203
3. *Tobacco* [b])	$-\ 947 + 48.92\,x$	9 182	12 074	14 783
4. *Clothing and footwear*	$7\,731 + 72.92\,x$	22 827	27 740	31 177
5. *Household durables*	$-\ 3\,533 + 37.92\,x$	4 318	6 559	8 659
6. *Non durable household goods and miscellaneous personal services* [b])	$-\ 214 + 37.27\,x$	7 503	9 706	11 770
7. *Fuel and electric power*	$-\ 5\,458 + 55.85\,x$	6 107	9 408	12 501
8. *Dwellings*	$2\,676 +\ 9.03\,x$	4 546	5 081	5 581
9. *Health and hygiene*	$866 + 28.18\,x$	6 701	8 366	9 926
10. *Communications*	–	7 366	10 058	12 580
communications	$-\ 1\,945 + 17.93\,x$	1 768	2 828	3 821
public transport services [b])	$-\ 119 + 27.61\,x$	5 598	7 230	8 759
11. *Private transport (purchase)* [b])	$-\ 2\,914 + 29.87\,x$	3 271	5 037	6 691
12. *Private transport (operation)*	$-\ 11\,376 + 84.87\,x$	6 197	11 214	15 913
13. *Miscellaneous*	–	19 201	25 416	31 237
hotels and public catering places	$-\ 1\,625 + 34.08\,x$	5 431	7 445	9 332
books and newspapers [b])	$-\ 958 + 21.83\,x$	3 562	4 853	6 061
entertainment [b])	$-\ 1\,517 + 27.59\,x$	4 196	5 827	7 354
other recreational expenses [b])	$841 +\ 9.08\,x$	2 721	3 258	3 761
other [b])	$690 + 12.56\,x$	3 291	4 033	4 729
Total	–	204 681	257 345	302 419
Differences	–	2 376	8 832	19 125
Aggregate expenditure	–	207 057	266 177	321 544

[a]) The calculation was made attributing to the functions' independent variable the values of Lit. 207 057/1 000 for 1958, Lit. 266 177/1 000 for 1965, and Lit. 321 544/1 000 for 1970.

[b]) Items requiring the calculation of new functions, due to the correction of basic data made by ISTAT after the publications of the SVIMEZ study. In this calculation we have used also the data of the years 1959 and 1960.

Table IX - Summary of forecasts obtained with the three different methods of analysis
used in the SVIMEZ study - *Per capita* values
(1953 lire for the first two methods and 1954 lire for the third method)

Expenditure item	1st method			2nd method			3rd method		
	1958	1965	1970	1958	1965	1970	1958	1965	1970
1-2. Food and beverages [a])	100 501	119 664	136 470	109 964	130 075	146 633	107 462	126 686	141 601
3. Tobacco	5 695	7 138	8 398	5 776	7 147	8 265	9 182	12 074	14 783
4. Clothing and footwear	32 420	46 148	59 065	32 560	44 503	56 022	22 827	27 740	31 177
5. Household durables	8 838	12 736	16 805	7 530	11 363	15 330	4 318	6 559	8 659
6. Non durable household goods and miscellaneous personal services	4 274	4 984	5 710	4 314	5 234	6 064	7 503	9 706	11 770
7. Fuel and electric power	9 315	11 669	13 794	9 155	11 530	13 640	6 107	9 408	12 501
8. Dwellings	7 251	10 108	12 681	6 985	8 385	10 755	4 546	5 081	5 581
9. Health and hygiene	5 878	7 746	9 416	5 498	7 278	8 907	6 701	8 366	9 926
10. Communications	3 130	4 574	5 943	2 657	4 029	5 454	7 366	10 058	12 580
11. Private transport (purchase)	4 071	6 522	9 349	3 200	5 500	8 100	3 271	5 037	6 691
12. Private transport (operation)	1 824	3 160	4 559	1 355	2 398	3 613	6 197	11 214	15 913
13. Miscellaneous	20 572	30 647	40 535	16 024	25 034	34 522	19 201	25 416	31 237
Total	203 769	265 095	322 725	204 018	262 476	317 305	204 681	257 345	302 419
Differences	- 39	- 1 478	- 2 350	- 288	- 1 141	3 070	2 376	8 832	19 125
Aggregate expenditure	203 730	263 617	320 375	203 730	263 617	320 375	207 057	266 177	321 544

[a]) For a better comparison of results in this table we have aggregated items 1 and 2 (in fact, non alcoholic beverages are under item 1 in the analysis made with the first two methods, and under item 2 in the analysis made with the third method).

Table X - Aggregate regional private consumption from 1951 to 1961 at 1954 prices (ISTAT data, billion lire)

Expenditure item	1951	1952	1953	1954	1955	1956	1957	1958	1959	1960	1961
a. *Mezzogiorno*											
1-2. Food and beverages	1 205.0	1 275.1	1 320.1	1 356.5	1 384.4	1 467.3	1 513.0	1 562.0	1 614.8	1 684.7	1 794.3
3. Tobacco	88.6	92.7	100.7	106.2	112.2	117.0	123.0	130.1	134.9	142.0	149.0
4. Clothing and footwear	239.6	228.4	293.2	264.6	266.1	278.0	287.5	289.9	300.6	319.2	336.1
5-8. Dwellings and related expenditures	172.7	179.6	194.6	206.0	211.6	222.0	249.4	261.2	286.0	316.5	343.9
9. Health and hygiene	68.0	70.5	73.5	73.7	80.0	85.5	95.6	99.6	112.8	143.8	158.7
10-12. Transport and communications	85.5	97.2	114.3	130.4	146.0	161.4	163.8	171.2	181.8	208.0	227.4
13. Miscellaneous	143.7	153.4	171.8	182.6	192.5	200.0	205.9	206.8	227.4	238.2	253.3
Total	2 003.1	2 096.9	2 268.2	2 320.0	2 391.8	2 531.2	2 638.2	2 720.8	2 858.3	3 052.4	3 262.7
b. *North*											
1-2. Food and beverages	2 976.0	3 122.9	3 243.9	3 323.5	3 432.6	3 502.7	3 615.0	3 717.0	3 904.2	4 125.3	4 400.7
3. Tobacco	234.4	243.3	260.3	272.8	284.8	299.0	318.0	332.9	345.1	361.0	384.0
4. Clothing and footwear	696.4	663.6	780.8	741.4	741.9	795.0	822.5	826.1	865.4	913.8	956.9
5-8. Dwellings and related expenditures	581.3	604.4	665.4	703.0	718.4	753.0	812.6	867.6	958.0	1 051.5	1 137.1
9. Health and hygiene	216.0	216.5	219.5	213.3	231.0	238.5	266.4	276.4	309.2	378.2	418.3
10-12. Transport and communications	352.5	391.8	463.7	496.6	572.0	613.6	636.2	657.8	713.2	800.0	882.6
13. Miscellaneous	533.3	570.6	627.2	642.4	675.5	699.0	713.1	719.2	740.6	785.8	839.7
Total	5 589.9	5 816.1	6 260.8	6 393.0	6 656.2	6 900.8	7 183.8	7 397.2	7 835.7	8 415.6	9 019.3

Table XI - Regional *per capita* private consumption from 1951 to 1961 at 1954 prices [a]) (Italian lire)

Expenditure item	1951	1952	1953	1954	1955	1956	1957	1958	1959	1960	1961
a. Mezzogiorno											
1-2. Food and beverages	69 027	72 705	74 904	76 587	77 780	82 055	84 210	86 509	88 970	92 368	97 889
3. Tobacco	5 075	5 286	5 714	5 996	6 247	6 543	6 846	7 205	7 433	7 786	8 129
4. Clothing and footwear	13 725	13 023	16 636	14 939	14 950	15 546	16 002	16 056	16 562	17 501	18 336
5-8. Dwellings and related expenditures	9 893	10 241	11 042	11 631	11 888	12 415	13 881	14 466	15 757	17 353	19 762
9. Health and hygiene	3 895	4 020	4 170	4 161	4 495	4 781	5 321	5 516	6 215	7 884	8 658
10-12. Transport and communications	4 898	5 542	6 486	7 362	8 203	9 026	9 117	9 482	10 017	11 404	12 406
13. Miscellaneous	8 232	8 746	9 748	10 309	10 815	11 184	11 459	11 453	12 528	13 060	13 818
Total	114 745	119 563	128 700	130 985	134 378	141 550	146 836	150 687	157 482	167 356	177 998
b. North											
1-2. Food and beverages	99 980	104 539	108 018	109 948	112 966	114 877	118 038	120 568	125 598	131 921	139 798
3. Tobacco	7 875	8 144	9 668	9 025	9 373	9 806	10 383	10 798	11 102	11 544	12 199
4. Clothing and footwear	23 396	22 214	26 000	24 527	24 416	26 073	26 856	26 796	27 840	29 222	30 398
5-8. Dwellings and related expenditures	19 529	20 333	22 157	23 257	23 642	24 696	26 533	28 149	30 819	33 625	36 122
9. Health and hygiene	7 257	7 247	7 309	7 056	7 602	7 822	8 698	8 966	9 946	12 094	13 288
10-12. Transport and communications	11 842	13 116	15 441	16 428	18 825	20 124	20 773	21 337	22 944	25 583	28 038
13. Miscellaneous	17 916	19 101	20 885	21 252	22 231	22 925	23 284	23 329	23 824	25 129	26 675
Total	187 795	194 694	208 478	211 493	219 055	226 323	234 565	239 943	262 073	269 118	286 518

[a]) *Per capita* values were calculated on the basis of the data of Table **X**, taking the de facto population into account.

Tableau I
Population et PNB, tendances récentes et hypothèses retenues.

	1958			Tendances passées			Projections de 1957-59 sur 1969-71									
	Population à la moitié de l'année (millions)	PNB par habitant (dollars E.U.)1)	PNB (milliards de dollars E.U.)1)	Population	PNB par habitant 3)	PNB 3)	Population	PNB par habitant B	PNB par habitant H	PNB B	PNB H	Population	PNB par habitant B	PNB par habitant H	PNB B	PNB H
				(pourcentage annuel)								(Indices 1969-71 (1957-59 = 100))				
PAYS A REVENU ELEVE	653.0	1426	931	1.3	3.0	4.3	1.2	2.6	3.8	3.9	5.0	115	137	156	158	179
Amérique du Nord	191.8	2190	420	1.9	1.2	3.1	1.8	1.3	2.5	3.1	4.4	124	116	135	144	167
Canada	17.0	1720	29.3	2.7	1.2	3.9	2.1	1.3	2.5	3.4	4.8	129	116	135	150	176
Etats-Unis	174.8	2235	391	1.8	1.2	3.0	1.7	1.3	2.5	3.0	4.3	123	116	135	143	166
Océanie	12.1	1570	19.0	2.3	1.6	3.9	2.0	1.0	2.0	3.0	4.0	127	113	127	143	160
Australie	9.8	1575	15.4	2.3	1.9	4.3	2.0	1.0	2.0	3.0	4.0	127	113	127	143	160
Nouvelle-Zélande	2.3	1560	3.6	2.3	-0.2	2.1	1.9	1.0	2.0	2.9	3.9	125	113	127	141	159
Europe occidentale	320.0	1180	378	0.8	4.2	5.0	0.7	3.5	4.5	4.2	5.2	109	151	169	165	184
- C.E.E. 2)	169.1	1285	217	0.9	4.9	5.8	0.7	3.9	4.7	4.7	5.5	109	158	174	173	190
Belgique 2)	9.4	1395	13.1	0.6	2.2	2.8	0.6	2.0	3.1	2.6	3.6	107	127	144	136	154
Luxembourg 2)				1.8	2.1	3.0	}									
France 2)	44.8	1405	62.9	0.9	3.4	4.3	0.8	3.6	4.4	4.4	5.2	110	154	168	169	185
Allemagne occidentale 2)	54.7	1490	81.6	1.1	6.5	7.6	0.9	4.0	4.8	4.9	5.7	108	161	176	174	190
Italie 2)	48.9	925	45.2	0.6	5.0	5.6	0.6	4.4	5.2	5.0	5.9	108	168	184	181	198
Pays-Bas 2)	11.3	1260	14.2	1.3	3.6	4.9	1.0	4.1	4.9	5.1	5.9	112	163	177	183	199
- Pays méditerranéens	65.1	575	37.6	1.0	5.9	6.9	1.0	3.9	5.2	4.9	6.2	112	159	184	178	206
Grèce	8.2	520	4.2	0.9	6.1	7.0	1.1	4.0	5.0	5.1	6.2	114	160	180	183	205
Portugal	9.0	490	4.4	0.8	2.9	3.7	0.5	2.5	3.5	3.0	4.0	106	135	151	142	160
Espagne	29.7	525	15.7	0.8	5.3	6.1	0.9	4.0	5.0	4.9	5.9	111	160	180	177	200
Yougoslavie	18.2	730	13.3	1.3	7.6	8.9	1.2	4.5	6.0	5.7	7.2	115	169	201	194	231
- Autres pays	86.6	1440	125	0.5	2.6	3.1	0.4	2.3	3.3	2.7	3.7	105	132	148	139	155
Autriche	7.0	1235	8.6	0.2	5.9	6.1	0.2	4.0	5.0	4.2	5.2	102	160	180	163	183
Danemark	4.5	1410	6.3	0.7	2.2	2.9	0.6	2.0	3.0	2.6	3.6	108	127	143	137	154
Finlande	4.4	1200	5.3	1.1	3.1	4.2	0.9	3.0	4.0	3.9	4.9	111	143	160	159	178
Irlande	2.9	770	2.2	-0.5	1.5	1.0	0.0	2.0	3.0	2.0	3.0	100	127	143	127	143
Norvège	3.5	1460	5.1	0.9	2.4	3.3	0.9	2.0	3.0	2.9	3.9	111	127	143	140	158
Suède	7.4	1475	10.9	0.6	2.9	3.5	0.6	2.5	3.5	3.1	4.1	107	135	151	144	162
Suisse	5.2	1480	7.7	1.2	4.3	5.5	0.6	3.0	4.0	3.6	4.6	107	143	160	153	172
Royaume-Uni	51.7	1515	78.4	0.4	2.1	2.5	0.4	2.0	3.0	2.4	3.4	105	127	143	133	150
Japon	91.8	910	83.5	1.3	6.1	7.5	0.7	5.3	6.3	6.0	7.0	109	186	208	202	226
Afrique du Sud	14.4	835	12.1	1.9	3.1	5.0	1.9	1.5	3.0	3.4	5.0	126	120	143	150	179
Argentine et Uruguay	22.9	825	18.8	2.0	0.1	2.1	1.7	1.3	2.0	3.0	3.7	117	127	143	142	154

1) PNB converti en dollars E.U. sur la base de parités de pouvoir d'achat calculées aux prix E.U. de 1955 d'après une estimation officieuse de l'IBRD.

2) Pour les six pays de la Communauté, les projections s'appliquent aux dépenses totales de consommation et non pas au PNB; elles reposent sur des estimations provisoires établies par le Secrétariat de la Communauté.

3) Les tendances passées du PNB ont été tirées des sources suivantes:
Amérique du Nord et Europe occidentale (à l'exclusion de la Finlande): "La croissance économique durant les années cinquante", Tableau 9, p. 21, CPE/WP 2 (61)5, Annexe 1, OECE, 6 juillet 1961.
Australie: PIB (on s'est servi des moyennes de 1950/51 et 51/52 comme base), "Etude sur l'économie mondiale - 1960", Tableau 1.1, Nations Unies.
Nouvelle-Zélande: Revenu réel disponible (même base que pour l'Australie), "Etude sur l'économie mondiale - 1960", Tableau 1.8.
Afrique du Sud: PIB (1953-59), "Etude sur l'économie mondiale - 1960", Tableau 2.1.
Finlande, Turquie et U.R.S.S.: PIB, "Annuaire des statistiques des comptabilités nationales", O.N.U., 1960, Tableau 2, pp. 266 et 268.
Japon: estimations ECAFE.

B = hypothèse basse, H = hypothèse haute.

Tableau II

Consommation alimentaire par habitant selon les principaux groupes de produits, 1957-59.

	Céréales 1)	Racines féculentes	Légumineuses et noix	Sucre 2)	Légumes 3)	Fruits (équivalent de fruits frais)	Matières grasses	Lait — Matières grasses	Lait — Protéines	Viande 4)	Oeufs	Poisson 5)	Calories (par jour)	Protéines animales (g par jour)	Café	Thé	Cacao
	(en kg per an)														(en kg per an)		
PAYS A REVENU ELEVE																	
Amérique du nord	67	48	7	41	95	95	21	8	9	91	20	5	3118	66	6.8	0.3	1.53
Canada	71	61	5	44	76	91	19	8	9	77	17	6	3100	62	3.3	1.1	1.58
Etats-Unis	67	47	7	41	97	95	21	8	9	92	20	5	3120	66	7.2	0.3	1.52
Océanie	87	55	4	50	65	73	17	8	7	113	12	4	3250	62	0.9	2.8	1.37
Australie	87	54	4	51	63	76	16	7	6	116	11	3	3220	60	0.9	2.7	1.33
Nouvelle-Zélande	86	57	4	42	75	59	20	11	10	106	15	7	3380	71	0.6	3.1	1.54
Europe occidentale																	
C.E.E.	109	103	7	27	93	70	20	5	6	49	11	5	1850	41	3.3	0.1	1.23
Belgique/Luxembourg	92	145	4	32	68	45	21	5	7	58	15	6	2920	46	5.8	0.04	1.95
France	108	104	6	30	126	53	17	6	7	71	11	5	2900	49	4.3	0.04	1.10
Allemagne occidentale	88	145	4	28	45	86	25	6	7	53	12	7	2980	45	3.3	0.1	1.85
Italie	142	49	13	19	128	74	15	4	4	25	11	4	2620	25	1.8	0.03	0.35
Pays-Bas	86	90	4	40	66	64	25	8	9	44	11	5	2940	43	4.3	0.8	1.92
Pays méditerranéens	141	91	14	15	95	76	15	3	4	18	4	10	2655	23	0.6	0.02	0.40
Grèce	166	41	16	11	117	106	18	4	5	21	5	8	2860	25	0.9	0.01	0.27
Portugal	121	103	10	17	105	68	15	1	1	16	3	20	2460	25	1.2	0.07	0.10
Espagne	113	116	17	16	114	82	18	5	3	15	5	5	2550	20	0.5	0.01	0.70
Yougoslavie	194	67	10	13	50	57	10	4	5	24	3	2	2830	25	0.3	0.01	0.13
Autres pays	89	97	5	46	56	61	22	8	8	63	13	10	3217	47	2.9	2.8	1.64
Autriche	115	91	4	34	65	84	18	7	8	52	10	3	2990	44	1.5	0.09	1.59
Danemark	81	129	4	47	66	57	27	9	8	72	9	15	3420	55	8.6	0.3	1.23
Finlande	113	102	2	41	20	23	18	12	12	31	11	11	3130	54	7.5	0.09	0.41
Irlande	117	142	3	42	63	24	21	8	11	58	15	4	3490	56	0.1	3.3	1.45
Norvège	83	104	4	38	36	66	25	12	9	37	8	19	3060	50	7.6	0.1	1.15
Suède	75	100	4	41	27	69	21	10	9	52	10	18	2940	52	9.2	0.1	1.33
Suisse	92	73	10	40	77	122	19	10	10	54	10	3	3150	52	5.1	0.2	2.92
Royaume-Uni	85	93	6	50	60	56	22	7	7	71	15	10	3280	51	0.9	4.4	1.75
Japon	153	66	17	13	76	21	3	1	–	5	4	22	2220	16.6	0.1	0.8	0.11
Afrique du Sud	145	17	4	43	37	37	6	3	3	44	3	7	2690	31.3	0.8	0.9	0.20
Argentine et Uruguay	118	82	3	31	42	75	16	4	4	105	7	2	3100	65.2	1.4	0.1	0.28

1) En équivalent de farine et de riz usiné.
2) En équivalent de sucre raffiné, sirop et miel.
3) En équivalent de produit frais, mais comprend de petites quantités de légumes traités.
4) En poids carcasse, graisses d'abattage non comprises.
5) Poids comestible estimé.
Source: Bilans des disponibilités alimentaires établis par la FAO et l'OCED.

Tableau III

Coefficients d'élasticité-revenu de la demande par principaux groups d'aliments, en termes de quantités.

	Céréales	Racines féculentes	Légumineuses et noix	Sucre	Légumes et fruits	Matières grasses (y compris le beurre)	Lait et produits laitiers	Viande	Oeufs	Poisson	Total alimentation			Café	Cacao
											Calories	Protéines animales	Valeur à la ferme		
PAYS A REVENU ELEVE															
Amérique du nord	-0.5	-0.7	-0.3	0.0	0.3	0.0	0.08 1)	0.4	0.02	0.3	-0.03	0.23	0.16	0.3	0.1
Canada	-0.5	-0.7	-0.3	0.0	0.35	0.03	0.10 1)	0.4	0.15	0.3	0	0.28	0.21	0.6	0.1
Etats-Unis	-0.5	-0.7	-0.3	0.0	0.25	0.0	0.05 1)	0.35	0.0	0.3	-0.03	0.22	0.15	0.3	0.1
Océanie	-0.5	-0.5	-0.2	-0.05	0.4	0.1	0.1 1)	0.1	0.2	0.25	-0.06	0.14	0.10	1.0	0.1
Australie	-0.5	-0.5	-0.2	-0.05	0.4	0.2	0.2 1)	0.1	0.2	0.3	-0.07	0.15	0.11	1.0	0.1
Nouvelle-Zélande	-0.4	-0.5	-0.2	0.0	0.45	0.0	0.0 1)	0.2	0.15	0.15	-0.05	0.13	0.07	1.0	0.1
Europe occidentale															
C.E.E.															
Belgique/Luxembourg	-0.3	-0.3		0.5	0.6	0.16	0.3	0.7	0.8	0.5	0.10	0.57	0.47	0.6	0.3
France	-0.4	-0.5		0.4	0.8	0.1	-0.2	0.6	0.4	0.7	0.07	0.60	0.35	0.4	
Allemagne occidentale	-0.2	-0.2		0.3	0.4	0.2	0.4	0.4	0.9	0.6	0.09	0.50	0.33	0.5	
Italie	-0.3	-0.5		0.2	0.6	0.0	0.2	1.4	0.6	0.5	0.22	0.40	0.42	0.6	
Pays-Bas	-0.2	0.3		1.1	0.7	0.4	0.6	0.7	0.7	1.0	0.07	0.43	0.71	0.8	0.5
Pays méditerranéens	-0.3	-0.3	0.1	0.4	0.5	0.5 1)	0.8	1.1	1.1	0.5	0.18	0.90	0.48	0.4	
Grèce	-0.3	0.0	0.1	0.8	0.4	0.4 1)	0.7	1.0	1.0	0.7	0.12	0.87	0.55	1.0	
Portugal	-0.2	0.3	0.2	1.0	0.3	0.4 1)	1.2	1.3	1.4	0.6	0.21	0.91	0.49	1.0	
Espagne	-0.2	0.0	0.1	0.8	0.4	0.4 1)	1.0	1.2	1.0	0.5	0.23	0.97	0.60	1.0	
Yougoslavie	-0.3	0.0	0.1	0.9	0.6	0.8 1)	0.6	1.0	1.2	1.0	0.14	0.88	0.56	1.0	
Autres pays															
Autriche	-0.4	-0.3	0.0	0.06	0.5	0.06	0.06	0.4	0.3	0.2	0.01	0.26	0.23	0.5	0.2
Danemark	-0.4	-0.2	0.0	0.3	0.4	0.3	0.05	0.5	0.5	0.5	0.07	0.33	0.33	1.0	
Finlande	-0.3	-0.4	0.0	0.2	0.5	-0.05	-0.06	0.6	0.3	0.2	-0.01	0.27	0.19	0.2	
Irlande	-0.4	-0.3	0.0	0.1	0.5	0.1	-0.01	0.5	0.6	0.3	-0.02	0.17	0.22	0.25	
Norvège	-0.35	-0.5	0.0	0.2	0.4	0.02	0.03	0.5	0.5	0.5	-0.02	0.23	0.23	0.25	
Suède	-0.4	-0.25	0.0	0.0	0.4	-0.1	-0.02	0.5	0.6	0.3	-0.01	0.24	0.14	0.25	
Suisse	-0.45	-0.3	0.0	0.0	0.35	-0.05	-0.09	0.5	0.3	0.1	0.03	0.21	0.20	0.2	
Royaume-Uni	-0.4	-0.3	0.0	0.0	0.5	-0.03	0.09	0.4	0.4	0.4	0.04	0.28	0.24	0.4	0.0
Japon	-0.17	-0.15	0.3	0.8	0.5	1.1 1)	2.0	1.7	1.0	0.5	0.20	0.94	0.58	1.5	0.7
Afrique du Sud	0.1	0.0	0.1	0.3	0.5	0.8 1)	0.6	0.5	0.5	0.6	0.29	0.59	0.48	0.8	0.3
Argentine et Uruguay	-0.3	-0.2	0.0	0.3	0.6	0.35 1)	0.4	0.15	0.1	0.4	0.04	0.22	0.17	1.2	

1) A l'exclusion du beurre.

N.B. Depuis la préparation de ces tableaux, dix des pays mentionnés ci-dessus nous ont adressé des commentaires qui sont reproduits intégralement dans les documents CCP 63/7/3 et Add I. Il est noté que les coefficients d'élasticité sont probablement un peu trop élevés pour la viande en Suède et au Royaume Uni; les chiffres de 0.25 et 0.2 sont indiqués comme plus vraisemblables. Toujours d'après ces commentaires, le coefficient d'élasticité pour les légumes et fruits paraît trop faible pour la Suède et le coefficient pour l'ensemble de la demande alimentaire un peu fort pour le Royaume Uni.

Tableau IV

Nombre-indices de la demande projetée par habitant, d'après les principaux groupes de produits alimentaires (effet-revenu seulement). Indice 1970 (1958 = 100).

	Céréales B	Céréales H	Racines féculentes B	Racines féculentes H	Légumineuses et noix B	Légumineuses et noix H	Sucre B	Sucre H	Légumes et fruits B	Légumes et fruits H	Matières grasses y compris le beurre B	Matières grasses H	Viande B	Viande H	Oeufs B	Oeufs H	Poisson B	Poisson H	Lait et produits laitiers B	Lait et produits laitiers H	Calories B	Calories H	Protéines animales B	Protéines animales H	Valeur à la ferme B	Valeur à la ferme H	Café B	Café H	Thé B	Thé H	Cacao 3) B	Cacao 3) H
PAYS A REVENU ELEVE	91	89	90	87	105 4)	106 4)	110	112	115	121	...	...	115	121	115	119	115 4)	120 4)	110	112	103	103	113	118	111	114	...	...	...	...	...	109
Amérique du Nord																																
Canada	93	88	91	83	96	93	100	100	104	108	100	100	105	111	100	100	105	109	101 1)	102 1)	100	99	103	106	102	104	104	109	88	104	109	109
Etats-Unis	93	88	91	83	96	93	100	100	104	108	100	100	106	111	102	104	105	109	101 1)	103 1)	100	99	103	106	102	104	112	124	93	100	115	115
Océanie																																
Australie	95	90	94	90	96	96	99	99	105	110	102	103	101	103	102	104	103	106	101 1)	101 1)	99	99	102	103	101	102	...	...	...	...	...	...
Nouvelle-Zélande	96	92	94	90	96	96	100	100	105	111	102	104	102	105	102	103	104	107	101 1)	103 1)	99	99	101	103	101	101	...	...	...	...	...	...
Europe occidentale																																
C.E.E. 2)	90	89	92	90	...	...	112	115	121	127	...	...	123	130	125	132	...	...	102 1)	104 1)	103	103	119	124	113	118	123	128	96	102	127	129
Belgique/Luxembourg	90	89	89	87	...	...	119	123	125	132	106	107	130	139	132	140	...	...	100 1)	100 1)	104	104	123	128	118	122	127	132	102	118	132	134
France	91	91	83	80	...	...	121	121	122	128	107	109	111	122	138	147	...	...	109	112	102	102	114	120	105	111	...	...	...	...	...	...
Allemagne occidentale	87	87	85	83	...	...	112	112	112	120	100	100	115	120	127	133	...	...	112	115	102	104	115	122	116	120	...	...	...	...	...	...
Italie	92	91	115	115	105	105	105	110	135	142	118	121	171	184	143	150	...	...	95	95	110	111	144	151	132	138	...	...	...	...	...	...
Pays-Bas	87	85	90	85	...	...	155	164	123	127	135 1)	150 1)	135	140	129	134	129	130	108	117	102	103	117	121	121	123	...	...	...	...	...	...
Pays méditerranéens	91	88	94	91	104	105	115	120	118	125	118 1)	124 1)	150	167	152	169	122	130	135	147	106	109	138	151	122	129	141	154	...	...	143	151
Grèce	89	88	112	114	104	105	135	145	114	118	116 1)	119 1)	147	154	146	156	133	141	133	141	104	106	138	147	120	125	...	...	...	...	...	...
Portugal	95	94	100	100	105	107	146	156	115	121	111 1)	119 1)	139	154	143	161	118	125	136	150	105	107	126	136	126	122	...	...	...	...	...	...
Espagne	93	92	100	100	104	105	123	131	119	123	116 1)	119 1)	157	170	146	156	124	129	147	159	109	111	144	154	123	128	115	120	...	...	120	123
Yougoslavie	89	85	100	100	104	105	135	143	128	142	135 1)	150 1)	147	170	157	183	147	170	128	142	105	107	138	156	122	134	...	...	...	...	...	...
Autres pays	91	88	93	92	100	100	140	157	113	118	102	102	112	117	109	112	107	110	102	102	100	100	106	109	106	108	115	120	...	...	120	123
Autriche	86	84	92	89	100	100	102	102	119	123	112	115	124	129	121	125	124	129	102	115	103	103	113	116	113	113	...	...	...	...	...	...
Danemark	92	89	91	89	100	100	112	114	112	118	99	99	110	114	109	105	105	105	102	102	100	100	106	108	104	106	...	...	...	...	...	...
Finlande	91	89	90	86	100	100	100	100	114	119	103	104	121	128	120	125	111	114	99	98	101	101	105	107	105	107	...	...	...	...	...	...
Irlande	92	89	95	93	100	100	106	108	110	114	101	101	112	118	109	113	118	124	100	100	100	100	105	108	103	104	...	...	...	...	...	...
Norvège	93	89	90	89	100	100	102	103	112	117	97	96	115	121	114	120	107	111	101	101	100	99	106	108	105	107	...	...	...	...	...	...
Suède	90	87	83	90	100	100	104	106	112	117	99	98	118	124	108	111	103	104	100	100	99	99	106	108	106	108	...	...	99	104	117	117
Suisse	87	85	91	89	100	100	100	100	112	118	99	99	110	114	113	116	114	119	97	97	100	100	106	109	105	107	...	...	126	139	160	168
Royaume-Uni	92	89	94	91	100	100	100	100	112	118	101	101	110	114	107	109	105	107	102	103	100	100	106	109	105	107	...	...	114	128	122	127
Japon	96	95	91	89	119	122	156	166	131	137	168 1)	180 1)	205	224	162	173	131	137	224	226	110	111	153	163	130	135	437	546	111	119	122	127
Afrique du sud	102	103	100	100	102	103	106	111	109	118	115 1)	129 1)	102	104	109	118	111	111	111	122	105	109	110	119	116	116	114	128				
Argentine et Uruguay	95	93	97	95	100	100	104	107	110	118	105 1)	108 1)	102	104	102	102	106	110	106	110	101	101	103	105	102	104						

1) A l'exclusion du beurre.
2) Estimations provisoires reposant sur des données établies par le Secrétariat de la C.E.E.
3) Compte tenu également de l'effet de la baisse de prix prévue.
4) Non compris les estimations de la C.E.E.
5) Estimations basées sur l'extrapolation des tendances de la consommation par tête et non sur l'effet revenu considéré comme négligeable.

Tableau V

Nombres-indices de la demande totale projetée, d'après les principaux groupes de produits alimentaires (effet-revenu et effet-population). Indice 1970 (1958 = 100).

	Céréales B	Céréales H	Racines féculentes B	Racines féculentes H	Légumineuses et noix B	Légumineuses et noix H	Sucre B	Sucre H	Légumes et fruits B	Légumes et fruits H	Matières grasses y compris le beurre B	Matières grasses y compris le beurre H	Lait et produits laitiers B	Lait et produits laitiers H	Viande B	Viande H	Oeufs B	Oeufs H	Poisson B	Poisson H	Total alimentation Calories B	Calories H	Protéines animales B	Protéines animales H	Valeur à la ferme B	Valeur à la ferme H	Café B	Café H	Thé 5) B	Thé 5) H	Cacao 3) B	Cacao 3) H
PAYS A REVENU ELEVE	104	102	103	100	120 4)	121 4)	126	128	131	137	...	...	125	128	133	139	131	135	133 4)	138 4)	117	118	130	135	126	130	...	...	...	...	...	...
Amérique du Nord																																
Canada	114	108	112	102	118	114	123	123	128	133	123	123	124 1)	126 1)	130	137	123	124	129	134	123	123	127	131	126	129	129	134	...	...	135	135
Etats-Unis	120	113	117	108	124	119	129	129	136	143	130	130	131 1)	132 1)	129	136	134	135	135	141	123	129	134	139	133	136			109	129	135	
Océanie																																
Australie	120	114	119	114	124	121	125	125	133	139	129	131	128 1)	130 1)	128	130	129	132	130	134	126	125	129	131	128	129	142	157	118	127	145	146
Nouvelle-Zélande	120	114	120	114	124	122	126	126	133	139	130	125	130 1)	133 1)	129	130	132	133	132	132	126	125	131	131	129	130						146
Europe occidentale																																
C.E.E. 2)	98	96	100	98	...	...	122	126	134	139	...	117	119	122	135	142	136	144	...	...	112	113	129	135	124	128			105	111		
Belgique/Luxembourg	96	95	97	94	...	...	130	134	136	143	115	117	122	125	141	148	144	152	...	...	113	113	134	139	134	139	134	140	111	128	**138**	**141**
France	98	98	96	96	...	...	129	129	130	137	110	110	102	102	118	130	115	126	...	...	109	110	122	128	112	119	138	143			**143**	**146**
Allemagne occidentale	95	95	98	90	...	...	121	121	121	130	116	118	119	129	125	130	137	144	...	...	113	113	130	134	121	126						
Italie	99	98	93	87	124	124	115	121	139	146	108	108	117	119	143	150	154	162	...	...	108	108	125	134	126	130						
Pays-Bas	98	96	101	96	122	120	129	135	138	142	127	130	152	159	183	198	145	151	137	145	119	116	155	162	143	149						
Pays méditerranéens	102	99	112	112	116	117	151	162	133	140	132 1)	138 1)	151	164	153	157	171	189	152	161	119	122	132	138	135	138						
Grèce	102	100	128	130	118	119	166	178	130	134	132 1)	136 1)	152	161	168	187	166	178	125	132	112	120	155	169	136	144	158	173			160	169
Portugal	101	90	106	106	112	113	130	139	122	128	117 1)	121 1)	144	158	168	181	152	170	137	143	112	114	157	168	137	142						
Espagne	103	101	111	111	115	116	150	158	132	137	129 1)	132 1)	163	176	147	163	161	173	169	195	120	123	133	144	133	142						
Yougoslavie	102	99	115	115	119	121	161	180	147	163	155 1)	172 1)	147	163	173	189	180	210	...	...	121	124	159	171	136	143						
Autres pays	96	93	98	96	106	106	107	117	119	124	107	107	107	107	169	195	114	118	112	115	106	106	158	179	142	155	121	126			126	129
Autriche	88	86	95	93	102	102	114	117	121	126	114	117	104	104	118	123	123	128	126	132	105	105	112	115	111	114						
Danemark	99	96	99	96	108	108	108	108	121	127	107	107	110	110	126	132	115	113	113	113	105	105	115	118	115	118						
Finlande	102	100	102	100	111	114	118	120	127	132	115	116	109	109	118	123	133	140	123	127	108	112	114	117	114	115						
Irlande	92	89	90	86	100	100	102	103	112	118	101	101	100	98	135	143	126	132	118	124	112	112	117	118	118	120						
Norvège	103	100	105	103	111	111	116	118	121	126	108	105	112	106	112	118	121	115	99	99	111	111	105	107	105	107						
Suède	97	94	99	97	107	107	107	107	120	125	106	106	107	106	123	129	121	125	110	110	106	105	113	116	112	114						
Suisse	94	91	98	98	107	107	107	107	121	125	106	106	104	103	126	132	115	120	122	127	105	105	112	114	114	116						
Royaume-Uni	97	93	97	96	105	105	105	105	118	124	106	106	107	108	115	120	121	125	120	113	105	105	111	114	110	113						
Japon	104	103	98	97	129	132	169	180	142	148	182 1)	196 1)	243	267	222	243	175	188	142	148	120	121	167	177	120	121			104	109	123	123
Afrique du Sud	128	130	126	126	128	130	133	140	138	149	144 1)	162 1)	140	153	138	149	138	149	140	153	132	138	139	150	142	147	476	595	137	151	174	183
Argentine et Uruguay	116	113	118	116	122	122	127	130	133	139	128 1)	132 1)	129	133	125	126	124	125	129	133	123	123	126	128	125	126	143	161			154	160

1) A l'exclusion du beurre.
2) Estimations provisoires reposant sur des données établies par le Secrétariat de la C.E.E.
3) Compte tenu également de la baisse de prix prévue.
4) Non compris les estimations de la C.E.E.
5) Voir note 5 tableau IV.

Tableau VI

Résumé des projections de la demande et comparaison avec les pays à revenu faible.

	Asie et Extrême-Orient (excl. Japon)		Proche-Orient et Afrique (excl. Union S.Africaine)		Amérique latine (excl. Argentine et Uruguay)		Japon		Europe méditerranéenne		C.E.E.		Autres pays d'Europe occidentale		Argentine et Uruguay		Océanie		Amérique du Nord	
	B*	H*	B	H	B	H	B	H	B	H	B	H	B	H	B	H	B	H	B	H
1. Valeurs absolues relevées en 1957/-59/ et projetées pour 1969/-71/																				
Population (en millions) 1957/-59/	736		275		173		92		65		169		87		23		12		192	
1969/-71/	972		368		240		100		73		184		91		28		15		238	
PNB par habitant (en $ par an 1)) 1957/-59/	165		260		491		910		575		1285		1440		825		1570		2190	
1969/-71/	190	220	310	360	620	680	1690	1890	915	1060	2030	2235	1900	2130	965	1050	1775	2000	2540	2955
Consommation de principes nutritifs p.p.j.																				
Calories 1957/-59/	1980		2400		2300		2220		2650		2850		3220		3100		3250		3120	
1969/-71/	2150	2320	2560	2690	2470	2540	2430	2470	2820	2880	2940	2955	3220	3330	3120	3130	3220	3210	3110	3100
dont: provenant des céréales 1957/-59/	1300		1495		950		1435		1370		1060		870		1115		865		670	
1969/-71/	1390	1460	1560	1600	980	990	1380	1360	1250	1210	930	910	800	770	1060	1040	820	780	620	580
protéines animales (en g) 1957/-59/	7		13		17		17		23		41		47		65		62		66	
1969/-71/	9	10	16	18	20	21	26	28	32	35	51	53	50	51	67	68	63	64	68	70
2. Élasticité-revenu 2) de la demande de tous produits alimentaires, en termes de:																				
Calories	0.6		0.4		0.3		0.2		0.2		0.1		0.01		0.04		-0.06		-0.03	
Protéines animales	1.5		1.2		0.8		0.9		0.9		0.6		0.3		0.22		0.14		0.23	
Prix à la ferme	0.9		0.7		0.6		0.6		0.55		0.5		0.2		0.17		0.1		0.16	
3. Taux moyens annuels de croissance projetés entre 1957/-59/ et 1969/-71/ (taux composés)																				
3.1. Hypothèses de base:																				
Population	2.3		2.5		2.7		0.7		1.0		0.7		0.4		1.7		2.0		1.8	
PNB par habitant	1.3	2.5	1.5	2.8	2.0	2.8	5.3	6.3	3.9	5.2	3.9	4.7	2.3	3.3	1.3	2.0	1.0	2.0	1.3	2.5
PNB	3.6	4.9	4.0	5.3	4.7	5.6	6.0	7.0	4.9	6.2	4.7	5.5	2.7	3.7	3.0	3.7	3.0	4.0	3.1	4.1
3.2. Accroissement potentiel 3) de la demande par habitant de tous produits alimentaires en termes de:																				
Calories	0.7	1.3	0.5	1.0	0.6	0.8	0.8	0.9	0.5	0.7	0.3	0.4	0.0	0.03	0.06	0.07	-0.07	-0.1	-0.04	-0.06
Protéines animales	1.8	3.3	1.6	2.8	1.4	1.9	3.6	4.1	2.7	3.9	1.9	2.2	0.5	0.7	0.3	0.4	0.14	0.25	0.25	0.5
Prix à la ferme	1.0	1.9	1.0	1.6	1.0	1.3	2.2	2.5	1.6	2.1	1.4	1.7	0.5	0.6	0.3	0.3	0.09	0.18	0.16	0.35
3.3. Accroissement potentiel de la demande totale de tous produits alimentaires en termes de:																				
Calories	3.1	3.7	3.0	3.4	3.3	3.5	1.5	1.6	1.5	1.7	1.1	1.1	0.5	0.5	1.7	1.8	1.9	1.9	1.7	1.7
Protéines animales	4.1	5.7	4.1	5.3	4.1	5.3	4.4	4.9	3.7	4.5	2.6	2.9	1.0	1.2	1.9	2.1	2.1	2.2	2.0	2.3
Prix à la ferme	3.4	4.3	3.5	4.1	3.7	4.1	2.9	3.3	2.6	3.1	2.1	2.4	0.9	1.1	1.9	2.0	2.1	2.2	1.9	2.1
4. Rapport entre l'effet du revenu et celui de la population sur la demande totale de la population en termes de prix à la ferme	0.4	0.8	0.4	0.6	0.3	0.5	3.3	3.9	1.8	2.4	2.1	2.6	1.0	1.4	0.1	0.2	0.04	0.1	0.1	0.2

1) Converti en dollars E.U. sur la base de parités de pouvoir d'achat calculées aux prix E.U. de 1955.

2) Valeur de l'élasticité-revenu durant la période de base 1957/-59/. Ces valeurs ont été dérivées de la demande projetée pour chaque groupe de produits dans chaque pays ou groupe de pays.

3) Ces accroissements résultent de la combinaison des élasticités-revenu (rubrique 2) et des pourcentages d'accroissement du PNB par habitant (rubrique 3.1). On s'est servi d'une fonction de demande log-inverse fondée sur l'hypothèse d'élasticité décroissante; il s'ensuit que les pourcentages d'augmentation de la demande sont quelque peu inférieure au produit des élasticités-revenu durant la période de base par les pourcentages d'accroissement du PNB par habitant.

B = hypothèse basse, H = hypothèse haute.

Tableau VII
Produits pour boissons et fruits tropicaux.

Produits		Valeur à l'importation CIF Moy. 1) (% min. et max.) 2)	Droits et taxes internes Moy. 1) (% min. et max.) 2)	Transformation et vente Moy. 1) (% min. et max.) 2)	Prix de détail	Accroissement 3) des importations en 1970 dans le cas d'une réduction des droits d'importation et des taxes internes					
		(% du prix de détail en 1961)				(en million de $ E.U.)			(en pourcentage)		
						20%	50%	100%	20%	50%	100%
C.E.E., Royaume-Uni, Danemark, Suède, Norvège, Suisse, Autriche	Café	37 (23-53)	20 (0-38)	43 (32-66)	100	18	50	104	2	5.1	11
Idem	Cacao	15 (9-22)	9 (1-40)	76 (50-84)	100	3.6	13	30	1	3.5	8
Idem	Thé	61 (19-64)	2 (0-36)	37 (28-62)	100	0.2	0.7	2.1	0.1	0.2	0.6
C.E.E. (non compris l'Italie), Suède et Norvège	Agrumes (oranges et mandarines)	49 (45-57)	11 (6-15)	40 (34-45)	100	7.2	18.9	38.7	2	5.3	11
C.E.E.	Bananes	40 (28-45)	4 (3-26)	56 (37-65)	100	1	2.5	5.2	1	2.4	5.1

1) Pourcentage pour chaque pays pondéré par les quantités importées en 1960.
2) Pourcentages minima et maxima enregistrés dans les pays étudiés.
3) Accroissement calculé en supposant que les marges de transformation et de commercialisation restent constantes en termes de dollars et en partant des prix moyens à l'exportation ayant prévalu en 1957–59.

Printed by

Offizin Andersen Nexö

in Leipzig